AF898411

The Federal Anti-Kickback Statute and Safe Harbors:

A HISTORY AND PRACTICE GUIDE, SECOND EDITION

GEOFFREY R. KAISER AND ADA JANOCINSKA

AMERICAN BAR ASSOCIATION
Health Law Section

Cover design by Sara Wadford/ABA Design

Printed in the United States of America.

27 26 25 24 23   5 4 3 2 1

Library of Congress Cataloging-in-Publication Data

Names: Kaiser, Geoffrey R, author. | Janocinska, Ada, author. | American Bar Association. Health Law Section sponsoring body
Title: The federal Anti-Kickback Statute and safe harbors / Geoffrey R. Kaiser, Ada Janocinska.
Description: Second edition. | Chicago, Illinois: ABA Publishing, American Bar Association, [2023] | Includes index. | Summary: "*The Federal Anti-Kickback Statute and Safe Harbors* is a comprehensive reference book for one of the nation's most commonly cited, investigated and enforced health care fraud and abuse laws. The book offers practical guidance to health care attorneys in understanding the law's origin, purpose and requirements."-- Provided by publisher.
Identifiers: LCCN 2023018644 (print) | LCCN 2023018645 (ebook) | ISBN 9781639053599 (paperback) | ISBN 9781639053605 (epub)
Subjects: LCSH: United States. Anti-Kickback Statute. | Medical care--Finance--Law and legislation--United States--Criminal provisions. | Medical referral--Law and legislation--United States--Criminal provisions. | Medicare fraud--Law and legislation. | Medicaid fraud--Law and legislation.
Classification: LCC KF9457 .K35 2023 (print) | LCC KF9457 (ebook) | DDC 345.73/0268--dc23
LC record available at https://lccn.loc.gov/2023018644
LC ebook record available at https://lccn.loc.gov/2023018645

Contents

Chapter 3:

Appendices

Appendices are available for download at www.ambar.org/FAKS2e.

About the Authors of the First and Second Editions

Geoffrey R. Kaiser

Senior Counsel

Geoffrey (Jeff) R. Kaiser, who has extensive experience in enforcement matters affecting the health care industry, concentrates his legal practice on health care fraud and regulatory compliance issues, white collar criminal defense, False Claims Act litigation, integrity monitoring, and internal investigations. As head of the Compliance, Investigations and White Collar Practice Group, and senior counsel in the Health Services Practice Group, Jeff is frequently called upon to handle matters implicating a range of health care fraud and abuse laws, including the False Claims Act and the Anti-Kickback Statute.

Before joining Rivkin Radler, Jeff served for nearly 10 years in the Criminal Divisions of the U.S. Attorney's Office for the Eastern District of New York and the U.S. Attorney's Office for the Southern District of New York. While at the Justice Department, he directed many white collar investigations and prosecutions, including with respect to health care fraud, securities fraud, mortgage fraud, mail and wire fraud, and bank fraud.

As Chief of Health Care Fraud Prosecutions and Deputy Chief of Public Integrity in the Eastern District U.S. Attorney's Office, Jeff directed investigations against individuals and corporations facing health care fraud allegations under a variety of criminal and civil statutes. In many instances, those investigations were rooted in allegations brought by whistleblowers under the False Claims Act. Jeff also exercised oversight responsibilities within the Public Integrity Section for all health care fraud cases within the Eastern

District of New York. He received many recognitions and honors for his efforts as a federal prosecutor.

After leaving the Justice Department, Jeff served as a managing director with Navigant Consulting, Inc., a global expert services firm, in two of its practice groups, Disputes and Investigations and Healthcare Disputes, Compliance and Investigations. While at Navigant, Jeff led teams performing internal investigations and integrity monitorships of individuals and organizations in various industries, including the health care industry.

Jeff received his B.A. with Honors from the University of Virginia, where he also graduated Phi Beta Kappa. He earned a J.D. from New York University School of Law, where he served on the Moot Court Board. After graduating from law school, Jeff served for two years as law clerk to the Hon. Fritz W. Alexander II, an associate judge on New York State's highest court, the New York Court of Appeals.

A frequent writer and speaker on a range of legal topics, particularly in the areas of health care fraud and compliance, Jeff was named a Super Lawyer in the Metro New York area, 2012–2022. Jeff is an adjunct professor of law at St. John's University School of Law, where he teaches Health Care Fraud.

The prestigious Chambers and Partners named Jeff a "Ranked Lawyer" in Band 5 in 2022. The Health Services Practice has been recognized in the Chambers USA directory in the Healthcare category and has also been listed in the prestigious Legal 500.

Ada Janocinska

Partner

Ada Janocinska concentrates her practice on regulatory and transactional matters within the health care industry.

A partner in Rivkin Radler's Health Services Practice Group, Ada represents health care providers, medical groups, hospitals, outpatient facilities, and other business entities that serve the health care industry. She advises clients on a wide variety of legal matters, including formation of business entities, joint ventures, employment negotiations, and compliance programs involving Medicaid and Medicare, Stark and Anti-Kickback Law, and the False Claims Act.

Ada also practices in Rivkin Radler's Privacy, Data & Cyber Law Practice Group, where she advises clients inside and outside of the health care industry on complying with HIPAA and the Health Information Technology for Economic and Clinical Health Act, and responding to any threats or breaches to an organization's privacy and cybersecurity.

She was honored by the *Long Island Business News* as a 2018 "30 Under 30" award recipient, and by the Huntington Township Chamber of Commerce as one of 30 "Celebrate Long Island's Young Professionals" honorees in 2017.

Ada is a frequent contributor to the firm's electronic health law news bulletin, *Rivkin Rounds*.

Ada previously served as a Senior Fellow for the Gitenstein Institute for Health Law and Policy, where she worked on several community outreach projects that strived to improve access to quality care and pave the way for positive change in the health care delivery system.

During law school, Ada earned a certificate in health law and served on the Editorial Board of *Hofstra Law Review*. She also received an award for outstanding achievement in the Health Law and Policy Clinic at Hofstra, where she worked as a student-attorney and represented a nonprofit health services organization in implementing internal scope of practice and risk management policies for community health workers.

Ada has been recognized in Ones to Watch by *Best Lawyers in America®* from 2021 to 2023. Ones to Watch is a recognition given to attorneys who are earlier in their careers for outstanding professional excellence in private practice.

Ada was also named a 2020 to 2022 New York Metro Super Lawyers Rising Star. The Rising Stars list is comprised of the top 2.5 percent of lawyers under the age of 40.

Additionally, *Long Island Business News* recognized Ada with the Leadership in Law Associate Award in 2020.

Additional Contributors to the Second Edition

Ashley Algazi, Lindsay Brocki, Joseph DiBella, Jeffrey Ehrhardt, Benjamin P. Malerba, Benjamin Wisher

About the Authors of the First Edition

Eric D. Fader

Partner

Eric Fader has represented health care providers and other corporate clients in connection with business planning and contractual issues, transactional matters, and federal and state regulatory compliance for more than 30 years. His clients include providers of intraoperative neurophysiologic monitoring (IONM) services, telehealth and telepharmacy companies, urgent care facilities, imaging centers, and private practices of all types. Eric has also represented insurers and third-party administrators, provider networks, medical device suppliers, equipment vendors, and providers of electronic medical records and other online health care services in contractual and regulatory matters.

Eric advises on billing and reimbursement questions, federal and state anti-kickback and self-referral issues, HIPAA compliance (including privacy and data breaches), payor audits, hospital privilege and medical staff issues, and state licensure and certificate of need matters. His work also includes organizational matters, corporate governance and structuring/restructuring advice, operating agreements, shareholder and partnership agreements and disputes, labor and employment law issues, private securities offerings, joint ventures, mergers and acquisitions.

A frequent writer and commentator on health care issues, Eric has written for and has been quoted in *Bloomberg BNA, Law360,* and *Thomson Reuters Westlaw*, among many others. Eric is the Editor of *Rivkin Rounds*, an electronic news bulletin for businesses, professionals, investors, and stakeholders in the health care industry.

Eric is a member of the American Society of Neurophysiological Monitoring (ASNM) and has been a webinar and symposium speaker for the ASNM. He served on the Board of Directors of Stayhealthy, Inc., a privately owned health solutions company committed to changing the way the world measures health and fitness.

Eric began his legal career as a securities lawyer and moonlighted for several years as a professional microcap stock trader. This activity afforded him unusual insights into the over-the-counter markets, which he has used in representing small public companies and those that invest in them.

Christopher J. Kutner

Partner

Christopher J. Kutner represents managed care organizations, physician groups, hospitals, and ancillary service providers, including laboratories, health care benefit administrators, and suppliers of medical equipment.

As partner in the Health Services Practice Group, Chris represents national and regional health plans in the acquisition of similar plans. He recently coordinated the acquisition and integration of a Connecticut managed care plan by a larger, New York City–based health maintenance organization. He is representing a multi-facility alcohol and substance abuse service provider in a stock sale transaction. He also represented a regional boutique laboratory in an asset sale. Moreover, a regional laboratory-management company hired Chris to advise on acquisitions, state and federal regulatory compliance, and managed care contracting. He advises health care providers with managed care contracting and dispute resolution and with respect to compliant practice structures and permissible arrangements concerning, among other issues, referrals.

He has represented a national managed care company in connection with its acquisition of managed long-term care plans and a county government in the sale of its Medicaid managed care plan including eight outpatient treatment facilities. His managed care experience makes him well suited for advising health care consumers with benefit and medical necessity opinions as well as assisting with external appeals with state regulators.

A partner in Rivkin Radler's Compliance, Investigations & White Collar Practice Group, Chris represents health care providers who are being audited or investigated by, among others, the New York State Department of Health's Office of Professional Medical Conduct, the New York State Medicaid Inspector General, the U.S. Department of Health and Human

Services' Office of Inspector General, the New York Attorney General and the U.S. Attorney's Offices for all districts in New York and New Jersey.

His practice includes advising providers in western and northern New York, and he is admitted, and practices law, in Connecticut.

Beginning his career as a commercial litigator, Chris represented local, national, and global companies in complex civil litigation in state and federal courts. In 1998, he accepted an in-house counsel position with Vytra Health Plans, a managed care organization and client he represented in private practice. For eight years, Chris worked inside managed care. Among his accomplishments: He implemented Vytra's first corporate compliance program and served as compliance and privacy officer. He ultimately served as special assistant and counsel to the president and chief executive officer, focusing on health care strategic planning, product development, and regulatory compliance. He served as corporate counsel and regulatory compliance counsel for Vytra's parent organization, HIP, while assuming the role of general counsel at Vytra, where he was instrumental in working with state and federal law enforcement on investigations of individuals and entities based on health care fraud, among other claims.

Chris enlisted in the U.S. military at age 19 and served active duty in the U.S. Air Force while attending college. He earned the Air Force Commendation Medal and was honorably discharged after four years of active military service to pursue a bachelor's of mechanical engineering degree from SUNY Stony Brook, which he earned in 1987.

Chris has been named to Best Lawyers in America in Healthcare by U.S. News & World Report from 2017 to 2020. The Health Services Practice Group has been listed in the prestigious Legal 500. The practice also has been included in the Chambers USA directory in the Healthcare category. Chris was named a Super Lawyer in the Metro New York Area in Health Care for 2014, 2015, 2018, and 2019.

Benjamin P. Malerba

Partner

Benjamin P. Malerba is a partner in the Health Services and Privacy, Data & Cyber Law Practice Groups. Ben counsels a cross-section of health care providers and facilities, including independent physician associations, accountable care organizations, provider networks, ambulatory surgery centers, diagnostic and treatment centers, dialysis facilities, and hospitals and federally qualified health centers, on general health care business transactions, state licensing issues, corporate practice of medicine and fee-splitting prohibitions, regulatory compliance, disputes with managed care companies, federal and state anti-kickback statutes, self-referral statutes, and federal and state privacy laws. His practice also covers data breach and response, cybersecurity and data security, with a particular focus on security breaches related to HIPAA.

Ben has particular experience representing ambulatory surgery centers (ASCs) and ambulatory surgery management companies, counseling them on a wide variety of corporate and commercial transactions, including mergers and acquisitions of existing ASCs, the establishment of de novo centers, and syndications. He regularly represents ASCs and other facilities before the New York State Department of Health and the New York State Public Health and Health Planning Council. He also has represented clients before federal and state government agencies, including the Department of Health and Human Services' Office for Civil Rights in its investigations into HIPAA-related security breaches. Ben also counsels clients on the development and implementation of compliance programs for health care providers and business associates under HIPAA and on preparing for and responding to HIPAA breaches and investigations.

A frequent lecturer, Ben delivers presentations on health care issues before provider networks, hospitals, ASCs, medical groups, and state professional associations. He has also written articles and delivered presentations on the topic of medical marijuana. Ben has participated in the Volunteer Lawyers Project, representing tenants in landlord/tenant proceedings. He serves on the board of directors of The Guidance Center of Westchester, whose mission is to improve the well-being of people of all ages through innovative and effective programs that enable everyone to learn, work, and thrive. Ben has also served on the board of directors of The Early Years Institute, a not-for-profit organization that promotes the impact of the early years of life on later success.

Ben has been named to Best Lawyers in America in Healthcare by *U.S. News & World Report* for 2018 through 2020. He was named a Top Healthcare Transaction Lawyer in 2015 and 2017 by the Ambulatory M&A Advisor. In 2011, *Long Island Business News* named him one of its "40 Rising Stars Under 40."

The Health Services Practice Group has been listed in the prestigious Legal 500. The practice also has been included in the Chambers USA directory in the Healthcare category.

1
An Introduction to the Anti-Kickback Statute

1.1. The Text and Import of the Anti-Kickback Statute

The Anti-Kickback Statute (AKS) is a criminal law that states:

(1) Whoever knowingly and willfully solicits or receives any remuneration (including any kickback, bribe, or rebate) directly or indirectly, overtly or covertly, in cash or in kind—

(A) in return for referring an individual to a person for the furnishing or arranging for the furnishing of any item or service for which payment may be made in whole or in part under a Federal health care program, or

(B) in return for purchasing, leasing, ordering, or arranging for or recommending purchasing, leasing, or ordering any good, facility, service, or item for which payment may be made in whole or in part under a Federal health care program, shall be guilty of a felony and upon conviction thereof, shall be fined not more than $25,000 or imprisoned for not more than five years, or both.

(2) Whoever knowingly and willfully offers or pays any remuneration (including any kickback, bribe, or rebate) directly or indirectly, overtly or covertly, in cash or in kind to any person to induce such person—

(A) to refer an individual to a person for the furnishing or arranging for the furnishing of any item or service for which

payment may be made in whole or in part under a Federal health care program, or

(B) to purchase, lease, order, or arrange for or recommend purchasing, leasing, or ordering any good, facility, service, or item for which payment may be made in whole or in part under a Federal health care program, shall be guilty of a felony and upon conviction thereof, shall be fined not more than $25,000 or imprisoned for not more than five years, or both.[1]

The AKS accordingly defines as felony conduct the solicitation, receipt, payment, or offer of payment of any "remuneration" to induce or in return for the referral of any individual to a person for furnishing or arranging for the furnishing of an item or service reimbursable under a federal health care program. The statute also bars a person from doing any of those things to induce or in return for purchasing, leasing, ordering, or arranging for or recommending purchasing, leasing, or ordering any item or service reimbursable under a federal health care program. An AKS violation is punishable by up to five years of imprisonment and a fine of up to $25,000. There are no exceptions to what may constitute "remuneration" under the AKS,[2] which is broadly construed to mean "anything of value."[3] The meaning of "federal health care program" is likewise broad, and includes, in addition to obvious federal health insurance programs like Medicare and Medicaid, virtually

1. 42 U.S.C. § 1320a-7b(b).

2. In this respect, the AKS is very different from, for example, the Civil Monetary Penalties Law (CMP; 42 U.S.C. § 1320a-7a). The CMP authorizes the imposition of civil penalties and sanctions for various types of health care fraud and abuse, including but not limited to violations of the AKS. Unlike the AKS, however, the CMP contains various exceptions to the definition of remuneration, and the U.S. Department of Health and Human Services, Office of Inspector General has taken the position that an exchange of remuneration having only "nominal value" will not trigger administrative sanctions under the CMP. *See* 42 U.S.C. § 1320a-7a(i)(6); OIG Special Advisory Bulletin, "Offering Gifts and Other Inducements to Beneficiaries" (Aug. 2002). Such exceptions, however, have no application to the AKS. *See* Narco Freedom, 2015 WL 1499265 at *8-9 (distinguishing the CMP from the AKS and noting that exceptions to the definition of remuneration as used in the CMP do not apply to the AKS).

3. *See, e.g.*, United States v. Narco Freedom, Inc., 2015 WL 1499265 at *8 (S.D.N.Y. 2015) (remuneration under AKS is anything of value and not limited to traditional bribes; remuneration may include an "in kind benefit [i.e., subsidized housing] provided at below market value to Medicaid beneficiaries"); Ameritox, Ltd. v. Millennium Labs., Inc., 20 F.Supp.3d 1348, 1356 (M.D. Fla. 2014) ("[T]he AKS does not contain exceptions to the broad definition of remuneration."); United States ex rel. McDonough v. Symphony Diagnostic Servs., 36 F.Supp.3d 773 (S.D. Ohio 2014) (remuneration can be "anything of value"); Klaczak v. Consol. Med. Transp., 458 F.Supp.2d 622, 678 (N.D. Ill. 2006) ("Remuneration, for purposes of the AKS, is defined broadly, meaning 'anything of value.'").

any plan or program providing health benefits which receives some degree of federal funding.[4]

To violate the AKS, a person's conduct, whether direct or indirect, covert or overt, must be knowing and willful (i.e., performed purposefully with the intention of inducing or rewarding referrals of items or services payable by a federal health care program).[5] Provided the conduct is knowing and willful, there is no requirement that the defendant have actual knowledge of or a specific intention to violate 42 U.S.C. § 1320a-7b(b) in order to trigger liability.[6]

In addition to the criminal penalties accompanying an AKS violation, violating the AKS implicates other laws as well. Conviction under the AKS brings mandatory exclusion from federal health care programs.[7] Additionally, when a person violates the AKS, the US Department of Health and Human Services, Office of Inspector General (HHS-OIG) may initiate administrative proceedings under the Civil Monetary Penalties Law (CMPL) to impose civil monetary penalties.[8] Furthermore, violating the AKS can result in liability under the Federal False Claims Act[9] for any claims submitted to federal health care programs that include any items or services resulting from a violation of the AKS. Indeed, the Patient Protection and Affordable Care Act[10] amended the AKS to state that any claim submitted in violation of the AKS "constitutes a false or fraudulent claim" for purposes of the False Claims Act.[11]

---

4. The AKS defines a federal health care program as: "(1) any plan or program that provides health benefits, whether directly, through insurance, or otherwise, which is funded directly, in whole or in part, by the United States Government (other than the health insurance program under chapter 89 of title 5); or (2) any State health care program, as defined in section 1320a–7(h) of this title."

5. Six Circuit Courts of Appeal that have considered the issue have held that only one purpose of the exchange of remuneration need be the inducement or reward of referrals in order to trigger the statute's provisions. This has become known as the "one purpose test." *See, e.g.*, United States v. Nagelvoort, 856 F.3d 1117, 1129-30 (7th Cir. 2017); United States v. Krikheli, 461 Fed. Appx. 7 at **3 (2d Cir. 2012); United States v. McClatchey, 217 F.3d 823, 834-35 (10th Cir. 2000); United States v. Davis, 132 F.3d 1092, 1094 (5th Cir. 1998); United States v. Kats, 871 F.2d 105, 108 (9th Cir. 1989); United States v. Greber, 760 F.2d 68, 69 (3d Cir. 1985), *cert. denied*, 474 U.S. 988 (1985); *Compare* United States v. Bay State Ambulance & Hops. Rental Serv. Inc., 874 F.2d 20, 29 (1st Cir. 1989) (affirming conviction on jury instruction requiring that jury find that "primary purpose" was to induce referrals, but leaving open the question whether the "one purpose test" is, in fact, the proper test).

6. 42 U.S.C. § 1320a-7b(h).

7. 42 U.S.C. § 1320a-7(a); 42 CFR Part 1001.

8. 42 U.S.C. § 1320a-7a(a)(7); 42 CFR §§ 1003.300 *et seq.*

9. 31 U.S.C. §§ 3729 *et seq.*

10. 42 U.S.C. §§ 18001 *et seq.*

11. 42 U.S.C. § 1320a-7b(g).

The AKS contains certain statutory and regulatory exceptions or "safe harbors" that protect selected business arrangements from prosecution under the statute.[12] Full compliance with a safe harbor is required to receive its benefits. A failure to comply with any required term of the approved business arrangement negates safe harbor protection.[13] Failing to satisfy a safe harbor, however, does not automatically result in AKS liability, which must be independently analyzed under the AKS statutory provisions.[14]

1.2. Legislative History and Public Policies Underlying the Anti-Kickback Statute and Safe Harbors

The AKS was first enacted through the Social Security Amendments of 1972 in order to combat fraud and abuse in the Medicare and Medicaid Programs.[15] The legislative history makes clear that these provisions were

12. *See, e.g.*, United States *ex rel.* Bartlett v. Ashcroft, 39 F. Supp. 3d 656, 676 (W.D. Pa. 2014) ("safe harbors protect certain business arrangements that might otherwise violate the Anti-Kickback Statute"); United States *ex rel.* Armfield v. Gills, 2012 WL 5340131 at *3 (M.D. Fla. 2012) (government has "promulgated regulations establishing a safe harbor for certain arrangements between healthcare providers which remove them from the scope of the Anti-Kickback Act"); United States v. Rogan, 459 F. Supp. 2d 692, 715 (N.D. Ill. 2006) (safe harbors "[list] various circumstances under which a financial relationship between a provider and a referral source would not give rise to liability under the Anti-Kickback Statute").

13. *See, e.g.*, Ashcroft, 39 F. Supp. 3d at 677 (W.D. Pa. 2014) (defendant "must prove strict compliance with a safe harbor to avoid liability for an arrangement that might otherwise violate the statute"); *Gills*, 2012 WL 5340131 at *5 ("The burden is on the party seeking protection under a safe harbor provision to demonstrate strict compliance with each and every element of the safe harbor."); United States *ex rel.* Westmoreland v. Amgen, Inc., 812 F.Supp.2d 39, 80 (D. Mass. 2011) ("To receive protection, a business arrangement must fit squarely within a safe harbor; substantial compliance is not enough . . . .").

14. *See, e.g.*, Gills, 2012 WL 5340131 at *8 n.6 (failure to satisfy a safe harbor does not mean the AKS is violated); *Westmoreland*, 812 F. Supp. 2d at 47 (safe harbor compliance "is voluntary and failure to comply is not a per se violation of the statute"); Feldstein v. Nash Cmty. Health Servs., 51 F. Supp. 2d 673, 687 (E.D.N.C. 1999) ("The failure to fall within a safe harbor . . . 'does not necessarily mean that the conduct/relationship is prohibited by the . . . anti-kickback statute.'") (citation omitted); HHS-OIG Federal Anti-Kickback Law and Regulatory Safe Harbors Fact Sheet, Nov. 1999, accessible at https://oig.hhs.gov/fraud/docs/safeharborregulations/safefs.htm ("Failure to comply with a safe harbor provision does not mean that an arrangement is *per se* illegal. Compliance with safe harbors is voluntary, and arrangements that do not comply with a safe harbor must be analyzed on a case-by-case basis for compliance with the anti-kickback statute."); Medicare and State Health Care Programs: Fraud and Abuse; Clarification of the OIG Safe Harbor Anti-Kickback Provisions, 59 Fed. Reg. 37202, 37203 (July 21, 1994) ("Whether a particular payment practice violates the statute is a question that can only be resolved by an analysis of the elements of the statute as applied to that set of facts."); Medicare and State Health Care Programs: Fraud and Abuse; OIG Anti-Kickback Provision, 56 Fed. Reg. 35952, 35955 (July 29, 1991) ("[T]he gravamen of a violation of the statute is 'inducement' and not necessarily the structure of the arrangement," and thus "case by case inquiries must necessarily focus on the intent of the parties.").

15. *See* Pub. L. No. 92-603, §242(b), 86 Stat. 1329, 1419 (1972).

intended to strengthen the legal framework for combatting practices that had "long been regarded by professional organizations as unethical, which are unlawful in some jurisdictions, and which contribute significantly to the cost of the [Medicare and Medicaid] programs."[16]

The AKS was amended in 1977 to make violations a felony, bolstering the penalties against "illegal practices by some individuals who provide services under Medicare and Medicaid" and which "contribute significantly to the cost of the programs."[17] The amendments expanded the AKS's reach to cover "*any remuneration* (including any kickback, bribe or rebate), directly or indirectly, overtly or covertly, in cash or kind,"[18] and were motivated by a rise in various health care fraud and abuse activities, including financial incentives to induce referrals of program business, medically unnecessary services, and the "*steering*" of patients to "*particular*" providers, thus violating the "*policy of freedom of choice*."[19] In 1997, additional amendments made the AKS applicable, not just to Medicare and Medicaid, but to *all* health care programs receiving federal funding.[20]

Generally, the purpose of the AKS is to remove the corrupting effects of kickbacks in health care by outlawing behavior designed to game the system through the use of financial incentives intended to direct patient referrals to particular health care providers and away from other providers rendering the same type of care. The HHS-OIG, which together with the US Department of Justice (DOJ), has primary responsibility for enforcing the AKS, has explained that violating the AKS increases risks associated with "overutilization, increased program costs, corruption of medical decision-making, patient steering and unfair competition."[21]

The AKS codifies several exceptions to the statutory prohibition, providing at 42 U.S.C. § 1320a-7b(b)(3) that the AKS "shall not apply to" the following:

> *(A) a discount or other reduction in price obtained by a provider of services or other entity under a Federal health care program if the reduction in price is properly disclosed and appropriately reflected*

---

16. H.R. Rept. No. 92-231 at p. 107 (1971).
17. H.R. 95-393 at p. 48 (1977); Pub. L. 95-142, 91 Stat. 1175 (1977).
18. *Id.* (emphasis added).
19. *Id.* at pp. 44-48 (emphasis added).
20. 42 U.S.C. §1320a-7b(f), as amended by Pub. L. No. 104-191, §204, 110 Stat. 1999-2000 (1996).
21. *See* the discussion of the AKS on the OIG website (http://oig.hhs.gov/compliance/physician-education/01laws.asp).

in the costs claimed or charges made by the provider or entity under a Federal health care program;

(B) *any amount paid by an employer to an employee (who has a bona fide employment relationship with such employer) for employment in the provision of covered items or services;*

(C) *any amount paid by a vendor of goods or services to a person authorized to act as a purchasing agent for a group of individuals or entities who are furnishing services reimbursed under a Federal health care program if—*

(i) *the person has a written contract, with each such individual or entity, which specifies the amount to be paid the person, which amount may be a fixed amount or a fixed percentage of the value of the purchases made by each such individual or entity under the contract, and*

(ii) *in the case of an entity that is a provider of services (as defined in section 1395x (u) of this title), the person discloses (in such form and manner as the Secretary requires) to the entity and, upon request, to the Secretary the amount received from each such vendor with respect to purchases made by or on behalf of the entity;*

(D) *a waiver of any coinsurance under part B of subchapter XVIII of this chapter by a Federally qualified health care center with respect to an individual who qualifies for subsidized services under a provision of the Public Health Service Act [42 U.S.C. 201 et seq.];*

(E) *any payment practice specified by the Secretary in regulations promulgated pursuant to section 14(a) of the Medicare and Medicaid Patient and Program Protection Act of 1987 or in regulations under section 1395w–104 (e)(6)* [1] *of this title;*

(F) *any remuneration between an organization and an individual or entity providing items or services, or a combination thereof, pursuant to a written agreement between the organization and the individual or entity if the organization is an eligible organization under section 1395mm of this title or if the written agreement, through a risk-sharing arrangement, places the individual or entity at substantial financial risk for the cost or utilization of the items or services, or a combination thereof, which the individual or entity is obligated to provide;*

(G) *the waiver or reduction by pharmacies (including pharmacies of the Indian Health Service, Indian tribes, tribal organizations, and urban Indian organizations) of any cost-sharing imposed under part D of subchapter XVIII of this chapter, if the conditions described in clauses (i) through (iii) of section 1320a–7a (i)(6)(A) of this title are met with respect to the waiver or reduction (except that, in the case of such a waiver or reduction on behalf of a subsidy eligible individual (as defined in section 1395w–114 (a)(3) of this title), section 1320a–7a (i)(6)(A) of this title shall be applied without regard to clauses (ii) and (iii) of that section);*

(H) *any remuneration between a federally qualified health center (or an entity controlled by such a health center) and an MA organization pursuant to a written agreement described in section 1395w–23 (a)(4) of this title;*

(I) *any remuneration between a health center entity described under clause (i) or (ii) of section 1396d (l)(2)(B) of this title and any individual or entity providing goods, items, services, donations, loans, or a combination thereof, to such health center entity pursuant to a contract, lease, grant, loan, or other agreement, if such agreement contributes to the ability of the health center entity to maintain or increase the availability, or enhance the quality, of services provided to a medically underserved population served by the health center entity; and*

(J) *a discount in the price of an applicable drug (as defined in paragraph (2) of section 1395w–114a (g) of this title) of a manufacturer that is furnished to an applicable beneficiary (as defined in paragraph (1) of such section) under the Medicare coverage gap discount program under section 1395w–114a of this title.*

HHS was mandated, through legislation passed in 1987, to promulgate regulations establishing additional "safe harbors" for business arrangements and payment practices that would not be subject to prosecution under the

AKS.[22] By statute, in "modifying and establishing safe harbors," HHS may consider any of the following factors:[23]

(A) An increase or decrease in access to health care services.
(B) An increase or decrease in the quality of health care services.
(C) An increase or decrease in patient freedom of choice among health care providers.
(D) An increase or decrease in competition among health care providers.
(E) An increase or decrease in the ability of health care facilities to provide services in medically underserved areas or to medically underserved populations.
(F) An increase or decrease in the cost to Federal health care programs (as defined in section 1320a–7b(f) of this title).
(G) An increase or decrease in the potential overutilization of health care services.
(H) The existence or nonexistence of any potential financial benefit to a health care professional or provider which may vary based on their decisions of—
(i) whether to order a health care item or service; or
(ii) whether to arrange for a referral of health care items or services to a particular practitioner or provider.
(I) Any other factors the Secretary deems appropriate in the interest of preventing fraud and abuse in Federal health care programs (as so defined).

In 1991, HHS promulgated the initial group of ten regulatory safe harbors, several of which constituted regulatory versions of statutory exceptions enacted at the time of the original AKS legislation.[24] The first group included safe harbors for investment interests, space rental, equipment rental, personal services and management contracts, sale of practice, referral services, warranties, discounts, employees, and group purchasing organizations. As HHS noted in promulgating the original regulatory safe harbors, "[t]he clear congressional intent behind the development of these

22. *See* 42 U.S.C. §1320a-7d(a); AKS regulatory safe harbors are codified at 42 CFR § 1001.952.

23. *Id.*

24. Final Rule: OIG Anti-Kickback Provisions (56 Fed. Reg. 35952; July 29, 1991): Final rulemaking promulgating the ten original safe harbor provisions.

safe harbor provisions is to define *innocuous arrangements* that should not be prosecuted, including the statutory exceptions."[25] The DOJ has argued the same position, maintaining that "[t]he Anti-Kickback Statute is designed to prohibit the intentional sale of patient referrals" and that "[t]he safe harbors aren't intended to undermine that principle, but, rather, to assure that legitimate economic relationships between parties who also have a referral relationship are not questioned."[26]

Over the next quarter century, additional safe harbors were created for waiver of copayment, coinsurance, and deductible amounts;[27] increased coverage, reduced cost-sharing amounts, or reduced premium amounts offered by health plans;[28] price reductions offered to health plans;[29] investment interests in rural areas;[30] practitioner recruitment;[31] obstetrical malpractice insurance subsidies;[32] investments in group practices;[33] cooperative hospital service organizations;[34] ambulatory surgical centers;[35] referral arrangements for specialty services;[36] price reductions offered to eligible managed care

25. 56 Fed. Reg. at 35957 (emphasis added); *see also* 64 Fed. Reg. 63519 (Nov. 19, 1999) (safe harbors designed to protect certain "payment and business practices" that might be seen as "technically covered" by "broad" statutory language if they are "*potentially capable* of inducing referrals of business"; explaining that "safe harbors provide a means of assuring that payment practices are not illegal . . . Payment practices that do not fully comply with a safe harbor *may still be lawful if no purpose of the payment practice is to induce referrals of Federal health care program business.*") (emphasis added); 72 Fed. Reg. 56632, 56640 (Oct. 4, 2007) (safe harbors are "meant to protect arrangements that do not pose undue risk for Federal health care programs or beneficiaries; they are not meant to protect arrangements that pose high risks to Federal health care programs.").

26. United States v. Kuchipudi, Case No. 13 CR 312 (N.D. Ill. 2016), "Government's Response to Defendant's Consolidated Post-Trial Motions," at pp. 5, 6-7, 9 (May 18, 2016).

27. Interim Final Rule: Safe Harbors for Protecting Health Plans (57 Fed. Reg. 52723; Nov. 5, 1992); Final Rule: Safe Harbors for Protecting Health Plans (61 Fed. Reg. 2122; Jan. 25, 1996): Revised final rule addressing the three managed care safe harbors originally promulgated in the Nov. 5, 1992 interim final rule; Final Rule: Medicare and State Health Care Programs: Fraud and Abuse; Revisions to the Safe Harbors Under the Anti-Kickback Statute and Civil Monetary Penalty Rules Regarding Beneficiary Inducements (81 Fed. Reg. 88368; Dec. 7, 2016).

28. *Id.*

29. *Id.*

30. Final Rule: Clarification of the Initial OIG Safe Harbor Provisions and Establishment of Additional Safe Harbor Provisions Under the Anti-Kickback Statute (64 Fed. Reg. 63518; Nov. 19, 1999).

31. *Id.*

32. *Id.*

33. *Id.*

34. *Id.*

35. *Id.*

36. *Id.*

organizations;[37] price reductions offered by contractors with substantial financial risk to managed care organizations;[38] ambulance replenishing;[39] health centers;[40] electronic prescribing items and services;[41] electronic health records items and services;[42] federally qualified health centers and Medicare Advantage organizations;[43] Medicare coverage gap discount program;[44] and local transportation.[45]

Each AKS safe harbor will be examined individually in Chapter 2.[46]

1.3. Key Sources of Interpretive Guidance

A. The Advisory Opinion Process

HHS is explicitly mandated by statute[47] to issue Advisory Opinions interpreting the requirements of the AKS and safe harbors, including the following:

> *(A) What constitutes prohibited remuneration within the meaning of section 1320a–7b(b) of this title [AKS] or section 1320a–7a(i)(6) of this title [CMPL].*
>
> *(B) Whether an arrangement or proposed arrangement satisfies the criteria set forth in section 1320a–7b(b)(3) of this title [Statutory Exceptions to the AKS] for activities which do not result in prohibited remuneration.*

---

37. Interim Final Rule: Federal Health Care Programs, Fraud and Abuse, Statutory Exception to the Anti-Kickback Statute for Shared Risk Arrangements (64 Fed. Reg. 63504; Nov. 19, 1999).

38. *Id.*

39. Final Rule: Ambulance Replenishing Safe Harbor Under the Anti-Kickback Statute (66 Fed. Reg. 62979; Dec. 4, 2001).

40. Final Rule: Safe Harbor for Federally Qualified Health Centers Arrangements Under the Anti-Kickback Statute (72 Fed. Reg. 56632; Oct. 4, 2007).

41. Final Rule: Safe Harbors for Certain Electronic Prescribing and Electronic Health Records Under the Anti-Kickback Statute (71 Fed. Reg. 45110; Aug. 8, 2006); Final Rule: Medicare and State Health Care Programs: Fraud and Abuse; Electronic Health Records Safe Harbor Under the Anti-Kickback Statute (78 Fed. Reg. 79202; Dec. 27, 2013).

42. *Id.*

43. Final Rule: Medicare and State Health Care Programs: Fraud and Abuse; Revisions to the Safe Harbors Under the Anti-Kickback Statute and Civil Monetary Penalty Rules Regarding Beneficiary Inducements (81 Fed. Reg. 88368; Dec. 7, 2016).

44. *Id.*

45. *Id.*

46. OIG issued proposed rules in 2019 that would revise several AKS safe harbors and add some new ones as well. The proposed changes may be found at 84 Fed. Reg. 55694 and 84 Fed. Reg. 2340. Once these rules are finalized, the authors will update this guidance.

47. 42 U.S.C. § 1320a-7d(b)(2); 42 C.F.R. pt. 1008.

(C) *Whether an arrangement or proposed arrangement satisfies the criteria which the Secretary has established, or shall establish by regulation for activities which do not result in prohibited remuneration [Safe Harbors].*

(D) *What constitutes an inducement to reduce or limit services to individuals entitled to benefits under subchapter XVIII or subchapter XIX within the meaning of section 1320a–7a(b) of this title.*

(E) *Whether any activity or proposed activity constitutes grounds for the imposition of a sanction under section 1320a–7 [Exclusions], 1320a–7a [CMPL], or 1320a–7b [AKS] of this title.*

HHS is prohibited from opining on the fair market value of goods, services, or property, or on whether any individual is a *bona fide* employee within the requirements of the Internal Revenue Code, 26 U.S.C. § 3121(d)(2).[48] An Advisory Opinion concerning a proposed business arrangement is binding only on HHS and the party requesting the Advisory Opinion, and a party's failure to request an Advisory Opinion may not be used as evidence that the party intended to violate the AKS or the provisions of 42 U.S.C. § 1320a-7a (CMPL) or 42 U.S.C. § 1320a-7 (Exclusions).[49] Advisory Opinions are nonetheless a major source of interpretive guidance concerning the scope and limits of the AKS and the safe harbors, and they are routinely consulted for this purpose by health law practitioners.

B. *Notice and Comment Rulemaking*

Another key source of interpretive guidance for the AKS may be found in the preambles and responses of HHS to comments from the public that are made as part of the Notice and Comment procedure required for the adoption and modification of AKS safe harbors. Given that these agency interpretive comments are made in the exercise of safe harbor rulemaking authority delegated by Congress, and against the backdrop of broad statutory authority from Congress tasking HHS with opining on what constitutes prohibited remuneration under the AKS and on whether business arrangements will be found to satisfy safe harbor requirements, these comments are likely entitled to a significant degree of deference.[50]

48. 42 U.S.C. § 1320a-7d(b)(3).
49. 42 U.S.C. § 1320a-7d(b)(4).
50. *See, e.g.*, Chevron v. Natural Res. Def. Council, Inc., 467 U.S. 837 (1984).

C. *Special Fraud Alerts and Special Advisory Bulletins*

The OIG is charged by statute with the responsibility of issuing Special Fraud Alerts in response to a request "for a notice which informs the public of practices which [the OIG] considers to be suspect or of particular concern" under Medicare, Medicaid, or any other qualifying state health care program.[51] Upon receiving such a request, the OIG is required to investigate and determine whether a special fraud alert should be issued, and if so, the alert is published in the *Federal Register*.[52] In issuing a Special Fraud Alert, the OIG is permitted to consider "whether and to what extent" as well as the "volume and frequency" of the practices to be addressed in the alert might result in any of the consequences that are identified in the law as appropriate considerations for HHS in deciding whether to modify or adopt new AKS safe harbors.[53] Special Advisory Bulletins are another form of periodic notice utilized by the OIG to warn the health care industry against suspect practices under the AKS. These OIG advisories contain useful analysis and guidance concerning business practices that the OIG believes may violate the AKS and/or not fall within the protections of any AKS safe harbor.

D. *Case Law*

In addition to the administrative sources already described, courts are a vital source of interpretive guidance concerning the AKS and safe harbors. As previously noted, the prevailing "one purpose test," holding that just one purpose of an arrangement involving the payment or receipt of remuneration need be inducing referrals to trigger the AKS, is a product of case law development. The meaning of key statutory terms such as "remuneration," the need for strict compliance with safe harbor requirements, and whether those requirements are satisfied in particular cases likewise are issues that have been clarified in judicial opinions.

51. 42 U.S.C. § 1320a-7d(c)(1)(A).
52. 42 U.S.C. § 1320a-7d(c)(1)(B).
53. 42 U.S.C. § 1320a-7d(c)(2)(A) and (B).

2
Statutory Exceptions and Safe Harbors

2.1. Investment Interests

The Anti-Kickback Statute (AKS) includes a safe harbor for certain investment interests under special conditions.

An "investment interest" is defined to include both debt and equity and extends to any "security issued by an entity," including "shares in a corporation, interests or units in a partnership or limited liability company, bonds, debentures, notes, or other debt instruments."[54]

Who qualifies as an "investor" under the investment interest safe harbor is broadly defined by the US Department of Health and Human Services (HHS), and includes "both individuals and entities who either directly or indirectly hold an investment interest in an entity."[55] Thus, "a family member of a referring physician may hold the investment interest in the joint venture entity, or a referring physician may have a legal or beneficial interest in an entity, such as his or her group practice, a trust or a holding company, where that entity directly holds the investment interest in the joint venture entity."[56] In such cases, HHS will deem the physician "as having the ownership interest in the joint venture entity."[57]

54. 42 C.F.R. § 1001.952(a)(4).
55. Final Rule: HHS Anti-Kickback Provisions (56 Fed. Reg. 35952, 35963; July 29, 1991): Final rulemaking promulgating the ten original safe harbor provisions.
56. *Id.* at 35964.
57. *Id.*

The safe harbor distinguishes between active and passive investors. An active investor is defined as either one "who is responsible for the day-to-day management of the entity and is a bona fide general partner in a partnership . . . or who agrees in writing to undertake liability for the actions of the entity's agents acting within the scope of their agency."[58] A passive investor is defined as one "who is not an active investor, such as a limited partner in a partnership . . . a shareholder in a corporation, or a holder of a debt security."[59]

HHS will frequently distinguish between investors doing business with the investment entity and those who are only seeking a return on their investment. HHS deems an investor doing business "in any manner" with the investment entity to be "an investor who is in a position to make or influence referrals to, furnish items or services to, or otherwise generate business for the entity."[60] This classification is not limited to those who actually make referrals to the entity, but rather focuses "on the status of the investor and the ability to make or influence the referral stream or level of business activity for the entity."[61] These investors may include physicians, hospitals, or any other entities able to influence referrals.[62]

An investor "doing business with the entity" includes "those investors who furnish items and services to the entity" and also "those investors who otherwise generate business for the entity."[63] However, investors such as "retired physicians [who] no longer make or influence referrals," or "a physician who resides and practices in a separate service area from the entity" and likewise cannot make or influence referrals, or an investor who has agreed as a matter of contract not to make or influence referrals, may not qualify as an "investor doing business with the entity" for purposes of the safe harbor.[64] It is a fact-dependent inquiry.

Generally, HHS "will accept a written stipulation that for the life of the investment the investor will not make referrals to, furnish items or services for, or otherwise generate business for the entity."[65] Due to the potential for abuse in using such a stipulation, however, HHS has stated that "the

58. 42 C.F.R. § 1001.952(a)(4).
59. *Id.*
60. *Id.*
61. *Id.*
62. *Id.*
63. *Id.*
64. *Id.*
65. *Id.*

investor must be bound to [the] agreement for the life of the investment as long as he or she remains an investor."[66] Generally, the investment interest safe harbors "protect against possible illegal remuneration by ensuring that Interested Investors are not in a position to dominate the joint venture's business, thereby increasing the likelihood that the joint venture has an independent and legitimate business purpose, and that any return on investment derives predominately from such business."[67] "Interested investors" are investors "who make referrals or who are in a position to make referrals or furnish items or services to the entity."[68]

A. *Large Publicly Traded Entities*

The safe harbor for investment interests is codified at 42 C.F.R. § 1001.952(a). The first category of investment interest is set forth at subparagraph (1) and applies to large, publicly traded entities:

> (a) *Investment interests.* As used in section 1128B of the Act, "remuneration" does not include any payment that is a return on an investment interest, such as a dividend or interest income, made to an investor as long as all of the applicable standards are met within one of the following three categories of entities:
>
> (1) If, within the previous fiscal year or previous 12 month period, the entity possesses more than $50,000,000 in undepreciated net tangible assets (based on the net acquisition cost of purchasing such assets from an unrelated entity) related to the furnishing of health care items and services, all of the following five standards must be met -
>
> (i) With respect to an investment interest that is an equity security, the equity security must be registered with the Securities and Exchange Commission under 15 U.S.C. 78l(b) or (g).
>
> (ii) The investment interest of an investor in a position to make or influence referrals to, furnish items or services to, or otherwise generate business for the entity must be obtained on terms (including any direct or

66. *Id.*

67. Advisory Opinion No. 98-12, 1998 WL 35287767 at *4 (Sept. 16, 1998).

68. Final Rule: Clarification of the Initial OIG Safe Harbor Provisions and Establishment of Additional Safe Harbor Provisions Under the Anti-Kickback Statute (64 Fed. Reg. 63518, 63533; Nov. 19, 1999).

indirect transferability restrictions) and at a price equally available to the public when trading on a registered securities exchange, such as the New York Stock Exchange or the American Stock Exchange, or in accordance with the National Association of Securities Dealers Automated Quotation System.

(iii) The entity or any investor must not market or furnish the entity's items or services (or those of another entity as part of a cross referral agreement) to passive investors differently than to non-investors.

(iv) The entity or any investor (or other individual or entity acting on behalf of the entity or any investor in the entity) must not loan funds to or guarantee a loan for an investor who is in a position to make or influence referrals to, furnish items or services to, or otherwise generate business for the entity if the investor uses any part of such loan to obtain the investment interest.

(v) The amount of payment to an investor in return for the investment interest must be directly proportional to the amount of the capital investment of that investor.

This category of investment interest was "proposed for investment interests in large public corporations where such investments are available to the general public" and requires a "minimum number of shareholders and a minimum number of assets the company must have in order to qualify."[69] HHS's intent was "to protect profit distributions made to referring investors in large publicly traded corporations where the investment interest was obtained at fair market value through trading on a publicly regulated exchange," reasoning that "[t]he remuneration received by these investors is so tangentially related to their referrals that the potential for abuse is minimal."[70] To comply with the safe harbor, the assets of the entity must be measured within the previous fiscal year or twelve-month period, which means that "growing entities will be protected as soon as they reach

69. Final Rule: HHS Anti-Kickback Provisions (56 Fed. Reg. 35952, 35953; July 29, 1991): Final rulemaking promulgating the ten original safe harbor provisions.

70. *Id.* at 35964; *see also* Advisory Opinion No. 98-12, 1998 WL 35287767 at *4 ("The requirements of the safe harbor for investments in large publicly traded entities ensure that referring investors will own such a small share of the total stock issuance that the return on investment is, at most, tangentially related to any referrals.").

compliance with all the preconditions and standards" in the safe harbor.[71] In addition, the safe harbor permits an entity "to retain safe harbor protection for a limited time period even though it is no longer in compliance with the $50 million threshold" and will be afforded "the opportunity to bring itself back into compliance."[72]

The entity further must possess that $50 million in assets in the form of undepreciated net tangible assets, which "removes many assets which [HHS] never intended to include within the scope of protection," including "all intangible assets such as the company's valuation of its name recognition and stock and other forms of goodwill."[73] HHS explained the exclusion of such assets, stating that "their valuation is too subject to 'creative' accounting or appraisal techniques."[74] Assets must also be reduced by any liabilities, such as outstanding loan obligations, but not by depreciation, as HHS decided it was "inappropriate for an entity to lose safe harbor protection as a result of the aging of its assets," and it also did not want to create incentives to replace equipment needlessly just to regain safe harbor protection.[75] The reporting of net tangible assets "must be based on net acquisition costs of purchasing such assets from an unrelated entity," a generally accepted accounting principle, and may not be based upon "a company's use of current market valuations of assets."[76] Assets that are "unrelated to a company's health care line of business cannot be used in the calculation of assets."[77] Health care–related means health care items, devices, supplies, and services as well as items or services reasonably related to the furnishing of such things, including, among other things, "non-emergency transportation, patient education, attendant services, social services . . . utilization review, quality assurance, and practice management services."[78] Marketing services are not included.[79] HHS further noted that although diversified assets could, in some cases, minimize incentives from investor referral sources, HHS "continue[d] to believe that arrangements involving ventures between

71. *Id.*
72. *Id.* at 35965.
73. *Id.*
74. *Id.*
75. *Id.*
76. *Id.*
77. *Id.*
78. Final Rule: Clarification of the Initial OIG Safe Harbor Provisions and Establishment of Additional Safe Harbor Provisions Under the Anti-Kickback Statute (64 Fed. Reg. 63518, 63522; Nov. 19, 1999).
79. *Id.*

health care businesses and non-health care businesses pose an increased risk of program abuse." As an example, HHS stated that it "would be an obvious sham, inconsistent with our original intent, if a joint venture could merge with a non-health care business and have those non-health care assets, and the revenues derived from that non-health care line of business counted for the purposes of qualifying for safe harbor protection."[80] Tangible assets that are used to furnish items and services may be counted even if they are not allowable costs under Medicare.[81]

Addressing the specific elements of the safe harbor, HHS stated that element (a)(1)(i) "applies only to an investment interest in an equity security, and requires such a security to be registered with the SEC," noting that requiring actual registration "provides a clear bright-line rule, and is an indication of good-faith entry into the public securities markets, which is a significant factor underlying the rationale for this safe harbor."[82] Actual registration is also required so that certain exempt securities, which may be actively traded without being registered or subject to SEC oversight, will not receive protection under the safe harbor.[83] The registration requirement, however, does not apply to debt securities because "[p]ublicly traded debt instruments, although protected under this safe harbor, are not the type of investment interests that are the focal point of the rule," and while "the potential for abuse is present," HHS was not aware of actual abuse relating to debt securities and determined "that their usefulness as instruments for inducing investors' referrals is more limited than equity investment interests."[84]

HHS next addressed element (a)(1)(ii), commenting that the standard requiring that an investor in a position to make or influence referrals obtain his or her investment interest on terms equally available to the public through a national securities exchange was intended "to preclude safe harbor protection for securities traded through the so-called 'pink sheets' or those 'non-NASDAQ' securities that are traded through the OTC Bulletin Board Service."[85] HHS noted that this requirement

80. *Id.*
81. Final Rule: HHS Anti-Kickback Provisions (56 Fed. Reg. 35952, 35965; July 29, 1991): Final rulemaking promulgating the ten original safe harbor provisions.
82. *Id.*
83. *Id.*
84. *Id.*
85. *Id.*

> follow[ed] [its] original intent to assure that the investment interests of physicians or others in a position to influence referrals must be obtained through the kind of arms-length trading that is normally associated with actively traded public securities at . . . fair market value through a publicly regulated exchange. Such public trading assures that the entity does not obtain capital by self-selecting investors based on their status as sources of referrals.[86]

Regarding the meaning of "on terms equally available," HHS has stated that "an investment interest is obtained on equally available terms if it is obtained at the same price as is available to the general public trading on a registered exchange through a broker and is not subject to restrictions on transferability."[87] On this subject, HHS identified "two significant concerns" in relation to investments in health care–related businesses:

> First, we are concerned that limited transferability or other restrictions on the sale or disposition of stock may serve to "lock" interested investors into specific investments, thereby increasing the incentives for those investors to refer Federal health care program business to the investment entity. Second, we are concerned that interested investors who are potential referral sources for the investment entity not be permitted to obtain their investment interests at insider prices or at prices more favorable than those available to the general public when purchasing stock from a registered national securities exchange through a broker. Such favorable treatment could potentially be disguised remuneration for referrals. For example, we are aware of certain public offerings of health care companies that involve simultaneous acquisitions of physician practices in exchange for stock in the newly-public company, with the stock valued in a manner that results in the selling physician obtaining the stock at a lower price or on more advantageous terms than offered to the public. The economic benefit conferred on the physician in such an arrangement potentially violates the anti-kickback statute if one purpose of the benefit is to reward or

86. *Id.*

87. Final Rule: Clarification of the Initial OIG Safe Harbor Provisions and Establishment of Additional Safe Harbor Provisions Under the Anti-Kickback Statute (64 Fed. Reg. 63518, 63522; Nov. 19, 1999).

induce referrals. The investment would not fall within the large entity investment safe harbor.[88]

HHS announced its intention to "closely scrutinize attempts to circumvent this standard," commenting that "any investment interest obtained before an entity becomes publicly traded is not protected under this provisions" and that "an investor is not protected by exchanging a limited partnership interest for shares in a newly formed entity that is publicly traded."[89] HHS further noted that the safe harbor will not protect investment interests "where physicians are afforded the opportunity to buy the available shares of an entity before other members of the public have the opportunity to invest in that entity," noting that such an entity "would have only physicians as investors" and that HHS did not wish to protect payments from that type of entity.[90] The public must have a legitimate opportunity to invest and "[w]here referring sources (or their immediate families) hold a large proportion of the shares, [HHS] will presume that this standard has not been met."[91]

Regarding element (a)(1)(iii), HHS explained that "although an entity may seek referrals or other business from passive investors, it must promote and furnish its items or services to investors and non-investors in the same manner," and "[a]n entity may not use a separate marketing approach or provide a different level of service to passive investors as opposed to non-investors" by, for example, referring to one's position as an investor or offering "special arrangements" to investors that are not offered to noninvestors.[92] Also, HHS commented that "[a]ny distribution to passive investors of individual or aggregate referral patterns" would not be protected and that "the entity or any investor must not promote the items or services of other entities as part of a cross referral agreement."[93]

Explaining the requirement in (a)(1)(iv), HHS stated that "[w]e do not believe protection should be afforded where an investor is loaned money from the entity, or from a parent or subsidiary corporation (or is guaranteed a loan by the entity or a related organization), and the investor makes an investment

88. *Id.*

89. Final Rule: HHS Anti-Kickback Provisions (56 Fed. Reg. 35952, 35965; July 29, 1991): Final rulemaking promulgating the ten original safe harbor provisions.

90. *Id.*

91. *Id.*

92. Final Rule: HHS Anti-Kickback Provisions (56 Fed. Reg. 35952, 35966; July 29, 1991): Final rulemaking promulgating the ten original safe harbor provisions.

93. *Id.*

based on that loan. . . . In such a situation, the investor is adding no real capital to the entity."[94] This prohibition "includes any such loan from another investor or a person acting on behalf of the entity or any investor."[95] HHS conceded, however, that "safe harbor protection is available where the investor borrows from other sources, such as from his or her broker or a bank."[96] Finally, addressing (a)(1)(v), HHS stated that "the amount of payment in return for the investment interest must be directly proportional to the amount of the capital investment" because "such payments are consistent with the type of corporate dividend payment that [HHS] is trying to protect."[97]

B. Small Entities Owned by Active or Passive Investors

The safe harbor for investment interests in small entities owned by active or passive investors is codified at 42 C.F.R. § 1001.952(a)(2):

> (2) If the entity possesses investment interests that are held by either active or passive investors, all of the following eight applicable standards must be met -
>
> (i) No more than 40 percent of the value of the investment interests of each class of investment interests may be held in the previous fiscal year or previous 12 month period by investors who are in a position to make or influence referrals to, furnish items or services to, or otherwise generate business for the entity. (For purposes of paragraph (a)(2)(i) of this section, equivalent classes of equity investments may be combined, and equivalent classes of debt instruments may be combined.)
>
> (ii) The terms on which an investment interest is offered to a passive investor, if any, who is in a position to make or influence referrals to, furnish items or services to, or otherwise generate business for the entity must be no different from the terms offered to other passive investors.
>
> (iii) The terms on which an investment interest is offered to an investor who is in a position to make or influence referrals to,

94. *Id.*

95. Final Rule: Clarification of the Initial OIG Safe Harbor Provisions and Establishment of Additional Safe Harbor Provisions Under the Anti-Kickback Statute (64 Fed. Reg. 63518, 63521; Nov. 19, 1999).

96. Final Rule: HHS Anti-Kickback Provisions (56 Fed. Reg. 35952, 35966; July 29, 1991): Final rulemaking promulgating the ten original safe harbor provisions.

97. *Id.*

furnish items or services to, or otherwise generate business for the entity must not be related to the previous or expected volume of referrals, items or services furnished, or the amount of business otherwise generated from that investor to the entity.

(iv) There is no requirement that a passive investor, if any, make referrals to, be in a position to make or influence referrals to, furnish items or services to, or otherwise generate business for the entity as a condition for remaining as an investor.

(v) The entity or any investor must not market or furnish the entity's items or services (or those of another entity as part of a cross referral agreement) to passive investors differently than to non-investors.

(vi) No more than 40 percent of the entity's gross revenue related to the furnishing of health care items and services in the previous fiscal year or previous 12-month period may come from referrals or business otherwise generated from investors.

(vii) The entity or any investor (or other individual or entity acting on behalf of the entity or any investor in the entity) must not loan funds to or guarantee a loan for an investor who is in a position to make or influence referrals to, furnish items or services to, or otherwise generate business for the entity if the investor uses any part of such loan to obtain the investment interest.

(viii) The amount of payment to an investor in return for the investment interest must be directly proportional to the amount of the capital investment (including the fair market value of any pre-operational services rendered) of that investor.

This safe harbor is intended to "protect payments from investment in small entities, particularly limited and general partnership interests."[98] HHS noted that due to "the significant business investment activities in these small entities—typically joint ventures—and the advantages of permitting them in

98. *Id.* HHS further noted that the small entity investment interest safe harbor was developed, in part, based on the agency's experience enforcing the AKS, including "investigations of abusive joint venture arrangements, our Fraud Alert describing suspect features of these arrangements [*see* discussion, *infra*], and our Report to Congress entitled 'Financial Arrangements Between Physicians and Health Care Businesses' (OIG, Office of Analysis and Inspections, May 1989). [The report] disclosed in detail both the extensive ownership of joint ventures by physicians, and the additional services received by patients of these physicians as compared to all Medicare patients in general." *Id.* at 35967.

certain situations, we believe that safe harbor protection is warranted."[99] HHS, however, also sounded its alarm over "widespread abuses in many of these joint ventures," commenting that "we believe that a large number of these newly formed entities are designed to have physicians as investors specifically to induce them to use the entity in which they have invested" and that, accordingly, "any safe harbor protection must include significant safeguards to minimize any corrupting influence the investment interest may have on the physician-investor's decision where to refer a patient."[100]

HHS classified investors as either "active" or "passive":

> The definition of an "active" investor includes two categories of persons. The first category is modeled after a bona fide general partner in a partnership under the Uniform Partnership Act who is responsible for the day-to-day management of the entity.
>
> We are including a second way to qualify as an "active" investor: the individual or entity must agree in writing to undertake the liability for the partnership, including the acts of its agents acting within the scope of their agency. We believe that such an affirmative act will assure that the individual or entity performs many of the same functions that general partners do who actively manage the day-to-day operations of the joint venture entity. For example, these active investors undertake the business risk that a typical general partner does, and will be interested in assuring that the day-to-day managers of the entity engage in sound business practices and not run afoul of the statute as well as other Federal and State laws and regulations.
>
> "Passive" investors are those investors who are not active investors, such as limited partners in a partnership or shareholders in a corporation.[101]

HHS stressed that "the standards for this safe harbor must be met by all the investors in the entity" and that "to the extent that one class of investors, such as active investors, qualifies, but the passive investors do not meet one of the standards, safe harbor protection is not given to payments to any investors in the entity."[102] As an example, HHS explained that if a group of individuals were passive investors in an entity that was itself an

99. *Id.* at 35966.
100. *Id.*
101. *Id.* at 35967.
102. *Id.*

active investor in another entity, then the first entity would have to meet all requirements for active investors and the group of individuals would have to meet all requirements for passive investors.[103]

Describing its development of the small entity safe harbor standards, HHS commented:

> The standards for this provision are structured into three categories that we have identified as being of concern to us in joint venture arrangements: (1) The manner in which investors are selected and retained, (2) the nature of their business structure, and (3) the financing and profit distributions. To the extent possible, we have adopted bright line rules. We believe that this approach will facilitate compliance because investors will be able to determine easily whether they meet the conditions of safe harbor protection.[104]

The five standards contained in subparagraphs (a)(2)(i)–(v) of the safe harbor are intended to address the first category of concern. HHS explained that the first standard, limiting those "in a position to make or influence referrals to, furnish items or services to, or otherwise generate business for the entity" to 40 percent of the value of the investment interests in the entity, "requires not only that a bona fide opportunity to invest has been afforded to people not in a position to make referrals, but that these individuals hold at least 60 percent of the value of the investment interests in each class of investments."[105] HHS described this as an "outcome measure" that would "provide a bright line test which will assist all the parties to the joint venture and [HHS] in determining whether compliance with this first standard has been achieved."[106] HHS commented that "classifying investors who provide items and services together with investors who make or influence referrals to the entity" was necessary to prevent an outside vendor (e.g., durable medical equipment [DME] supplier) from forming a joint venture with referring physicians under circumstances in which all of the joint venture owners "would be doing business with the joint venture by either furnishing items or making referrals."[107] Classifying both categories of investor together means that "at least 60 percent of the value

---

103. *Id.*
104. *Id.*
105. *Id.* at 35968.
106. *Id.*
107. *Id.*

of the investment interests must be held by investors who will neither make referrals nor engage in business activity with the entity."[108]

In ensuring conformity with this requirement, "the joint venture is free to use any internal accounting principles it chooses to adopt so long as it uses such principles consistently over time so that it is not manipulating data to obscure its noncompliance."[109] The standard permits two different measurement periods. The joint venture may use either its prior fiscal year or the previous twelve-month period. If a calendar year is the venture's fiscal year, then it may look at "the number and status of investors" either in the prior year, or in the twelve-month period immediately preceding the current date.[110] HHS stressed, however, that it would be "highly unlikely" to pursue an investigation of a joint venture where it is out of compliance with the 60 and 40 percent standard based on its prior fiscal year "but is making a good-faith effort to reach compliance with this standard based on data showing compliance on a monthly basis for the most recent months of operation."[111]

The next two standards contained in (a)(2)(ii) and (a)(2)(iii) "address the problems of discriminatory marketing strategies that result in the offer of better deals, for example, more shares or a better price, to individuals who will refer a high volume of patients."[112] Standard (a)(2)(ii) "focuses on the *status* of investor and bars safe harbor protection where the terms of investment opportunities depend on whether a passive investor is in a position to influence referrals, furnish items or services, or otherwise generate business for the entity."[113] Investments may only be offered to such investors "on the same terms as those offered to other passive investors not in a position to influence the flow of business to the entity."[114] The standard does not apply to active investors in view of the fact that "it is precisely because of a physician's familiarity with the health care field that he or she may be chosen as a general partner and offered different investment terms from those offered to passive investors."[115]

Standard (a)(2)(iii) "assumes that an investment interest is being offered to a person in a position to make referrals, but bars the offering of favorable

108. *Id.*
109. *Id.*
110. *Id.*
111. *Id.*
112. *Id.*
113. *Id.*
114. *Id.*
115. *Id.*

terms based on his or her past or expected referrals or amount of business otherwise generated for the entity."[116] This standard applies to both active and passive investors based on the view of HHS that "it is inappropriate to protect all investment interests where any investor, even general partners, can obtain more shares because they can be expected to generate more business for the entity."[117]

Standards (a)(2)(iv) and (v) relate to how investors are retained:

> The fourth standard bars the entity from requiring passive investors to make referrals or remain in a position to make referrals as a condition for retaining their investment. The fifth standard parallels the new standard for publicly traded entities and requires the entity and investors not to market or furnish items or services to passive investors in any manner differently than to non-investors. . . .
>
> [The] fifth standard also requires the entity and any investor not to promote the services of other entities as part of a cross referral agreement.[118]

These two standards apply only to passive investors in recognition of the fact that "active investors are often sought out because they will help generate business for the joint venture."[119]

Standard (a)(2)(vi) relates to the second category of HHS concern (i.e., the nature of the business structure). The requirement that no more than 40 percent of the joint venture's revenue come from investor referrals stems from HHS's concern over situations in which "the referrals from investing physicians dominate the joint venture's business so that it does not have to compete for outside business and that it cannot survive without such referrals from its investing physicians," with the result that "the business purpose of the joint venture becomes suspect."[120] This sixth standard, combined with the first standard imposing a 60 and 40 percent ownership requirement, "provide clear rules which assure that no protection is afforded to joint ventures that operate primarily on the referrals of physician investors."[121] As explained by HHS:

116. *Id.*
117. *Id.*
118. *Id.* at 35969.
119. *Id.*
120. *Id.*
121. *Id.*

> By requiring that no more than 40 percent of the joint venture's revenue come from investors' referrals, we help assure that revenues of these joint ventures come from a wider group than referrals from physician investors. And by limiting the number of investors who make referrals, we help assure that the profits from these entities are distributed to a wider group than referring physician investors. Thus, these two standards will help assure that joint ventures are not dependent on the capital and referrals of physician-investors.[122]

This standard, like the first 40 percent standard, allows "a joint venture to use any internal accounting principle it chooses to adopt so long as it uses such principles consistently" and is "not manipulating the data to obscure its non-compliance."[123] Also, as with the first standard, the joint venture entity can measure its compliance by reference to its prior fiscal year or the previous twelve-month period.[124] And, again, HHS noted that it would be highly unlikely to initiate an investigation where the joint venture is in compliance with the other standards but is not in compliance with this standard based on prior fiscal year data, provided that it is making a "good-faith effort" to comply "based on data showing compliance on a monthly basis for the most recent months of operation."[125] HHS reiterated that in applying both 40 percent standards in situations in which the joint venture entity is owned by other entities, HHS

> will examine the ownership structure of these other entities to determine whether they are owned by physicians who are referring to the joint venture entity. In such a situation, these physicians are considered to be investors of the joint venture entity, and their ownership interest must be offset by non-referring owners and the revenue they generate for the joint venture must be offset by referrals from non-investors.

Standards (a)(2)(vii) and (viii) relate to the third category of HHS concern (i.e., financing and profit distributions). Standard (a)(2)(vii) is intended "to assure that the investments are bona fide, i.e., that investors' funds are genuinely at risk."[126] Accordingly, although the joint venture entity "may

---

122. *Id.*
123. *Id.*
124. *Id.*
125. *Id.*
126. *Id.* at 35970.

borrow from the investor, and investors may borrow from other sources to obtain funds to use for the capital investment," the entity "cannot lend the funds or guarantee loans used to make the investment."[127] This is because if the investment is made with capital provided by the entity, the investor is "adding no real capital to it," and the purpose of the standard is to "help assure that physicians and other investors in fact provide new needed capital and that the joint venture is not in reality a sham to facilitate the distribution of payments for referrals."[128] Moreover, HHS noted that "it is useful to analyze joint ventures on a case-by-case basis to determine what the real capital needs of the project are, and whether the capital that has been invested is merely a sham to pay investors for referrals."[129]

Standard (a)(2)(viii) provides that, in order to receive protection, "dividend payments can only be tied to the number of shares owned by an investor, and not to his or her referrals," and where investors "contribute capital in the form of pre-operational services or sweat equity, their dividend payments may reflect the fair market value of those services rendered."[130] This standard does not protect "payments to active investors for operational services they provide to the joint venture" but only "payments that represent a return on investment."[131] Protection for payments made in return for personal services is governed by the personal services and management contracts safe harbor, not the investment interests safe harbor.

The HHS, Office of Inspector General (OIG) has issued Special Fraud Alerts to discuss joint venture arrangements that it considers to be suspect and potentially violative of the AKS and outside the protection of this safe harbor. The first such Special Fraud Alert was issued in 1989 and announced that the OIG had "become aware of a proliferation of arrangements between those in a position to refer business, such as physicians, and those providing items or services for which Medicare or Medicaid pays," including "clinical diagnostic laboratory services, durable medical equipment (DME), and other diagnostic services."[132] The OIG went on to describe the nature of joint ventures and how they may be found to violate the AKS:

---

127. *Id.*
128. *Id.*
129. *Id.*
130. *Id.*
131. *Id.*
132. Special Fraud Alert: Joint Venture Arrangements (Issued Aug. 1989).

> A joint venture may take a variety of forms: it may be a contractual arrangement between two or more parties to cooperate in providing services, or it may involve the partnership or closely held corporation, to provide such services. Of course, there may be legitimate reasons to form a joint venture, such as raising necessary investment capital. However, [OIG] believes that some of these joint ventures may violate the [AKS].
>
> Under these suspect joint ventures, physicians may become investors in a newly formed joint venture entity. The investors refer their patients to this new entity, and are paid by the entity in the form of "profit distributions." These [suspect] joint ventures may be intended not so much to raise investment capital legitimately to start a business, but to lock up a stream of referrals from the physician investors and to compensate them indirectly for these referrals. Because physician investors can benefit financially from their referrals, unnecessary procedures and tests may be ordered or performed, resulting in unnecessary program expenditures.

The OIG identified a nonexclusive set of factors that, viewed separately or collectively, could indicate the existence of a joint venture that violates the AKS:

1. Investor

- Investors are chosen because they are in a position to make referrals.
- Physicians who are expected to make a large number of referrals may be offered a greater investment opportunity in the joint venture than those anticipated to make fewer referrals.
- Physician investors may be actively encouraged to make referrals to the joint venture, and may be encouraged to divest their ownership interest if they fail to sustain an "acceptable" level of referrals.
- The joint venture tracks its sources of referrals, and distributes this information to the investors.
- Investors may be required to divest their ownership interest if they cease to practice in the service area, for example, if they move, become disabled, or retire.
- Investment interests may be nontransferable.

2. Business Structure

- The structure of some joint ventures may be suspect. For example, one of the parties may be an ongoing entity already engaged in a particular line of business. That party may act as the reference laboratory or DME supplier for the joint venture. In some of these cases, the joint venture can be best characterized as a "shell."

- In the case of a shell laboratory joint venture, for example:
  - It conducts very little testing on the premises, even though it is Medicare certified.
  - The reference laboratory may do the vast bulk of the testing at its central processing laboratory, even though it also serves as the "manager" of the shell laboratory.
  - Despite the location of the actual testing, the local "shell"' laboratory bills Medicare directly for these tests.
- In the case of a shell DME joint venture, for example:
  - It owns very little of the DME or other capital equipment; rather, the ongoing entity owns them.
  - The ongoing entity is responsible for all day-to-day operations of the joint venture, such as delivery of the DME and billing.

3. Financing and Profit Distribution

- The amount of capital invested by the physician may be disproportionately small and the returns on investment may be disproportionately large when compared to a typical investment in a new business enterprise.
- The amount of capital invested by the physician may be disproportionately small and the returns on investment may be disproportionately large when compared to a typical investment in a new business enterprise.
- Physician investors may invest only a nominal amount, such as $500 to $1500.
- Physician investors may be permitted to "borrow" the amount of the "investment" from the entity and pay it back through deductions from profit distributions, thus eliminating even the need to contribute cash to the partnership.
- Investors may be paid extraordinary returns on the investment in comparison with the risk involved, often well over 50 to 100 percent per year.[133]

---

133. *Id.*

The OIG returned to the subject of suspect joint ventures in April 2003, when it issued a Special Advisory Bulletin on "Contractual Joint Ventures."[134] Referencing its 1989 bulletin, the OIG stated that it had observed the continued proliferation of joint ventures despite its prior warning. Defining a "joint venture" to be "any common enterprise with mutual economic benefit," the 2003 Special Advisory Bulletin focused on "questionable contractual arrangements where a health care provider in one line of business . . . expands into a related health care business by contracting with an existing provider of a related item or service . . . to provide the new item or service to the [first provider's] existing patient population."[135] In such arrangements, the second provider frequently "not only manages the new line of business, but may also supply it with inventory, employees, space, billing, and other services."[136] In this way, the first provider (typically an owner of the related line of business) effectively "contracts out substantially the entire operation of the related line of business" to the second provider, who might otherwise have been a competitor, and in return receives the profits of the business, including revenues earned as a result of federal health care program referrals.[137]

The OIG offered several examples of these kinds of contractual joint ventures, including (1) a hospital that establishes a DME subsidiary and contracts out the entire operation to an existing DME company; (2) a DME company that forms its own mail order pharmacy to supply nebulizer drugs and contracts with an existing mail order pharmacy to run the entire operation and sell nebulizer drugs to the DME company pharmacy for inventory; and (3) a nephrology group that establishes a wholly owned company to provide dialysis supplies to dialysis patients, and the company contracts out the entire operation to an existing home dialysis supplier.[138]

The OIG identified certain "common elements" to such suspect joint ventures:

1. the owner is expanding into a related line of business (either organized separately or as part of an existing entity) that is dependent on owner-generated referrals or other business and which serves the owner's existing patient base;

134. Special Advisory Bulletin: Contractual Joint Ventures (Issued April 2003).
135. *Id.*
136. *Id.*
137. *Id.*
138. *Id.*

2. the owner does not operate or commit significant financial or other resources to the new business, but contracts out substantially all the operations to another party that supplies management services and everything else needed to run the business, including inventory, personnel, space, and billing, which is done in the name of the owner. Contracts may include non-competition provisions that result in an exclusive dealing arrangement, and the owner does not assume meaningful business risk as a result of its ability to influence referrals to the new business.
3. the manager of the new line of business is an established provider of the same services and would, absent the joint venture, be a competitor of the new line of business, providing and billing for those services in its own name.
4. the owner and manager share in the economic benefits of the new line of business, with the manager earning revenues through its various contracts with the owner, and the owner receiving residual profits from the new line of business.
5. payments to the manager, particularly for goods and services, typically vary with the value or volume of referrals or other business generated by the owner, as will the owner's profits.[139]

The OIG warned that these suspect joint ventures may not be protected under any safe harbor, despite efforts "to carve otherwise problematic contracting arrangements into several different contracts for discrete items or services . . . and then qualify each separate contract for protection under a 'safe harbor'."[140] The OIG commented that, to the extent a manager is selling items or services to an owner as a discount, it is not protected by the discount safe harbor, which "does not protect—and has never protected—prices offered by a seller to a buyer in connection with a common enterprise."[141] Such a price reduction must be based on an arms-length transaction, and "the provision of items or services to a joint venture by a participant in the venture is not an 'arms length' transaction."[142]

The OIG also pointed out that any safe harbors that do apply would only protect the compensation flowing from the owner to the manager for actual services rendered but would not protect remuneration that "is often the

139. *Id.*
140. *Id.*
141. *Id.*
142. *Id.*

difference between the money paid by the Owner to the Manager/Supplier and the reimbursement received from the federal health care programs" since the manager, in "agreeing effectively to provide services it could otherwise provide in its own right for less than the available reimbursement . . . is providing the Owner with the opportunity to generate a fee and a profit."[143] That business opportunity "is itself remuneration that may implicate the anti-kickback statute."

The OIG summarized a nonexclusive list of characteristics that, viewed together and/or separately, potentially indicate a prohibited arrangement: (1) the new business is an expansion into a new line of health care business that can be provided to an owner's existing patients; (2) the new business is designed to exclusively or predominantly service an existing, captive patient base of the owner; (3) the owner's primary contributions are the referrals, with the entire operation delegated to the manager, and the owner taking on no real business risk and making little or no financial investment; (4) the manager/supplier would normally compete for the owner's referrals and has the ability to provide the same services and bill in its own name; (5) the manager/supplier provides all or most key services to the new business; (6) the practical effect of the arrangement is to permit the owner to bill insurers and patients for business otherwise provided by the manager/supplier; and (7) a noncompete clause exists that prohibits the owner from providing items or services to outside patients and/or prohibits the manager/supplier from providing services in its own right to the owner's patients.[144]

A significant number of Advisory Opinions have opined on the safe harbor for small entity investment interests in the context of proposed business arrangements or joint ventures.[145] One example of a venture that the OIG determined presented an unacceptable risk of violating the AKS is discussed in Advisory Opinion No. 11-15.[146] There, the OIG addressed a proposed arrangement in which a physician-owned and physician-managed company (Company A) would contract with another company that either currently operated or would form a Medicare-certified clinical anatomic pathology

143. *Id.*

144. *Id.*

145. There is also case law discussing the requirements of this safe harbor in the context of a False Claims Act lawsuit in which joint venture partners in a pharmacy business who also owned nursing homes were alleged to have arranged the investment opportunity for the purpose of securing pharmacy referrals. *See* United States *ex rel.* Nehls v. Omnicare, Inc., 2013 WL 3819671 at **14-15 (July 23, 2013, N.D. Ill.).

146. Advisory Opinion 11-15 (Issued Oct. 3, 2011).

laboratory (Company B). The physician certified that he would not refer the physician's own patients or otherwise generate business in connection with the arrangement. Company B would enter into a management services contract with Company A for at least a three-year term. Under the contract, Company A would provide Company B with all required services, including utilities, furniture, fixtures, use of lab space and equipment, marketing, billing, and nonphysician support staff. Company B would pay Company A a usage fee based on a percentage of Company B's income, fixed in advance for one year, generally corresponding to the volume of Company B's use of Company A's services. Company A certified that the usage fee would represent fair market value for the use of its services. The physician would offer the opportunity to invest in Company A to other physicians, most of whom would have little or no experience in clinical laboratory services, but he would hire others with the appropriate experience as employees or contractors. Physician investors in a position to refer lab specimens to Company A would account for more than 40 percent of the value of all investment interests in Company A, and more than 40 percent of Company A's gross revenue would be sourced to the referrals of such physician investors, although there would be no requirement that physician investors refer to Company A. Membership interests would be purchased based on the book value of Company A multiplied by the pro rata share purchased, and profit distributions would correspond to an investor's percentage membership interest in Company A.[147]

As the fact pattern involves "ownership of a non-public entity by interested investors," the OIG noted that the small entity investment safe harbor was "potentially applicable."[148] The OIG quickly concluded, however, that the safe harbor could not apply on these facts since both 40 percent requirements were not satisfied, commenting that "[a]s the result of noncompliance with these elements, the small entity safe harbor would be inapplicable and would not protect [Company A's] profit distributions to the new physician investors and the [physician owner/manager]."[149] The OIG

147. *Id.*

148. *Id.*

149. *Id.* The OIG further noted that the contract arrangements for all of the services provided to Company B would not satisfy other safe harbors for space rental, equipment rental, or personal services and management contracts because the compensation would not be set in advance but would instead "be calculated based on a percentage of [Company B's income]," which would impermissibly "take into account the volume or value of business generated for [Company B] by the physician investors in the form of lab referrals." *Id.*

went on to explain, concerning the risk involved, that "[t]he absence of limits on such involvement by interested investors or other safeguards to restrain the Proposed Arrangement's reliance on investor-generated business further underscores the already-noted risks of overutilization, distorted medical decision-making, and increased program costs."[150] Furthermore, the OIG noted that given the lack of any relevant experience in clinical lab services by the physician owners of the entity providing such services, but who nonetheless have the ability to refer patients for those services, the proposed arrangement "appears to have no business purpose other than to permit the physician investors to profit from the business they generate" for Company B in the form of lab specimen referrals. Further, "[t]he fact that the profits would be obtained indirectly, because [Company B], rather than [Company A], would bill for the clinical laboratory services, is immaterial."[151]

Other Advisory Opinions declined to impose administrative sanctions on proposed arrangements even though they did not comply with the small entity investment safe harbor, and despite some concerning elements that might have violated the AKS if an intent to reward or induce referrals were present. A review of these opinions reveals a variety of mitigating factors that led the OIG to conclude in a given case that the particular arrangement under review posed an acceptably low level of risk, notwithstanding its failure to comply fully with the safe harbor and despite a fact pattern that could potentially reward or induce referrals. The OIG's restraint in these cases was based on some combination of the following elements:

- Absence of individual physician investors or physician investors who were not direct referral sources[152]
- Limited number of referrals coming from joint venture partners[153]
- Affirmative measures taken by joint venture partners to limit the ability to direct or influence referrals, including not requiring or encouraging physicians to refer patients; not tracking referrals; or not compensating potential referral sources based on the volume or value of referrals[154]

---

150. *Id.*

151. *Id.*

152. *See* Advisory Opinion No. 10-15 (Issued Aug. 31, 2010); Advisory Opinion 03-12 (Issued May 22, 2003).

153. *See* Advisory Opinion No. 05-12 (Issued Oct. 31, 2005); Advisory Opinion No. 97-5 (Issued Oct. 6, 1997).

154. *See* Advisory Opinion No. 10-15 (Issued Aug. 31, 2010); Advisory Opinion No. 05-12 (Issued Oct. 31, 2005); Advisory Opinion No. 03-12 (Issued May 22, 2003); Advisory Opinion No. 98-19 (Issued Dec. 14, 1998); Advisory Opinion No. 97-5 (Issued Oct. 6, 1997).

- Return on investment that was proportional to capital investment and not based on previous or expected volume of referrals, services furnished, or amount of business that might otherwise be generated[155]
- Any ancillary service agreements were based on fair market value and did not add appreciable risk to the arrangement[156]
- Joint venture partners that were all part of one academic medical center, where the structure of the proposed arrangement would facilitate efficient integration of their respective clinical, research, and teaching missions[157]
- Inability or a limited ability to control or influence referral frequency or volume[158]
- Business opportunity that was obtained through a competitive bidding process[159]
- Arrangement promoted a public service in a location where such a service had historically been deficient or failed financially[160]
- Investor referrals well below 40 percent so that there was a low risk the arrangement relied primarily on owner referrals[161]
- Investors assumed genuine business risk by committing financial resources and agreeing to guarantee a bank line of credit[162]
- Certification that a physician, whose family members owned 70 percent of an independent diagnostic testing facility (IDTF), would not make referrals or generate business for entity, and neither physician nor IDTF would supply DME that might create incentive for physician to slant test interpretations to support medical necessity and thus risk overutilization[163]
- Fewer than 5 percent of entity patients were beneficiaries of federal health care programs, and the vast majority of such group were referred

155. *See* Advisory Opinion No. 10-15 (Issued Aug. 31, 2010); Advisory Opinion No. 05-12 (Issued Oct. 31, 2005); Advisory Opinion No. 03-13 (Issued June 16, 2003); Advisory Opinion No. 03-12 (Issued May 22, 2003); Advisory Opinion No. 98-19 (Issued Dec. 14, 1998); Advisory Opinion No. 97-5 (Issued Oct. 6, 1997).

156. *See* Advisory Opinion No. 03-12 (Issued May 22, 2003).

157. *See* Advisory Opinion No. 10-15 (Issued Aug. 31, 2010).

158. *See* Advisory Opinion No. 09-17 (Issued Sept. 30, 2009); Advisory Opinion No. 03-12 (Issued May 22, 2003); Advisory Opinion No. 98-19 (Issued Dec. 14, 1998); Advisory Opinion No. 97-5 (Issued Oct. 6, 1997).

159. *See* Advisory Opinion No. 09-17 (Issued Sept. 30, 2009).

160. *See id.*

161. Advisory Opinion No. 03-13 (Issued June 16, 2003).

162. *See* Advisory Opinion No. 09-17 (Issued Sept. 30, 2009).

163. *See* Advisory Opinion No. 12-08 (Issued June 22, 2012).

by noninvestors, with any investor referrals required to undergo an independent evaluation by one whose compensation did not depend on evaluation results[164]

- Low risk of cross-referrals among physician investors, where each had independent practice providing similar services, and competed with each other[165]
- Low risk of overutilization of items or services, where federal health care program beneficiaries all belonged to capitated Medicaid health maintenance organization (HMO) plans, and no more than 2 percent of federally sourced revenues resulted from investor referrals[166]

C. Entities Located in Underserved Areas

The safe harbor for entities located in underserved areas is codified at 42 C.F.R. § 1001.952(a)(3):

> (3) (i) If the entity possesses investment interests that are held by either active or passive investors and is located in an underserved area, all of the following eight standards must be met -
>
> (A) No more than 50 percent of the value of the investment interests of each class of investments may be held in the previous fiscal year or previous 12-month period by investors who are in a position to make or influence referrals to, furnish items or services to, or otherwise generate business for, the entity. (For purposes of paragraph (a)(3)(i)(A) of this section, equivalent classes of equity investments may be combined, and equivalent classes of debt instruments may be combined.)
>
> (B) The terms on which an investment interest is offered to a passive investor, if any, who is in a position to make or influence referrals to, furnish items or services to, or otherwise generate business for the entity must be no different from the terms offered to other passive investors.
>
> (C) The terms on which an investment interest is offered to an investor who is in a position to make or influence referrals to, furnish items or services to, or otherwise generate business for the entity must not be related to the previous or expected

164. Advisory Opinion No. 05-12 (Issued Oct. 31, 2005).
165. *See id.*
166. *See id.*

volume of referrals, items or services furnished, or the amount of business otherwise generated from that investor to the entity.

(D) There is no requirement that a passive investor, if any, make referrals to, be in a position to make or influence referrals to, furnish items or services to, or otherwise generate business for the entity as a condition for remaining as an investor.

(E) The entity or any investor must not market or furnish the entity's items or services (or those of another entity as part of a cross-referral agreement) to passive investors differently than to non-investors.

(F) At least 75 percent of the dollar volume of the entity's business in the previous fiscal year or previous 12-month period must be derived from the service of persons who reside in an underserved area or are members of medically underserved populations.

(G) The entity or any investor (or other individual or entity acting on behalf of the entity or any investor in the entity) must not loan funds to or guarantee a loan for an investor who is in a position to make or influence referrals to, furnish items or services to, or otherwise generate business for the entity if the investor uses any part of such loan to obtain the investment interest.

(H) The amount of payment to an investor in return for the investment interest must be directly proportional to the amount of the capital investment (including the fair market value of any pre-operational services rendered) of that investor.

(ii) If an entity that otherwise meets all of the above standards is located in an area that was an underserved area at the time of the initial investment, but subsequently ceases to be an underserved area, the entity will be deemed to comply with paragraph (a)(3)(i) of this section for a period equal to the lesser of:

(A) The current term of the investment remaining after the date upon which the area ceased to be an underserved area or

(B) Three years from the date the area ceased to be an underserved area.

The OIG initially proposed this safe harbor after learning that entities in many rural areas found it difficult with the two 60-40 tests in the small entity investment interest safe harbor.[167] The OIG commented that "[e]ntities located in rural areas may have an especially difficult time complying with these two standards, because in many cases physicians may be the primary sources of capital in the area, and those physicians may have no alternative facility to which they can refer."[168] The primary concern of the OIG was to ensure "that beneficiaries have adequate access to quality health care" given the reality that "certain communities experience shortages of health care services."[169] The safe harbor was "designed to balance the interests of those communities in facilitating the development of health care services with the anti-fraud interests that are the basis of the anti-kickback statute."[170]

The OIG observed that joint ventures in underserved areas raise the same AKS concerns as other joint ventures, namely, whether the joint venture is a *bona fide* business enterprise, whether distributions from the joint venture are merely payments for referrals from investors, and whether distributions are merely payments for referrals from one investor to another.[171] Accordingly, the OIG was mindful that "any safe harbor contain adequate safeguards and conditions against fraud and abuse," while also providing "additional flexibility for investments in underserved areas that may experience a shortage of available capital from non-referral source investors."[172] The safe harbor as adopted defines "an underserved area as any defined geographic area that is designated as a MUA [Medically Underserved Area]" by regulation, including both rural and urban areas.[173]

Other key features of the safe harbor are as follows: (1) a rule that 75 percent of the volume of the entity's business must be derived from residents of underserved areas; (2) a three-year grace period for entities that comply with the safe harbor initially but subsequently fall out of compliance; and (3) a rule requiring that at least 50 percent of the investment interests be held by nonreferral source investors.[174] The need for a grace period arises from the possibility that an entity meeting all other safe harbor requirements might be located in an area that loses its MUA designation after initially

167. Final Rule: Clarification of the Initial OIG Safe Harbor Provisions and Establishment of Additional Safe Harbor Provisions under the Anti-Kickback Statute (64 Fed. Reg. 63518, 63530; Nov. 19, 1999).
168. *Id.* at 63532.
169. *Id.*
170. *Id.*
171. *Id.*
172. *Id.*
173. *Id.*
174. *Id.*

being classified as a MUA. The grace period is designed to "afford entities that wish to maintain safe harbor protection an opportunity to restructure so as to qualify for the small entity investment interest safe harbor."[175]

Regarding the 75 percent rule found at (a)(3)(i)(F), the OIG conveyed its belief the 75 percent requirement "would adequately protect against abuses and further the purpose of this safe harbor . . . [by] requiring that at least 75 percent of the dollar volume of the entity's business in the previous fiscal year or previous 12-month period be derived from services provided to persons residing in an underserved area or persons who are member of a MUP."[176] The OIG further explained its decision to eliminate entirely the 60-40 revenue rule of the small entity investment interest safe harbor for entities operating in underserved areas, while retaining a modified interested investor rule:

> [W]e are persuaded that eliminating both 60-40 rules, and in particular the 60-40 investor rule, may lead to inappropriate financial incentives and unfair competition in some areas by allowing referral source investors, primarily physicians, to "lock up" the market for particular services in those areas. Ensuring fair competition in the health care marketplace is one of the goals of the anti-kickback statute. We are also concerned that an excessive proliferation of particular services in rural or urban underserved areas could lead to overutilization by entities competing for scarce revenue and could prompt protected entities to develop revenue streams from patients not residing in underserved areas, in contravention of the intent and spirit of the safe harbor . . .
>
> . . .
>
> In this final rule, we are adopting our original proposal to eliminate the 60-40 revenue rule, but we are retaining a modified limitation on the number of interested investors. Specifically, we are requiring, as a condition for protection, that investors who make referrals or who are in a position to make referrals or furnish items or services to the entity not own more than 50 percent of the value of investment interest within each class of investment in the entity. As with the 60-40 investor rule in the small entity investment safe harbor, we are permitting equivalent classes of stock to be aggregated for purposes of determining safe harbor compliance.

175. *Id.* at 63533.
176. *Id.* at 63534.

> We believe that eliminating the 60-40 revenue rule, thereby permitting entities to draw 100 percent of their revenue from referrals by investor-owners should make investment in such entities sufficiently attractive to non-referral source investors so as to permit the entities to meet the new 50-50 investor test.[177]

The OIG rejected a request that it allow compliance with this safe harbor in situations where an entity has certified its inability to satisfy the 60-40 standards of the small entity investment interest safe harbor despite "best efforts," commenting that "[a] mere 'best efforts' exception to the small entity investment interests safe harbor based on a certification from the investment entity would be insufficient to protect against abusive arrangements and would be impractical in application."[178] The OIG went on to say that if an entity cannot comply with the 50-50 investor rule of this safe harbor, it would still "have recourse to the advisory opinion process for guidance about their specific arrangements."[179]

There have been Advisory Opinions addressing the safe harbor for investments in underserved area entities. Advisory Opinion No. 03-13[180] analyzed a joint venture involving ownership of a magnetic resonance imaging (MRI) center that served residents of a three-county rural area that was not also designated a MUA. More than 85 percent of the MRI center's patients were residents of this region, which had not had MRI services available prior to the establishment of the center. In order to raise capital for the MRI center, limited partnership interests were offered to members of the medical community and former board members of the three area hospitals. One hospital and its supporting foundation purchased 30 percent of the partnership units. Others in a position to influence or generate referrals or provide items or services to the MRI center owned another 30 percent of the center. The remaining 40 percent of the center was owned by those who are not in a position to influence or generate referrals. The percentage of non-referring investors had increased over time. All investors were offered the opportunity to invest on the same terms, without reference to their ability to refer to or generate business for the MRI center, and return on investment was directly proportional to investor capital contributions. More than

177. *Id.* at 63533.
178. *Id.*
179. *Id.*
180. Advisory Opinion No. 03-13 (Issued June 16, 2003).

60 percent of the revenues of the MRI center was generated from referrals made by disinterested parties. Ancillary management service and space lease agreements were certified to be compliant with safe harbor requirements.

Against this factual backdrop, the OIG concluded that since 60 percent of the venture was owned by interested investors, no investment interest safe harbor was available to protect the arrangement. The small entity safe harbor requires that no more than 40 percent of the venture be owned by such investors, and while the MRI center was located in a rural area, the facility was not located in a MUA and had more than 50 percent interested investors. The OIG nonetheless determined that it would not impose administrative sanctions, as the below-enumerated factors led it to conclude that the risk of fraud and abuse was sufficiently low:

- The arrangement had indicia of a legitimate, *bona fide*, business because all investors were offered the opportunity to invest on the same terms and conditions, returns on investment interests were proportional to capital contributions, and, most important, less than 40 percent of the revenue of the MRI center was derived from interested investors.
- The structure of the arrangement did not contain any suspect characteristics identified in the OIG's 1989 Special Fraud Alert on joint ventures and would have complied with the safe harbor for rural entities proposed in 1993 (although not with the final rule adopted in 1999).
- The arrangement was developed as a community-oriented effort to provide access to MRI services in the three-county region and has provided a substantial community benefit.
- The ancillary agreements have been certified as safe harbor compliant.

Advisory Opinion No. 07-20[181] involved an arrangement proposed by a physician in a Louisiana parish who had operated a medical clinic that was destroyed by Hurricane Katrina. The physician then opened a new medical practice in the parish to serve the residents there. The sole hospital in the parish had also been destroyed in the hurricane and had not reopened. The number of physicians practicing in the parish also declined precipitously after the hurricane. The physician certified that no medical imaging services were available in the parish and that patients who needed such services were required to travel outside the parish, although the health care infrastructure outside the parish was also significantly reduced after the storm. The physician proposed

181. Advisory Opinion No. 07-20 (Issued Dec. 27, 2007).

establishing an imaging center (the Center) in the same building as his medical practice. The physician and his brother would each contribute 50 percent of the capital needed to fund the Center, and they would each own 50 percent. The brother would function as the business manager and would be a *bona fide* employee receiving a salary at fair market value and unrelated to the volume or value of business generated for the Center. The physician further certified that (1) he and his brother would be active investors on terms unrelated to referral or business generation; (2) the Center would be located in a MUA and at least 75 percent of the Center's revenues would be derived from individuals residing in a MUA or who are members of a MUA population; (3) neither the Center nor any investor (or anyone acting on behalf of the Center or any investor) would loan funds to or guarantee a loan for an interested investor; and (4) returns on investment would be directly proportionate to the amount of the capital investment of the investors. The physician estimated that 35 percent of patients receiving services from the Center would be referred by him, and 65 percent would come from outside referrals, with that percentage increasing as more physicians return to the parish. The physician also certified that a proposed ancillary space lease agreement would be safe harbor compliant.

The OIG first noted that the proposed arrangement would not comply with the underserved area entity safe harbor because 100 percent of the investment interests would be held by interested investors (i.e., the physician and his brother) in a position to make or influence referrals to, furnish items or services, or generate business for the Center. The OIG concluded, however, that the risk of fraud and abuse was not materially increased by the brother's investment interest, "particularly when viewed in light of the Proposed Arrangement's substantial potential community benefits."[182] Specifically, the OIG noted:

- The brother, who was not then in the health care business, would not be compensated in any manner that depends on his generating business for the Center and would receive a fair market value salary for actual and necessary services, which would reduce the usual risk that the investor would charge the venture below-market rates to boost returns to interested investors.
- The brother would put up real capital and receive proportional returns, and the terms of investment would be unrelated to referrals, items or services furnished, or business generation.

182. *See id.*

- Because the physician already had reasons to refer patients to the Center, the sibling relationship was not viewed as likely to increase such referrals.
- Any residual risk was offset by the special conditions in which the proposed arrangement would be implemented, as an effort to improve access to care in the aftermath of Hurricane Katrina and the devastation inflicted on the local health care infrastructure.

2.2. Space Rental

The regulatory safe harbor for space rental arrangements is codified at 42 C.F.R. § 1001.952(b), which states:

> (b) *Space Rental.* As used in [the AKS], "remuneration" does not include any payment made by a lessee to a lessor for the use of premises, as long as all of the following six standards are met—
>
> (1) The lease agreement is set out in writing and signed by the parties.
>
> (2) The lease covers all of the premises leased between the parties for the term of the lease and specifies the premises covered by the lease.
>
> (3) If the lease is intended to provide the lessee with access to the premises for periodic intervals of time, rather than on a full-time basis for the term of the lease, the lease specifies exactly the schedule of such intervals, their precise length, and the exact rent for such intervals.
>
> (4) The term of the lease is for not less than one year.
>
> (5) The aggregate rental charge is set in advance, is consistent with fair market value in arms-length transactions and is not determined in a manner that takes into account the volume or value of any referrals or business otherwise generated between the parties for which payment may be made in whole or in part under Medicare, Medicaid or other Federal health care programs.
>
> (6) The aggregate space rented does not exceed that which is reasonably necessary to accomplish the commercially reasonable business purpose of the rental.
>
> Note that for purposes of paragraph (b) of this section, the term fair market value means the value of the rental property for general commercial purposes, but shall not be adjusted to reflect the

> additional value that one party (either the prospective lessee or lessor) would attribute to the property as a result of its proximity or convenience to sources of referrals or business otherwise generated for which payment may be made in whole or in part under Medicare, Medicaid and all other Federal health care programs.

This safe harbor was part of the original safe harbors enacted by HHS in 1991.[183] It was intended to protect against sham rental arrangements that purport to lease space that does not exist, is not actually used for the intended purpose, or is not large enough or otherwise suitable for its intended purpose.[184] Thus, compliance with the safe harbor predominantly turns on whether a referral relationship exists between the lessor and lessee and whether the rental fee is consistent with fair market value and does not take into account the value or volume of patients referred between the parties.

In order to determine whether a referral relationship exists, it is important to understand the direction in which referrals and remuneration flow.[185] For example, in one Advisory Opinion,[186] HHS explained that an arrangement is not suspect under the AKS when remuneration and referrals "run the same way." The proposed arrangement analyzed in the Advisory Opinion involved suppliers of DME using consignment closets in hospitals free of charge.[187] The hospitals referred patients to the suppliers, but they did not receive anything of value from the suppliers. Although the suppliers received remuneration from the hospitals in the form of free closet space, they were not in a position to refer patients to the hospital. Thus, HHS concluded that the arrangement did not implicate the AKS because there was no reason to believe that the free closet space was in fact a kickback in disguise.[188] As shown in Figure 2.1 (*see* Illustration 1), the remuneration (i.e., the free closet space) and the referrals of patients ran in the same direction (i.e., from the hospital to the supplier).

183. Final Rule: OIG Anti-Kickback Provisions (56 Fed. Reg. 35952, 35953; July 29, 1991) (Final rulemaking promulgating the ten original safe harbor provisions).

184. *Id.* at 35972 (providing a common example of a sham lease arrangement pursuant to which a physician rented a small, unsuitable space, such as a closet, and claimed to use the space for laboratory services, yet the space contained no laboratory equipment or personnel at any time).

185. *Id.* ("[W]here the lessor is a real estate developer or other entity *not involved in the delivery of health care services*, any arrangements that encourage referrals between the lessee and other third parties would *not be scrutinized by the OIG*." [emphasis added]).

186. OIG Advisory Opinion No. 08-20 (Nov. 19, 2008).

187. *Id.*

188. *Id.*

Illustration 1

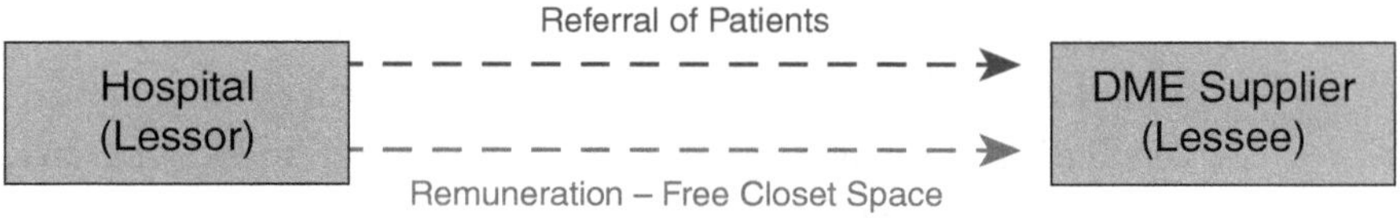

Illustration 2

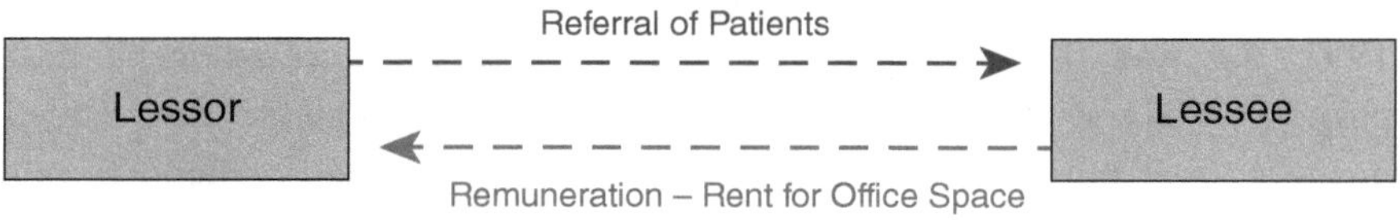

Illustration 3

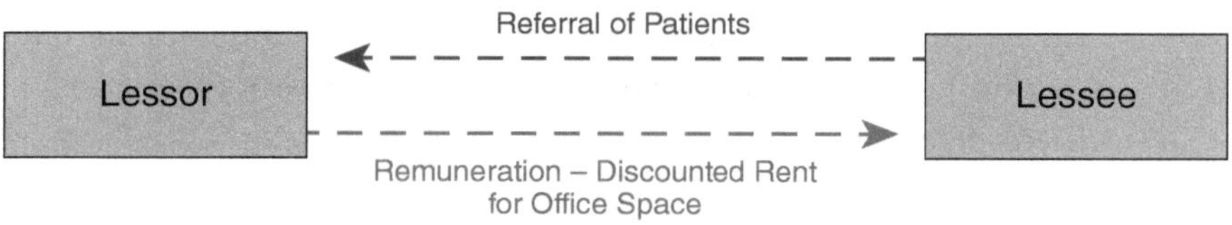

Figure 2.1

When a referral relationship does exist and the party receiving the remuneration is in a position to refer patients to the other party (see, e.g., Illustration 2 in Figure 2.1), then the AKS may be implicated because the remuneration, or a portion thereof, may be viewed as remuneration for referred patients. This analysis would apply to common rental arrangements where the lessor is in a position to refer patients to the lessee, and the lessee is giving remuneration (i.e., the rental fee) to the lessor (see Illustration 2 in Figure 2.1). However, it may also apply when the lessee is in a position to refer patients to the lessor, and the lessor is giving remuneration to the lessee by accepting a discounted rental fee from the lessee, in which case such discounted amount may be viewed as a kickback for patient referrals (see Illustration 3 in Figure 2.1).[189] In order to avoid AKS implications, such arrangements should satisfy all elements of the space rental safe harbor.

---

189. *See* United States *ex rel.* Bingham v. HCA, Inc., 2016 U.S. Dist. LEXIS 10178 at *22 (S.D. Fla. 2016) (citing United States *ex rel.* Osheroff v. Tenet Healthcare Corp., 2013 U.S. Dist. LEXIS 44235 at *9 (S.D. Fla. 2013) and explaining that a reasonable inference can be made that a landlord would not enter into a below-market rate lease if some other consideration was not involved, such as the referral of patients to the landlord).

The first element requires that the rental arrangement be set out in a written agreement that is signed by both parties.[190] In order to satisfy the second element, the written agreement must also cover all of the space leased between the parties, which would include office space leased for exclusive use and common areas to which the lessee may have access. All such leased areas must be specifically identified in the written agreement.[191]

The third element of the safe harbor states that when space is leased for periodic intervals of time, rather than a full-time basis, such intervals and the rental fee per interval must be specified in the written agreement. This requirement prohibits rental arrangements on an "as needed" basis, thereby reducing the risk that parties will modify their arrangement based on their referral patterns.[192] It is generally recommended for part-time lease agreements to include a detailed schedule, including specific days and times, when the leased space will be made available to the lessee. However, HHS has recognized that in certain circumstances it may be difficult for parties to establish a predetermined schedule for reasons other than the parties' referral patterns. Although such cases would fall outside the safe harbor protections, they would be analyzed by HHS on a case-by-case basis as to whether they are vulnerable to abuse and violation of the AKS.[193]

The fourth element of the safe harbor requires the lease agreement to be for a term of at least one year. This requirement is intended to reduce the risk that parties will periodically renegotiate short-term leases to account for changes in referral patterns.[194] Accordingly, HHS has clarified that compliance with the safe harbor does not require the services (i.e., the leased space) to be provided for at least one year, but that the terms of the lease cannot

---

190. *See e.g.*, United States *ex rel.* Singh v. Bradford Reg'l Med. Ctr., 752 F. Supp. 2d 602, 635-39 (W.D. Pa. 2010) (concluding that a contract proposal and preliminary invoice initialed by the parties did not constitute a formal, signed writing for purposes of compliance with the AKS safe harbor).

191. *See e.g.*, United States *ex rel.* Armfield v. Gills, 2012 U.S. Dist. LEXIS 154749 at *17-18 (M.D. Fla. 2012) (concluding that the lease at issue sufficiently specified the premises covered by the lease by identifying the total amount of square feet of the rented space, and explaining that the rented space included such office space that was sufficient and necessary for operation of physician's practice and specifically included examination rooms, waiting areas, and kitchen and bathroom facilities).

192. Final Rule: OIG Anti-Kickback Provisions, 56 Fed. Reg. 35952, 35974 (July 29, 1991) (Final rulemaking promulgating the ten original safe harbor provisions).

193. *Id.*

194. *Id.* at 35973.

be modified for such time.[195] Similarly, the lease may be terminated with or without cause by the parties prior to the expiration of the first year.[196] In the event of such early termination, the parties should refrain from entering into the same type of arrangement on substantially the same terms until the one-year period expires to ensure that the second lease is not viewed as a modification of the first, prior to expiration of the initial one-year period, which would fall outside the safe harbor protection.

The fifth element of the safe harbor relates to the rental fee. It states that the fee must be set in advance, consistent with fair market value in an arms-length transaction, and cannot be determined in a manner that takes into account the volume or value of any referrals or other business generated between the parties.[197]

With respect to the fair market value requirement, the rental fee should fall within a reasonable commercial range that does not take into account any additional value that the space may have due to its proximity or convenience to referral sources and/or patients.[198] HHS has explained that a fair inference can be drawn that payments for referrals are impermissibly disguised as rental payments when the rent is substantially higher than the cost of renting the same-sized space at a nearby location.[199] However, HHS has also acknowledged that the rental fee for space used for health care–related purposes can be justifiably higher than the fee for similar commercial property that is used for non-health care purposes.[200] For example, leasehold improvements may be required to make the space suitable for medical use, such as installation of extra plumbing and greater electrical costs due to medical equipment used at the location.[201] Such items can be considered when calculating fair market value.

In a Special Fraud Alert issued in 2000, HHS further explained that common rental arrangements involving rental of space in a physician's

---

195. *Id.* (recognizing that certain short-term arrangements, such as an academic physician visiting a medical university for only one semester and renting office space from the university for such time, are unlikely to implicate the AKS).

196. *Id.*

197. *See generally,* United States *ex rel.* Goodstein v. McLaren Reg'l Med. Ctr., 202 F. Supp. 2d 671 (E.D. Mich. 2002) (analyzing expert testimony regarding fair market value of a rental fee and concluding that the parties negotiated the fee at arm's length).

198. Final Rule: OIG Anti-Kickback Provisions, 56 Fed. Reg. 35952, 35971-72 (July 29, 1991) (Final rulemaking promulgating the ten original safe harbor provisions).

199. *Id.*

200. *Id.*

201. *Id.*

office to referral sources, such as other practitioners or suppliers of medical equipment, are suspect under the AKS. When analyzing such arrangements, HHS considers the following factors: (i) the appropriateness of the rental agreement, (ii) the rental amount, and (iii) time and space considerations.[202]

With respect to the first factor, a threshold question for analyzing any rental arrangement is whether payment of rent is appropriate or it is in fact a disguised kickback.[203] A common example would be payment of rent for space that is traditionally provided for free or nominal charge, such as a consignment closet used for storage of medical equipment and supplies.[204] Even when payment of a fee is appropriate, the second factor also required that fee to be consistent with fair market value.[205] As a general matter, the fee should not exceed the rent paid by the physician-lessor under the underlying lease for the premises.[206] The third factor considers the amount of space that is rented and the duration of the rental arrangement. Consistent with the sixth element of the space rental safe harbor, HHS explains that the time and space should be reasonable and necessary to achieve a commercially reasonable business purpose.[207] Moreover, the rental fee should be a ratio of the length of time during which the space is rented and the amount of space that is actually used by the lessee.[208] In addition, when the lessee has exclusive use of the space then such lessee should be responsible for one hundred percent of the fair market value fee, but when use of the space is not exclusive (for example, when the lessee shares space with others, including common areas like lobbies and patient waiting rooms) the

202. *Special Fraud Alert: Rental of Space in Physician Offices by Persons or Entities to Which Physicians Refer*, Off. Inspector Gen., Feb. 2000. https://oig.hhs.gov/fraud/docs/alertsandbulletins/office%20space.htm.

203. *Id.*

204. *Id.*; *see also* OIG Advisory Opinion No. 06-02 (Mar. 21, 2006) (stating that there is a long-standing concern that rental payments for a consignment closet may exceed fair market value and may be a disguised kickback).

205. *Special Fraud Alert: Rental of Space in Physician Offices by Persons or Entities to which Physicians Refer*, Off. Inspector Gen., Feb. 2000, https://oig.hhs.gov/fraud/docs/alertsandbulletins/office%20space.htm.

206. *Id.*

207. *Id.* Examples of unreasonable and unnecessary rental arrangements that would not qualify for the safe harbor protection include (i) when lessee only requires use of one patient examination room to meet patient demand, yet the rental payment is calculated based on use of the entire office; (ii) the rental payment includes payment for times when the space is not actually used by the lessee; and (iii) the rental payment is calculated based on the fair market value of the entire space but lessee's occupancy is not exclusive. In such shared space arrangements, fair market value should be adjusted proportionally based on the lessee's actual use of the space. *Id.*

208. *Id.*

lessee should only be responsible for his proportionate share of such shared space.[209]

By way of example, HHS has provided the following formula for calculating annual rent for *exclusive* space:

$$\frac{\text{Annual rent of underlying lease}}{\text{Number of work days per year}} \times \frac{\text{Sq. ft. used exclusively by lessee}}{\text{Total sq. ft.}} \times \frac{\text{Number of hours per day that Lessee uses the space}}{\text{Total work hours per day}} \times \text{Number of days per year that Lessee uses the space}$$

$$= \text{TOTAL ANNUAL RENT FOR EXCLUSIVE SPACE}$$

Rent for *nonexclusive* space should be apportioned among all lessees who share the space.

It is also important to note that, to meet the requirements of the space rental safe harbor, the aggregate rental fee must be set in advance. Fees that are subject to fluctuation, such as percentage or "per use" fees, would not satisfy this requirement because the aggregate fee paid through the term of the lease would not be fixed (i.e., "set in advance").[210]

HHS has clarified that such percentage or "per use" rental fees are not *per se* violations of the AKS but would have to be analyzed on a case-by-case basis.[211] By way of example, the U.S. District Court in Illinois has interpreted this guidance to mean that "time-based or unit-of-service-based payments [are intended to] be protected [under the AKS], so long

209. *Id.*

210. *See* OIG Advisory Opinion No. 11-15 (Oct. 3, 2011) (analyzing a management services relationship that included the rental of office space for a fee that was based on a percentage of the lessee's income which not only did not meet the requirements of the safe harbor but also presented a substantial risk for fraud and abuse under the AKS because the fee took into account the volume and/or value of business generated between the parties).

211. Final Rule: OIG Anti-Kickback Provisions, 56 Fed. Reg. 35952, 35973 (July 29, 1991) (Final rulemaking promulgating the ten original safe harbor provisions). "[HHS] recognize[s] that legitimate considerations, such as the depreciation of equipment [or rental space], could result in some part of the payment to be based on a percentage or 'per use' payment arrangement without these payments influencing or being influenced by Medicare or Medicaid referrals. However, the more the payments appear to reflect the volume of referrals from the financially-interested party, the more suspect the arrangement becomes and the more likely [HHS] will need to examine it carefully." *Id.*

as the payment per unit is at fair market value at inception and does not subsequently change during the lease term in any manner that takes into account DHS referrals."[212] In other words, a fixed "per use" rental fee (e.g., $100 for each hour the lessee actually uses the leased space) is unlikely to violate the AKS if it is consistent with fair market value, is not increased or decreased during the term of the lease to account for changes in patient referrals, and otherwise meets the other elements of the safe harbor.

Finally, to satisfy the sixth and final element of the space harbor, the aggregate of the rented space cannot exceed what would be considered reasonable and necessary to accomplish the commercially reasonable business purpose for the rental arrangement.

Arrangements that implicate the space rental safe harbor may often implicate other safe harbors as well. For example, it is common for a lessor not only to provide office space to a lessee but to also lease medical equipment located at the premises and/or provide administrative or maintenance services necessary to operate the premises. HHS has noted that each part of such arrangement must meet the requirements of the applicable safe harbor.[213] HHS has also noted that hospitals may sometimes offer rent concessions to staff physicians which may not fall within the space rental safe harbor.[214] Such remuneration, however, may be protected under the physician recruitment safe harbor when it is offered as part of a hospital's recruitment effort.

---

212. United States *ex rel.* Perales v. St. Margaret's Hosp., 243 F. Supp. 2d 843 (C.D. Ill. 2003) (*citing* Final Rule: Medicare and Medicaid Programs; Physicians' Referrals to Health Care Entities With Which They Have Financial Relationships, 66 Fed. Reg. 856, 876 (Jan. 4, 2001)).

213. Final Rule: OIG Anti-Kickback Provisions, 56 Fed. Reg. 35952, 35972 (July 29, 1991) (Final rulemaking promulgating the ten original safe harbor provisions). To the extent rental payments include payment for office space and other equipment or services provided by the lessor, then such rental payment must reflect the fair market value of all such space, equipment, and/or services in order to qualify for each applicable safe harbor. In order to ensure that this requirement is met, parties to such arrangements may prefer to enter into multiple written agreements—a separate agreement for the space, equipment, and/or services provided—and analyze each agreement individually under its applicable safe harbor. Alternatively, if one master agreement is executed, then the fees payable under the agreement should be clearly defined and distinct based on each space/equipment/service provided. The portion of the fee attributable to the applicable space/equipment/service should reflect fair market value (FMV) of such space/equipment/services. *See also* United States *ex rel.* Armfield v. Gills, 2012 U.S. Dist. LEXIS 154749 at *14 (M.D. Fla. 2012) ("Where [ ] a single payment is made for multiple purposes (i.e., payment for rent and compensation for services), each separate aspect of the payment must comply with the respective safe harbor provisions.").

214. *Id.*

2.3. Equipment Rental

The regulatory safe harbor for equipment rental arrangements is codified at 42 C.F.R. § 1001.952(c), which states:

> (c) *Equipment Rental.* As used in [the AKS], "remuneration" does not include any payment made by a lessee of equipment to the lessor of the equipment for the use of the equipment, as long as all of the following six standards are met—
>
> (1) The lease agreement is set out in writing and signed by the parties.
>
> (2) The lease covers all of the equipment leased between the parties for the term of the lease and specifies the equipment covered by the lease.
>
> (3) If the lease is intended to provide the lessee with use of the equipment for periodic intervals of time, rather than on a full-time basis for the term of the lease, the lease specifies exactly the schedule of such intervals, their precise length, and the exact rent for such interval.
>
> (4) The term of the lease is for not less than one year.
>
> (5) The aggregate rental charge is set in advance, is consistent with fair market value in arms-length transactions and is not determined in a manner that takes into account the volume or value of any referrals or business otherwise generated between the parties for which payment may be made in whole or in part under Medicare, Medicaid or all other Federal health care programs.
>
> (6) The aggregate equipment rental does not exceed that which is reasonably necessary to accomplish the commercially reasonable business purpose of the rental.
>
> Note that for purposes of paragraph (c) of this section, the term fair market value means that the value of the equipment when obtained from a manufacturer or professional distributor, but shall not be adjusted to reflect the additional value one party (either the prospective lessee or lessor) would attribute to the equipment as a result of its proximity or convenience to sources of referrals or business otherwise generated for which payment may be made in whole or in part under Medicare, Medicaid or other Federal health care programs.

Much like the space rental safe harbor, this safe harbor was included in the original safe harbors enacted by HHS in 1991 as an effort to prevent sham rental arrangements for use of diagnostic and other medical equipment that are merely "a vehicle to provide reimbursement for referrals."[215]

The elements of this safe harbor mirror the elements of the space rental safe harbor.[216] If a referral relationship exists between a lessor and lessee who are parties to a rental arrangement for equipment, in order for such arrangement to be protected under the safe harbor, it must be set forth in a written agreement that (i) covers and specifically identifies all of the equipment leased between the parties, (ii) is for a term of at least one year, and (iii) provides for payment of a rental fee that is (A) set in advance, (B) consistent with fair market value of the leased equipment, and (C) not determined in a manner that takes into account the volume or value of referrals or other business generated between the parties.[217] In addition, the aggregate equipment rented by the lessee cannot exceed what is reasonably necessary to achieve the commercially reasonable business purpose of the rental arrangement.

If the equipment is leased for periodic intervals of time, rather than a full-time basis, the written agreement must also specify the exact intervals and the rental fee for each interval.[218] HHS has clarified that "per use" (or "per click") arrangements, in which the aggregate rental fee is not fixed and set in advance, but instead fluctuates based on the actual use of the equipment,

215. Final Rule: OIG Anti-Kickback Provisions, 56 Fed. Reg. 35952, 35953 (July 29, 1991) (Final rulemaking promulgating the ten original safe harbor provisions).

216. For a more detailed discussion of each element, see discussion on the space rental safe harbor *supra* at Chapter 2.2. *See also* OIG Advisory Opinion No. 98-18 (Nov. 25, 1998) (concluding that a rental arrangement for certain telemedicine equipment satisfied all of the elements of the equipment rental safe harbor).

217. *See generally*, United States *ex rel.* Armfield v. Gills, 2012 U.S. Dist. LEXIS 154749 at *20-22 (M.D. Fla. 2012); United States *ex rel.* Perales v. St. Margaret's Hosp., 243 F. Supp. 2d 843, 860-64 (C.D. Ill. 2003); *see also* OIG Advisory Opinion 11-17 (Nov. 16, 2011) (concluding that an arrangement that included the rental of equipment, among other things, for a fee based on percentage of collections of the lessee was not protected under the safe harbor and created a substantial risk of violating AKS).

218. *See, e.g.*, OIG Advisory Opinion No. 10-14 (Aug. 30, 2010) (explaining that a fixed "per-test" fee did not violate AKS because it was consistent with fair market value and, when taken individually and not in the aggregate, it did not take into account the value or volume of referrals or other business generated between the parties); OIG Advisory Opinion No. 04-08 (June 23, 2004) (explaining that an arrangement that involved the rental of space and equipment on an "as needed" basis failed to satisfy the elements of the applicable safe harbors and presented a substantial risk of fraud and abuse). "[P]eriodic, sporadic, or part-time leases must specify precisely the timing and duration of the rental periods and the compensation charged for each rental period." OIG Advisory Opinion No. 04-08 (June 23, 2004).

are not protected under the safe harbor and must be analyzed on a case-by-case basis.[219]

Take, for example, an arrangement where medical equipment is leased by a lessor that is in a position to refer patients to the lessee, and the aggregate rental fee increases based on the amount of procedures that are performed by the lessee that utilize the equipment. Even if the "per use" rental fee is a fixed amount consistent with fair market value, since the exact intervals of when the equipment is made available to the lessee are not predetermined at the outset of the arrangement (but instead provided on an as-needed basis), the aggregate rental fee is not "set in advance" and, therefore, does not satisfy the elements of the safe harbor. Moreover, such arrangements are considered suspect under AKS for potential fraud and abuse because they create a clear incentive for overutilization—the lessor would be incentivized to increase the amount of patient referrals that are sent to the lessee which, in turn, would increase the lessee's utilization of the equipment and the amount paid to the lessor.[220]

Similarly, some equipment rental arrangements may include "wear and tear" clauses, pursuant to which the rental fee is increased based on utilization of the equipment to account for ordinary wear and tear and depreciating value of the equipment each time it is used. However, consistent with its position on "per use" arrangements, HHS has explained that, while it "recognize[s] that equipment becomes less valuable the more it is used, and that its owner deserves compensation for such wear and tear[,] . . . it is also a relatively easy matter to disguise such a wear and tear payment as a payment for referrals."[221]

Accordingly, equipment rental fees that are based on utilization of the equipment are generally considered suspect under AKS because they present a substantial risk of fraud and abuse.

---

219. Final Rule: OIG Anti-Kickback Provisions, 56 Fed. Reg. 35952, 35973 (July 29, 1991) (Final rulemaking promulgating the ten original safe harbor provisions).

220. *See id.*; *see also* OIG Advisory Opinion No. 10-23 (Oct. 28, 2010) (analyzing an arrangement under which a hospital would provide sleep testing equipment and related services to a sleep testing provider for a "per test" fixed rental fee). In this Opinion, OIG concluded that the arrangement presented a high risk of fraud and abuse under AKS because the aggregate rental fee was not set in advance, which fell outside of the safe harbor protections, and the hospital was also providing marketing services to the sleep testing provider, which put the hospital in a position to generate patient referrals and directly linked the success of the sleep testing business to the amount of rental fees that were paid to the hospital. *Id.* at 4-6.

221. *See id.* at 35955.

2.4. Personal Services and Management Contracts and Outcome-Based Payment Arrangements

The regulatory safe harbor for personal services and management contracts and outcome-based payment arrangements, modified by 85 FR 77684, is codified at 42 C.F.R. § 1001.952(d), which states:

(d) Personal services and management contracts and outcomes-based payment arrangements.

(1) As used in section 1128B of the Act, "remuneration" does not include any payment made by a principal to an agent as compensation for the services of the agent, as long as all of the following standards are met:

(i) The agency agreement is set out in writing and signed by the parties.

(ii) The agency agreement covers all of the services the agent provides to the principal for the term of the agreement and specifies the services to be provided by the agent.

(iii) The term of the agreement is not less than 1 year.

(iv) The methodology for determining the compensation paid to the agent over the term of the agreement is set in advance, is consistent with fair market value in arm's-length transactions, and is not determined in a manner that takes into account the volume or value of any referrals or business otherwise generated between the parties for which payment may be made in whole or in part under Medicare, Medicaid, or other Federal health care programs.

(v) The services performed under the agreement do not involve the counseling or promotion of a business arrangement or other activity that violates any State or Federal law.

(vi) The aggregate services contracted for do not exceed those which are reasonably necessary to accomplish the commercially reasonable business purpose of the services.

(2) As used in section 1128B of the Act, "remuneration" does not include any outcomes-based payment as long as all of the

standards in paragraphs (d)(2)(i) through (viii) of this section are met:

(**i**) To receive an outcomes-based payment, the agent achieves one or more legitimate outcome measures that:

(**A**) Are selected based on clinical evidence or credible medical support; and

(**B**) Have benchmarks that are used to quantify:

(**1**) Improvements in, or the maintenance of improvements in, the quality of patient care;

(**2**) A material reduction in costs to or growth in expenditures of payors while maintaining or improving quality of care for patients; or

(**3**) Both.

(**ii**) The methodology for determining the aggregate compensation (including any outcomes-based payments) paid between or among the parties over the term of the agreement is: Set in advance; commercially reasonable; consistent with fair market value; and not determined in a manner that directly takes into account the volume or value of any referrals or business otherwise generated between the parties for which payment may be made in whole or in part by a Federal health care program.

(**iii**) The agreement between the parties is set out in writing and signed by the parties in advance of, or contemporaneous with, the commencement of the terms of the outcomes-based payment arrangement. The writing states at a minimum: A general description of the services to be performed by the parties for the term of the agreement; the outcome measure(s) the agent must achieve to receive an outcomes-based payment; the clinical evidence or credible medical support relied upon by the parties to select the outcome measure(s); and the schedule for the parties to regularly monitor and assess the outcome measure(s).

(**iv**) The agreement neither limits any party's ability to make decisions in their patients' best interest nor induces any party to reduce or limit medically necessary items or services.

(v) The term of the agreement is not less than 1 year.

(vi) The services performed under the agreement do not involve the counseling or promotion of a business arrangement or other activity that violates any State or Federal law.

(vii) For each outcome measure under the agreement, the parties:

(A) Regularly monitor and assess the agent's performance, including the impact of the outcomes-based payment arrangement on patient quality of care; and

(B) Periodically assess, and as necessary revise, benchmarks and remuneration under the arrangement to ensure that the remuneration is consistent with fair market value in an arm's length transaction as required by paragraph (d)(2)(ii) of this section during the term of the agreement.

(viii) The principal has policies and procedures to promptly address and correct identified material performance failures or material deficiencies in quality of care resulting from the outcomes-based payment arrangement.

(3) For purposes of this paragraph (d):

(i) An agent of a principal is any person other than a bona fide employee of the principal, who has an agreement to perform services for or on behalf of the principal.

(ii) Outcomes-based payments are limited to payments between or among a principal and an agent that:

(A) Reward the agent for successfully achieving an outcome measure described in paragraph (d)(2)(i) of this section; or

(B) Recoup from or reduce payment to an agent for failure to achieve an outcome measure described in paragraph (d)(2)(i) of this section.

(iii) Outcomes-based payments exclude any payments:

(A) Made directly or indirectly by the following entities:

(1) A pharmaceutical manufacturer, distributor, or wholesaler;

(2) A pharmacy benefit manager;

(3) A laboratory company;
(4) A pharmacy that primarily compounds drugs or primarily dispenses compounded drugs;
(5) A manufacturer of a device or medical supply as defined in paragraph (ee)(14)(iv) of this section;
(6) A medical device distributor or wholesaler that is not otherwise a manufacturer of a device or medical supply, as defined in paragraph (ee)(14)(iv) of this section; or
(7) An entity or individual that sells or rents durable medical equipment, prosthetics, orthotics, or supplies covered by a Federal health care program (other than a pharmacy or a physician, provider, or other entity that primarily furnishes services); or

(B) Related solely to the achievement of internal cost savings for the principal; or
(C) Based solely on patient satisfaction or patient convenience measures.

The safe harbor for personal services and management contracts was modified, effective as of January 19, 2021, to provide greater flexibility for part-time or sporadic arrangements and arrangements for which the aggregate compensation could not be set in advance.[222] The modifications also provided new safe harbor protection for outcome-based payment arrangements.[223]

A. *Elimination of Requirement to Set Aggregate Compensation in Advance*

Prior to the modifications, the safe harbor for personal services and management contracts required the aggregate compensation for such arrangements to be set in advance. OIG has replaced this requirement by stating that the methodology for determining compensation (as opposed to the aggregate compensation) must be set in advance for an arrangement to fall

222. Final Rule: Medicare and State Health Care Programs: Fraud and Abuse; Revisions to Safe Harbors Under the Anti-Kickback Statute, and Civil Monetary Penalty Rules Regarding Beneficiary Inducements 85 FED. REG. 77684, 77839 (Dec. 2, 2020).

223. *Id.*

under the safe harbor.[224] This change provides greater flexibility for providers to undertake more innovative arrangements, such as arrangements that promote care coordination and a transition to value-based arrangements.[225] OIG explained that this increased flexibility does not increase the risk for fraud and abuse because the arrangements must nonetheless satisfy the other unmodified requirements of the safe harbor, which provide sufficient protection (such as the requirement for the compensation to not be determined in a manner that takes into account the volume or value of referrals or other business generated between the parties).[226]

An example of a permissible compensation structure, for which the methodology would be set in advance, would be an hourly rate (provided that it satisfies all of the other requirements of the safe harbor as well).[227] OIG also considered whether a fee structure based on the costs incurred by a party would satisfy the modified "set in advance" compensation requirement. OIG explained that it would have to consider the facts of a particular arrangement to determine whether a cost-based methodology for calculating compensation is in fact set in advance.[228] Take, for example, a hospital that leases a physician on a part-time basis from the physician's practice and pays a percentage of the practice's actual expenses in employing the physician, and such expenses include the physician's salary, fringe benefits, and malpractice insurance—Each of these components for calculating the fee would likely be set in advance and can satisfy the requirement of the safe harbor. In comparison, if the practice's expenses in employing the physician include a discretionary bonus, for which the methodology is not set in advance, then the hospital's payment of a percentage of such bonus would also not be considered set in advance. This bonus component of the fee would have to be structured in a way that satisfies all elements of the safe harbor, including the requirement that the methodology for calculating the bonus is set in advance and that it does not take into account the volume or value of referrals or other business generated by the parties.

It is also important to remember that the compensation must be consistent with fair market value. OIG did not make any changes to this requirement, and it also declined to provide a specific definition or

224. *Id.* at 77839–40.
225. *Id.*
226. *Id.*
227. *Id.*
228. *Id.*

appropriate methodologies for determining fair market value. That said, OIG did acknowledge that fair market value may vary based on region, setting, and other factors.[229]

B. *Elimination of Requirement to Specify Schedule of Part-Time Arrangements*

In the modified safe harbor, OIG also eliminated the requirement that part-time or sporadic arrangements must specify the schedule, length, and exact charge for each scheduled intervals.[230] This change was also intended to provide increased flexibility for value-based and care coordination arrangements. OIG does not believe that additional requirements are necessary for part-time or sporadic arrangements, as opposed to full-time arrangements, because the other requirements of the safe harbor are sufficient to protect against potential fraud and abuse.[231]

C. *Protection of Outcomes-Based Payment Arrangements*

The modified safe harbor was also renamed as the safe harbor for "personal services and management contracts *and outcome-based payment arrangements*" because OIG added new paragraphs that provide safe harbor protection for outcome-based payment arrangements. Under the modified regulations, outcome-based payments, which are intended to improve quality of care, promote coordination across all patient care settings, and reduce overall health care costs, are not considered impermissible remuneration under the anti-kickback statute (AKS) if they satisfy eight elements, many of which are similar to the requirements for personal services and management contracts.[232]

First, the agent who receives the outcome-based payment must achieve one or more legitimate outcome measures that (i) are selected based on clinical evidence or credible medical support, and (ii) have benchmarks that are used to quantify improvements in quality of care and/or material reductions in costs or expenditures of payors while maintaining or improving such

229. *Id.*

230. *Id.* at 77841. One commenter praised this change as being particularly beneficial to dialysis facilities and other services that have relatively unpredictable demand.

231. *Id.*

232. *Id.* at 77841–48.

quality of care for patients.[233] OIG believes that the requirement to rely on "clinical evidence" and "credible medical support" provides sufficient flexibility for parties to select measures that improve patient care and reduce costs in a manner that is scientifically valid, measurable, and transparent.[234] In addition, the requirement to achieve "legitimate" outcome measures is intended to prevent sham arrangements that offer remuneration for maintaining the status quo because such remuneration would not fall under the safe harbor protection.[235] OIG also noted that the outcome measures must be based on improving quality of care, reducing cost of care, or both. Patient satisfaction, for example, although an important factor in overall patient care, is not a proper outcome measure because it does not provide sufficient protection against abusive or sham arrangements. Similarly, reductions in internal costs incurred by a provider, although relevant to obtaining practice efficiencies, pose a risk to reducing quality of care, which outweighs the potential efficiencies that can be achieved. As such, the safe harbor explicitly excludes patient satisfaction and reduction in internal provider costs as appropriate measures for outcome-based payments.[236]

The second requirement for outcome-based payment arrangements is consistent with the compensation requirement for personal services and management contracts. It states that the methodology for determining the aggregate compensation, which includes any outcome-based payments, must be (i) set in advance, (ii) commercially reasonable, (iii) consistent with fair market value, and (iv) not determined in a manner that directly takes into account the volume or value of any referrals or other business generated between the parties.[237] OIG also explained that the safe harbor specifically covers remuneration "between or among" the parties, as

233. *Id.* It should be noted that OIG interprets the term "outcome measure" under this safe harbor to have the same meaning as under any other safe harbor that uses it, including, for example, the new safe harbor for value-based arrangements at paragraph 1001.952(ee), but with the understanding that different safe harbors protect different types of remuneration, include different safeguards, and use additional terminology. For example, outcome measures under this safe harbor must include benchmarks for improving quality of care or reducing costs, or both, whereas a different safe harbor may have different benchmark requirements for a target patient population. OIG explained: "[W]e note that this safe harbor is not the only option for protecting payments under alternative payment models. Participants in such models may be able to look to the safe harbor for CMS-sponsored models at paragraph 1001.952(ii), or the value-based safe harbors at paragraphs 1001.952(ee)-(gg)."

234. *Id.*

235. *Id.*

236. *Id.*

237. *Id.*

opposed to remuneration that only flows one way from the principal to the agent, because the safe harbor is intended to encompass payment in the form of recoupment or reduction in payment to the agent if certain outcome measures are not achieved. The safe harbor explicitly clarifies that outcome-based payments include rewards to the agent for successfully achieving an outcome measure *or* recoupment or reduction in payment to the agent for failure to achieve an outcome measure.[238]

The third requirement is that the agreement between the parties must be set out in writing and signed by the parties in advance of, or contemporaneously with, the commencement of the arrangement.[239] The writing must, at a minimum, include a general description of the services to be performed, the outcome measures that the agent must achieve, the clinical evidence or credible medical support relied upon to select the outcome measures, and a schedule for the parties to regularly monitor and assess their performance with the outcome measures.[240] OIG recognized that, at the outset of an arrangement, the parties may not be aware of every step that will be necessary to achieve an identified outcome and the actual services may vary over time, which is why the agreement only needs to provide a "general description" of the services.[241] It is also worth noting that OIG is not requiring the parties to identify a specific timeframe for achieving the outcome measures because it recognizes that such a timeframe can vary greatly and would be difficult to predict.

The fourth element of the safe harbor prohibits the agreement from limiting a party's ability to make decisions in the patients' best interests or inducing a party to limit medically necessary services.[242] OIG noted that certain arrangements that promote "product standardization," such as establishing an outcome measure that requires an exclusive or minimum use level for a product to obtain an outcome-based payment, are not necessarily precluded from the safe harbor as long as they do not interfere with the parties' ability to make decisions in the best interest of their patients and as long as they can satisfy the other elements of the safe harbor.[243]

238. *Id.*

239. *Id.*

240. *Id.*

241. *Id.* This is distinct from the requirements for personal services and management contracts, which require the agreement to specify all of the services to be provided by the agent during the term of the agreement.

242. *Id.*

243. *Id.*

As with personal services and management contracts, the fifth and sixth elements of the safe harbor require outcome-based payment agreements to be for a term of not less than one year and to not involve counseling or promoting a business activity that violates state or federal law.[244]

The seventh requirement for outcome-based arrangements is that the parties must regularly monitor the agent's performance, including the impact of the arrangement on quality of patient care, and periodically assess and revise, as necessary, the benchmarks and remuneration under the arrangement to ensure that the remuneration is at all times consistent with the fair market value in an arm's-length transaction.[245] Such monitoring and assessment is a key element of the safe harbor because it ensures that the arrangement continues to meet all of the other requirements of the safe harbor at all times. For example, once a benchmark is achieved and there is no room for further improvement, then the parties may establish new benchmarks. All such new benchmarks must be assessed for compliance with all of the elements of the safe harbor. OIG did not identify a specific mechanism for monitoring and assessing performance. Instead, it explained that the "parties may conduct and document such monitoring in any way that makes sense for the particular arrangement."[246]

Finally, the eighth requirement states that the principal to the arrangement must have policies and procedures in place to promptly address and correct any material performance failures or deficiencies in quality of care resulting from the outcome-based arrangement.[247]

OIG did not limit the applicability of this safe harbor to a particular list of outcome-based arrangements. Instead, it took a broader approach by stating that the safe harbor can potentially apply to a wide variety of stakeholders and arrangements in the health care industry. However, the safe harbor explicitly excludes outcome-based payments made directly or indirectly by the following types of entities: (i) pharmaceutical manufacturer, distributor, or wholesaler; (ii) pharmacy benefit manager; (iii) laboratory company; (iv) pharmacy that primarily compounds drugs or primarily dispenses compounded drugs; (v) manufacturer of a device or medical supply; (vi) medical device distributor or wholesaler that is not otherwise a

244. *Id.*
245. *Id.*
246. *Id.* at 77844.
247. *Id.*

manufacturer of a device or medical supply; or (vii) an entity or individual that sells or rents durable medical equipment, prosthetics, orthotics, or supplies covered by a federal health care program (other than a pharmacy or a physician, provider, or other entity that primarily furnishes services).[248] These are the same entities that are ineligible for the new value-based safe harbors and are excluded from the definition of a "value based enterprise participant." As OIG explained, these entities were excluded from the safe harbors because "they are heavily dependent on prescriptions and referrals and might use outcomes-based payments primarily to market their products to providers and patients."[249] OIG was concerned that such entities may rely on the safe harbor inappropriately to enter into sham arrangements that incentivize providers to utilize their products and provide medically unnecessary services or items.[250]

2.5. Sale of Practice

The safe harbor for sale of practice, codified at 42 C.F.R. § 1001.952(e), states:

(e) *Sale of practice.*

(1) As used in [the AKS], "remuneration" does not include any payment made to a practitioner by another practitioner where the former practitioner is selling his or her practice to the latter practitioner, as long as both of the following two standards are met -

(i) The period from the date of the first agreement pertaining to the sale to the completion of the sale is not more than one year.

(ii) The practitioner who is selling his or her practice will not be in a professional position to make referrals to, or otherwise generate business for, the purchasing practitioner for which payment may be made in whole or in part under Medicare, Medicaid or other Federal health care programs after 1 year from the date of the first agreement pertaining to the sale.

(2) As used in [the AKS], "remuneration" does not include any payment made to a practitioner by a hospital or other entity where

248. *Id.*
249. *Id.*
250. *Id.*

the practitioner is selling his or her practice to the hospital or other entity, so long as the following four standards are met:

(iii) The period from the date of the first agreement pertaining to the sale to the completion date of the sale is not more than three years.

(iv) The practitioner who is selling his or her practice will not be in a professional position after completion of the sale to make or influence referrals to, or otherwise generate business for, the purchasing hospital or entity for which payment may be made under Medicare, Medicaid or other Federal health care programs.

(v) The practice being acquired must be located in a Health Professional Shortage Area (HPSA), as defined in Departmental regulations, for the practitioner's specialty area.

(vi) Commencing at the time of the first agreement pertaining to the sale, the purchasing hospital or entity must diligently and in good faith engage in commercially reasonable recruitment activities that:

(A) May reasonably be expected to result in the recruitment of a new practitioner to take over the acquired practice within a one year period and

(B) Will satisfy the conditions of the practitioner recruitment safe harbor in accordance with paragraph (n) of this section.

In proposing this safe harbor, HHS noted that it would "exist for the sale of physician practices when occurring as the result of retirement or some other event that removes the physician from the practice of medicine or from the service area in which he or she was practicing, but not when the sale is for the purpose of obtaining an ongoing source of patient referrals."[251] As an example of a transaction not protected by the safe harbor, HHS described the purchase of a physician practice by a hospital to assure itself a steady stream of referrals for both physician and hospital services.[252] In such a transaction, HHS noted that the patients

251. Proposed Rule: OIG Anti-Kickback Provisions, 54 Fed. Reg. 3088, 3091 (Jan. 23, 1989) (Proposed original ten safe harbor provisions).

252. Another example offered by HHS of a problematic transaction was the purchase by an ophthalmologist of an optometry practice, where "the optometrist keeps practicing, only now

may be unaware of the sale, and that it may "often involve much higher rates of compensation [than] would be the case if a retiring physician sold a comparable practice to another physician," with the extra compensation "reflect[ing] the value of the referrals."[253] HHS specifically rejected the idea that these kinds of transactions deserve protection, stating that "such practices lead to increased program costs and potential conflicts between the patient's best interests and the physician's business relationship to the hospital."[254]At the same time, HHS acknowledged that "in ordinary circumstances, a hospital is not in violation of the statute if it purchases the practice of a retiring physician who no longer makes referrals to that hospital."[255] The scope of this particular safe harbor, however, is not intended to cover purchases by hospitals or other entities, except in the limited context of a rural hospital and physician recruitment, as discussed below.[256]

HHS declined to extend the period for completing the sale beyond one year given the risk of abuse, and noted that "[o]ften, sales and option agreements are designed solely to ensure referrals, and payments for the sale or option agreement are actually payments for referrals."[257] The one-year limit was designed to "protect sales where the sale occurs because the physician is no longer going to be practicing and not because the purchaser seeks an ongoing stream of referrals."[258] Payments from the sale, however, need not be completed within one year, so long as the other requirements of the safe harbor are satisfied.[259] Referrals are permitted within the one-year period.[260]

---

substantially salaried by the ophthalmologist" and where "[t]he only purpose of [the] sale [is] to lock up referrals." *Id.*

253. *Id.*

254. Final Rule: OIG Anti-Kickback Provisions (56 Fed. Reg. 35952, 35975; July 29, 1991): Final rulemaking promulgating the ten original safe harbor provisions.

255. *Id.*

256. In a letter from D. McCarty Thornton of OIG to the Internal Revenue Service (IRS) commenting on hospital acquisitions of physician practice groups, Mr. Thornton states that "[i]n the final safe harbor regulations, we expressly declined to expand the scope of the safe harbor to cover purchases of physician practices by hospitals or other types of entities or to situations where the seller remains in a continuing position to make referrals or influence referrals to the buyer because of our concerns that many of such purchases were in fact merely attempts to provide remuneration in return for a fuure stream of referrals." Letter from D. McCarty Thornton to T. J. Sullivan (Dec. 22, 1992).

257. Final Rule: OIG Anti-Kickback Provisions (56 Fed. Reg. 35952, 35975; July 29, 1991): Final rulemaking promulgating the ten original safe harbor provisions.

258. *Id.*

259. *Id.*

260. *Id.*

HHS declined to extend safe harbor protection to the sale of an individual practice to a group practice or the sale of part of a practice to a group practice or another physician when the provider is changing the scope of his or her practice, reasoning that although "some buy-out arrangements are not abusive," the agency "was also aware of abusive purchase arrangements," whereby "the sale becomes another mechanism for the buyer to profit from the stream of referrals made to the seller who previously practiced independently without dividing profits with the new 'partner.'"[261]

HHS also clarified the relationship between the sale of practice safe harbor and the employee safe harbor, explaining that "[w]here a practitioner purchases another practitioner's practice, makes payments to that other practitioner which continue for some period of time, and retains that other practitioner on his or her staff as an employee, we believe that such payments are not protected under this provision or the employee exception."[262] The payments in question are not protected by the sale of practice safe harbor because the seller "remains in a position to make referrals" and they are not protected by the employee safe harbor because "that provision only protects payments 'for employment in the provision of covered items or services' . . . [but here] these payments relate to the purchase of a practice and not to services provided pursuant to employment for the provision of items or services."[263] HHS noted, however, that if a *bona fide* employment relationship existed and the employer was making other payments for employment services, such payments could be protected.[264] If a party were attempting to comply with two separate safe harbors, then HHS stated that it "would expect separate justifications for compliance with each provision."[265]

In 1999, HHS modified the sale of practice safe harbor to protect payments made to a practitioner by a hospital or other entity to purchase the practitioner's practice in certain circumstances "to accommodate transactions involving the rural hospital purchase of a physician practice as part of a practitioner recruitment program. . . ."[266] HHS was "persuaded that a need exists to protect certain practice acquisitions by hospitals and other entities

---

261. *Id.*
262. *Id.*
263. *Id.*
264. *Id.*
265. *Id.*
266. Final Rule: Clarification of the Initial OIG Safe Harbor Provisions and Establishment of Additional Safe Harbor Provisions Under the Anti-Kickback Statute (64 Fed. Reg. 63518, 63550; Nov. 19, 1999).

located in rural and urban underserved areas that are engaged in practitioner recruitment programs" in circumstances in which the practitioner sellers are "retiring or relocating a distance that would preclude them from being in a position to make referrals to the purchasing entity, if the acquisitions occur as part of a practitioner recruitment program that qualifies for protection under the safe harbor for practitioner recruitment."[267] HHS noted that the provider must "be retired from the practice of medicine or otherwise no longer in a position to generate referrals for the hospital" because otherwise the transaction "might result in abusive payments to induce referrals of business from the physician's new practice."[268] HHS further commented that "[r]elocation a significant distance from the practice being sold is an indicator that a physician is no longer in a position to refer patients."[269] HHS rejected calls to protect practice sales related to acquisitions by "integrated health care delivery systems," concluding that "many such arrangements may provide incentives for overutilization, increased billings to the Federal programs, and inappropriate steering of patients in circumstances where the Federal health care programs pay on a fee-for-service basis."[270] HHS also rejected a request to permit valuation of all tangible and *intangible* assets that could be used to determine a practice's fair market value, reasoning that "we remain of the opinion that payments for 'intangibles' can easily be used to disguise payments for referrals of Federal health care program business, and therefore we are unwilling to provide safe harbor protection for any particular valuation methodology."[271]

2.6. Referral Services and Referral Arrangements for Specialty Services

A. Referral Services

There are two safe harbors for referral services. The first, codified at 42 C.F.R. § 1001.952(f), states:

> (f) *Referral services.* As used in [the AKS], "remuneration" does not include any payment or exchange of anything of value between an

267. *Id.*
268. *Id.*
269. *Id.*
270. *Id.*
271. *Id.*

individual or entity ("participant") and another entity serving as a referral service ("referral service"), as long as all of the following four standards are met -

(1) The referral service does not exclude as a participant in the referral service any individual or entity who meets the qualifications for participation.

(2) Any payment the participant makes to the referral service is assessed equally against and collected equally from all participants and is based only on the cost of operating the referral service, and not on the volume or value of any referrals to or business otherwise generated by either party for the other party for which payment may be made in whole or in part under Medicare, Medicaid, or other Federal health care programs.

(3) The referral service imposes no requirements on the manner in which the participant provides services to a referred person, except that the referral service may require that the participant charge the person referred at the same rate as it charges other persons not referred by the referral service, or that these services be furnished free of charge or at reduced charge.

(4) The referral service makes the following five disclosures to each person seeking a referral, with each such disclosure maintained by the referral service in a written record certifying such disclosure and signed by either such person seeking a referral or by the individual making the disclosure on behalf of the referral service -

    (i) The manner in which it selects the group of participants in the referral service to which it could make a referral;

    (ii) Whether the participant has paid a fee to the referral service;

    (iii) The manner in which it selects a particular participant from this group for that person;

    (iv) The nature of the relationship between the referral service and the group of participants to whom it could make the referral; and

    (v) The nature of any restrictions that would exclude such an individual or entity from continuing as a participant.

The safe harbor for "Referral Services," was enacted in 1991 as part of the original set of safe harbors to protect service fees paid to "professional societies" and "consumer-oriented" groups that operate referral services, but instituted certain protections "to safeguard against abuse," including "by persons who would attempt to operate exclusive or selective referral services for which they would impose high participation fees."[272] The rule protects remuneration between an entity serving as a referral service and an entity or individual such as a physician participating in such a service, provided, *inter alia*, that any payment made to the referral service "is assessed equally against and collected equally from all participants, and is only based on the cost of operating the referral service, and not on the volume or value of any referrals to or business otherwise generated by either party for the other party" for which payment may be made under a federal health care program.[273]

The safe harbor also required certain disclosures to patients seeking a referral, including "[w]hether the participant has paid a fee to the referral service" and "[t]he manner in which it selects a particular participant from this group for that person."[274] HHS regarded such disclosures as essential, given that "[r]eferral services help beneficiaries make their initial contact with the health care system before a relationship of trust is established with a particular health care provider" and that without such disclosures "a consumer has very little information upon which to base his or her trust" in the provider, making the disclosures "an ethical duty" bearing upon "a patient's freedom of choice and quality of care" and which "may be necessary to enable a patient to give informed consent."[275]

HHS further noted that the safe harbor's requirements apply both to direct and indirect forms of remuneration, including in an employment setting:

> The [AKS] is implicated not only where direct payments are made in return for referrals, but also where indirect forms of remuneration are

272. Final Rule: OIG Anti-Kickback Provisions, 56 Fed. Reg. 35952, 35954 (July 29, 1991) (Final rulemaking promulgating the ten original safe harbor provisions); Proposed Rule: OIG Anti-Kickback Provisions, 54 Fed. Reg. 3088, 3091 (Jan. 23, 1989) (Proposed original ten safe harbor provisions).

273. 42 C.F.R. § 1001.952(f)(2).

274. 42 C.F.R. § 1001.952(f)(4)(ii), (iii).

275. Final Rule: OIG Anti-Kickback Provisions, 56 Fed. Reg. 35952, 35960 (July 29, 1991) (Final rulemaking promulgating the ten original safe harbor provisions).

> given for referrals. For example, hospitals often operate free referral services for members of their medical staffs as one of the benefits that comes with being on that hospital's staff. In return for the benefits of staff privileges (including the free referral service), physicians have a variety of obligations, such as sitting on various hospital committees. Depending on the circumstances, the services physicians furnish a hospital to assist in its operations may constitute a form of remuneration to the hospital for providing the referral service, and would be covered by the statute . . . "Giving a person an opportunity to earn money may well be an inducement to that person to channel potential Medicare payments towards a particular recipient." . . . Therefore, staff physicians and hospitals seeking safe harbor protection must comply with this provision when they are engaged in a referral service that does not charge a specific fee.[276]

The safe harbor for referral services applies not only to physicians but also to payments by other providers, including but not limited to chiropractors, dentists, podiatrists, psychologists, and nursing homes, to entities providing referral services.[277] Regarding the requirement that the referral service may not exclude any participant who is "qualified" for participation, HHS stated that the "determination as to whether a particular health care provider is 'qualified' to participate in the service may be made by the referral service according to its own criteria" but that it "must apply the eligibility criteria equally to all participants in the referral service."[278] Additionally, "the referral service must disclose to all persons seeking a referral the criteria it uses to determine who is qualified as a participant . . . [including] the manner in which it selects the pool of participants."[279] This includes whether the provider to whom the person is being referred "has paid a fee to participate."[280] The referral service must also disclose how the particular provider was selected for the referral (e.g., Is there a rotation system?), and what relationship exists between the provider and the referral service (e.g., Is the provider employed by the organization that operates the referral

276. *Id.* at 35976 (quoting United States v. Bay State Ambulance & Hosp. Rental Serv., Inc., 874 F.2d 20, 29 (1st Cir. 1989)).
277. *Id.* at 35975.
278. *Id.* at 35975-76.
279. *Id.* at 35976.
280. *Id.*

service?).[281] Further, the referral service must disclose the criteria used to exclude a provider from participation in the service (e.g., Are there quality of care concerns?).[282] Addressing the form of the disclosure, HHS has stated that there is no one particular form that is mandated, but that it must be "effective disclosure," which "requires that the relevant information is communicated in time for the information to be used by the beneficiary before an important decision is made."[283] Accordingly, HHS has indicated that "it is unlikely that disclosure after the referral has been made would constitute effective disclosure if the beneficiary had already seen the health care provider, or in some cases, if the appointment had already been made."[284]

A written record certifying that these disclosures were made to each person seeking a referral must be maintained. The record "must be signed by either the person seeking the referral or by the individual making the disclosure on behalf of the referral service," and it will be insufficient to maintain only "a blank copy of the disclosure form or instructions to staff on how to make the disclosure."[285] The safe harbor also permits a referral service to prohibit discriminatory pricing practices by a provider participant or require that services be provided at no charge or at a reduced charge.[286] Regarding the fees that may be charged by the referral service, HHS has clarified that the safe harbor protects payments "that are related only to the cost of operating the referral service" and does not protect "fees that in any manner are based on the volume or value of Medicare or Medicaid referrals or business otherwise generated by the participant for the referral service."[287] Fees, however, need not be paid in full before referrals are made.[288] Further, the requirements of the AKS, and hence the safe harbor, apply irrespective of whether providers are charged for referral services, and the safe harbor applies to both direct and indirect forms of remuneration in exchange for referrals.[289]

This safe harbor has been addressed several times in Advisory Opinions. In Advisory Opinion No. 11-06,[290] the OIG addressed a business arrangement

281. *Id.*
282. *Id.*
283. *Id.*
284. *Id.*
285. *Id.*
286. *Id.*
287. *Id.*
288. *Id.*
289. *Id.*
290. OIG Advisory Opinion No. 11-06 (May 13, 2011).

in which a for-profit company operated an online referrals service that provided hospitals with access to a nationwide listing of post-acute care providers. Hospitals would use the service to identify and select providers for hospital patients about to be discharged and to send referral requests to selected providers. The hospitals paid a fee for the service that was equal to fair market value and not based on the volume or value of referrals or other business generated between the parties. Under the proposed arrangement, providers, who had previously not been charged for the service, would be charged a one-time implementation fee as well as a monthly fee to electronically receive or respond to hospital referral requests. Those fees would not vary based on the volume or value of referrals or other business generated between the parties, but they would be beyond the ability of some providers to pay. Although providers who elected not to pay the fees would continue to be listed by the service, they would not be able to electronically receive or respond to hospital referral requests and would be notified of such requests via facsimile, while having to respond to the requests via telephone or facsimile, thereby disadvantaging those providers and preventing them from timely communicating with hospitals.

The OIG found that the proposed arrangement did not satisfy safe harbor requirements, including the requirement that referral fees be assessed uniformly against all participants and be based only on the cost of operating the service. The OIG further determined that the arrangement posed more than a minimal risk of fraud and abuse under the AKS because the arrangement: (1) created a significant competitive advantage of paying providers over nonpaying providers in allowing the former to receive patient referrals electronically; (2) required that patient referrals be sent to non-paying providers via facsimile even though it was more expensive to do so in order to provide paying providers a competitive advantage; and (3) generated pressure to recoup the costs associated with participation in the referral service that could create incentives for paying providers to provide medically unnecessary services or inflate medical costs, thereby increasing costs to federal health care programs.[291]

Other Advisory Opinions examining arrangements under this safe harbor, however, have concluded that, despite failing to meet all of the requirements

---

291. The safe harbor has also been referenced in several court decisions. *See, e.g.*, United States *ex rel.* Young v. Suburban Homes Physicians, 2017 WL 6625940 at *2 (Dec. 28, 2017 N.D. Ill.); United States *ex rel.* DeCesare v. Americare In Home Nursing, 2011 WL 607390 at *2 (Feb. 10, 2011 E.D. Va.); Mittal v. United States, 2005 WL 2036023 at *14 n.1 (Aug. 24, 2005 S.D.N.Y.).

of the safe harbor, the arrangement at issue posed no more than a minimal risk of fraud and abuse. For example, Advisory Opinion No. 09-16[292] addressed a fact pattern in which a chiropractic association entered into an arrangement with a for-profit referral service. Under the arrangement, the cost of participation in the referral network was set at $60 per month for association members, which represented a $40 discount off the usual rate, and the network would pay the association $10 per month for each of the association's members who participated in the network, which fee would be in exchange for the association promoting the network with members and nonmembers.

While the OIG concluded that the arrangement did not fall within the safe harbor because the referral fees did "not meet the requirement that referral fees be assessed uniformly against all participants," it determined that it would not impose administrative sanctions because the arrangement posed only a minimal risk of fraud or abuse.[293] In reaching that conclusion, the OIG first noted that the arrangement was not a "typical, non-profit referral service operating for the convenience and support of patients," for which the safe harbor was designed.[294] The OIG then commented that, although not all participants would pay the same fee, the variance was not based on referrals of federal health care program business, and the providers receiving the referrals would be selected on a rotating basis by geographic area and would not be influenced by such variance. The OIG further observed that the $10 monthly fee for participating association members, while varying with the amount of business generated for the network, would not vary with referrals and that, in fact, the network did not provide reimbursable items or services, and therefore the payment did not implicate the AKS.[295] Finally, the OIG noted that the referral service would be open to participation by any state-licensed chiropractor, participating providers would receive referrals on an equal basis, there would be no requirements on the manner in which providers could furnish services, and all disclosures required by the referral services safe harbor would be made.[296]

Consistent with the OIG's reasoning in Advisory Opinion No. 09-16, those Advisory Opinions that have determined not to impose administrative sanctions on arrangements, notwithstanding the failure to meet all of

292. OIG Advisory Opinion No. 09-16 (Sept. 17, 2009).
293. *Id.* at 2.
294. *Id.* at 4.
295. *Id.* at 5.
296. *Id.*

the requirements of the safe harbor, have relied on some combination of the following factors:

- Fees paid by providers did not vary based on the volume or value of referrals and were unrelated to inducement of referrals.[297]
- Notices to prospective patients indicated that the provider was not being endorsed and advised of patients' freedom of choice.[298]
- There was a low risk of a cross-referral arrangement between parties to the arrangement.[299]
- No extra charge was to be included in a provider network.[300]
- Although fees charged in connection with referrals were on a "per click" basis, such transaction-based pricing was charged each time an ordering provider made a referral, regardless of whether the patient followed through and actually received items or services from the receiving provider—not a "success" fee.[301]
- Fees charged to ordering providers in a referral service were low and also capped, making it unlikely to influence the ordering provider's referral decisions.[302]
- There were no artificial limitations on which providers may participate in referral network, which was intended to be as complete as possible, and therefore there was no negative impact on patient or provider freedom of choice.[303]
- The fee structure of the referral service did not provide those participating in the service with enhanced access to a patient referral stream.[304]

B. *Referral Arrangements for Specialty Services*

The second referral services safe harbor, codified at 42 C.F.R. § 1001.952(s), states:

> (s) *Referral arrangements for specialty services.* As used in [the AKS], "remuneration" does not include any exchange of value among

---

297. OIG Advisory Opinion No. 11-18 (Nov. 30, 2011); OIG Advisory Opinion No. 09-16 (Sept. 17, 2009).
298. OIG Advisory Opinion No. 99-8 (July 6, 1999).
299. *Id.*
300. OIG Advisory Opinion No. 11-18 (Nov. 30, 2011).
301. *Id.*
302. *Id.*
303. *Id.*
304. *Id.*

individuals and entities where one party agrees to refer a patient to the other party for the provision of a specialty service payable in whole or in part under Medicare, Medicaid or any other Federal health care programs in return for an agreement on the part of the other party to refer that patient back at a mutually agreed upon time or circumstance as long as the following four standards are met -

(1) The mutually agreed upon time or circumstance for referring the patient back to the originating individual or entity is clinically appropriate.

(2) The service for which the referral is made is not within the medical expertise of the referring individual or entity, but is within the special expertise of the other party receiving the referral.

(3) The parties receive no payment from each other for the referral and do not share or split a global fee from any Federal health care program in connection with the referred patient.

(4) Unless both parties belong to the same group practice as defined in paragraph (p) of this section, the only exchange of value between the parties is the remuneration the parties receive directly from third-party payors or the patient compensating the parties for the services they each have furnished to the patient.

The safe harbor for specialty services was adopted in 1999 to allow for the referral of patients to those with specialized medical knowledge. In discussing the need for the safe harbor, HHS noted that patient freedom of choice could be compromised if patients are not given access to specialty care and that physicians might decline to make such referrals for fear of permanently losing patients to specialists.[305] For that reason, the safe harbor protects an agreement between general and specialized providers by which the general provider refers a patient to the specialist for needed treatment, provided that the specialist refers the patient back to the general provider when the specialty treatment is completed.[306] HHS made clear, however, that "protection

---

305. Final Rule: Clarification of the Initial OIG Safe Harbor Provisions and Establishment of Additional Safe Harbor Provisions Under the Anti-Kickback Statute, 64 Fed. Reg. 63518, 63548 (Nov. 19, 1999).

306. *Id.*

under this safe harbor is limited to referral arrangements for patients of the physician making referrals to the specialist" and that the "safe harbor does not protect generalized cross-referral arrangements of the 'you send me your patients and I'll send you mine' variety."[307] Instead, the safe harbor "protects an agreement to refer patients to a specialist in return for an agreement or understanding that the specialist will refer those *same* patients back at the agreed upon time or circumstance (*e.g.*, completion of the specialist services for which the patient was referred)."[308]

The safe harbor applies to solo practitioners as well as members of group practices, with the difference being that members of group practices who refer among themselves "may share revenues from specialty services performed as a result of the intra-group referrals," whereas solo practitioners "may not give anything of value to a specialist in exchange for the referral back of his or her original patient, except for the opportunity to receive compensation for services directly from third parties or patients."[309]

When the rule was first proposed in 1993, HHS commented on the criteria developed for satisfying the safe harbor, emphasizing the importance of permitting payments only for the services rendered, and not for the referrals themselves, commenting that "[t]he . . . standard[s] . . . proposed prohibit[] any actual *payment* to be made between the parties for the referral [and] requires that the only exchange of value between the parties . . . is the opportunity to obtain monetary remuneration directly from third-party payors or the patient, as compensation for his or her respective professional services."[310] In the final rule, HHS commented on the importance of prohibiting referral payments to ensure "preservation of patient freedom of choice" and stated that referral arrangements protected by the safe harbor posed only a minimal risk of abuse, provided that "no payment is made between the referring and receiving parties."[311] HHS expressed particular concern with "the potential for abuse when the referring physician and the specialty physician receiving the referral split a global payment from a Federal health

307. *Id.*

308. *Id.*

309. *Id.* at 63549.

310. Proposed Rule: Additional Safe Harbor Provisions Under the Anti-Kickback Statute, 58 Fed. Reg. 49008, 49012 (Sept. 21, 1993) (Proposed rule designed to incorporate seven additional safe harbor provisions) (emphasis in original).

311. Final Rule: Clarification of the Initial OIG Safe Harbor Provisions and Establishment of Additional Safe Harbor Provisions Under the Anti-Kickback Statute, 64 Fed. Reg. 63518, 63548 (Nov. 19, 1999).

care program," citing complaints from ophthalmology providers about certain abusive arrangements with optometrists who use their ability to control referrals to insist on the right to receive the postoperative portion of the Medicare global fee for eye surgery.[312] The final version of the safe harbor excluded such remuneration from protection.[313] In making that exclusion, HHS noted that it was not suggesting that all referral arrangements involving the splitting of a global fee violate the AKS, which would depend, *inter alia*, on "whether the specialty services are medically necessary, whether the timing of the referrals is clinically appropriate, and whether the services performed are commensurate with the portion of the global fee received."[314]

In adopting the final rule, HHS noted, in response to concerns that the safe harbor could encourage arrangements that required patients to be referred back to the primary physician regardless of clinical appropriateness, that "clinical appropriateness should be the touchstone of all referrals, specialty or otherwise," and inserted a requirement that referrals back to the primary provider must be clinically appropriate.[315] HHS declined, however, to define "clinically appropriate," concluding that "whether a referral is clinically appropriate will depend on the particular facts and circumstances."[316]

2.7. Warranties

The modified safe harbor for warranties is codified at 42 C.F.R. § 1001.952(g):

> (g) *Warranties.* As used in section 1128B of the Act, "remuneration" does not include any payment or exchange of anything of value under a warranty provided by a manufacturer or supplier of one or more items and services (provided the warranty covers at least one item) to the buyer (such as a health care provider or beneficiary) of the items and services, as long as the buyer complies with all of the following standards in paragraphs (g)(1) and (2) of this section and the manufacturer or supplier complies with all of the following standards in paragraphs (g)(3) through (6) of this section:
>
> (1) The buyer (unless the buyer is a Federal health care program beneficiary) must fully and accurately report any price

312. *Id.*
313. *Id.*
314. *Id.* at 63548-49.
315. *Id.* at 63548.
316. *Id.*

reduction of an item or service (including a free item or service) that was obtained as part of the warranty, in the applicable cost reporting mechanism or claim for payment filed with the Department or a State agency.

(2) The buyer must provide, upon request by the Secretary or a State agency, information provided by the manufacturer or supplier as specified in paragraph (g)(3) of this section.

(3) The manufacturer or supplier must comply with either of the following standards:

(i) The manufacturer or supplier must fully and accurately report any price reduction of an item or service (including free items and services) that the buyer obtained as part of the warranty on the invoice or statement submitted to the buyer and inform the buyer of its obligations under paragraphs (g) (1) and (2) of this section.

(ii) When the amount of any price reduction is not known at the time of sale, the manufacturer or supplier must fully and accurately report the existence of a warranty on the invoice or statement, inform the buyer of its obligations under paragraphs (g)(1) and (g)(2) of this section, and when any price reduction becomes known, provide the buyer with documentation of the calculation of the price reduction resulting from the warranty.

(4) The manufacturer or supplier must not pay any remuneration to any individual (other than a beneficiary) or entity for any medical, surgical, or hospital expense incurred by a beneficiary other than for the cost of the items and services subject to the warranty.

(5) If a manufacturer or supplier offers a warranty for more than one item or one or more items and related services, the federally reimbursable items and services subject to the warranty must be reimbursed by the same Federal health care program and in the same Federal health care program payment.

(6) The manufacturer or supplier must not condition a warranty on a buyer's exclusive use of, or a minimum purchase of, any of the manufacturer's or supplier's items or services.

(7) For purposes of this paragraph (g), the term warranty means:
   (i) Any written affirmation of fact or written promise made in connection with the sale of an item or bundle of items, or services in combination with one or more related items, by a manufacturer or supplier to a buyer, which affirmation of fact or written promise relates to the nature of the quality of workmanship and affirms or promises that such quality or workmanship is defect free or will meet a specified level of performance over a specified period of time;
   (ii) Any undertaking in writing in connection with the sale by a manufacturer or supplier of an item or bundle of items, or services in combination with one or more related items, to refund, repair, replace, or take other remedial action with respect to such item or bundle of items in the event that such item or bundle of items, or services in combination with one or more related items, fails to meet the specifications set forth in the undertaking which written affirmation, promise, or undertaking becomes part of the basis of the bargain between a seller and a buyer for purposes other than resell of such item or bundle of items; or
   (iii) A manufacturer's or supplier's agreement to replace another manufacturer's or supplier's defective item or bundle of items (which is covered by an agreement made in accordance with this paragraph (g)), on terms equal to the agreement that it replaces.

Effective January 19, 2021, the warranties safe harbor was modified to protect warranties covering services that are related to one or more items if certain conditions are met. Before this modification, only warranties for items, and not services, were protected under the warranties safe harbor. The "items only" element of the old warranties safe harbor precluded an arrangement in Advisory Opinion 01-08 from receiving safe harbor protection, where a manufacturer agreed to reimburse a nursing facility for insurance deductibles paid by the facility as a result of judgments for skin care or wound care deficiencies. There, OIG noted that the arrangement did not fall under the warranty safe harbor because "the 'product' [was] a combination of items (i.e., the support surfaces, skin and wound care products, and protocols) and some services (i.e., the wound specialist's advice and in-service training)."[317] We believe that such an arrangement could in fact qualify under the warranty safe harbor as now modified.

Importantly, the safe harbor does not provide protection to warranties that cover services alone, a decision by OIG based on an identified heightened potential for fraud and abuse. The warranty protections are subject to certain conditions, such as that all federally reimbursable items and services subject to bundled warranty arrangements must be reimbursed by the same federal health care program and in the same payment. In addition, the modified rule bars arrangements that condition warranties on exclusive use or minimum purchasing requirements.

As modified, the warranty safe harbor now explicitly excludes beneficiaries from the reporting requirements regarding price reductions applicable to buyers who receive certain warranties. No specific reporting timeline for buyers or sellers regarding price reductions in connection with warranties was added by the modified rule, though OIG noted it expects reporting in a "timely" manner. Finally, the modified rule now defines "warranty" directly rather than by reference, as an affirmation of fact or written promise relating to bundled items and related services.[318] We now turn to specific comments, responses, and insights regarding the warranty safe harbor modifications addressed or provided by OIG during the rule-making process.

A. Inclusion of Services in Bundled Warranties

With the modified rule, OIG intends to protect warranties that warranty a bundle of items or a bundle of items and services. This modification offers greater flexibility to buyers and sellers to enter "innovative arrangements that warranty the value of an entire bundle of items or that include bundled items and services."[319] For example, under the safe harbor, a drug manufacturer could offer to a hospital a warranty covering the clinical effectiveness of a self-injected drug contingent on the patient receiving post-prescribing

317. Advisory Opinion No. 01-08 (Issued July 3, 2001).

318. Final Rule: Medicare and State Health Care Programs: Fraud and Abuse; Revisions to Safe Harbors Under the Anti-Kickback Statute, and Civil Monetary Penalty Rules Regarding Beneficiary Inducements 85 Fed. Reg. 77684, 77848 (Dec. 2, 2020); 42 C.F.R. § 1001.952(g)(7).

319. 85 Fed. Reg. 77684, 77848–49.

product administration and the use of education through nurse support offered by the manufacturer.[320] OIG agreed with one commenter who noted that "sellers and buyers, such as health systems, would have greater flexibility under the safe harbor to protect related services that are often integral to determining whether the terms of a warranty, such as a clinical outcome, have been met."[321] OIG reiterated that warranties for services, which are not tied to one or more related items, could present heightened fraud and abuse risks and, as such, would not be protected.[322]

Commenters expressed concern that bundled warranties could harm competition and limit clinician and patient choice if sellers conditioned a warranty on the purchase of a bundle of products and services.[323] In response, OIG confirmed its opinions that the safeguards being finalized in the rule, including prohibiting exclusivity and minimum-purchase requirements, discussed further below, and limiting the scope of what may be included in a bundled warranty, provide meaningful protection against anticompetitive behavior.[324]

Despite certain risks, OIG declined to impose any restriction on the way warrantied medication adherence services may be provided when offered as part of a bundled warranty.[325] Further, OIG is "declining to impose a requirement that warrantied medication adherence services must either be provided via an independent intermediary or subject to the approval of a licensed medical professional."[326] However, OIG emphasized that the warranties safe harbor would not protect the provision of free or reduced-cost medication adherence services furnished by a seller.[327]

B. Requirement for Federally Reimbursable Items and Services Subject to Bundled Warranty Arrangements to Be Reimbursed by the Same Federal Health Care Program and in the Same Payment

According to OIG, the bundling of items and services that are reimbursed under different methods could create incentives for inappropriate utilization

320. *Id.* at 77849.
321. *Id.* at 77849.
322. *Id.* at 77849.
323. *Id.* at 77849.
324. *Id.* at 77850.
325. *Id.* at 77850.
326. *Id.* at 77850.
327. *Id.* at 77850.

and overutilization or the potential for cost-shifting. The modified safe harbor protects warranties that apply to one or more items and related services, and only if the federally reimbursable items and services subject to the warranty arrangement are reimbursed by the same federal health care program and in the same federal health care program payment.[328] One commenter expressed concern that the same program/same payment requirement would prohibit warranty safe harbor protection for an episode of care involving a joint replacement that occurs in a hospital or ambulatory surgical center followed by discharge to a skilled nursing facility or to home health care. In response, OIG reiterated their concerns that a bundle of products paid for separately and potentially across different payment systems poses an increased risk of inappropriate utilization and overutilization.[329] OIG noted, however, that such arrangements may qualify for protection under the value-based safe harbors described in the final rule.[330]

Commenters noted that the bundled warranty arrangement approved under Advisory Opinion No. 18-10 would not meet the revised safe harbor because some of the items in the bundle were separately reimbursable under certain states' Medicaid programs.[331] OIG noted that Advisory Opinion No. 18-10 included the possibility that bundled devices could be separately reimbursed by state Medicaid programs; however, and notwithstanding the Advisory Opinion, OIG reiterated that warranty remuneration paid resulting from the failure of a separately reimbursable item or service would not be covered by the warranties' safe harbor.[332] OIG acknowledged that due to the same program/same payment requirement, the warranty safe harbor protection would not be available for an arrangement consisting of a particular federally reimbursed drug product when used in conjunction with a companion diagnostic where the drug would be reimbursed under Medicare at the negotiated price (for a Part D drug) or at ASP plus 6 percent (for a Part B drug), while the companion diagnostic would be reimbursed under the clinical laboratory fee schedule.[333]

---

328. *Id.* at 77851.
329. *Id.* at 77852.
330. *Id.* at 77852; 42 C.F.R. 1001.952(ee), (ff), and (gg).
331. *Id.* at 77852.
332. *Id.* at 77852.
333. *Id.* at 77853.

OIG eased the concerns of one commenter who was under the impression that the new rule would foreclose even one-drug warranties given that drugs are virtually always reimbursed by Medicare and Medicaid (and usually additional federal health care programs), with each program having different payment methodologies for outpatient drugs.[334] It is important to remember that the "same program/same payment" requirement only applies when a manufacturer or supplier offers a warranty for more than one item or one or more items and related services, and would not apply to single-item warranties.

C. Capped Amount of Warranty Remedies

Prior to the modification, the safe harbor for warranties limited the amount of remuneration a manufacturer or supplier could pay to any individual (other than a beneficiary) or entity for any medical, surgical, or hospital expense incurred by a beneficiary to the cost of the item itself.[335] That limitation has been expanded to accommodate the safe harbor's expanded protection of bundled warranties, such that now the rule provides for a cap on warranty remuneration for any medical, surgical, or hospital expense incurred by a beneficiary at the cost of the *items and services* subject to the warranty.[336]

The cap helps safeguard against excess remuneration to providers to induce referrals, while still offering sellers more flexibility by protecting a broader scope of warranties and a potentially higher amount of warranty remuneration. The rule allows sellers to offer a remedy to their customers if a product fails to meet a clinical outcome guarantee, as long as the total warranty remuneration provided, including the cost of any replacement items, would be limited to the original cost of the items and services incurred by the buyer.[337] Without a cap on warranty remuneration, a vendor could pay for a wide range of consequential expenses resulting from the failure of a device including, for example, hospitalization expenses, and revision surgery, in addition to providing a replacement for the faulty device, which according to OIG, would provide too great an opportunity for sellers to offer generous remuneration to buyers.[338]

---

334. *Id.* at 77853.
335. *Id.* at 77853.
336. *Id.* at 77853.
337. *Id.* at 77854.
338. *Id.* at 77854.

D. *Prohibition on Exclusivity and Minimum-Purchase Requirements*

The warranty safe harbor precludes warranty arrangements from being conditioned on the exclusive use or minimum purchase of one or more items or services. Although exclusivity and minimum-purchase requirements may allow for certain efficiencies, OIG noted that such requirements tied to the offer of a warranty could potentially lead to interference with clinical decision-making, overutilization or inappropriate utilization, or other anticompetitive effects.[339] In essence, the potential for sellers to require exclusivity and minimum-purchase requirements in exchange for a warranty may lock buyers into a particular item (and, under the modified safe harbor, multiple items or items and services) and thereby could result in, for example, a buyer using a particular item in a given case that is not in the patient's best interest.[340]

OIG noted that the revised safe harbor is not intended to impact those arrangements in which providers agree to the exclusive purchase of a particular item or designate an item as "preferred" in exchange for favorable commercial terms. Rather, OIG interprets the "conditioned on" standard as a causal connection between receiving a warranty and maintaining exclusivity or minimum-purchase levels.[341] The safe harbor does not prohibit exclusive-use or minimum-purchase provisions that are conditioned upon commercial terms unrelated to the offer of a warranty.[342]

E. *Reporting Requirements*

In response to expressed concerns over the reporting requirements for the safe harbor, OIG clarified that the safe harbor can be used to protect warranty arrangements that span multiple years. The final rule changed the term "the price reduction" to "any price reduction" for clarity that more than one price reduction may occur pursuant to a warranty arrangement. In addition, the modified rule expressly clarifies that buyers, *other than federal health care program beneficiaries*, are obligated under the safe harbor to report price reductions in a manner compatible with the reimbursement methodology for the item(s) or service(s) that, as a commenter pointed out, may not in all circumstances be reported in a "cost reporting mechanism" or

339. *Id.* at 77854.
340. *Id.* at 77854.
341. *Id.*
342. *Id.*

a "claim for payment."[343] The reporting requirement applies to buyers even when buyers do not have an express obligation to report a price reduction or replacement product under applicable requirements of the federal health care program payor making payment for the warrantied item or service to which the price reduction relates. OIG noted that if a payor does not provide any mechanism for reporting of costs, such reporting is not required for a buyer to obtain safe harbor protection.[344]

Commenters requested clarification whether multiple warranty payments related to the same item or bundle of items and services could be reported at various points throughout a warranty arrangement. OIG responded by stating that such reports could in fact be made at various points throughout the arrangement.[345] In addition, OIG noted that it recognizes there may be some circumstances in which remuneration paid pursuant to a bundled warranty will be related to more than one item or service that fails to meet the specifications set forth in the warranty undertaking. In most of those cases, OIG believes that a warranty remedy paid pursuant to a bundled warranty should be reported proportionately to the cost of each bundled item or service.[346] However, the safe harbor does not set forth a specific methodology to allocation reporting across multiple items or services, and instead OIG allows flexibility for buyers to adopt different but reasonable allocation methodologies in circumstances in which, for example, the failure of the bundle to meet the agreed specifications results disproportionately from the failure of a particular item or service.[347]

OIG noted that while the rule did not add a timeline to report any price reduction of an item or service, it expects buyers and sellers to fulfill reporting obligations under paragraphs 42 C.F.R. §§ 1001.952(g)(1) and 1001.952(g)(3) in a timely manner.[348]

F. *Definition of "Warranty"*

As noted above, instead of referencing definitions in other statutes (i.e., 15 U.S.C. 2301(6)), the new rule directly defines "warranty" as an affirmation of fact or written promise relating to bundled items and related

343. *Id.* at 77856.
344. *Id.* at 77856.
345. *Id.* at 77856.
346. *Id.* at 77856.
347. *Id.* at 77856.
348. *Id.* at 77856.

services.[349] The new definition parallels the prior definition's language requiring a written promise that an item, bundle of items, or bundle of items and services is defect-free or will meet a specified level of performance over a specified period of time. By defining "warranty" directly, the rule makes it clear that the warranties safe harbor is available for drugs and devices regulated under the Federal Food, Drug, and Cosmetic Act, whereas the definition set forth in 15 U.S.C. 2301(6) potentially excludes Food and Drug Administration–regulated drugs and devices.[350]

The warranties safe harbor remains silent on whether a warranty arrangement protected under the safe harbor can have a single triggering condition or multiple triggering conditions. OIG noted that a warranty arrangement that qualifies for safe harbor protection could have multiple triggering conditions based on specifications set forth in the warranty undertaking as long as the seller complies with paragraph 42 C.F.R. § 1001.952(g)(4) in determining the maximum amount that it may offer for remuneration.[351]

2.8. Discounts

On November 30, 2020, OIG published a final rule amending the discount safe harbor at 42 C.F.R. § 101.952(h) to remove safe harbor protection for reductions in price in connection with the sale or purchase of prescription pharmaceutical products from manufacturers to plan sponsors under Part D, either directly or through pharmacy benefit managers (PBMs) acting under contract with them, unless the reduction in price is required by law.[352] The discount safe harbor amendment appears at § 1001.952(h)(5)-(9) and states:

> (h) *Discounts . . .*
>
> . . .
>
> (5) For purposes of this paragraph, the term ***discount*** means a reduction in the amount a buyer (who buys either directly or through a wholesaler or a group purchasing organization) is

349. 42 C.F.R. § 1001.952(g)(7).

350. *Id.* at 77856.

351. *Id.* at 77857.

352. The original effective date of this safe harbor amendment was January 1, 2022. However, as a result of a lawsuit challenging the final rule that was filed in the U.S. District Court for the District of Columbia, the effective date of the amendment was delayed by court order to January 1, 2023. Congress then extended that date in a series of legislative enactments ending with the Inflation Reduction Act of 2022, which, on August 16, 2022, extended the moratorium on implementation, administration, or enforcement of the final rule until January 1, 2032.

charged for an item or service based on an arms-length transaction. The term *discount* does not include—

. . .

(viii) A reduction in price or other remuneration in connection with the sale or purchase of a prescription pharmaceutical product from a manufacturer to a plan sponsor under Medicare Part D either directly to the plan sponsor under Medicare Part D, or indirectly through a pharmacy benefit manager acting under contract with a plan sponsor under Medicare Part D, unless it is a price reduction or rebate that is required by law.

(6) For purposes of this paragraph (h), the term manufacturer carries the meaning ascribed to it in Social Security Act section 1927(k)(5).

(7) For purposes of this paragraph (h), the terms wholesaler and distributor are used interchangeably and carry the same meaning as the term "wholesaler" defined in Social Security Act section 1927(k)(11).

(8) For purposes of this paragraph (h), the term pharmacy benefit manager or PBM means any entity that provides pharmacy benefit management on behalf of a health plan that manages prescription drug coverage.

(9) For purposes of this paragraph (h), a prescription pharmaceutical product means either a drug or biological product as those terms are described in Social Security Act section 1927(k)(2)(A), (B), and (C).

OIG commented that "[a]s a threshold matter, to be protected under the discount exception, an arrangement must involve a reduction in price."[353] Accordingly, "an arrangement between a manufacturer and a plan sponsor to increase the amount of the rebate to the plan sponsor by increasing the list price of the drug would be suspect and subject to scrutiny under the statute."[354] OIG noted that because many rebate arrangements created in recent years "are not reductions in price," it has been determined that

353. Final Rule: Removal of Safe Harbor Protection for Rebates Involving Prescription Pharmaceuticals and Creation of New Safe Harbor Protection for Certain Point-of-Sale Reductions in Price on Prescription Pharmaceuticals and Certain Pharmacy Benefit Manager Service Fees, 85 FED. REG. 76666, 76690 (Nov. 30, 2020).

354. *Id.*

"rebates to Part D plan sponsors do not pose a low risk of fraud and abuse and should not be protected by a regulatory safe harbor."[355]

OIG commented that the price reductions excluded from the discount definition, if they are in the form of upfront discounts, rather than after-sale rebates, are eligible for protection under the new safe harbor for point-of-sale reductions in price for prescription pharmaceutical products at § 1001.952(cc).[356] OIG reiterated that "the discount safe harbor protects only the reduction in the amount a buyer is charged for an item or service; it does not protect payments for services."[357] OIG stressed, moreover, that the new amendment to the discount safe harbor "has no impact on the statutory [discount] exception."[358]

OIG also commented that the discount safe harbor amendment does not apply to prescription pharmaceutical products payable under Medicare Part B since Part B drugs are reimbursed based on average sales price, which already accounts for rebates and other price concessions.[359] OIG reiterated that it intends for the discount safe harbor to continue protecting discounts on prescription pharmaceutical products offered to Medicaid managed care organizations (MCOs) or their pharmacy benefit managers (PBMs), together with other entities such as "wholesalers, hospitals, physicians, pharmacies, and third-party payors in other Federal health care programs."[360] OIG also clarified that "protection is available for these discounts (including rebates) even if the prescription pharmaceutical product is ultimately dispensed to a Part D enrollee (provided all safe harbor conditions are met)."[361]

OIG further commented that although discounts "offered or given to pharmacies owned by a plan sponsor under Part D or a PBM generally could qualify under the discount safe harbor" if the safe harbor elements are fully satisfied, other remuneration "that is labeled as a 'discount' but that is given to pharmacies or other entities owned by or affiliated with a plan sponsor under Part D or a PBM to reward the plan or the PBM for referrals of other Federal health care program business would be suspect" as such arrangements "would appear to have many of the same features as problematic swapping arrangements. . . ."[362]

355. *Id* at 76690, 76691.
356. *Id* at 76667.
357. *Id* at 76694.
358. *Id* at 76691.
359. *Id* at 76693.
360. *Id* at 76694, 76705.
361. *Id* at 76694.
362. *Id.*

2.9. Employees

Although Congress intended that "remuneration" under the AKS be construed "broadly,"[363] the 1977 legislation also included several exceptions, commonly known as "safe harbors," from AKS prosecution. One such exception, codified at 42 U.S.C. §1320a-7b(b)(3)(B), states as follows:

> *(3) [The AKS] shall not apply to-*
>
> . . .
>
> *(B) any amount paid by an employer to an employee (who has a bona fide employment relationship with such employer) for employment in the provision of covered items or services. . . .*

The initial set of safe harbors published in the 1991 final rule included a regulatory version of this exception, which may be found at 42 C.F.R. § 1001.952(i). The regulatory safe harbor generally tracks the statutory language:

> *As used in [the AKS], "remuneration" does not include any amount paid by an employer to an employee, who has a bona fide employment relationship with the employer, for employment in the furnishing of any item or service for which payment may be made in whole or in part under Medicare, Medicaid or other Federal health care programs. For purposes . . . of this section, the term employee has the same meaning as it does for purposes of [the Internal Revenue Code].*

Thus, the safe harbor has two independently mandated elements: (1) there must be a *bona fide* employment relationship; and (2) the remuneration paid must be for employment in the furnishing or provision of items or services reimbursable under a federal health care program.

Regarding the first requirement, the regulatory safe harbor states that "the term employee has the same meaning as it does for purposes" of the Internal Revenue Code.[364] HHS, however, is barred by statute from opining, during the Advisory Opinion process, on whether an individual is a *bona fide* employee within the meaning of the IRS Code provision.[365]

---

363. H.R. 95-393 at p. 49 (1977).

364. 42 C.F.R. § 1001.952(i) ("the term *employee* has the same meaning as it does for purposes of 26 U.S.C. § 3121(d)(2)"); 26 U.S.C. § 3121(d)(2) ("[T]he terms "employee" means . . . an individual who, under the usual common law rules applicable in determining the employer-employee relationship, has the status of an employee").

365. 42 U.S.C. § 1320a-7d(b)(3)(B).

Regarding the second requirement, there has been disagreement in the case law over its precise meaning and scope, with some courts ruling that a *bona fide* employee may be paid in any manner chosen by an employer, which may even include payments for referrals,[366] while other courts have ruled that the safe harbor only protects payments to employees that are tied to the employees' furnishing or provision of items and services reimbursable under a federal health care program, and not simply payments made in exchange for referrals.[367]

Some have taken the view that the latter position is more consistent with the legislative purpose and design of the AKS and the other safe harbors, with HHS interpretations of the employee safe harbor and with the text of the employee safe harbor itself. On this view, permitting an employer's purchase of patient referrals from an employee who otherwise qualified as *bona fide* within the meaning of the safe harbor could allow the employee safe harbor to undermine the remedial purposes of the AKS by effectively permitting employers to hire their co-conspirators and swallowing the general statutory prohibition against making payments to induce or reward referrals. Furthermore, such an interpretation arguably does not make sense by reference to the text of the safe harbor itself. Under this reasoning, if the intent of the safe harbor were to allow referral payments, there would have been no need to limit the reach of the safe harbor by requiring that payment be for "employment in the furnishing [or provision]" of covered items or services, a clause presumably meant to tie the specific remuneration paid to an employee's "furnishing" or "providing" particular reimbursable items or services, which do not include referrals. Instead, the safe harbor could simply have required evidence of a *bona fide* employment relationship, with no additional showing needed. The inclusion of that additional language, this reasoning continues, was not an inadvertence, but a requirement that compensation, even that paid to *bona fide* employees, must be for the furnishing or providing of covered items and services in order to receive safe harbor protection. Additionally, if the employee safe harbor were intended

366. *See, e.g.*, Wall v. Vista Hospice Care Inc., 2016 WL 3449833 (N.D. Tex. June 20, 2016) (upholding legality of referral payments under employee safe harbor); United States v. Crinel, 2015 WL 3755896 (E.D. La. June 16, 2015) (upholding legality of referral payments under employee safe harbor, provided services rendered are otherwise reimbursable under federal health care program).

367. *See, e.g.*, Obert-Hong v. Advocate Health Care, 211 F.Supp.2d 1045, 1050-51 (N.D. Ill. 2002) (employee safe harbor protects "typical hospital-physician employment relationships," provided that compensation arrangements are "based on personally performed services" and are not "directly related to referrals").

to shield referral payments, one might expect to see exceptions included in other safe harbors permitting such payments to *bona fide* employees. Yet, one will search in vain for any such exceptions. For example, a safe harbor for free or discounted local transportation services that became effective on January 6, 2017, contains an explicit prohibition against paying drivers transporting patients on a "per head" basis, and that safe harbor contains no exception for *bona fide* employee drivers of health care organizations offering such transportation services.[368]

These are some of the reasons that a persuasive argument can be made in support of the view that the employee safe harbor is an exception intended to protect, not the purchase of patient referrals at the expense of patient choice and other competing providers in the health care marketplace, but rather traditional compensation arrangements such as those between physicians and employers like hospitals and group practices which, even while compensating the employee for personally performed services, might still be "potentially capable of inducing referrals of business under Medicare."[369]

To protect these kinds of arrangements, Congress and HHS required not only that there be a *bona fide* employment relationship but also that the money paid by the employer be for employment in the furnishing or provision of covered items and services. On this view, satisfying the former requirement without satisfying the latter requirement will not trigger the safe harbor's protections. Nor would it be sufficient to invoke the safe harbor for a *bona fide* employee to receive a fee in connection with a patient referral unless that fee has some relation to covered items or services that are being personally furnished by that employee. Where the fee is disconnected from the furnishing by the employee of any covered item or service outside the referral itself, such that the fee can only be reasonably viewed as a referral payment (i.e., a payment made solely for the purpose of inducing or rewarding a decision to steer a patient to a particular provider), the protections of the safe harbor would not be available.

The view that the safe harbor does not protect payments made only for referrals and for no other purpose finds support in multiple judicial decisions

368. 42 C.F.R. § 1001.952(b)(b).

369. Proposed Rule: OIG Anti-Kickback Provisions, 54 Fed. Reg. 3088 (Jan. 23, 1989); *See* Obert-Hong v. Advocate Health Care, 211 F. Supp. 2d 1045, 1050-51 (N.D. Ill. 2002) (employee safe harbor protects "typical hospital-physician employment relationships," provided that compensation arrangements are "based on personally performed services" and are not "directly related to referrals").

as well as by opinions issued by the agency charged by statute with the safe harbor's interpretation and enforcement.

Among judicial decisions, one particularly lucid discussion may be found in a district court decision from the Southern District of Florida, *United States v. Luis*.[370] In *Luis*, the government moved for a preliminary injunction in a case seeking to restrain the assets of a defendant under criminal prosecution for health care fraud and violating the AKS by paying employee nurses to recruit Medicare patients. Opposing the motion, the defendant argued that the payments were protected by the employee safe harbor. The court, relying both on the text of the safe harbor and the Eleventh Circuit's 1998 decision in *United States v. Starks*,[371] rejected this argument:

> For either safe-harbor provision to apply, the remuneration must have been made to the employee for furnishing or providing covered items or services or for items or services payable under Medicare. This is evident from the text of the safe-harbor provisions, as well as the Eleventh Circuit's decision in [*Starks*]. The text of the safe-harbor provision upon which Luis relies states that "remuneration" does not include "any amount paid by an employer to an employee . . . *in the furnishing* of any item or service for which payment may be made in whole or in part under Medicare." 42 C.F.R. §1001.952 (emphasis added). Similarly, the safe harbor contained in §1320a–7b states that it will apply to "any amount paid by an employer to an employee . . . *for employment in the provision* of covered items or services." §1320a–7b(b)(3)(B) (emphasis added). The emphasized language in both of these provisions makes clear that the safe-harbor provisions will only apply when payments made to an employee compensate the employee for furnishing or providing covered items or services or items or services payable by Medicare, not simply for referring patients.
>
> This was also the Eleventh Circuit's view in [*Starks*] where the court considered a vagueness challenge to the employee safe-harbor provisions. In that case, two individuals (Angela Starks and Barbara Henry) were paid for referring patients to Future Steps, Inc. [a drug addiction services business owned by Andrew Siegel] . . . Although Starks and Henry referred patients, they did not personally provide any medical

370. United States v. Luis, 966 F. Supp. 2d 1321 (S.D. Fla. 2013) (Huck, J.), *aff'd*, 564 Fed. Appx. 493 (11th Cir. 2014), *vacated and remanded on other grounds*, 136 S.Ct. 1083 (2016).

371. United States v. Starks, 157 F.3d 833 (11th Cir. 1998).

> services . . . Starks and Siegel appealed their [Anti-Kickback Statute] convictions, arguing that the [employee safe harbor] . . . is unconstitutionally vague. Rejecting this argument the court found that, even if Starks and Siegel believed they were bona fide employees, the safe-harbor was not vague, as applied, because Starks and Henry were not compensated for providing "covered items or services." . . .
>
> . . .
>
> Here, Special Agent Warren's declaration states that [the nurse employees] were paid for recruiting patients. Even if these patients ultimately received legitimate medical care, payments to these nurse/recruiters for referring patients . . . violate the Anti-kickback statute . . . Therefore, it is irrelevant whether the nurses were bona fide employees paid for "covered items or services" because the payments to them were, at least in part, for their illegal patient referrals.[372]

Advisory Opinions issued by HHS likewise have consistently interpreted the safe harbor as requiring that compensation qualifying for its protections must be paid for the employee's furnishing or provision of covered items or services.[373] That is significant because, as previously discussed, HHS is

---

372. *Luis*, 966 F. Supp. 2d at 1330-31 (emphasis added); *see also* United States v. Jackson, 220 Fed. Appx. 317 (5th Cir. 2007) (affirming conviction under the AKS based on payments for patient referrals that were paid to employee in checks separate from employee's regular payroll checks written for patient-related services).

373. *See, e.g.*, Advisory Opinion No. 12-08, 2012 WL 4753655 (issued June 22, 2012) (analyzing proposed compensation arrangement between a physician and an independent diagnostic testing facility providing home sleep testing services in which facility would pay physician to read and perform sleep studies and perform administrative duties and, after assuming physician would be *bona fide* employee, concluding arrangement was protected under safe harbor because the physician "*would be compensated for furnishing a service for which payment may be made in whole or in part under Medicare, Medicaid or other Federal health care program*") (emphasis added); Advisory Opinion No. 04-09, 2004 WL 5701854 (issued July 15, 2004) (proposed arrangement between geriatric practice group and referring primary care physicians under which the latter would provide consulting services at an hourly rate was protected under employee safe harbor because, assuming *bona fide* status of employees, physicians would be paid "*for the furnishing of covered items and services*"; noting that AKS "*disfavors payment structures that tie compensation, even for services, to patients referred by the compensated party*" but creates exception where services are furnished by *bona fide* employees) (emphasis added); Advisory Opinion No. 98-9, 1998 WL 35287764 (issued July 13, 1998) (proposed arrangement under collective bargaining agreement, whereby nurse employees would receive additional compensation based on the number of union members and dependents admitted to hospital as inpatients over set periods, was protected under employee safe harbor because, assuming nurses were *bona fide* employees, the compensation was based on the performance of covered "*nursing and other health care related services,*" the extra compensation was "*tied to aggregate admissions and not to specific admissions or services,*" and to be eligible to receive the money, a nurse could not be "*in a position to refer patients to the Hospital*") (emphasis added).

statutorily mandated, as part of the Advisory Opinion process, to opine on "[w]hat constitutes prohibited remuneration within the meaning of section 1320a-7b(b) [i.e., the AKS]."[374] Thus, interpretive guidance from the agency concerning what kinds of remuneration are and are not protected by the safe harbor is likely entitled to substantial deference.[375]

However, the need to link employee compensation to the furnishing or provision of covered items or services in order to trigger the employee safe harbor does not mean that employee compensation formulas may not contain incentive elements that could potentially induce patient referrals. On the contrary, this is where the real impact of the safe harbor is felt by providing broad discretion to employers in how they choose to compensate their employees for furnishing or providing those covered items or services.

The reason underpinning this grant (both statutory and regulatory) of employer autonomy is alluded to in HHS commentary within the final rule promulgating the original regulatory safe harbors. HHS declared its confidence "that the employer-employee relationship is unlikely to be abusive, in part because the employer is generally fully liable for the actions of its employees and is therefore more motivated to supervise and control them."[376]

In other commentary, HHS has stated that the safe harbor "permits an employer to pay an employee in whatever manner he or she chooses for having that employee assist in the solicitation of . . . health care program business" and "if individuals and entities desire to pay a salesperson on the basis of the amount of business they generate, then to be exempt from civil or criminal prosecution, they should make these salespersons employees where they can and should exert appropriate supervision for the individual's acts."[377]

In some quarters, this commentary has been construed as supporting virtually unlimited discretion by employers in devising compensation formulas, to include payments to employees in exchange for patient referrals. As discussed earlier, however, such a view might be a "bridge too far" in interpreting the scope and reach of the employee safe harbor. The commentary may

374. *See* 42 U.S.C. § 1320a-7d(b)(2)(A) (emphasis added).

375. *See, e.g.*, Chevron v. Natural Res. Def. Council, Inc., 467 U.S. 837 (1984).

376. Final Rule: OIG Anti-Kickback Provisions (56 Fed. Reg. 35952; July 29, 1991): Final rulemaking promulgating the ten original safe harbor provisions.

377. Proposed Rule: OIG Anti-Kickback Provisions (54 Fed. Reg. 3088; Jan. 23, 1989): Proposed original ten safe harbor provisions. Medicare and Medicaid Programs, Fraud and Abuse OIG Anti-Kickback Provisions, 54 Fed. Reg. 3088, 3093 (Jan. 23, 1989).

also be understood as speaking to an employer's flexibility in structuring employee compensation for furnishing covered items or services, rather than an employer's authority to pay for referrals alone. Notably, the cited commentary does not purport to address the safe harbor's requirement that the remuneration be tied to the furnishing or provision of covered items or services but instead focuses on the employer's freedom in structuring the compensation even where the compensation formula is related to "the solicitation of . . . health care program business." That would be consistent, for example, with paying physician employees based on a percentage of revenue collections generated from their personally performed services,[378] or with permitting such employees to participate in a bonus pool composed of revenues related to their personally performed services.[379] It is also consistent with an employer paying commissions to an employed sales force responsible for selling various reimbursable "items" (e.g., DME, pharmaceuticals, etc.) directly to medical providers.

Whereas one can at least understand a rationale for not protecting under the employee safe harbor a payment that is solely and exclusively for referrals, and not related to any covered item or service, what of a payment that is made for both reasons? For example, it is certainly conceivable that a hospital employer could choose to structure an employed physician's compensation, both to compensate the physician for personally performed services and also to encourage the physician to refer more patients to his or her hospital employer. Both motivations could underlie a hospital employer's decision to allow a physician to participate in a bonus pool composed of collections by the hospital on the physician's personally performed services. Does the motivation to encourage the physician to refer more patients to the hospital taint the entire compensation formula under the AKS? A strict application of the "one purpose test" might suggest so, and there is some case law and Advisory Opinion language that could support such an outcome, focusing on whether *any* purpose of the remuneration is to induce referrals.[380] Such

378. Obert-Hong v. Advocate Health Care, 211 F. Supp. 2d 1045, 1051 (N.D. Ill. 2002) (approving compensation formula based on percentage of collections).

379. Baklid-Kunz v. Halifax Hosp., 2013 WL 6196562 at *2 (M.D. Fla. Nov. 26, 2013) (approving compensation formula involving payments to medical oncologists consisting of revenues from "outpatient medical oncology services" including "physician services" of the oncologists and paid out of an "Incentive Compensation pool [that] was divided . . . based on each individual oncologist's personally performed services.").

380. *See* United States v. Borrasi, 639 F.3d 774, 782 (7th Cir. 2011) (payments intended to induce referrals violated AKS "even if the payments were also intended to compensate for professional services").

an interpretation might, however, intrude upon the legislative and regulatory scope of the employee safe harbor by allowing prosecution under the AKS for payments made to *bona fide* employees, even if those payments are intended to compensate for an employee's furnishing of covered items or services, so long as the payments are also intended to induce referrals. Yet, since the employee safe harbor contains no specific language requiring that the remuneration paid, in order to receive protection, be paid *exclusively* for the purpose of providing covered items or services, it is fair to ask whether a more commonsense interpretation would require only that at least one purpose of the compensation be for the furnishing of a covered item or service. On this view, if the facts indicated that the sole purpose of the compensation was to reward or induce referrals, the employee safe harbor would not apply, but if the remuneration had a dual purpose to compensate for personally performed services and also to induce referrals to the employer, the payment could still receive protection under the safe harbor.

Another situation involves compensation that is paid only for a single purpose (i.e., personally performed services) but that may fall within more than one safe harbor (e.g., employee safe harbor and personal services safe harbor). In such a situation, HHS has stated that if the payment practice does not qualify for protection under the employee safe harbor, "it still may receive safe harbor protection under the personal services and management contract safe harbor," and "if the payment practice fits into either one of the safe harbors, it is exempt from criminal prosecution and program exclusion."[381]

Concerning the relationship between the employee safe harbor and the safe harbor for sale of practice, in cases where a practitioner purchases another's practice and retains the other practitioner on staff as an employee, HHS has stated that payments to the other practitioner for the practice

381. Final Rule: OIG Anti-Kickback Provisions (56 Fed. Reg. 35952, 35957; July 29, 1991): Final rulemaking promulgating the ten original safe harbor provisions. It is important to distinguish whether an AKS analysis involves *one* arrangement that may fall within multiple safe harbors or *multiple* arrangements between the same parties, whereby each separate arrangement would fall under a different safe harbor. In the example discussed here, a compensation arrangement (i.e., a single arrangement) can fall under multiple safe harbors, including the safe harbor for employee compensation and personal services arrangements. In such an example, only one applicable safe harbor must be satisfied for the arrangement to be protected under AKS. By comparison, when parties have multiple arrangements in place, for example, a landlord may provide office space and certain administrative services to a tenant, then each part of the arrangement must fall within an applicable safe harbor. In this example, the provision of office space would need to fall under the space rental safe harbor, and the administrative services would need to fall under the personal services safe harbor. *See supra* note 209.

itself do not qualify under either safe harbor because those payments are made to one who is still in a position to make referrals (see Chapter 2.5 on Sale of Practice), and they are not payments made "for employment in the provision of covered items or services" since the payments "relate to the purchase of a practice and not to services provided pursuant to employment for the provision of items or services."[382] However, any salary payments to the practitioner for services, assuming the existence of a *bona fide* employment relationship, would be protected under the employee safe harbor.[383]

In explaining the decision to defer to the IRS definition of "employee," HHS stated that the IRS definition "is a longstanding one that has been developed by both agency and court rulings" and that the definition "is sufficiently narrow that it excludes certain types of relationships that we believe tend to be associated with violations of the statute."[384] HHS clarified that the meaning of "employee" will be defined not only by the IRS Code (26 U.S.C. § 3121(d)(2)), "but also by the IRS's interpretation of that provision as codified in its regulations and other interpretive sources."[385] Part-time as well as full-time employment can qualify for protection.[386] Independent contractor relationships are not protected by the safe harbor, although they may receive protection under the safe harbor for personal services (see Chapter 2.4 on Personal Services and Management Contracts).[387]

2.10. Group Purchasing Organizations

The safe harbor for group purchasing organizations is codified both in statute and regulation. 42 U.S.C. § 1320a-7b(b)(3)(C) states:

> (C) any amount paid by a vendor of goods or services to a person authorized to act as a purchasing agent for a group of individuals or entities who are furnishing services reimbursed under a Federal health care program if—
>
> (i) the person has a written contract, with each such individual or entity, which specifies the amount to be paid the person, which amount may be a fixed amount or a fixed percentage

382. *Id.* at 35975.
383. *Id.*
384. *Id.* at 35981.
385. *Id.*
386. *Id.*
387. *Id.* at 35981-82.

of the value of the purchases made by each such individual or entity under the contract, and

(ii) in the case of an entity that is a provider of services (as defined in section 1395x (u) of this title), the person discloses (in such form and manner as the Secretary requires) to the entity and, upon request, to the Secretary the amount received from each such vendor with respect to purchases made by or on behalf of the entity. . . .

The regulatory equivalent of this safe harbor is codified at 42 C.F.R. § 1001.952(j):

> (j) *Group purchasing organizations.* As used in [the AKS], "remuneration" does not include any payment by a vendor of goods or services to a group purchasing organization (GPO), as part of an agreement to furnish such goods or services to an individual or entity as long as both of the following two standards are met -
>
> (1) The GPO must have a written agreement with each individual or entity, for which items or services are furnished, that provides for either of the following -
>
> (i) The agreement states that participating vendors from which the individual or entity will purchase goods or services will pay a fee to the GPO of 3 percent or less of the purchase price of the goods or services provided by that vendor.
>
> (ii) In the event the fee paid to the GPO is not fixed at 3 percent or less of the purchase price of the goods or services, the agreement specifies the amount (or if not known, the maximum amount) the GPO will be paid by each vendor (where such amount may be a fixed sum or a fixed percentage of the value of purchases made from the vendor by the members of the group under the contract between the vendor and the GPO).
>
> (2) Where the entity which receives the goods or service from the vendor is a health care provider of services, the GPO must disclose in writing to the entity at least annually, and to the Secretary upon request, the amount received from each vendor with respect to purchases made by or on behalf of the entity. Note that for purposes of paragraph (j) of this section,

> the term *group purchasing organization* (GPO) means an entity authorized to act as a purchasing agent for a group of individuals or entities who are furnishing services for which payment may be made in whole or in part under Medicare, Medicaid or other Federal health care programs, and who are neither wholly-owned by the GPO nor subsidiaries of a parent corporation that wholly owns the GPO (either directly or through another wholly-owned entity).

As explained by Congress in adopting the statutory safe harbor:[388]

> Group Purchasing organizations (GPOs) purchase goods and services for participating hospitals and other institutions at costs below those which the members would be able to obtain individually. To cover costs, GPOs either charge administrative fees to member institutions, or they require vendors from whom they purchase services or supplies to pay them a fixed percentage of the value of the business that they refer to the vendors. The Inspector General of the Department of Health and Services has determined that this latter arrangement—the vendor-paid fee—represents a "technical" violation of the anti-kickback provisions. In the IG's view, both the vendor who agrees to such a condition and a GPO who solicits such an agreement are violating the law. The IG does not consider these payments exempt from criminal liability as "discounts" under sections 1877(b) and 1909(b) of the Act because they are not reductions in price, the value of which are passed on to the purchaser. Under group purchasing agreements, the amount paid by the vendor to the agent may not be passed along to the hospitals.
>
> Pending Congressional clarification on this point, the IG requested that the Justice Department announce it would refrain from prosecuting such arrangements, but the Department, by letter dated October 30, 1985, declined, arguing that "this would be tantamount to saying that conduct which Congress in its wisdom has made a crime is not a crime." It is clear that Congressional action is warranted.
>
> The Committee believes that GPOs can help reduce health care costs for the government and the private sector alike by enabling a group

388. H.R. Rep. 99-727, Omnibus Budget Reconciliation Act of 1986 (July 31, 1986) (1986 WL 31979 at **3662-63).

> of purchasers to obtain substantial volume discounts on the prices they are charged. The Committee understands that the amount of the price reductions exceeds the fees the vendors must pay the GPOs. The Committee can see no justification for prohibiting such cost-saving arrangements, and believes that the uncertainty resulting from the Justice Department's position on this issue should be eliminated.
>
> The Committee bill therefore creates an exception to the antikickback provisions for amounts paid by vendors of goods and services to authorized purchasing agents for groups of hospitals, nursing homes, or other entities receiving Medicare and Medicaid reimbursement, if the following conditions are met. First, the purchasing agent must have a written contract with each vendor and with each Medicare or Medicaid provider or practitioner in the group specifying the amount paid to the agent. The amount may be either a fixed sum or a fixed percentage (not to exceed 3 percent) of the value of the purchase made by each practitioner or provider under the contract. Second, the purchasing agent must disclose to each practitioner or provider in the group the amount received from each vendor with respect to that individual's or entities purchases. These limitations are intended to assure that only reasonable and above-board vendor-paid GPO fee arrangements receive the protection of this exclusion.
>
> The purpose of this provision is to assure GPOs and the vendors who contract with them, that they do not risk prosecution as a result of the fees the GPO's collection from the vendors. The provision is therefore effective with respect to payments made before, on, or after enactment.

In adopting the regulatory version of the GPO safe harbor, HHS commented that the safe harbor "was designed to apply to payments from vendors to entities authorized to act as a GPO for individuals or entities who are furnishing Medicare or Medicaid services. The exception required a written agreement between the GPO and the individual or entity that specifies the amounts vendors will pay the GPO."[389] In response to a comment, HHS clarified that the exception was not designed to protect a nursing home chain that requested payments from laboratories as GPO fees in return for laboratory referrals from member nursing homes:

389. Final Rule: OIG Anti-Kickback Provisions (56 Fed. Reg. 35952, 35953; July 29, 1991): Final rulemaking promulgating the ten original safe harbor provisions.

> [W]e do not believe it appropriate for a nursing home chain to qualify as a GPO and request "GPO fees" for referrals. If a nursing home directly requested such a fee it would appear to represent an illegal inducement. We see no reason how such a solicitation sanitizes the illegality when it is made indirectly by a wholly-owned subsidiary of the nursing home, instead of directly by the nursing home itself.
>
> In addition, we believe that Congress did not intend this exception to apply where it is the vendor and not the health care provider who is furnishing services and directly billing the Medicare or Medicaid program. For example, in addition to services furnished by the nursing home, other health care providers furnish many part B services to nursing home patients, such as laboratory services and durable medical equipment (DME). We believe that a GPO, acting on behalf of a group of nursing homes, is not serving as a GPO when it receives a "GPO fee" from a laboratory or DME supplier that is supplying goods or services to nursing home patients and billing Medicare or Medicaid directly.[390]

Responding to comments requesting that GPOs be permitted to specify a fee range rather than the actual fee amount, HHS agreed that "it is not necessary in all circumstances, to specify the exact fees the GPO will receive from its vendors as a result of a particular member's purchases."[391] To guard against excessive GPO fees, however, which HHS noted was a specific concern of Congress, HHS explained that a GPO "needs to specify the administrative fee it is paid from vendors only if any fee will be above 3 percent" and that "[i]n the event that the fee cannot be ascertained at the time of the contract or the fee is not fixed at 3 percent or less, the contract must state the maximum amount that could be paid to the GPO by the vendor."[392] HHS noted that "this mechanism will permit some flexibility in payments made to the GPO, yet retain the focus on excessive fees about which Congress was concerned."[393]

Addressing the relationship between the GPO safe harbor and the discount safe harbor, HHS noted that "[t]his is an example of an arrangement where two safe harbor provisions could apply, i.e., one applicable

390. *Id.* at 35982.
391. *Id.*
392. *Id.*
393. *Id.*

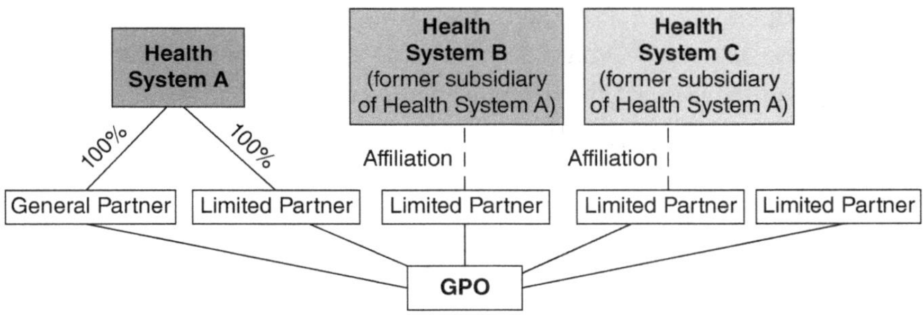

Figure 2.2

to discounts, and one applicable to GPOs" but that "the GPO provision applies only to payments made by a vendor of goods or services to a person authorized to act as a GPO [whereas] [p]ayments, such as discounts, made by vendors of goods or services to health care providers must qualify under the discount exception."[394]

Several Advisory Opinions have been issued on the subject of the GPO safe harbor. In Advisory Opinion No. 01-6, the OIG addressed a business arrangement (see Figure 2.2) involving a GPO organized as a limited partnership owned by entities affiliated with four health care systems that purchased items and services through the GPO, which negotiated discounted prices with vendors. The general partner and one of the limited partners were wholly owned by a health system (Health System) that owned a health care provider that purchased items and services through, and provided advisory and consulting services, space, and personnel to, the GPO. Two of the limited partners were affiliated with health care systems that were formerly subsidiaries of Health System, and the fourth limited partner was an entity having no affiliations with Health System or any other limited partner. In addition to the health care systems affiliated with the GPO, other nonaffiliated health care providers also contracted with the GPO to purchase health care products and services from vendors. Each purchaser entered into an agreement permitting the GPO to act as purchasing agent and disclosing that the GPO would receive quarterly fees from the vendors in connection with purchases made through the GPO. The party requesting the opinion certified that (a) the GPO agreement identified the vendors paying a fee of

394. *Id.*

3 percent or less to the GPO and, for those paying more than 3 percent, specified the exact percentage; (b) the GPO made an annual written disclosure to purchasers of the amounts received from each vendor relating to purchases attributable to each purchaser; (c) none of the purchasers was wholly owned by the GPO or was a subsidiary of a parent corporation that wholly owned the GPO; and (d) the GPO would promptly advise the Affiliated Purchasers that the regulations governing costs to related organizations (42 C.F.R. § 413.17) might apply to them. Finding that all of the requirements of the GPO safe harbor would be satisfied under the facts certified, the OIG concluded that the GPO fees paid by the vendors would not constitute prohibited remuneration under the AKS.

In Advisory Opinion No. 12-01, the OIG addressed a somewhat different GPO fact pattern (see Figure 2.3) that did not elicit the same unqualified approval from the OIG but still avoided the prospect of administrative sanctions in the absence of any intention to induce or reward referrals. The fact pattern involved a corporate parent (Parent Organization) of a national health system consisting of multiple nonprofit corporations operating local health care facilities (Nonprofits). Each of the Nonprofits was a separate legal entity and indirect subsidiary of the Parent Organization. A direct subsidiary of the Parent Organization (Subsidiary) exercised oversight over the Nonprofits and wholly owned another entity (LLC) that was responsible for supply chain, resource, and materials management functions on behalf

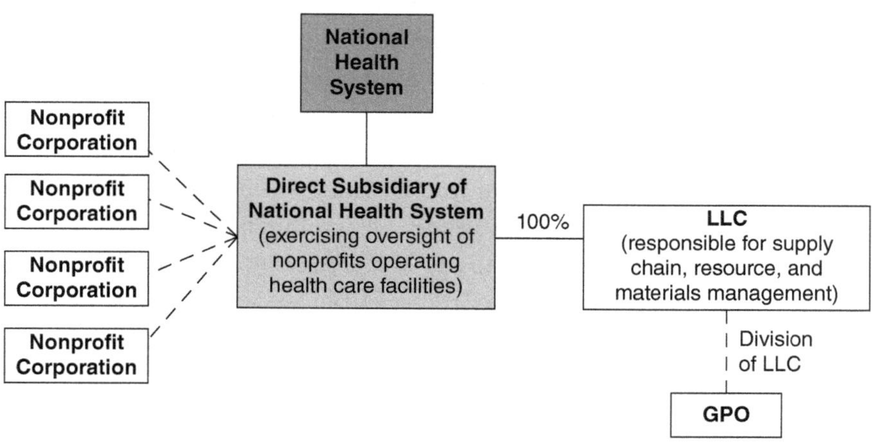

Figure 2.3

of the Parent Organization, Subsidiary, and the Nonprofits. The LLC sought to form and operate a GPO, as a division of the LLC, to benefit the Nonprofits and other affiliated organizations in the health care industry, while continuing through a separate division to be responsible for resource and supply management functions. The initial participants of the GPO would likely be the Nonprofits and other affiliates of the Parent Organization or Subsidiary, but the GPO would also be open to participation by unrelated health systems and organizations (affiliated and nonaffiliated entities, collectively "Participants"). The LLC would not charge GPO participation fees to the Participants. To accomplish its goals, the GPO represented, among other things, that it would enter into written agreements with Participants and suppliers, pursuant to which the GPO would arrange for discounts. The GPO might also provide rebates to Participants by distributing administrative fees to Participants that it collects in excess of its costs, and it would inform vendors directly of this practice.

The OIG concluded that the administrative fees paid to the GPO would *not* be protected by the GPO safe harbor "because the Proposed GPO and most of the Affiliated Participants would be wholly owned by the Parent Organization or the Subsidiary," which is not permitted under the safe harbor and which creates "an increased risk that administrative fees collected by the GPO could be illegal inducements to induce referrals or recommendations." Notwithstanding this fact, however, the OIG determined that the proposed arrangement "present[ed] an acceptably low level or risk to Federal health care programs" because (a) the Nonprofits are separate legal entities, the GPO would function as a purchasing agent for those entities and charge vendors fees for those services, and the GPO would not retain all of the administrative fees but would distribute fees exceeding its costs to Participants, which, in turn, would be required to report their fees as rebates under the discount safe harbor, thereby removing any incentive for the GPO to negotiate higher fees in lieu of discounts; (b) there was a certification that all Medicare cost reporting rules would be satisfied by affiliated participants and thus there was no risk that those participants would not fully account for their distributions from the GPO, and nonaffiliated participants would be provided with the information necessary to accurately report their costs; (c) vendors would be informed that administrative fees in excess of the GPO's costs may be passed through to participants, and thus vendors would be on notice to obtain specific information regarding passed-through fees in order to comply with their own price

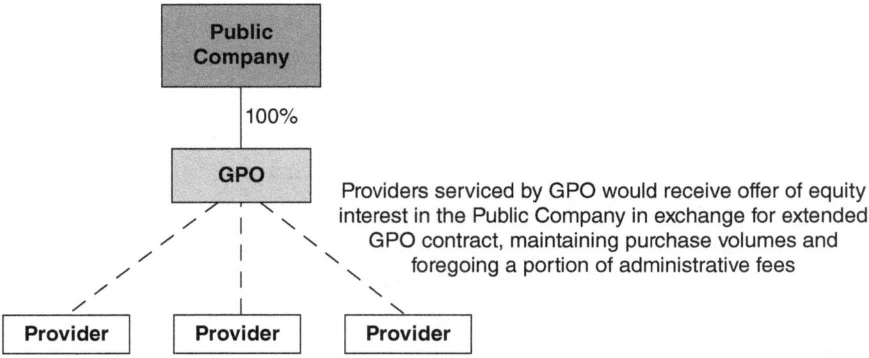

Figure 2.4

reporting requirements; (d) there was a certification that the GPO would not be restricted to affiliated participants, and its expanded roster of participants would serve as additional motivation for the GPO to be competitive in the marketplace and seek out the best prices and services; and (e) there was a certification that the Parent Organization would continue to direct its purchasing volume through independent GPOs whenever those independent GPOs could obtain better value from suppliers, and the LLC would continue to contract directly on behalf of the Nonprofits whenever necessary to meet their needs, thereby ensuring that multiple resources would be used to obtain the best value for Participants, whether or not that was through the proposed GPO, which made it more likely that Participants would receive the benefits intended by Congress.

Advisory Opinion No. 13-09 involved a publicly traded company (the "Company") that provided financial and performance improvement products and services to hospitals and health systems (see Figure 2.4). A wholly owned subsidiary of the Company operated a GPO. The GPO served various providers, the largest among them being hospital and integrated delivery systems. The GPO accounted for about 60 percent of the Company's revenues. The GPO's fees paid by vendors range from 0.25 to 3 percent. The GPO has different contract models: a fee-for-service model under which members pay the GPO a negotiated fee but have no minimum purchase requirements, and the GPO passes 100 percent of the administrative fees paid by vendors through to members; and a "shareback" model, under which the GPO passes through to members a negotiated percentage (usually 50 percent) of the administrative fees collected from vendors, and although members often do have minimum purchase requirements, they do not pay any fees to the GPO. If the member does not meet its minimum purchase requirements, then the percentage pass-through of administrative fees is reduced. The GPO pass-through fees are treated as discounts under both models. Under the new proposed arrangement, the Company wanted to offer current and prospective GPO members an equity interest in the Company in exchange for the member extending the existing (or, in the case of a new member, entering into a new) GPO agreement for five to seven years and committing not to decrease the volume of its purchases through the GPO. Those members accepting the equity interest would forgo a portion of the administrative fees that they otherwise would have received. The new arrangement would be presented as an option, with the member also being allowed to keep its current arrangement with no change, accept 66 percent of the current "shareback" amount and receive equity approximating the market value of the forfeited shareback, or accept 33 percent of the current shareback and receive equity approximating the market value of the forfeited shareback. Fee-for-service members would be permitted to enter into shareback arrangements under these terms.

The OIG concluded that the offer of an equity interest in the Company was a form of remuneration to induce members to order federally reimbursable products under the GPO's contracts and to extend those contracts under new terms. The OIG determined that this particular form of remuneration did not meet any safe harbor and could not be said to present a minimal risk of fraud and abuse. The OIG noted that while administrative fees passed through to GPO members could be treated as discounts and members could meet reporting requirements under the discount safe harbor, the same was not true of the equity interest. The OIG cited Government Accountability Office (GAO) reports raising concerns that the "financial flows between hospitals, GPOs, and vendors might result in divergent interests between GPOs and hospitals" and that GPOs might "have an incentive not to seek the lowest price, because the GPO could earn higher administrative fees on higher-priced products."[395]

OIG observed that when administrative fees are passed through to members, savings to federal health care programs may still be realized even when the GPO is not obtaining the lowest cost on products and services, because those distributions must be treated as either discounts or rebates, but if the

395. Advisory Opinion 13-09 at pp. 5-6.

distributions take the form of equity in the Company, that equity would have no potential to benefit payers. Additionally, OIG noted that under the proposed arrangement, equity received was tied to past purchases and members would be required to extend their contracts by five to seven years and could not reduce their volume of purchases, regardless of whether the GPO was obtaining the best price. Further, even though return on investment in the Company would not be directly tied to future purchases, since the GPO's revenues were a substantial percentage of the Company's revenues, and the GPO would be retaining more administrative fees, that might increase Company revenue and result in higher returns for investors referring to the GPO. OIG, therefore, ultimately concluded that the proposed arrangement was non-compliant since it would use Company equity to reward past referrals and induce members to continue purchasing items through the GPO for an extended period of time.

Advisory Opinion No. 16-06 involved a national GPO with more than 84,000 members, including hospitals, nursing facilities, clinics, physician practices, laboratories, and home care or equipment organizations (*see* Figure 2.5). Through a series of corporate transactions, the GPO was 95 percent owned by a health system (Health System) and 5 percent by another holding company (Holdings). Under the proposed arrangement, the Health System would purchase the remaining ten shares of the GPO currently held by Holdings. It was certified that the GPO would continue to serve the same market in the same way, "including negotiating with vendors regarding products and pricing to be offered to the GPO . . . members, and receiving administrative fee from vendors based on a small percentage of the value of

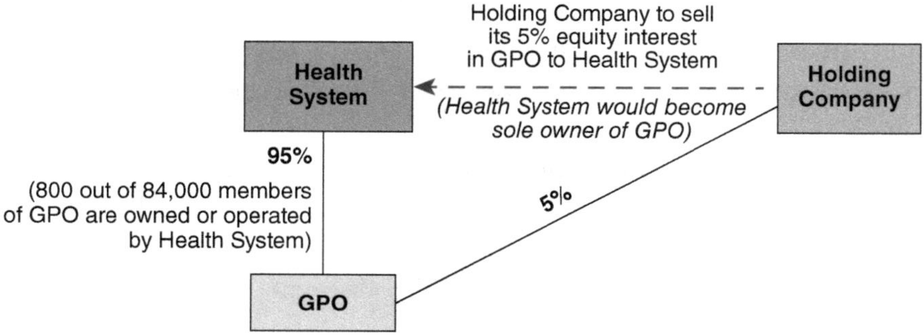

Figure 2.5

sales to members."[396] It was further certified that members of the GPO "that are owned or operated by the Health System . . . are, and would continue to be, subject to GPO contract terms and conditions negotiated on the same basis as members unaffiliated with the Health System," and that various other requirements of the GPO and discount safe harbors would be satisfied, except "that the GPO . . . would be wholly owned by the same entity that also wholly owns approximately one percent of the pool of the [GPO's] members."[397]

The OIG first commented that, even if discounts offered and given to members and administrative fees passed through to members qualified for protection under the discount safe harbor, that safe harbor would not protect the administrative fees received by the GPO from vendors, because those fees must be analyzed under the GPO safe harbor. The OIG then acknowledged that under the proposed arrangement, the GPO would no longer meet the regulatory requirement that the GPO members not be either "wholly-owned by the GPO nor [be] subsidiaries of a parent corporation that wholly owns the GPO" since Health System owned the GPO as well as some of the GPO members (about 800 out of 84,000 members). The OIG, however, determined that this circumstance did not create a heightened risk. The OIG noted that even though the GPO would be wholly owned by the same entity that owns some of the GPO's members, those wholly owned members only comprised 1 percent of the GPO's total membership, and all the members would continue to be subject to GPO "contract terms and conditions negotiated on the same basis as members unaffiliated with the Health System."[398] Accordingly, the GPO "would continue to operate as a purchasing agent for a group of individuals and entities, the vast majority of which are unrelated to the GPO."[399]

2.11. Waiver of Beneficiary Copayment, Coinsurance and Deductible Amounts

The regulatory safe harbor for space rental arrangements is codified at 42 C.F.R. § 1001.952(k), which states:

> (k) *Waiver of beneficiary copayment, coinsurance and deductible amounts.* As used in [the AKS], "remuneration" does not

396. Advisory Opinion No. 16-06, at p. 3.
397. *Id.*
398. *Id.* at pp. 6-7.
399. *Id.*

include any reduction or waiver of a Federal health care program beneficiary's obligation to pay copayment, coinsurance or deductible (for purposes of this subparagraph (k) "cost-sharing") amounts as long as all the standards are met within one of the following categories of health care providers or suppliers.

(1) If the cost-sharing amounts are owed to a hospital for inpatient hospital services for which a Federal health care program pays under the prospective payment system, the hospital must comply with all of the following three standards:

(i) The hospital must not later claim the amount reduced or waived as a bad debt for payment purposes under a Federal health care program or otherwise shift the burden of the reduction or waiver onto a Federal health care program, other payers, or individuals;

(ii) The hospital must offer to reduce or waive the cost-sharing amounts without regard to the reason for admission, the length of stay of the beneficiary, or the diagnostic related group for which the claim for reimbursement is filed; and

(iii) The hospital's offer to reduce or waive the cost-sharing amounts must not be made as part of a price reduction agreement between a hospital and a third-party payer (including a health plan as defined in paragraph (l)(2) of this section), unless the agreement is part of a contract for the furnishing of items or services to a beneficiary of a Medicare supplemental policy issued under the terms of section 1882(t)(1) of the [Social Security Act].

(2) If the cost-sharing amounts are owed by an individual who qualifies for subsidized services under a provision of the Public Health Services Act or under Titles V or XIX of the [Social Security Act] to a federally qualified health care center or other health care facility under any Public Health Services Act grant program or under Title V of the [Social Security Act], the health care center or facility may reduce or waive the cost-sharing amounts for items or services for which payment may be made in whole or in part by a Federal health care program.

(3) If the cost-sharing amounts are owed to a pharmacy (including, but not limited to, pharmacies of the Indian Health Service, Indian tribes, tribal organizations, and urban Indian organizations) for cost-sharing imposed under a Federal health care program, the pharmacy may reduce or waive the cost-sharing amounts if:
  (i) The waiver or reduction is not offered as part of an advertisement or solicitation; and
  (ii) Except for waivers or reductions offered to subsidy-eligible individuals (as defined in section 1860D-14(a)(3)) to which only requirement in paragraph (k)(3)(i) of this section applies:
    (A) The pharmacy does not routinely waive or reduce cost-sharing amounts; and
    (B) The pharmacy waives the cost-sharing amounts only after determining in good faith that the individual is in financial need or after failing to collect the cost-sharing amounts after making reasonable collection efforts.

(4) If the cost-sharing amounts are owed to an ambulance provider or supplier for emergency ambulance services for which a Federal health care program pays under a fee-for-service payment system and all the following conditions are met:
  (i) The ambulance provider or supplier is owned and operated by a State, a political subdivision of a State, or a tribal health care program, as that term is defined in section 4 of the Indian Health Care Improvement Act;
  (ii) The ambulance provider or supplier engaged in an emergency response, as defined in 42 CFR 414.605;
  (iii) The ambulance provider or supplier offers the reduction or waiver on a uniform basis to all of its residents or (if applicable) tribal members, or to all individuals transported; and
  (iv) The ambulance provider or supplier must not later claim the amount reduced or waived as a bad debt for payment purposes under a Federal health care program or otherwise shift the burden of the reduction or waiver

onto a Federal health care program, other payers, or individuals.

The cost-sharing waiver safe harbor was included as part of the original safe harbors that were enacted by HHS in 1991.[400] HHS has made numerous amendments to the safe harbor since its enactment. As it currently stands, the safe harbor protects waivers and reductions[401] of cost-sharing amounts that are offered by the following four types of providers and suppliers, as long as all of the requirements of the safe harbor are met: (1) hospitals for inpatient services, (2) federally qualified health centers (FQHCs) or other health care facilities under a Public Health Services Act grant program or under Title V of the Social Security Act ("Qualifying Facilities"), (3) pharmacies, and (4) ambulance provider or supplier of emergency ambulance services.[402]

A. *Cost-Sharing Waivers Offered by a Hospital*

The first category of providers and suppliers that are protected by the cost-sharing waiver safe harbor are hospitals. This category is further limited to waivers offered by hospitals for inpatient services only.

When enacting the safe harbor, HHS explained that it is aware that hospitals routinely waive deductibles and coinsurance charges in order to attract patients and that such practice is considered an inducement to utilize the hospital's services.[403] However, HHS also noted that such inducement can present a low risk of fraud and abuse if certain risk-mitigating factors are present. For example, HHS stated that there is a relatively fixed level of patient demand for hospital inpatient services. As such, permitting hospitals to waive a patient's deductible or coinsurance amount is not likely to significantly increase the utilization of hospital inpatient services. For this reason, HHS limited the applicability of the safe harbor to waivers for inpatient hospital services only.[404] Other risk-mitigating factors

400. Final Rule: OIG Anti-Kickback Provisions, 56 Fed. Reg. 35952.

401. Although the safe harbor is often referred to as the cost-sharing "waiver" safe harbor, it applies equally to both waivers and reductions of deductibles, copayments, and coinsurance amounts. *See* 81 Fed. Reg. 88368, 88374.

402. Originally, the safe harbor only applied to waivers of cost-sharing amounts offered by a hospital for inpatient services and by FQHCs and other Qualifying Facilities. *Id.* In 2016, it was expanded to also include protections for waivers offered by pharmacies and ambulance service providers. 81 Fed. Reg. 88368, at 88376.

403. 56 Fed. Reg. 35952.

404. *Id.* For this same reason, HHS declined to expand the safe harbor protections to other types of providers at the time the safe harbor was originally enacted in 1991. HHS believed that other types of providers did not have a fixed level of patient demand for their services

noted by HHS are addressed in the other three requirements of the safe harbor summarized below.[405]

The first requirement prohibits the hospital from claiming the waived amount as bad debt for payment purposes under a federal health care program or otherwise shifting the burden of the waived amount onto a federal health care program or other payor. By prohibiting hospitals from claiming the waived amount as bad debt, it ensures that the waiver "cause[s] no direct financial harm to the Medicare program [or other federal health care program or payor]."[406]

The second requirement of the safe harbor prohibits the hospital from taking into account the following factors when making decisions whether to waive cost-sharing amounts for a particular patient: (i) the patient's reason for admission, (ii) length of hospital stay, and (iii) the type of disease or diagnostic group for which the patient is seeking treatment and for which reimbursement will be sought.[407] HHS has long reiterated its position that hospital waiver policies should be applied uniformly to all patients and should not take into account the foregoing factors.[408]

The last requirement states that the waiver of cost-sharing amounts cannot be made as part of a price reduction agreement between a hospital and a third-party payor, including a health plan,[409] unless the agreement is part of a contract for the furnishing of items or services to a beneficiary of a Medicare supplemental policy issued under Section 1882(t)(1) of the Social

---

as hospitals did for inpatient services such that a waiver of cost-sharing amounts would not present a risk of overutilization. However, HHS also noted that it has no purpose in interfering with other providers or hospitals that offer waivers of cost-sharing amounts to indigent patient populations in order to promote access to care for such patient populations. Such practices "would not likely violate the statute so long as the partial forgiveness of the copayment obligation was strictly a pragmatic financial decision and not an inducement to patients to purchase medical services." *Id.*

405. HHS also declined to extend the safe harbor protections to other forms of remuneration that might be offered by hospitals to patients, such as free meals, presurgical overnight stays, sample products, or other free items or services because such inducements "could easily become excessive." *Id.* Unlike a waiver of coinsurance or deducible, which is limited to the fixed amount of the coinsurance or deductible, free items or services have "no distinct financial or other cut-off point below which [HHS] can be sure that [such] gifts remain non-abusive." *Id.*

406. 56 Fed. Reg. 35952.

407. *Id.*

408. *Id.*; *see also* 81 Fed. Reg. 88368, at 88373 (explaining that all decisions regarding waivers of cost-sharing amounts for "financial need" must be made "on a good faith, individualized, case-by-case basis in accordance with a reasonable set of income guidelines uniformly applied in all cases").

409. HHS enacted a separate safe harbor that protects reductions in cost-sharing amounts offered by health plans. *See* 42 C.F.R. § 1001.952(l) (summarized herein in Chapter 2.12).

Security Act. Generally speaking, the cost-sharing waiver safe harbor was only intended to protect waivers offered directly to patients and not third-party payors.[410] However, in 1992, HHS revised the safe harbor to provide one exception that permits cost-sharing waiver arrangements with a Medicare supplemental policy that is issued by Medicare SELECT insurers, provided that the first two requirements of the safe harbor are also satisfied.[411] HHS also clarified that the waiver arrangement with the Medicare SELECT insurer must only be applicable to beneficiaries covered by the insurer's Medicare SELECT policy.[412]

In addition, the OIG has often concluded that waivers offered to third-party payors, which do not satisfy the third requirement for safe harbor protection, can nonetheless present a low risk of fraud and abuse if the following factors are present:

1. The waiver will not affect payments made by a federal health care program (e.g., by increasing the amount owed by a federal health care program for the inpatient hospital service or otherwise shifting the burden of the waived amount);
2. The arrangement is unlikely to increase overutilization of a service;[413]
3. The arrangement will not unfairly affect competition among hospitals;
4. The arrangement is unlikely to affect professional medical judgment of providers; and
5. The arrangement would operate transparently, meaning that patients would be clearly informed about their freedom to choose any hospital to receive inpatient services.

Based on the OIG's position in numerous advisory opinions, if the foregoing factors are present in a proposed cost-sharing waiver arrangement

410. *See, e.g.*, OIG Advisory Opinion 18-04 (June 7, 2018) ("[The] safe harbor specifically excludes [coinsurance and deductible] waivers when they are part of an agreement with insurers.").

411. 57 Fed. Reg. 52723. Medicare SELECT policies are intended to reduce costs for beneficiaries by encouraging providers to become preferred providers of the plan in order to be able to treat Medicare SELECT patients in exchange for accepting a reduced payment for such treatment. *Id.* The safe harbor protection for waivers of coinsurance and deductions between hospitals and the plans is consistent with the plan's intent to reduce overall health care costs. *See id.; see also* 61 Fed. Reg. 2122 at 2127.

412. *Id.*

413. With respect to inpatient hospital services, the OIG notes that it has long held that due to the relatively fixed demand for inpatient services, waivers of cost-sharing amounts are unlikely to increase demand or utilization of such services. *See supra* note 5.

between a hospital and a third-party payor, such arrangement is unlikely to violate the AKS or result in sanctions imposed by the OIG.[414]

B. Cost-Sharing Waivers Offered by a Federally Qualified Health Center or Other Qualifying Facility

The second category under the safe harbor permits FQHCs and other Qualifying Facilities (as defined earlier) to waive cost-sharing amounts owed by patients for subsidized services for which payment may be made in whole or in part by a federal health care program.[415]

C. Cost-Sharing Waivers Offered by a Pharmacy

The third category under the cost-sharing waiver safe harbor applies to pharmacies. Pharmacies are permitted to reduce or waive cost-sharing amounts imposed under a federal health care program if the waiver or reduction is not offered as part of an advertisement or solicitation.

HHS explained that the terms "advertisement" and "solicitation" as used in the safe harbor should be interpreted in accordance with "their common usage in the health care industry," and "whether a particular means of communication constitutes an advertisement or solicitation will depend on the [particular] facts and circumstances."[416] By way of example, information posted on websites regarding cost-sharing waivers would likely be considered an advertisement.[417] In comparison, responding to a specific patient inquiry about cost-sharing waivers and/or discussing the patient's

---

414. *See, e.g.*, OIG Advisory Opinion 18-04 (June 7, 2018); OIG Advisory Opinion 18-12 (Oct. 22, 2018); OIG Advisory Opinion 18-09 (Aug. 14, 2018); OIG Advisory Opinion 18-06 (July 11, 2018); OIG Advisory Opinion 17-06 (Nov. 9, 2017); OIG Advisory Opinion 17-04 (Aug. 24, 2017); OIG Advisory Opinion 16-11 (Oct. 27, 2016); OIG Advisory Opinion 16-05 (Apr. 26, 2016); OIG Advisory Opinion 16-04 (Apr. 12, 2016); OIG Advisory Opinion 16-03 (Mar. 11, 2016); OIG Advisory Opinion 16-01 (Jan. 7, 2016); OIG Advisory Opinion 15-09 (July 16, 2015); OIG Advisory Opinion 15-08 (June 12, 2015); OIG Advisory Opinion 15-05 (Apr. 22, 2015); OIG Advisory Opinion 15-03 (Feb. 23, 2015); OIG Advisory Opinion 14-10 (Oct. 14, 2014); OIG Advisory Opinion 14-08 (Sept. 17, 2014); OIG Advisory Opinion 14-07 (Aug. 18, 2014); OIG Advisory Opinion 14-04 (Apr. 9, 2014); OIG Advisory Opinion 14-02 (Feb. 12, 2014); OIG Advisory Opinion 13-06 (June 20, 2013); OIG Advisory Opinion 13-01 (May 8, 2013); OIG Advisory Opinion 11-09 (July 14, 2011); OIG Advisory Opinion 10-21 (Sept. 21, 2010); OIG Advisory Opinion 10-01 (Feb. 12, 2010); OIG Advisory Opinion 09-10 (July 24, 2009); OIG Advisory Opinion 08-13 (Sept. 23, 2008); OIG Advisory Opinion 07-15 (Dec. 3, 2007); OIG Advisory Opinion 03-10 (May 8, 2003).

415. *See* 42 C.F.R. § 1001.952(k)(2); 57 Fed. Reg. 52723.

416. 81 Fed. Reg. 88368, at 88372.

417. *Id.*

financial needs would generally not be considered an advertisement or solicitation.[418]

In addition, in order to qualify for the safe harbor protection, the pharmacy offering the waiver must satisfy the following two requirements: (i) it cannot routinely waive or reduce cost-sharing amounts; and (ii) it can only waive or reduce cost-sharing amounts after (A) determining in good faith that the patient receiving the waiver or reduction is in financial need or (B) failing to collect the cost-sharing amounts from the patient after making reasonable collection efforts. However, the foregoing requirements in sub-clause (i) and (ii) are not applicable if the pharmacy offers the cost-sharing waiver to subsidy-eligible patients, as defined under Section 1860D-14(a)(3) of the Social Security Act. When cost-sharing waivers are offered to such subsidy-eligible patients, the pharmacy is permitted to make the waiver as long as the first element of the safe harbor is met (i.e., the waiver was not part of an advertisement or solicitation).[419]

With respect to the prohibition on "routine waivers," HHS has declined to explicitly define what constitutes a "routine" waiver.[420] However, it has stated that waivers should not become commonplace and should only be offered "occasionally" when patients meet certain objective criteria, such as financial need.[421] Yet, HHS has also declined to define a particular method for determining "financial need."[422] What constitutes a "routine waiver" or "financial need" will be determined by HHS on a case-by-case basis after considering the underlying facts and circumstances.

HHS has noted that, under the safe harbor, pharmacies must make a "good faith" determination of financial need. Such determinations should be made on a "case-by-case basis in accordance with a reasonable set of income guidelines [that are] uniformly applied."[423] Further, pharmacies should not only accept a patient's statement that they are in financial need but should perform an independent assessment of the patient's financial need.[424] Such assessment may include verifying the patient's financial resources and/or

418. *Id.*

419. *Id.* at 88371.

420. *Id.* at 88372.

421. *Id.*; *see also* OIG Special Fraud Alert (Dec. 19, 1994), https://oig.hhs.gov/fraud/docs/alertsandbulletins/121994.html.

422. *Id.* at 88373.

423. *Id.* The guidelines should be objective and appropriate for the applicable locality so as to ensure that inflated income guidelines are not used. *Id.*

424. *Id.* Although HHS acknowledges that performing a financial assessment may be costly, it also believes that it is an "important safeguard" in mitigating potential fraud and abuse.

collecting financial documents from the patient such as pay stubs, tax forms, or evidence of other expenses.[425]

As an alternative to performing a financial need assessment, the second element of the cost-sharing waiver safe harbor permits pharmacies to waive or reduce cost-sharing amounts after making reasonable collection efforts (and assuming that all other requirements of the safe harbor are satisfied). HHS defines "reasonable collection efforts" as "those efforts that a reasonable provider would undertake to collect amounts owed for items and services provided to patients."[426] HHS also relies on the collection guidelines established by the CMS *Provider Reimbursement Manual*, which requires providers to issue bills to patients and take other reasonable actions to collect payment for such bills, including issuance of subsequent bills, collection letters, telephone calls, and other contact with the patient.[427] In other words, to qualify for safe harbor protection, the pharmacies must make a "genuine" collection effort before waiving or reducing cost-sharing amounts.[428]

D. *Cost-Sharing Waivers Offered by an Emergency Ambulance Service Provider*

The fourth and final category of the cost-sharing waiver safe harbor applies to providers or suppliers of emergency ambulance services for which payment is made under a federal health care program. The safe harbor applies only to waivers or reductions of cost-sharing amounts offered by an ambulance provider or supplier that is owned and operated by a state, a political subdivision of a state, or a tribal health care program (as the term is defined under the Indian Health Care Improvement Act). The safe harbor does not apply to privately owned ambulance companies.[429]

In addition, the safe harbor protects only cost-sharing waivers for emergency ambulance services. "Emergency ambulance services" are defined

---

425. "By way of example only, one pharmacy might choose to apply a multiple of the poverty guidelines, which take into account family size, for determining financial need, while another pharmacy might prefer to take into account a combination of the poverty guidelines, adjusted for the cost of living in the pharmacy's locality, plus family medical expenses. We emphasize, however, whatever guideline is applied by the pharmacy must be reasonable and applied uniformly." *Id.* at 88374.

426. *Id.* (citing *Provider Reimbursement Manual* (CMS Pub. 15-1) § 310).

427. *Id.*

428. *Id.* HHS also noted that "[t]he amount of the copayment or historical inability to collect cost-sharing amounts for a particular beneficiary might be factors that are considered in determining what reasonable collection efforts are, but they do not justify forgoing all collection efforts." *Id.*

429. *Id.*

as ambulance transports initiated by a 911 call or other emergency access number.[430] Further, the ambulance provider or supplier must be engaged in an "emergency response" that is defined as a response to a 911 call or equivalent call system that requires BLS (basic life support) or ALS1 (advanced life support) level of service.[431]

Further, to qualify for the safe harbor protection, the cost-sharing waiver must be applied on a uniform basis to all patients. HHS has also clarified that the applicability of the waiver should not be based on patient-specific factors.[432] An ambulance provider cannot decide to waive cost-sharing amounts due to a patient's health condition, age, or insurance or financial status.[433] Notably, the latter prohibition is distinguishable from other categories of the cost-sharing waiver safe harbor. The category for pharmacies (discussed earlier), for example, states that, under certain circumstances, pharmacies are permitted to waive cost-sharing amounts only after determining the patient's financial need. Yet, under the same safe harbor, ambulance providers are prohibited from taking into account the financial need or insurance status of a patient.[434]

HHS has also stated that ambulance providers are not prohibited from considering the residency of a patient in a particular municipality or government unit when making cost-sharing waiver decisions.[435]

The final requirement of the safe harbor, as applicable to ambulance providers, is the same as the requirement applicable to hospitals (as discussed earlier)—the ambulance provider cannot claim the waived cost-sharing amount as bad debt for payment under a federal health care program, or otherwise shift the burden on to a federal health care program or other payor or individual.[436]

When analyzing proposed arrangements that did not meet all of the elements of the cost-sharing waiver safe harbor for ambulance services, the OIG

430. *Id.* at 88376; *see also* 42 C.F.R. § 1001.952(u)(i)(E)(4)(iv).

431. 42 C.F.R. § 1001.952(k); 42 C.F.R. § 414.605.

432. 81 Fed. Reg. 88368, at 88376.

433. *Id.*

434. *Id.*

435. *Id.* ("[A]n ambulance provider or supplier could waive cost-sharing amounts for all residents, but charge cost-sharing amounts to nonresidents. However, the ambulance provider or supplier cannot discriminate on the basis of any factor other than residency or, if applicable, tribal membership. For example, an ambulance provider or supplier cannot waive cost-sharing amounts for patients transported for an emergency that required only outpatient treatment, but charge cost-sharing amounts for patients transported for a condition that requires hospitalization (or vice versa)."); *see also* OIG Advisory Opinion 13-11 (Aug. 14, 2014).

436. 81 Fed. Reg. 88368, at 88376.

has considered whether the arrangement presented a risk of overutilization of services and increased costs to federal health care programs. Where the risk of overutilization is low, the OIG has concluded that there was a low risk of fraud and abuse under the AKS.[437] Generally speaking, routine waivers are likely to be considered suspect under the AKS, while "unscheduled and sporadic waivers" are less likely to present a risk of fraud and abuse.[438]

Similarly, the OIG has previously found that arrangements that do not influence demand for ambulance services would not be considered suspect under the AKS.[439] By way of example, one arrangement analyzed by the OIG involved an ambulance provider offering backup services to adjoining fire departments and waiving patient cost-sharing amounts.[440] The backup services were provided as needed by the fire departments and were not based on the value or volume of referrals between the parties.[441] Moreover, the ambulance provider would use the same billing practices as the fire departments for all backup services it provided.[442] The OIG concluded that the arrangement presented a low risk of fraud and abuse because it did not influence demand for ambulance services, since the services would have to be provided regardless if they were provided by the fire departments or as backup services, and in either event, they would be billed using the same billing practices, without potential for increasing costs to federal health care programs.[443]

2.12. Increased Coverage, Reduced Cost-Sharing Amounts, or Reduced Premium Amounts Offered by Health Plans

The safe harbor for price reductions offered to health plans is codified at 42 C.F.R. § 1001.952(l):

(l) *Increased coverage, reduced cost-sharing amounts, or reduced premium amounts offered by health plans.*

437. *See, e.g.*, OIG Advisory Opinion 13-11 (Aug. 14, 2014) (explaining that when waivers were offered on an "unscheduled and sporadic basis" they were unlikely to result in overutilization).

438. *Id.*

439. *See* OIG Advisory Opinion 18-08 (Aug. 7, 2018).

440. *Id.*

441. *Id.*

442. *Id.*

443. *Id.*

(1) As used in [the AKS], "remuneration" does not include the additional coverage of any item or service offered by a health plan to an enrollee or the reduction of some or all of the enrollee's obligation to pay the health plan or a contract health care provider for cost-sharing amounts (such as coinsurance, deductible, or copayment amounts) or for premium amounts attributable to items or services covered by the health plan, the Medicare program, or a State health care program, as long as the health plan complies with all of the standards within one of the following two categories of health plans:

(i) If the health plan is a risk-based health maintenance organization, competitive medical plan, prepaid health plan, or other health plan under contract with CMS or a State health care program and operating in accordance with section 1876(g) or 1903(m) of the Act, under a Federal statutory demonstration authority, or under other Federal statutory or regulatory authority, it must offer the same increased coverage or reduced cost-sharing or premium amounts to all Medicare or State health care program enrollees covered by the contract unless otherwise approved by CMS or by a State health care program.

(ii) If the health plan is a health maintenance organization, competitive medical plan, health care prepayment plan, prepaid health plan or other health plan that has executed a contract or agreement with CMS or with a State health care program to receive payment for enrollees on a reasonable cost or similar basis, it must comply with both of the following two standards -

(A) The health plan must offer the same increased coverage or reduced cost-sharing or premium amounts to all Medicare or State health care program enrollees covered by the contract or agreement unless otherwise approved by CMS or by a State health care program; and

(B) The health plan must not claim the costs of the increased coverage or the reduced cost-sharing or premium amounts as a bad debt for payment purposes under Medicare or a State health care program or otherwise shift the burden of the increased coverage or reduced cost-sharing or premium amounts to the extent that increased payments are claimed from Medicare or a State health care program.

(2) For purposes of paragraph (l) of this section, the terms -

Contract health care provider means an individual or entity under contract with a health plan to furnish items or services to enrollees who are covered by the health plan, Medicare, or a State health care program.

Enrollee means an individual who has entered into a contractual relationship with a health plan (or on whose behalf an employer, or other private or governmental entity has entered into such a relationship) under which the individual is entitled to receive specified health care items and services, or insurance coverage for such items and services, in return for payment of a premium or a fee.

Health plan means an entity that furnishes or arranges under agreement with contract health care providers for the furnishing of items or services to enrollees, or furnishes insurance coverage for the provision of such items and services, in exchange for a premium or a fee, where such entity:

(i) Operates in accordance with a contract, agreement or statutory demonstration authority approved by CMS or a State health care program;

(ii) Charges a premium and its premium structure is regulated under a State insurance statute or a State enabling statute governing health maintenance organizations or preferred provider organizations;

(iii) Is an employer, if the enrollees of the plan are current or retired employees, or is a union welfare fund, if the enrollees of the plan are union members; or

(iv) Is licensed in the State, is under contract with an employer, union welfare fund, or a company furnishing health insurance coverage as described in conditions (ii) and (iii) of this definition, and is paid a fee for the

> administration of the plan which reflects the fair market value of those services.

In 1992, the OIG published an interim final rule establishing a safe harbor for "Increased Coverage, Reduced Cost-sharing Amounts, or Reduced Premium Amounts Offered by Health Plans."[444] This was one of three safe harbor provisions protecting health plans and dealt "with the relationship of health plans to enrollees."[445] The OIG noted that while the AKS "is generally not implicated when a health plan offers a premium to a Medicare or State health care program beneficiary to provide an insurance package, the statute is implicated when discounts on premiums or other incentives are offered."[446] This safe harbor "was created to protect certain incentives to enrollees (including increased benefits and waiver of deductible and coinsurance amounts) offered by health plans . . . [and] contained two parts designed to protect incentives offered by health care plans under contract with the Health Care Financing Administration (HCFA) [now CMS] or a State health care program."[447]

According to the OIG, the "first part of this safe harbor protected risk-based health plans, like HMOs, competitive medical plans (CMPs) and prepaid health plans (PHPs)" and "the only standard for such health plans was that the health care plan could not discriminate in the offering of these incentives, but [had to] offer the same incentives to all enrollees unless otherwise specifically approved by HCFA or a State health care program."[448] The second part of the safe harbor "protected incentives offered to enrollees by HMOs, CMPs, PHPs and health care prepaid plans (HCPPs) . . . that are paid on a reasonable cost or similar basis" provided that "the same incentives [are] offered to all enrollees for all covered services" and that "the health plan [does] not claim the cost of these incentives as bad debts or otherwise shift the burden of these incentives onto Medicare, the State health care programs, other payers or individuals."[449]

---

444. Interim Final Rule: Safe Harbors for Protecting Health Plans (57 Fed. Reg. 52723, 52725; Nov. 5, 1992) (sets forth three new safe harbors addressing managed care plans through interim final rulemaking).

445. *Id.*

446. *Id.*

447. Final Rule: Safe Harbors for Protecting Health Plans (61 Fed. Reg. 2122, 2123; Jan. 25, 1996) (revised final rule addressing the three managed care safe harbors originally promulgated in the Nov. 5, 1992, interim final rule).

448. *Id.*

449. *Id.*

Regarding the safe harbor's requirement that incentives be provided to all enrollees, the OIG explained that its purpose was "to restrict the ability of health plans to target particular Medicare or Medicaid beneficiaries or groups of such beneficiaries and induce them to enroll in the plan by providing incentives."[450] The OIG did not want plans to "target health beneficiaries by offering them increased services or reductions in cost sharing and attempt to avoid older or sicker beneficiaries or those with expensive or chronic health conditions requiring a high utilization of services by offering only the same services available through a fee-for-service plan."[451] Nor did the OIG limit the safe harbor to any specific type of insurance product because it believed that "the same type of abuses could occur where health plans offered several different products."[452] In addition, the OIG required that any incentives offered by health plans "be offered to all Medicare or State health care program enrollees of the plan" in order to "safeguard against the possibility that health plans may improperly favor certain healthy beneficiaries or use incentives to improperly encourage utilization when the item or service is furnished."[453]

The OIG emphasized that the safe harbor did nothing to "change[] reimbursement rules" and that "[i]f a provider chooses to . . . comply with [the safe harbor], such action may very well have reimbursement implications." The OIG further commented:

> Many program beneficiaries are now served by a wide variety of managed care plans, such as various models of HMOs, CMPs, and health care prepayment plans (HCPPs) . . . and prepaid health plans (PHPs) . . . as well as PPOs, and we agree that additional safe harbor protection is warranted . . . We are promulgating . . . safe harbor provisions to protect the essential activities of prepaid health plans ("health plans") . . . [This safe harbor] protects the contractual relationships between health plans and "contract health care providers" for the furnishing of covered items and services at reduced prices.[454]

---

450. *Id.* at 2130.
451. *Id.*
452. *Id.*
453. *Id.*
454. *Id.* Definitions of key terms used in the safe harbor are as follows:
Contract health care provider means an individual or entity under contract with a health plan to furnish items or services to enrollees who are covered by the health plan, Medicare, or a State health care program.
Enrollee means an individual who has entered into a contractual relationship with a health plan (or on whose behalf an employer, or other private or governmental entity

The OIG noted that "health care providers will contract with health plans and agree to furnish items and services to enrollees of the health plan at a discount from the provider's usual fee in return for obtaining a large volume of patients."[455] As with the safe harbor codified at 42 CFR § 1001.952(l), "protecting incentives to enrollees," this safe harbor "is divided into two separate parts for risk-based and cost-reimbursed health plans that operate in accordance with a contract or agreement with [CMS] or a State health care program."[456] A third part of the safe harbor protects "other health plans that do not have [such] contracts or agreement . . . where additional standards are met."[457]

The remuneration protected by the safe harbor is a provider's reduction of its usual charges and "only applies to reductions in the total amount charged by" the provider, rather than "reductions which are applicable only to a specific part of portion of the health care provider's charge, such as coinsurance and deductibles."[458] The OIG continued:

> Furthermore, we are only protecting the remuneration which represents the price reduction offered by the contract health care provider to make clear that any other forms of remuneration offered or paid by a contract health care provider to a health plan are not protected under this safe harbor provision. Indeed, we will closely review any forms of other such remuneration to ensure that improper payments

---

> has entered into such a relationship) under which the individual is entitled to receive specified health care items and services, or insurance coverage for such items and services, in return for payment of a premium or a fee.
>
> *Health plan* means an entity that furnishes or arranges under agreement with contract health care providers for the furnishing of items or services to enrollees, or furnishes insurance coverage for the provision of such items and services, in exchange for a premium or a fee, where such entity:
>
> (i) Operates in accordance with a contract, agreement or statutory demonstration authority approved by CMS or a State health care program;
>
> (ii) Charges a premium and its premium structure is regulated under a State insurance statute or a State enabling statute governing health maintenance organizations or preferred provider organizations;
>
> (iii) Is an employer, if the enrollees of the plan are current or retired employees, or is a union welfare fund, if the enrollees of the plan are union members; or
>
> (iv) Is licensed in the State, is under contract with an employer, union welfare fund, or a company furnishing health insurance coverage as described in conditions (ii) and (iii) of this definition, and is paid a fee for the administration of the plan which reflects the fair market value of those services.

42 CFR § 1001.952(l).

455. *Id.* at 52726.

456. *Id.*

457. *Id.*

458. *Id.*

are not employed to induce the health plan to issue a contract or otherwise steer patients to the person paying the remuneration.[459]

The safe harbor's second requirement that the agreement with the parties be in writing "is intended to assist [HHS] in understanding the intent of the parties" and, if needed, the OIG "will look behind the contract to determine if the real intent of the parties is not fully disclosed in the written agreement."[460] A third requirement that the agreement must be for the sole purpose of having the provider furnish to enrollees items or services covered by the health plan, Medicare, or Medicaid is to ensure that the safe harbor does not protect contracts for services other than "covered benefits."[461]

Noncovered services such as "peer review," "marketing services," and "pre-enrollment screening" would need to satisfy another safe harbor, such as the safe harbor for personal services and management contracts, and "where protection is sought from more than one safe harbor, separate justifications must be clearly set forth for each provision for which protection is sought."[462] The OIG explained the need for this requirement as stemming from its "experience with some HMOs that have abused their contractual relationships with medical groups where individuals in the groups have engaged in abusive or illegal activities on behalf of the HMO . . . by conducting pre-enrollment screening."[463] The OIG indicated its intention to "use [its] authorities aggressively to monitor closely and penalize where appropriate any abusive relationships between health plans and contract health care providers to assure the medically necessary services of a high quality are available and accessible to all enrollees."[464]

The first part of the safe harbor was designed to protect risk-based HMOs, CMPs, and PHPs under contract with [CMS] or a State health care program and operating in accordance with specified provisions of the Social Security Act or under a federal demonstration authority or under other federal statutory or regulatory authority.[465] In addition to risk-based contract health plans having to satisfy the requirements described earlier, the interim final rule required that contract providers "not separately bill Medicare, Medicaid

459. *Id.*
460. *Id.*
461. *Id.*
462. *Id.*
463. *Id.*
464. *Id.*
465. *Id.*

or another State health care program for items or services furnished under the agreement with the health plan . . . [or] otherwise shift the burden of the agreement onto Medicare, Medicaid, other payors, or individuals."[466] Moreover, "[a]ny claim for reimbursement made directly to Medicare, Medicaid or other State health care program for items or services for which payment was made by the health plan would constitute an unlawful false claim."[467]

The second part of the safe harbor protected health plans that had executed a contract or agreement with the CMS or a state health care program to have payment made on a reasonable cost or similar basis, provided that any price reduction agreement satisfied four enumerated standards.

The third part of the safe harbor protected price reductions offered by contract health care providers to all other health plans, provided that six enumerated standards were satisfied.

In 1996, the OIG revised and clarified the rule in response to public comments.[468] In its general comments, the OIG clarified, in response to concerns that this and other safe harbors affecting health plans could "chill" the activities of such plans if they find themselves unable to fit within the safe harbor, that the safe harbors "did not expand the zone of illegal conduct" under the AKS and that "[l]egally and logically, the safe harbors can only make the zone of illegal conduct smaller."[469] The OIG further explained that "compliance with the safe harbors is completely voluntary" and "[i]f a practice or arrangement does not fall within a safe harbor, it has precisely the same legal risk that it had before the safe harbor was promulgated."[470] The safe harbors "are designed to provide a means through which plans and providers can be assured that their arrangements are immune from potential criminal and administrative sanctions under the anti-kickback statute."[471] The OIG further assured the public that the fact that certain activities of health plans are not referenced in the safe harbors does not mean the OIG regards such activities as unlawful or that they would be subjected to heightened scrutiny.[472] The OIG made clear that, being voluntary, the safe harbors "do not

---

466. *Id.* at 52727.

467. *Id.*

468. Final Rule: Safe Harbors for Protecting Health Plans (61 Fed. Reg. 2122; Jan. 25, 1996) (revised final rule addressing the three managed care safe harbors originally promulgated in the Nov. 5, 1992, interim final rule).

469. *Id.* at 2124.

470. *Id.*

471. *Id.*

472. *Id.*

create affirmative obligations on individuals or entities" and that "failure to comply with a safe harbor means only that the practice or arrangement does not have the absolute assurance of protection from [AKS] liability."

Addressing the overall need for the safe harbor, the OIG commented that

> Enrollment in a health plan falls within the scope of the anti-kickback statute where such enrollment involves Medicare or Medicaid beneficiaries and results from various incentives offered to these individuals by the managed care plan.
>
> The incentives offered to beneficiaries constitute remuneration with the meaning of the statute. Once enrolled, the plan is entitled to receive Medicare or Medicaid reimbursement for the services directly provided to program beneficiaries. Alternatively, the plan steers enrollees to certain providers who furnish reimbursable services. The incentives offered to program beneficiaries can be in return for obtaining reimbursable program business and, therefore, are covered by the statute.[473]

Responding to comments protesting the safe harbor's requirement that health plans not shift the burden of increased coverage, reduced cost-sharing, or price reductions to other payers, the OIG reaffirmed its view "that enrollee incentives and provider price reductions should be economically sensible, i.e., they should not be driven by a motive to shift costs to the government or other payers."[474] The OIG continued:

> A health plan should not be offering incentives or provider discounts unless they believe the cost of those incentives or discounts can be recovered through lower operating costs resulting from increased volume, economies of scale or other efficiencies. We also believe that practices should be protected only if they do not cause harm to the Medicare and Medicaid programs. Accordingly, we are only willing to protect incentives and price reductions that do not result in increased costs to the programs. In order to ensure that result, we believe it is necessary to include a requirement which prohibits cost shifting to the Medicare and Medicaid programs.[475]

The OIG did agree, however, that the bar against burden shifting did not need to be broader than necessary to protect Medicare and Medicaid and

473. *Id.*
474. *Id.* at 2126.
475. *Id.* at 2126-27.

thus narrowed the scope of the prohibition in the revised final rule to make clear that cost shifting occurs "when an arrangement or agreement results in increased payments being claimed from the Medicare or State health care programs."[476] The OIG declined to establish standards for determining when cost shifting has occurred but noted that "in any case where a plan or provider raises its costs or fees to others or reduces the services it provides to others as a result of an incentive or a discount, prohibited cost shifting has occurred" and that "[c]laiming certain costs, such as waivers of coinsurance or deductibles, as bad debt would also constitute impermissible cost shifting."[477]

2.13. Price Reductions Offered to Health Plans

The safe harbor for price reductions offered to health plans is codified at 42 C.F.R. § 1001.952(m):

> (m) *Price reductions offered to health plans.*
>
> (1) As used in section 1128B of the Act, "remuneration" does not include a reduction in price a contract health care provider offers to a health plan in accordance with the terms of a written agreement between the contract health care provider and the health plan for the sole purpose of furnishing to enrollees items or services that are covered by the health plan, Medicare, or a State health care program, as long as both the health plan and contract health care provider comply with all of the applicable standards within one of the following four categories of health plans:
>
> (i) If the health plan is a risk-based health maintenance organization, competitive medical plan, or prepaid health plan under contract with CMS or a State agency and operating in accordance with section 1876(g) or 1903(m) of the Act, under a Federal statutory demonstration authority, or under other Federal statutory or regulatory authority, the contract health care provider must not claim payment in any form from the Department or the State agency for items or services furnished in accordance with the agreement except as approved

476. *Id.* at 2127.
477. *Id.*

by CMS or the State health care program, or otherwise shift the burden of such an agreement to the extent that increased payments are claimed from Medicare or a State health care program.

(ii) If the health plan is a health maintenance organization, competitive medical plan, health care prepayment plan, prepaid health plan, or other health plan that has executed a contract or agreement with CMS or a State health care program to receive payment for enrollees on a reasonable cost or similar basis, the health plan and contract health care provider must comply with all of the following four standards -

(A) The term of the agreement between the health plan and the contract health care provider must be for not less than one year;

(B) The agreement between the health plan and the contract health care provider must specify in advance the covered items and services to be furnished to enrollees, and the methodology for computing the payment to the contract health care provider;

(C) The health plan must fully and accurately report, on the applicable cost report or other claim form filed with the Department or the State health care program, the amount it has paid the contract health care provider under the agreement for the covered items and services furnished to enrollees; and

(D) The contract health care provider must not claim payment in any form from the Department or the State health care program for items or services furnished in accordance with the agreement except as approved by CMS or the State health care program, or otherwise shift the burden of such an agreement to the extent that increased payments are claimed from Medicare or a State health care program.

(iii) If the health plan is not described in paragraphs (m)(1)(i) or (m)(1)(ii) of this section and the contract health care provider is not paid on an at-risk, capitated basis, both the health plan and contract health care provider must comply with all of the following six standards -

(A) The term of the agreement between the health plan and the contract health care provider must be for not less than one year;

(B) The agreement between the health plan and the contract health care provider must specify in advance the covered items and services to be furnished to enrollees, which party is to file claims or requests for payment with Medicare or the State health care program for such items and services, and the schedule of fees the contract health care provider will charge for furnishing such items and services to enrollees;

(C) The fee schedule contained in the agreement between the health plan and the contract health care provider must remain in effect throughout the term of the agreement, unless a fee increase results directly from a payment update authorized by Medicare or the State health care program;

(D) The party submitting claims or requests for payment from Medicare or the State health care program for items and services furnished in accordance with the agreement must not claim or request payment for amounts in excess of the fee schedule;

(E) The contract health care provider and the health plan must fully and accurately report on any cost report filed with Medicare or a State health care program the fee schedule amounts charged in accordance with the agreement and, upon request, will report to the Medicare or a State health care program the terms of the agreement and the amounts paid in accordance with the agreement; and

(F) The party to the agreement, which does not have the responsibility under the agreement for filing claims or requests for payment, must not claim or request payment in any form from the Department or the State health care program for items or services furnished in accordance with the agreement, or otherwise shift the burden of such an agreement to the extent that increased payments are claimed from Medicare or a State health care program.

(iv) If the health plan is not described in paragraphs (m)(1)(i) or (m)(1)(ii) of this section, and the contract health care provider is paid on an at-risk, capitated basis, both the health plan and contract health care provider must comply with all of the following five standards -

(A) The term of the agreement between the health plan and the contract health provider must be for not less than one year;

(B) The agreement between the health plan and the contract health provider must specify in advance the covered items and services to be furnished to enrollees and the total amount per enrollee (which may be expressed in a per month or other time period basis) the contract health care provider will be paid by the health plan for furnishing such items and services to enrollees and must set forth any copayments, if any, to be paid by enrollees to the contract health care provider for covered services;

(C) The payment amount contained in the agreement between the health care plan and the contract health care provider must remain in effect throughout the term of the agreement;

(D) The contract health care provider and the health plan must fully and accurately report to the Medicare and State health care program upon request, the terms of the agreement and the amounts paid in accordance with the agreement; and

(E) The contract health care provider must not claim or request payment in any form from the Department, a State health care program or an enrollee (other than copayment amounts described in paragraph (m)(2)(iv)(B) of this section) and the health plan must not pay the contract care provider in excess of the amounts described in paragraph (m)(2)(iv)(B) of this section for items and services covered by the agreement.

(2) For purposes of this paragraph, the terms *contract health care provider, enrollee,* and *health plan* have the same meaning as in paragraph (l)(2) of this section.

In 1992, the OIG published an interim final rule establishing a safe harbor for price reductions offered to health plans. The OIG emphasized that the safe harbor did nothing to "change[] reimbursement rules" and that "[i]f a provider chooses to . . . comply with [the safe harbor], such action may very well have reimbursement implications."[478] The OIG further commented:

> Many program beneficiaries are now served by a wide variety of managed care plans, such as various models of HMOs, CMPs, and health care prepayment plans (HCPPs) . . . and prepaid health plans (PHPs) . . . as well as PPOs, and we agree that additional safe harbor protection is warranted . . . We are promulgating . . . safe harbor provisions to protect the essential activities of prepaid health plans ("health plans") . . . [This safe harbor] protects the contractual relationships between health plans and "contract health care providers" for the furnishing of covered items and services at reduced prices.[479]

478. Interim Final Rule: Safe Harbors for Protecting Health Plans (57 Fed. Reg. 52723, 52724-25; Nov. 5, 1992) (sets forth three new safe harbors addressing managed care plans through interim final rulemaking).

479. *Id.* Definitions of key terms used in the safe harbor are as follows:

Contract health care provider means an individual or entity under contract with a health plan to furnish items or services to enrollees who are covered by the health plan, Medicare, or a State health care program.

Enrollee means an individual who has entered into a contractual relationship with a health plan (or on whose behalf an employer, or other private or governmental entity has entered into such a relationship) under which the individual is entitled to receive specified health care items and services, or insurance coverage for such items and services, in return for payment of a premium or a fee.

Health plan means an entity that furnishes or arranges under agreement with contract health care providers for the furnishing of items or services to enrollees, or furnishes insurance coverage for the provision of such items and services, in exchange for a premium or a fee, where such entity:

(i) Operates in accordance with a contract, agreement or statutory demonstration authority approved by CMS or a State health care program;

(ii) Charges a premium and its premium structure is regulated under a State insurance statute or a State enabling statute governing health maintenance organizations or preferred provider organizations;

(iii) Is an employer, if the enrollees of the plan are current or retired employees, or is a union welfare fund, if the enrollees of the plan are union members; or

(iv) Is licensed in the State, is under contract with an employer, union welfare fund, or a company furnishing health insurance coverage as described in conditions (ii) and (iii) of this definition, and is paid a fee for the administration of the plan which reflects the fair market value of those services.

42 CFR § 1001.952(l).

The OIG noted that "health care providers will contract with health plans and agree to furnish items and services to enrollees of the health plan at a discount from the provider's usual fee in return for obtaining a large volume of patients."[480] As with the safe harbor codified at 42 CFR § 1001.952(l), "protecting incentives to enrollees," this safe harbor "is divided into two separate parts for risk-based and cost-reimbursed health plans that operate in accordance with a contract or agreement with [CMS] or a State health care program."[481] A third part of the safe harbor protects "other health plans that do not have [such] contracts or agreement . . . where additional standards are met."[482]

The remuneration protected by the safe harbor is a provider's reduction of its usual charges and "only applies to reductions in the total amount charged by" the provider, rather than "reductions which are applicable only to a specific part of portion of the health care provider's charge, such as coinsurance and deductibles."[483] The OIG continued:

> Furthermore, we are only protecting the remuneration which represents the price reduction offered by the contract health care provider to make clear that any other forms of remuneration offered or paid by a contract health care provider to a health plan are not protected under this safe harbor provision. Indeed, we will closely review any forms of other such remuneration to ensure that improper payments are not employed to induce the health plan to issue a contract or otherwise steer patients to the person paying the remuneration.[484]

The safe harbor's second requirement that the agreement with the parties be in writing "is intended to assist [HHS] in understanding the intent of the parties" and, if needed, the OIG "will look behind the contract to determine if the real intent of the parties is not fully disclosed in the written agreement."[485] A third requirement that the agreement must be for the sole purpose of having the provider furnish to enrollees items or services covered by the health plan, Medicare or Medicaid is to ensure that the safe harbor does not protect contracts for services other than "covered benefits."[486]

---

480. *Id.* at 52726.
481. *Id.*
482. *Id.*
483. *Id.*
484. *Id.*
485. *Id.*
486. *Id.*

Noncovered services such as "peer review," "marketing services," and "pre-enrollment screening" would need to satisfy another safe harbor, such as the safe harbor for personal services and management contracts, and "where protection is sought from more than one safe harbor, separate justifications must be clearly set forth for each provision for which protection is sought."[487] The OIG explained the need for this requirement as stemming from its "experience with some HMOs that have abused their contractual relationships with medical groups where individuals in the groups have engaged in abusive or illegal activities on behalf of the HMO . . . by conducting pre-enrollment screening."[488] The OIG indicated its intention to "use [its] authorities aggressively to monitor closely and penalize where appropriate any abusive relationships between health plans and contract health care providers to assure the medically necessary services of a high quality are available and accessible to all enrollees."[489]

The first part of the safe harbor was designed to protect risk-based HMOs, CMPs, and PHPs under contract with [CMS] or a state health care program and operating in accordance with specified provisions of the Social Security Act or under a federal demonstration authority or under other federal statutory or regulatory authority.[490] In addition to risk-based contract health plans having to satisfy the requirements described earlier, the interim final rule required that contract providers "not separately bill Medicare, Medicaid or another State health care program for items or services furnished under the agreement with the health plan . . . [or] otherwise shift the burden of the agreement onto Medicare, Medicaid, other payors, or individuals."[491] Moreover, "[a]ny claim for reimbursement made directly to Medicare, Medicaid or other State health care program for items or services for which payment was made by the health plan would constitute an unlawful false claim."[492]

The second part of the safe harbor protected health plans that had executed a contract or agreement with the CMS or a state health care program to have payment made on a reasonable cost or similar basis, provided that any price reduction agreement satisfied four enumerated standards.

487. *Id.*
488. *Id.*
489. *Id.*
490. *Id.*
491. *Id.* at 52727.
492. *Id.*

The third part of the safe harbor protected price reductions offered by contract health care providers to all other health plans, provided that six enumerated standards were satisfied.

In 1996, the OIG revised and clarified the rule in response to public comments.[493] In its general comments, the OIG clarified, in response to concerns that this and other safe harbors affecting health plans could "chill" the activities of such plans if they find themselves unable to fit within the safe harbor, that the safe harbors "did not expand the zone of illegal conduct" under the AKS and that "[l]egally and logically, the safe harbors can only make the zone of illegal conduct smaller."[494] The OIG further explained that "compliance with the safe harbors is completely voluntary" and "[i]f a practice or arrangement does not fall within a safe harbor, it has precisely the same legal risk that it had before the safe harbor was promulgated."[495] The safe harbors "are designed to provide a means through which plans and providers can be assured that their arrangements are immune from potential criminal and administrative sanctions under the anti-kickback statute."[496] The OIG further assured the public that the fact that certain activities of health plans are not referenced in the safe harbors does not mean the OIG regards such activities as unlawful or that they would be subjected to heightened scrutiny.[497] The OIG made clear that, being voluntary, the safe harbors "do not create affirmative obligations on individuals or entities" and "failure to comply with a safe harbor means only that the practice or arrangement does not have the absolute assurance of protection from [AKS] liability."

Addressing the overall need for the safe harbor, the OIG commented that

> Enrollment in a health plan falls within the scope of the anti-kickback statute where such enrollment involves Medicare or Medicaid beneficiaries and results from various incentives offered to these individuals by the managed care plan.
>
> The incentives offered to beneficiaries constitute remuneration with the meaning of the statute. Once enrolled, the plan is entitled to receive Medicare or Medicaid reimbursement for the services directly provided

493. Final Rule: Safe Harbors for Protecting Health Plans (61 Fed. Reg. 2122; Jan. 25, 1996) (revised final rule addressing the three managed care safe harbors originally promulgated in the Nov. 5, 1992, interim final rule).

494. *Id.* at 2124.

495. *Id.*

496. *Id.*

497. *Id.*

> to program beneficiaries. Alternatively, the plan steers enrollees to certain providers who furnish reimbursable services. The incentives offered to program beneficiaries can be in return for obtaining reimbursable program business and, therefore, are covered by the statute.[498]

Responding to comments protesting the safe harbor's requirement that health plans not shift the burden of increased coverage, reduced cost-sharing, or price reductions to other payers, the OIG reaffirmed its view "that enrollee incentives and provider price reductions should be economically sensible, i.e., they should not be driven by a motive to shift costs to the government or other payers."[499] The OIG continued:

> A health plan should not be offering incentives or provider discounts unless they believe the cost of those incentives or discounts can be recovered through lower operating costs resulting from increased volume, economies of scale or other efficiencies. We also believe that practices should be protected only if they do not cause harm to the Medicare and Medicaid programs. Accordingly, we are only willing to protect incentives and price reductions that do not result in increased costs to the programs. In order to ensure that result, we believe it is necessary to include a requirement which prohibits cost shifting to the Medicare and Medicaid programs.[500]

The OIG did agree, however, that the bar against burden shifting did not need to be broader than necessary to protect Medicare and Medicaid and thus narrowed the scope of the prohibition in the revised final rule to make clear that cost shifting occurs "when an arrangement or agreement results in increased payments being claimed from the Medicare or State health care programs."[501] The OIG declined to establish standards for determining when cost shifting has occurred, but noted that "in any case where a plan or provider raises its costs or fees to others or reduces the services it provides to others as a result of an incentive or a discount, prohibited cost shifting has occurred" and that "[c]laiming certain costs, such as waivers of coinsurance or deductibles, as bad debt would also constitute impermissible cost shifting."[502]

---

498. *Id.*
499. *Id.* at 2126.
500. *Id.* at 2126-27.
501. *Id.* at 2127.
502. *Id.*

2.14. Practitioner Recruitment

The safe harbor for practitioner recruitment, codified at 42 C.F.R. § 1001.952(n),[503] states:

> (n) *Practitioner recruitment.* As used in [the Anti-Kickback Statute], "remuneration" does not include any payment or exchange of anything of value by an entity in order to induce a practitioner who has been practicing within his or her current specialty for less than one year to locate, or to induce any other practitioner to relocate, his or her primary place of practice into a Health Professional Shortage Area (HPSA) for his or her specialty area, as defined in Departmental regulations, that is served by the entity, as long as all of the following nine standards are met -
>
> (1) The arrangement is set forth in a written agreement signed by the parties that specifies the benefits provided by the entity, the terms under which the benefits are to be provided, and the obligations of each party.
>
> (2) If a practitioner is leaving an established practice, at least 75 percent of the revenues of the new practice must be generated from new patients not previously seen by the practitioner at his or her former practice.
>
> (3) The benefits are provided by the entity for a period not in excess of 3 years, and the terms of the agreement are not renegotiated during this 3-year period in any substantial aspect; provided, however, that if the HPSA to which the practitioner was recruited ceases to be a HPSA during the term of the written agreement, the payments made under the written agreement will continue to satisfy this paragraph for the duration of the written agreement (not to exceed 3 years).
>
> (4) There is no requirement that the practitioner make referrals to, be in a position to make or influence referrals to, or otherwise generate business for the entity as a condition for receiving the benefits; provided, however, that for purposes of this paragraph, the entity may require as a condition for receiving benefits that the practitioner maintain staff privileges at the entity.

503. 42 C.F.R. § 1001.952(n).

(5) The practitioner is not restricted from establishing staff privileges at, referring any service to, or otherwise generating any business for any other entity of his or her choosing.

(6) The amount or value of the benefits provided by the entity may not vary (or be adjusted or renegotiated) in any manner based on the volume or value of any expected referrals to or business otherwise generated for the entity by the practitioner for which payment may be made in whole or in part under Medicare, Medicaid or any other Federal health care programs.

(7) The practitioner agrees to treat patients receiving medical benefits or assistance under any Federal health care program in a nondiscriminatory manner.

(8) At least 75 percent of the revenues of the new practice must be generated from patients residing in a HPSA or a Medically Underserved Area (MUA) or who are part of a Medically Underserved Population (MUP), all as defined in paragraph (a) of this section.

(9) The payment or exchange of anything of value may not directly or indirectly benefit any person (other than the practitioner being recruited) or entity in a position to make or influence referrals to the entity providing the recruitment payments or benefits of items or services payable by a Federal health care program.

The safe harbor for practitioner recruitment was enacted in 1999 with the intent to "promote beneficiary access to quality health care by permitting communities that have difficulty attracting needed medical professionals to offer inducements to those professionals without running afoul of the anti-kickback statute."[504] This intention was an expansion of the original proposed rule of 1993, which sought only to protect recruitment in communities defined as "rural" by the Office of Management and Budget.[505] The final rule is intended to allow areas that have shown a need for the practitioners,

504. Final Rule: Clarification of the Initial OIG Safe Harbor Provisions and Establishment of Additional Safe Harbor Provisions Under the Anti-Kickback Statute, 64 Fed. Reg. 63518, 63541 (Nov. 19, 1999).

505. Proposed Rule: Additional Safe Harbor Provisions Under the Anti-Kickback Statute, 58 Fed. Reg. 49008 49010 (Sept. 21, 1993) (proposed rule designed to incorporate seven additional safe harbor provisions).

and for practitioners who "actually serve" the affected community.[506] HHS updated and clarified that the designation of demonstrated need is limited to HPSAs and MUAs, as defined by the Health Resources and Services Administration (HRSA), as opposed to simply a disproportionate share hospital (DSH) or the original "rural" designation. This is due to the fact that while DSH payments indicate the number of low-income patients, they do not necessarily indicate a shortage of practitioners.[507] In order to fit within the safe harbor, a physician's relocation must be to a HPSA; a service area consisting exclusively of areas designated as MUAs is not sufficient to satisfy the relocation standard.

HHS affirmatively stated that failure to meet the standards of this safe harbor does not determine whether or not an arrangement violates the AKS. Arrangements for remuneration to physicians for recruitment need to be evaluated on a case-by-case basis if they do not meet the standards of the safe harbor.[508]

In response to concerns over the meaning of the clause "the terms of the agreement are not renegotiated during this 3-year period in any substantial aspect," HHS clarified that "substantial aspect" means any manner that would materially affect the payments and benefits to be made to the practitioners that were recruited, per the written agreement.[509] The terms "payment" and "benefit" are used in §§ 1001.952(n)(1), (3), and (6). HHS clarified that these terms could not be given a definitive specification due to the necessity of evaluating the recruitment process and the degree of variation associated with it in each case. The three-year limit does not allow for incentives to be offered after that period for the purpose of retention.[510] "[P]ayments for retention purposes require closer scrutiny than initial recruitment payments."[511]

When the rule was proposed in 1993, it required a relocating practitioner to move at least 100 miles from the previous place of practice, and derive 85 percent of the new practice's revenue from new patients "not previously

506. Final Rule: Clarification of the Initial OIG Safe Harbor Provisions and Establishment of Additional Safe Harbor Provisions Under the Anti-Kickback Statute, 64 Fed. Reg. 63518, 63541 (Nov. 19, 1999).

507. *Id.* at 63542.

508. *Id.* at 63545.

509. *Id.* at 63543.

510. *Id.* at 63544.

511. *Id.* at 63543.

seen by the practitioner at his or her former practice."[512] The final version of the rule, when changing its methodology in determining which areas were to be covered, removed the 100-mile requirement as it could have led to arbitrary results in rural areas and made it difficult to serve urban areas in need. The enacted rule allows for even a short move, providing it is into a HPSA. HHS cautioned that the area of practitioner recruitment is particularly vulnerable to abuse, and "experienced practitioners" could relocate a short distance to a HPSA with the purpose of qualifying for the safe harbor rather than to serve the affected community.[513] This potential abuse would not have been mitigated with the proposed 85 percent new patient revenue. The final version rectifies this issue by requiring that "75 percent of the revenues of the new practice must be generated from patients residing in a HPSA or a MUA or who are members of a MUP." HHS further clarified where the patients of the new practice may come from: "The patients do not necessarily have to reside in the specific HPSA in which the practitioner's new practice is located, but may reside instead in a nearby MUA or HPSA. In sum, to qualify for the safe harbor, a new or relocating physician must substantially treat patients who are new to the physician's practice and who reside in underserved areas, or are members of medically-underserved populations designated by HRSA."[514]

For times when the recruitment process does not strictly meet the requirements of this safe harbor, the OIG has offered advisory opinions on how to move forward and whether or not a hospital would be subject to administrative sanctions. OIG Advisory Opinion No. 01-4[515] emphasized four points as being of particular importance:

> Whether there is documented evidence of an objective need for the practitioner's services . . . , Whether the practitioner has an existing stream of referrals within the recruiting entity's service area . . . , Whether the benefit is narrowly tailored so that it does not exceed that which is reasonably necessary to recruit a practitioner . . . , [and] Whether the remuneration directly or indirectly benefits other referral sources.[516]

512. Proposed Rule: Additional Safe Harbor Provisions Under the Anti-Kickback Statute, 58 Fed. Reg. 49008 49010 (Sept. 21, 1993) (proposed rule designed to incorporate seven additional safe harbor provisions).

513. *Id.* at 63543.

514. *Id.*

515. OIG Advisory Opinion No. 01-4 (May 10, 2001).

516. *Id.* at 8.

These factors are meant to weigh the level of risk of abuse presented by a given arrangement but are not determinative in and of themselves, as each case is subject to the OIG's discretion.[517]

2.15. Obstetrical Malpractice Insurance Subsidies

The safe harbor for obstetrical malpractice insurance subsidies is codified at 42 C.F.R. § 1001.952(o):

> (o) *Obstetrical malpractice insurance subsidies.* As used in [the AKS] "remuneration" does not include any payment made by a hospital or other entity to another entity that is providing malpractice insurance (including a self-funded entity), where such payment is used to pay for some or all of the costs of malpractice insurance premiums for a practitioner (including a certified nurse-midwife as defined in section 1861(gg) of the Act) who engages in obstetrical practice as a routine part of his or her medical practice in a primary care HPSA, as long as all of the following seven standards are met -
>
> (1) The payment is made in accordance with a written agreement between the entity paying the premiums and the practitioner, which sets out the payments to be made by the entity, and the terms under which the payments are to be provided.
>
> (2)
>
> (i) The practitioner must certify that for the initial coverage period (not to exceed one year) the practitioner has a reasonable basis for believing that at least 75 percent of the practitioner's obstetrical patients treated under the coverage of the malpractice insurance will either -
>
> (A) Reside in a HPSA or MUA, as defined in paragraph (a) of this section; or
>
> (B) Be part of a MUP, as defined in paragraph (a) of this section.
>
> (ii) Thereafter, for each additional coverage period (not to exceed one year), at least 75 percent of the practitioner's

517. The safe harbor has also been referenced in several court decisions. *See, e.g.*, McDonnell v. Cardiothoracic & Vascular Surgical Assoc., Inc., 2004 WL 3733402 at *7 (July 28, 2004 S.D. Ohio); United States v. AIDS Healthcare Found., Inc., 262 F. Supp. 3d 1353 (June 9, 2017 S.D. Fla.); United States *ex rel.* Jacobs v. CDS, P.A., 2015 WL 5698395 at *4 (Sept. 28, 2015 D. Idaho).

obstetrical patients treated under the prior coverage period (not to exceed one year) must have -

(A) Resided in a HPSA or MUA, as defined in paragraph (a) of this section; or

(B) Been part of a MUP, as defined in paragraph (a) of this section.

(3) There is no requirement that the practitioner make referrals to, or otherwise generate business for, the entity as a condition for receiving the benefits.

(4) The practitioner is not restricted from establishing staff privileges at, referring any service to, or otherwise generating any business for any other entity of his or her choosing.

(5) The amount of payment may not vary based on the volume or value of any previous or expected referrals to or business otherwise generated for the entity by the practitioner for which payment may be made in whole or in part under Medicare, Medicaid or any other Federal health care programs.

(6) The practitioner must treat obstetrical patients who receive medical benefits or assistance under any Federal health care program in a nondiscriminatory manner.

(7) The insurance is a bona fide malpractice insurance policy or program, and the premium, if any, is calculated based on a bona fide assessment of the liability risk covered under the insurance. For purposes of paragraph (o) of this section, *costs of malpractice insurance premiums* means:

(i) For practitioners who engage in obstetrical practice full-time, any costs attributable to malpractice insurance; or

(ii) For practitioners who engage in obstetrical practice on a part-time or sporadic basis, the costs:

(A) Attributable exclusively to the obstetrical portion of the practitioner's malpractice insurance and

(B) Related exclusively to obstetrical services provided in a primary care HPSA.

As explained by the OIG, "[t]his safe harbor is intended to facilitate access to obstetrical services for Federal health care program beneficiaries in primary care health professional shortage areas by protecting from the reach of the antikickback statute subsidized malpractice insurance for practitioners who are primarily engaged in obstetrical practices in those areas."[518]

The OIG noted that, by limiting such protection to obstetrical malpractice insurance subsidies, the safe harbor "does not call into question the legality of all other types of practitioner malpractice insurance subsidies" and that those subsidies "may qualify for protection under other safe harbors, such as practitioner recruitment, personal services contracts or employee compensation."[519] At the same time, however, the OIG noted "that malpractice insurance subsidies paid to or on behalf of potential referral sources may be suspect under the anti-kickback statute."[520] In proposing the rule, the OIG explained that "nothing in the safe harbor would authorize payment by the Federal health care programs to hospitals or other institutional providers for costs they may incur in providing malpractice insurance" and that "[a]ny allowable costs for such insurance are governed strictly by Federal health care program rules."[521]

The OIG noted that safe harbor protection is "appropriate for family practitioners and other physicians and certified nurse midwives who deliver babies as routine part of their medical practices."[522] The OIG defined "routine" as requiring "that the practitioner must provide substantial and regular obstetrical services; we do not intend to protect obstetrical insurance subsidies for practitioners who practice obstetrical medicine on only an occasional basis."[523] For certified nurse midwives and practitioners who do not practice obstetrical medicine full time, the safe harbor "will protect payments for *obstetrical* malpractice insurance only" and not "subsidies for other types of medical malpractice liability" so that "the protected subsidy will be the difference between the cost of malpractice insurance that includes obstetrical coverage and the cost of malpractice insurance that includes obstetrical coverage and the cost of malpractice insurance that does not include such coverage."[524] The safe harbor also protects insurance subsidies paid for practitioners who are engaged only in part-time obstetrical

518. Final Rule: Clarification of the Initial OIG Safe Harbor Provisions and Establishment of Additional Safe Harbor Provisions Under the Anti-Kickback Statute (64 Fed. Reg. 63518, 63545; Nov. 19, 1999).

519. *Id.* at 63546.

520. *Id.*

521. *Id.* at 63545.

522. *Id.*

523. *Id.*

524. *Id.*

practice within a health professional shortage area (HPSA), protecting subsidies for insurance coverage that is "related exclusively to services provided in the HPSA."[525] Further, "[i]f the practitioner is covered by a single insurance policy or program, the safe harbor covers subsidies for that portion of the insurance premium that is reasonably allocable to obstetrical services provided in a HPSA."[526] The OIG limited the safe harbor "to primary care HPSAs so as to ensure as much as possible that the benefits protected by this safe harbor are extended to practitioners in areas where there is a well-founded, documented shortage of obstetrical practitioners."[527] The OIG further commented that "nothing in this safe harbor prevents protection of malpractice insurance subsidies for practitioners engaged in practice outside primary care HPSAs as part of an arms-length, fair market value compensation package that meets the requirements of the personal services safe harbor or the employee compensation exception to the anti-kickback statute."[528]

Regarding the safe harbor's protection of "*bona fide*" insurance products, such as "*bona fide* self-funded obstetrical malpractice insurance programs, including risk-retention groups that qualify under the Liability Risk Retention Act, 15 U.S.C. 3901, and . . . *bona fide* offshore insurance products," the OIG stated that although it was "not defining the full scope of *bona fide* insurance products, [it] believe[s] that certification by a qualified actuary that the program is adequate relative to the risk insured would be an indicator of a *bona fide* insurance program."[529] Finally, responding to a comment raising concern that the safe harbor did not sufficiently protect group practices, the OIG commented that "[a] group practice that provides obstetrical malpractice insurance subsidies may qualify as an 'entity' for purposes of this safe harbor" but that the safe harbor "is not intended to protect group practices for any payment practice that does not satisfy all of the safe harbor criteria."[530]

This safe harbor also has been addressed in an Advisory Opinion. In Advisory Opinion No. 04-11,[531] the OIG elected not to impose administrative sanctions on an arrangement under which a medical center would subsidize malpractice insurance expenses for four community-based obstetricians. The

525. *Id.*
526. *Id.*
527. *Id.* at 63546.
528. *Id.*
529. *Id.* at 63547.
530. *Id.*
531. Advisory Opinion No. 04-11 (Issued Sept. 2, 2004).

medical center wished to provide the benefit because it was concerned that rising malpractice costs might cause the obstetricians to stop providing care, which would cause a sharp decrease in access to obstetrical care. The OIG acknowledged that the arrangement did not satisfy the requirements of the safe harbor because the obstetricians did not practice in a "primary care" HPSA, and instead practiced in a community having different HPSA designations for low-income populations, migrant agricultural workers, and homeless individuals. Nevertheless, the OIG concluded that this one discrepancy did not increase the risk of fraud and abuse and was consistent "with the intent of the safe harbor to ensure access to needed obstetrical care . . . in places and for populations that do not have sufficient access to care."[532] The OIG also determined that there were other factors that mitigated any residual risk, including that (1) the insurance subsidies were a response to sharply escalating premium costs and would only be provided on a temporary basis for a fixed period; (2) the subsidies would only cover a portion of the obstetricians' increased premium expense and would not result in a "windfall"; and (3) the subsidies would be provided irrespective of whether the obstetricians performed services at a facility affiliated with the medical center.

2.16. Investments in Group Practices

The safe harbor for investments in group practices is codified at 42 C.F.R. § 1001.952(p) and states:

> (p) *Investments in group practices.* As used in [the AKS], "remuneration" does not include any payment that is a return on an investment interest, such as a dividend or interest income, made to a solo or group practitioner investing in his or her own practice or group practice if the following four standards are met -
>
> (1) The equity interests in the practice or group must be held by licensed health care professionals who practice in the practice or group.
>
> (2) The equity interests must be in the practice or group itself, and not some subdivision of the practice or group.
>
> (3) In the case of group practices, the practice must:
>
> (i) Meet the definition of "group practice" in section 1877(h)(4) of the Social Security Act and implementing regulations; and

532. *Id.*

(ii) Be a unified business with centralized decision-making, pooling of expenses and revenues, and a compensation/profit distribution system that is not based on satellite offices operating substantially as if they were separate enterprises or profit centers.

(4) Revenues from ancillary services, if any, must be derived from "in-office ancillary services" that meet the definition of such term in section 1877(b)(2) of the Act and implementing regulations.

The safe harbor for investments in group practices was added in 1999 and "protects returns on investments in the group practice itself (i.e., not in separately owned health care services), if the group practice meets the Stark Law definition of a group practice . . . and if the group practice investors are all licensed professionals who practice in the group."[533] The safe harbor "also protects investments in solo practices where the practice is conducted through the solo practitioner's professional corporation or other separate legal entity."[534] While not viewing investments in group or solo practices as "suspect per se," the OIG recognized that the "plain language of the anti-kickback statute is sufficiently broad so as potentially to include payments from a group [or solo] practice to an investor in the practice."[535] Profits derived from in-office ancillary services, as defined under the Stark Law, are also protected.[536] Equity interests "may be held by an individual professional corporation if the corporation is exclusively owned by a single individual."[537] The safe harbor, however, "does not protect investments made jointly by group members in separate entities."[538] The OIG specifically chose not to use this safe harbor to protect group practice investments in outside entities providing ancillary services due to concerns over "anti-competitive effects and . . . abusive arrangements and incentives to overutilize" such services, but acknowledged that such investments could still receive protection under the small entity investment interest safe harbor.[539] The OIG further

533. Final Rule: OIG Anti-Kickback Provisions, 64 Fed. Reg. 63518, 63540 (Nov. 19, 1999) (Final Rule: Clarification of the Initial OIG Safe Harbor Provisions and Establishment of Additional Safe Harbor Provisions Under the Anti-Kickback Statute).

534. *Id.*

535. *Id.*

536. *Id.*

537. *Id.*

538. *Id.*

539. *Id.*

noted that, while the group practice safe harbor imposed no restrictions on whether the investment interest could be related to previous or expected referrals, since such a restriction was deemed unnecessary in the context of a physician group practice, the safe harbor still requires that any return on investment comply with the Stark Law, "which limits compensation to physician investors that is based on the volume or value of referrals by the physician."[540]

The OIG addressed the group practice investment safe harbor in Advisory Opinion No. 08-24.[541] There, the OIG was asked to opine upon a shared medical practice (the Practice) involving twenty-three physicians and podiatrists that offered medical care, consultation, diagnosis, and treatment services through shared office space, facilities, equipment, and personnel. Among other things, the Practice provided urgent care consultation on a walk-in basis, clinical laboratory services, and diagnostic radiology services. All the physician investors in the Practice, except for one, treated patients at the practice, but none of them worked there full time, instead spending time at different office locations that were not affiliated with the practice. Each investor owned a fixed percentage stake in the Practice and shared in profits or losses in direct proportion to that stake. The Practice had a central governing board that made key decisions, maintained control over assets and liabilities, handled finance-related matters, and developed clinical and nonclinical policies and procedures. The Practice also had a centralized accounting system and pooled all expenses and revenues. The Practice certified that it would shortly meet the definition of "group practice" under the Stark Law and that any revenues from ancillary services would meet the Stark Law definition of "in-office ancillary services."

The OIG noted that, since one of the physician investors (holding 1 percent equity) did not treat patients and performed only an administrative function, the Practice could not satisfy the group practice investment safe harbor. The OIG also noted that "it may be necessary, in order to meet the minimum percentage of physician-patient encounters conducted by practice members under [the group practice definition], for the Practice" to hire additional physicians.[542] The OIG, however, determined that the Practice would comply with

540. *Id.* at 63541.
541. Advisory Opinion No. 08-24 (Issued Dec. 29, 2008).
542. *See id.*, at n.3.

the safe harbor "in nearly all respects" and that several factors sufficiently reduced the risk of fraud and abuse:

- All equity interests, save for one, were held by health care professionals who work at the Practice.
- All equity interests are held in the Practice and not a subdivision, and each investor held a fixed percentage stake in the entire Practice, rather than in a specialty group or other subdivision.
- It was certified that the arrangement would comply fully in all respects with the requirements of the group practice definition under the Stark Law.
- It was certified that the ancillary service revenues were derived from "in-office ancillary services" that meet the Stark Law definition.

Given these facts, the OIG concluded that the lone physician investor who performed only administrative services at the Practice "[did] not pose appreciable additional risks," commenting that his returns were directly proportional to his investment interest that the provided "substantial services integral to the Practice's operation and administration, thus minimizing the risk that his small equity interest reflects referrals."[543] While the OIG did not specifically cite this factor as a justification, it nonetheless bears mentioning that the OIG's decision not to impose administrative sanctions in this case could have been influenced by the fact that the Practice at issue was located in a rural HPSA.[544]

2.17. Cooperative Hospital Service Organizations

The safe harbor for cooperative hospital service organizations is codified at 42 C.F.R. § 1001.952(q):

> (q) *Cooperative hospital service organizations.* As used in [the AKS], "remuneration" does not include any payment made between a cooperative hospital service organization (CHSO) and its patron-hospital, both of which are described in section 501(e) of the Internal Revenue Code of 1986 and are tax-exempt under section 501(c)(3) of the Internal Revenue Code, where the CHSO is wholly owned by two or more patron-hospitals, as long as the following standards are met -

543. *See id.*
544. *See id.*

(1) If the patron-hospital makes a payment to the CHSO, the payment must be for the purpose of paying for the bona fide operating expenses of the CHSO, or
(2) If the CHSO makes a payment to the patron-hospital, the payment must be for the purpose of paying a distribution of net earnings required to be made under section 501(e)(2) of the Internal Revenue Code of 1986.

The OIG proposed this safe harbor in 1993 "for most cooperative hospital service organizations (CHSOs) that qualify under section 501(c)(3) of the Internal Revenue Code."[545] Pursuant to that Code provision and related regulations (26 CFR 1.501(e)-1), "these organizations are formed by two or more tax exempt hospitals (known as "patron-hospitals") to provide specifically enumerated services, such as purchasing, billing, and clinical services solely for the benefit of its patron-hospitals."[546] The organizations also are "required to distribute 'all net earnings to patrons on the basis of services performed.'"[547]

The proposed provision was intended to "protect payments from a patron-hospital to a CHSO to support the CHSO's operational costs and those payments from a CHSO to a patron-hospital that are required under IRS rules."[548] In order for protection to attach, "the CHSO must be wholly owned by its patron-hospitals" since such a condition "protects against potentially abusive joint venture arrangements that are formed under the guise of CHSOs."[549]

The OIG explained that "[w]ith respect to the payments the CHSO makes to its patron-hospitals . . . the level of discretion given to these providers as to what payment formula to use warrants safe harbor protection."[550]

545. Proposed Rule: Additional Safe Harbor Provisions Under the Anti-Kickback Statute (58 Fed. Reg. 49008, 49012; Sept. 21, 1993) (proposed rule designed to incorporate seven additional safe harbor provisions); *see also* Final Rule: Clarification of the Initial OIG Safe Harbor Provisions and Establishment of Additional Safe Harbor Provisions Under the Anti-Kickback Statute (64 Fed. Reg. 63518, 63549; Nov. 19, 1999) (adopting proposed rule without modification).

546. *Id.*

547. *Id.*

548. *Id.*

549. *Id.*

550. *Id.* On the issue of discretion, the OIG commented: "Where a health care provider engages in an activity which is specifically required by another statutory provision and the provider is afforded no discretion in the manner of compliance, such a requirement is a valid defense to an alleged violation of the anti-kickback statute. However, where the health care provider is engaging in the activity to fulfill a general statutory obligation, but is afforded

The OIG also pointed out that "[t]o the extent a CHSO acts as a group purchasing organization or a patron-hospital obtains discounts as a result of the CHSO's activities, CHSOs and patron-hospitals must comply with the respective safe harbor provisions applicable to group purchasing organizations and discounts to be fully protected."[551]

The OIG declined to extend safe harbor protection to other cooperative organizations that do not qualify under section 501(e) of the Internal Revenue Code because there would be "no limits on the types of services that may be shared, nor are there restrictions on the identity of shareholders."[552] The OIG concluded that "the limitations imposed under section 501(e) are necessary to protect against potentially abusive joint ventures or referral arrangements."[553]

2.18. Ambulatory Surgical Centers

The regulatory safe harbor for ambulatory surgical centers (ASCs)[554] is codified at 42 C.F.R. § 1001.952(r), which states:

> (r) *Ambulatory surgical centers.* As used in section 1128B of the Act, "remuneration" does not include any payment that is a return on an investment interest, such as a dividend or interest income, made to an investor, as long as the investment entity is a certified ambulatory surgical center (ASC) under part 416 of this title, whose operating and recovery room space is dedicated exclusively to the ASC, patients referred to the investment entity by an investor are fully informed of the investor's investment interest, and all of the applicable standards are met within one of the following four categories –
>
> (1) Surgeon-owned ASCs – If all of the investors are general surgeons or surgeons engaged in the same surgical specialty, who

---

discretion in the manner of compliance, such a defense is not available because the provider's choice in the method of compliance may be motivated by an intent to generate program-related business." *Id.*

551. *Id.*

552. Final Rule: Clarification of the Initial OIG Safe Harbor Provisions and Establishment of Additional Safe Harbor Provisions Under the Anti-Kickback Statute (64 Fed. Reg. 63518, 63549; Nov. 19, 1999).

553. *Id.*

554. An ASC is defined as any distinct entity that operates exclusively for the purpose of providing surgical services to patients not requiring hospitalization and in which the expected duration of services would not exceed 24 hours following an admission. *See* 42 C.F.R. § 416.2.

are in a position to refer patients directly to the entity and perform surgery on such referred patients; surgical group practices (as defined in this paragraph) composed exclusively of such surgeons; or investors who are not employed by the entity or by any investor, are not in a position to provide items or services to the entity or any of its investors, and are not in a position to make or influence referrals directly or indirectly to the entity or any of its investors, all of the following six standards must be met –

(i) The terms on which an investment interest is offered to an investor must not be related to the previous or expected volume of referrals, services furnished, or the amount of business otherwise generated from that investor to the entity.

(ii) At least one-third of each surgeon investor's medical practice income from all sources for the previous fiscal year or previous 12-month period must be derived from the surgeon's performance of procedures (as defined in this paragraph).

(iii) The entity or any investor (or other individual or entity acting on behalf of the entity or any investor) must not loan funds to or guarantee a loan for an investor if the investor uses any part of such loan to obtain the investment interest.

(iv) The amount of payment to an investor in return for the investment must be directly proportional to the amount of the capital investment (including the fair market value of any pre-operational services rendered) of that investor.

(v) All ancillary services for Federal health care program beneficiaries performed at the entity must be directly and integrally related to primary procedures performed at the entity, and none may be separately billed to Medicare or other Federal health care programs.

(vi) The entity and any surgeon investors must treat patients receiving medical benefits or assistance under any Federal health care program in a nondiscriminatory manner.

(2) Single-Specialty ASCs – If all of the investors are physicians engaged in the same medical practice specialty who are in a position to refer patients directly to the entity and perform procedures on such referred patients; group practices (as defined in this paragraph) composed exclusively of such physicians; or investors who are not employed by the entity or by any investor, are not in a position to provide items or services to the entity or any of its investors, and are not in a position to make or influence referrals directly or indirectly to the entity or any of its investors, all of the following six standards must be met –

(i) The terms on which an investment interest is offered to an investor must not be related to the previous or expected volume of referrals, services furnished, or the amount of business otherwise generated from that investor to the entity.

(ii) At least one-third of each physician investor's medical practice income from all sources for the previous fiscal year or previous 12-month period must be derived from the surgeon's performance of procedures (as defined in this paragraph).

(iii) The entity or any investor (or other individual or entity acting on behalf of the entity or any investor) must not loan funds to or guarantee a loan for an investor if the investor uses any part of such loan to obtain the investment interest.

(iv) The amount of payment to an investor in return for the investment must be directly proportional to the amount of the capital investment (including the fair market value of any pre-operational services rendered) of that investor.

(v) All ancillary services for Federal health care program beneficiaries performed at the entity must be directly and integrally related to primary procedures performed at the entity, and none may be separately billed to Medicare or other Federal health care programs.

(vi) The entity and any physician investors must treat patients receiving medical benefits or assistance under any Federal health care program in a nondiscriminatory manner.

(3) Multi-Specialty ASCs – If all of the investors are physicians who are in a position to refer patients directly to the entity and perform procedures on such referred patients; group practices, as defined in this paragraph, composed exclusively of such physicians; or investors who are not employed by the entity or by any investor, are not in a position to provide items or services to the entity or any of its investors, and are not in a position to make or influence referrals directly or indirectly to the entity or any of its investors, all of the following seven standards must be met –

(i) The terms on which an investment interest is offered to an investor must not be related to the previous or expected volume of referrals, services furnished, or the amount of business otherwise generated from that investor to the entity.

(ii) At least one-third of each physician investor's medical practice income from all sources for the previous fiscal year or previous 12-month period must be derived from the physician's performance of procedures (as defined in this paragraph).

(iii) At least one-third of the procedures (as defined in this paragraph) performed by each physician investor for the previous fiscal year or previous 12-month period must be performed at the investment entity.

(iv) The entity or any investor (or other individual or entity acting on behalf of the entity or any investor) must not loan funds to or guarantee a loan for an investor if the investor uses any part of such loan to obtain the investment interest.

(v) The amount of payment to an investor in return for the investment must be directly proportional to the amount of the capital investment (including the fair market value of any pre-operational services rendered) of that investor.

(vi) All ancillary services for Federal health care program beneficiaries performed at the entity must be directly and integrally related to primary procedures performed at the entity, and none may be separately billed to Medicare or other Federal health care programs.

(vii) The entity and any physician investors must treat patients receiving medical benefits or assistance under any Federal health care program in a nondiscriminatory manner.

(4) Hospital/Physician ASCs – If at least one investor is a hospital, and all of the remaining investors are physicians who meet the requirements of paragraphs (r)(1), (r)(2) or (r)(3) of this section; group practices (as defined in this paragraph) composed of such physicians; surgical group practices (as defined in this paragraph); or investors who are not employed by the entity or by any investor, are not in a position to provide items or services to the entity or any of its investors, and are not in a position to refer patients directly or indirectly to the entity or any of its investors, all of the following eight standards must be met –

(i) The terms on which an investment interest is offered to an investor must not be related to the previous or expected volume of referrals, services furnished, or the amount of business otherwise generated from that investor to the entity.

(ii) The entity or any investor (or other individual or entity acting on behalf of the entity or any investor) must not loan funds to or guarantee a loan for an investor if the investor uses any part of such loan to obtain the investment interest.

(iii) The amount of payment to an investor in return for the investment must be directly proportional to the amount of the capital investment (including the fair market value of any pre-operational services rendered) of that investor.

(iv) The entity and any hospital or physician investor must treat patients receiving medical benefits or assistance under any Federal health care program in a nondiscriminatory manner.

(v) The entity may not use space, including, but not limited to, operating and recovery room space, located in or owned by any hospital investor, unless such space is leased from the hospital in accordance with a lease that complies with all the standards of the space rental safe harbor set forth in paragraph (b) of this section; nor may it use equipment owned by or services provided by the hospital unless such equipment is leased in accordance with a lease that complies with the equipment rental safe harbor set forth in paragraph (c) of this section, and such services are provided in accordance with a contract that complies with the personal services and management contracts safe harbor set forth in paragraph (d) of this section.

(vi) All ancillary services for Federal health care program beneficiaries performed at the entity must be directly and integrally related to primary procedures performed at the entity, and none may be separately billed to Medicare or other Federal health care programs.

(vii) The hospital may not include on its cost report or any claim for payment from a Federal health care program any costs associated with the ASC (unless such costs are required to be included by a Federal health care program).

(viii) The hospital may not be in a position to make or influence referrals directly or indirectly to any investor or the entity.

(5) For purposes of paragraph (r) of this section, procedures means any procedure or procedures on the list of Medicare-covered procedures for ambulatory surgical centers in accordance with regulations issued by the Department and group practice means a group practice that meets all of the standards of paragraph (p) of this section. Surgical group practice means a group practice that meets all of the standards of paragraph (p) of this section and is composed exclusively of surgeons who meet the requirements of paragraph (r)(1) of this section.

The ASC safe harbor has four categories: Surgeon-Owned ASCs, Single-Specialty ASCs, Multi-Specialty ASCs, and Hospital/Physician ASCs. In order to establish safe harbor protection, all requirements of a given category must be met. The following requirements are shared by all four categories:

(i) the ASC must be certified under 42 C.F.R. part 416;

(ii) loans from the ASC or other investors for the purpose of investing are prohibited;

(iii) investment interests must be offered on terms not related to the volume or value of referrals;
(iv) all ancillary services must be directly and integrally related to primary procedures performed at the ASC and none may be separately billed to Medicare or other Federal health care programs; and
(v) neither the ASC nor physicians practicing at the ASC are permitted to discriminate against Federal health care program beneficiaries.

Further, the ASC's operating and recovery room space must be exclusive to use by the ASC,[555] and physician investors must inform all patients referred to an ASC of the physician investor's ownership interest in such ASC with written notice prior to the date of a procedure at the ASC, absent exigent circumstances.

A. *Surgeon-Owned Ambulatory Surgical Centers*

The first category of the safe harbor is the Surgeon-Owned ASC. Generally, this category protects investments in ASCs where all physician investors are general surgeons or surgeons engaged in the same surgical specialty who are in a position to refer patients directly to the ASC to perform procedures on these patients, group practices that are composed of such physicians and who meet all requirements of the group practice safe harbor,[556] or investors who:

(i) do not provide services to the ASC or its investors;
(ii) are not employed by the ASC or any investor; and
(iii) are not in a position to refer patients directly or indirectly to, or generate business for, the ASC or any of its investors.[557]

Importantly, in order for surgeon investors to qualify for safe harbor protection, they must perform at least one-third of their medical practice income from all sources for the previous fiscal year or twelve-month period through the physician's performance of surgical procedures at an ASC or other hospital setting ("1/3 Income Test").[558]

555. *See* 42 C.F.R. § 1001.952(r).
556. *See* Group Practice Safe Harbor 42 C.F.R. § 1001.952(p).
557. *See* 64 Fed. Reg. 63518, at 63518-63519.
558. *See id.*

B. *Single-Specialty Ambulatory Surgical Centers*

The second category is the Single-Specialty ASC. This category protects investment entities in the same way the Surgeon-Owned ASC category does, without requiring the physician investor to be a general surgeon.[559] Generally, it is designed to protect ASC investments by physician investors engaged in the same medical practice specialty who perform ASC procedures as a significant part of their practice (e.g., gastroenterologists).[560] Specifically, it protects investments in ASCs by physicians who are in a position to refer patients directly to the ASC to perform procedures on these patients, group practices that are composed of such physicians and meet all requirements of the group practice safe harbor,[561] or investors who:

(i) do not provide services to the ASC or its investors;
(ii) are not employed by the ASC or any investor; and
(iii) are not in a position to refer patients directly or indirectly to, or generate business for, the ASC or any of its investors.[562]

As with the Surgeon-Owned ASC category, each physician investor must meet the 1/3 Income Test.[563]

C. *Multi-Specialty Ambulatory Surgical Centers*

The third category of the safe harbor is the Multi-Specialty ASC. Its requirements are similar to the Surgeon-Owned ASC and Single-Specialty ASC categories but allows for a variation in the types of physicians and their specialties that are eligible for protection.[564] Specifically, it extends protection to (a) both surgeons or nonsurgeons who are in a position to refer patients directly to the ASC and who perform procedures on these patients, (b) group practices that are composed of such physicians and meet all requirements of the group practice safe harbor,[565] or (c) investors who:

(i) do not provide services to the ASC or its investors;
(ii) are not employed by the ASC or any investor; and

---

559. Compare Surgeon-Owned ASC safe harbor with Single-Specialty ASC safe harbor.
560. *See* 64 Fed. Reg. 63518, 63518-19.
561. *See* Group Practice Safe Harbor, 42 C.F.R. § 1001.952(p).
562. *See* 64 Fed. Reg. 63518, 63518-19.
563. *See id.*
564. *See id.*
565. *See* Group Practice Safe Harbor, 42 C.F.R. §1001.952(p).

(iii) are not in a position to refer patients directly or indirectly to, or generate business for, the ASC or any of its investors.[566]

As with the previous two categories, each physician investor must meet the 1/3 Income Test[567] and, due to the increased risk of remuneration for referrals among physicians with different specialties, physicians in this category are also required to perform at least one-third (1/3) of their procedures that require an ASC or hospital surgical setting to be performed at the ASC in which the physician is investing ("1/3 Procedure Test"). The 1/3 Procedure Test helps to ensure that the ASC serves as an extension of the physician's office so as to mitigate concerns that the physician investors may be incentivized to refer surgical procedures to other investors in order to receive an additional return on their investment in the ASC from the referral.[568]

D. *Hospital/Physician Ambulatory Surgical Centers*

The fourth category is the Hospital/Physician ASC. It protects certain joint venture ASC investments by hospitals, physicians, and/or other investors. In order to qualify for protection, at least one investor must be a hospital and the other investors must be:

(i) physicians who meet the requirements of Surgeon-Owned ASCs, Single-Specialty ASCs, or Multi-Specialty ASCs, as applicable: or
(ii) non-referral source investors.[569]

Moreover, the hospital must not be in a position to refer patients directly or indirectly to any physician investor or to the ASC to be eligible. The ASC space must be for the exclusive use of the ASC,[570] and the space must not be used by the hospital for the hospital's inpatient or outpatient treatments.[571] Finally, the ASC may lease space and/or equipment owned by or located in a hospital investor's premises as long as the lease of space and the equipment meets all requirements of those respective safe harbors.[572]

566. *See* 64 Fed. Reg. 63518, 63518-19.
567. *See id.*
568. *See id.*
569. *See id.*
570. *See id.*
571. *See id.*
572. *See* Space Rental Safe Harbor at 42 C.F.R. §1001.952(b), and Equipment Rental Safe Harbor at 42 C.F.R. §1001.952(c).

E. Regulatory Guidance, Policy, and Advisory Opinions

The ASC safe harbor was included as an additional safe harbor proposed as an amendment by HHS in 1993.[573] As explained in the preamble to the final rule providing safe harbor protection for returns on investment interests in ASCs, the decision to extend this protection derives in large measure from HHS's long-standing policy of promoting greater utilization of ASCs, where appropriate, because of the substantial cost savings that the federal health care programs may achieve when procedures are performed in ASCs rather than in more costly hospital inpatient or outpatient facilities.[574] When promulgating the ASC safe harbor, the OIG stated that its chief concern was that "a return on investment in an ASC might be a disguised payment for referrals."[575] However, recognizing that some physician-owned ASCs may be beneficial to the federal health care programs and their beneficiaries, the OIG stated:

> The gravamen of an anti-kickback offense is payment of remuneration to induce the referral of Federal health care program business. In the context of an ASC, our chief concern is that a return on an investment in an ASC might be disguised as payment for referrals . . . [P]hysicians in specialties that typically refer to one another could jointly invest in an ASC so that they are positioned to earn a profit from such referrals or so that one physician specialty provides the ASC services and the other provides the referrals. In such cases, medical decision-making may be corrupted by financial incentives offered to potential referral sources who stand to profit from services provided by another physician.[576]

For example, indirect kickbacks might flow to investor physicians, by means of receiving a return through the ASC's profit distribution, who refer patients to other investors in an ASC that perform surgical procedures at that ASC.[577]

---

573. 64 Fed. Reg. 63518; *see also Fact Sheet: Federal Anti-Kickback Law and Regulatory Safe Harbors*, U.S. Off. Inspector Gen., Nov. 1999, https://oig.hhs.gov/fraud/docs/safeharborregulations/safefs.htm.

574. *See* 64 Fed. Reg. 63518, 63537; *see also* OIG Advisory Opinion No. 12-06 at 7 (June 1, 2012).

575. 64 Fed. Reg. 63518, 63536 (providing two illustrative examples of potentially problematic arrangements).

576. *Id.*

577. *See id.*

However, so long as an arrangement does not violate these core principles, coupled with the strong policy support for the promotion of ASCs, the OIG has ruled favorably in several advisory opinions notwithstanding the failure of the arrangement to meet each and every requirement of the applicable ASC safe harbor. In doing so, the OIG has recognized that the absence of safe harbor protection is not fatal provided that the arrangement would pose more than a minimal risk of fraud and abuse under the AKS. This is particularly the case "[w]here the ASC is functionally an extension of a physician's office, so that the physician personally performs services at the ASC on his or her own patients as a substantial part of his or her medical practice."[578] It is also important to note that while many ASC arrangements will fit within the advised safe harbor requirements, some legitimate ASC arrangements that do not meet the safe harbor requirements may still be protected under the small entity investments safe harbor or the safe harbor for investments in underserved areas.[579]

In Advisory Opinion 08-08, the OIG determined not to impose administrative sanctions on a proposed physician/hospital joint venture ASC that did not qualify for safe harbor protection.[580] Specifically, of the eighteen surgeon investors involved in the proposed ASC, only fourteen met the 1/3 Income Test and would regularly practice at the ASC. The four surgeons who would not be utilizing the ASC primarily performed surgeries at a hospital on an inpatient basis. In finding that the proposed arrangement posed little risk of fraud and abuse, the OIG reasoned that notwithstanding the failure of the four inpatient surgeons to meet the 1/3 Income Test, the ASC was unlikely to be a vehicle for them to profit from referrals.[581] This was because as practitioners in subspecialties of orthopedic surgery that require a hospital operating room setting, the inpatient surgeons rarely have occasion to refer patients for ASC-qualified procedures,

578. OIG Advisory Opinion No. 12-06 at 7 (June 1, 2012).

579. 64 Fed. Reg. 63518, 63536 (discussing the small entity investments safe harbor (42 C.F.R. § 1001.952(a)(2)-(3)).

580. *See* OIG Advisory Opinion No. 08-08 (July 25, 2008).

581. *See id.* at 5 (finding that the arrangement did not qualify for the protection of the hospital-/physician-owned ASC safe harbor because the surgeon investors did not hold their investment interests in the ASC either directly or through a group practice). However, the OIG opined that since the surgeon investor's ownership interest in the pass through entity "[was] proportioned to his or her capital investment, the surgeon's ownership interest in the ASC was, in turn, proportional to its capital investment." *Id.* As a result, the individual surgeon investors received a return in their ASC investments that was the same as if they had invested directly.

with the exception of pain management procedures.[582] Moreover, like the other surgeon investors, the inpatient surgeons were regularly engaged in a genuine surgical practice, deriving at least one-third of their medical practice income from procedures requiring a hospital operating room setting. The inpatient surgeons were qualified to perform surgeries at the ASC and had a choice to do so (and earn the professional fees) in medically appropriate cases. Also, the inpatient surgeons comprised a small proportion of the surgeon investors, and a majority of them would use the ASC on a regular basis as part of their medical practice. The OIG found that this arrangement was distinguishable from potentially riskier arrangements in which few investing physicians actually used the ASC on a regular basis or in which investing physicians were significant potential referral sources for other investors or the ASC, as when primary care physicians invest in a surgical ASC or cardiologists invest in a cardiac surgery ASC.

Similarly, in finding that a joint venture ASC between a hospital and physicians was unlikely to be a vehicle for the investors to profit from referrals where the proposed ASC did not satisfy all of the elements of the Hospital/Physician ASC safe harbor because the hospital was in a position to refer patients to either the ASC or its investors, the OIG ruled in Advisory Opinion 01-17 that four safeguards proposed by the hospital mitigated any concerns about the hospital's ability to direct or influence referrals to the ASC.[583] These safeguards included:

(i) the hospital's restraint from requiring or encouraging hospital-affiliated physicians from referring patients to the ASC, the investing ophthalmologists, or their group practices;
(ii) the hospital's commitment not to track referrals made by hospital-affiliated physicians to the ASC, investing ophthalmologists, or their group practices;
(iii) compensation paid to hospital-affiliated physicians was determined at arm's length and at a fair market value and not related to the volume or value of referrals or other business generated by these physicians

582. *See id.* at 6 (determining that the potential for abusive referrals was sufficiently mitigated by a stipulation from the requestors certifying that no surgeon investor would refer patients for pain management procedures to be performed at the ASC, unless the procedure would be performed personally by the referring surgeon investor).

583. *See* OIG Advisory Opinion No. 01-17 (Oct. 10, 2001).

to or for the ASC, the investing ophthalmologists, or their group practices; and

(iv) hospital-affiliated physicians were informed of these measures.[584]

With the implementation of these safeguards, the OIG found that the ASC was unlikely to be a vehicle for the investors to profit from referrals by the hospital. However, by way of comparison, in OIG Advisory Opinion No. 03-5, the OIG found that the proposed arrangement would pose more than a minimal risk of fraud and abuse under the AKS.[585] This was because the proposed ASC was to be owned by a multispecialty group comprised of surgeons and fourteen family practitioners, eleven internists, six pediatricians, five obstetricians/gynecologists, two general surgeons, three orthopedic surgeons, and two ophthalmologists. The OIG opined that since the group was a multispecialty group, there was a substantial likelihood of cross-specialty referrals for services performed in the ASC, principally because few of the physician owners would actually use the ASC on a regular basis as part of their medical practice. The proposed arrangement would allow those physician owners for whom the ASC was not an extension of their office practices to profit from their referrals to the ASC or to their partners who perform procedures there. In this respect, the OIG reasoned that the proposed arrangement posed the same risks as an ASC owned directly by surgeons and primary care physicians in the same community.[586]

2.19. Price Reductions Offered to Eligible Managed Care Organizations

The safe harbor for price reductions offered to eligible managed care organizations (MCOs) is codified in statute and regulation. The AKS, at 42 U.S.C. § 1320a-7b(b)(3)(F), states that the AKS will not apply to "any remuneration between an organization and an individual or entity providing items or services, or a combination thereof, pursuant to a written agreement between the organization and the individual or entity if the organization is an eligible

584. *See id.*; *see also* OIG Advisory Opinion No. 03-2 (Jan. 13, 2003) (determining that the OIG would not impose administrative sanctions on a proposed ASC arrangement that included safeguards that limited the risk of fraud and abuse).

585. OIG Advisory Opinion No. 03-5 (Feb. 6, 2003).

586. *See generally* OIG Adv. Op. No. 07-13 (concluding that the proposed arrangement composed of optometrists and ophthalmologists had "no discernible safeguards to minimize significant risk" that investment in the ASC was for the purpose of inducing or rewarding referrals).

organization under section 1395mm of this title [authorizing payments to health maintenance organizations and competitive medical plans]. . . ." Consistent with this statutory protection, 42 C.F.R. § 1001.952(t) provides as follows:

> (t) *Price reductions offered to eligible managed care organizations.*
>
> (1) As used in section 1128(B) of the Act, "remuneration" does not include any payment between:
>
> (i) An eligible managed care organization and any first tier contractor for providing or arranging for items or services, as long as the following three standards are met -
>
> (A) The eligible managed care organization and the first tier contractor have an agreement that:
>
> (1) Is set out in writing and signed by both parties;
>
> (2) Specifies the items and services covered by the agreement;
>
> (3) Is for a period of at least one year; and
>
> (4) Specifies that the first tier contractor cannot claim payment in any form directly or indirectly from a Federal health care program for items or services covered under the agreement, except for:
>
> *(i)* HMOs and competitive medical plans with cost-based contracts under section 1876 of the Act where the agreement with the eligible managed care organization sets out the arrangements in accordance with which the first tier contractor is billing the Federal health care program;
>
> *(ii)* Federally qualified HMOs without a contract under sections 1854 or 1876 of the Act, where the agreement with the eligible managed care organization sets out the arrangements in accordance with which the first tier contractor is billing the Federal health care program; or
>
> *(iii)* First tier contractors that are Federally qualified health centers that claim supplemental payments from a Federal health care program.
>
> (B) In establishing the terms of the agreement, neither party gives or receives remuneration in return for

or to induce the provision or acceptance of business (other than business covered by the agreement) for which payment may be made in whole or in part by a Federal health care program on a fee-for-service or cost basis.

(C) Neither party to the agreement shifts the financial burden of the agreement to the extent that increased payments are claimed from a Federal health care program.

(ii) A first tier contractor and a downstream contractor or between two downstream contractors to provide or arrange for items or services, as long as the following four standards are met -

(A) The parties have an agreement that:

(1) Is set out in writing and signed by both parties;

(2) Specifies the items and services covered by the agreement;

(3) Is for a period of at least one year; and

(4) Specifies that the party providing the items or services cannot claim payment in any form from a Federal health care program for items or services covered under the agreement.

(B) In establishing the terms of the agreement, neither party gives or receives remuneration in return for or to induce the provision or acceptance of business (other than business covered by the agreement) for which payment may be made in whole or in part by a Federal health care program on a fee-for-service or cost basis.

(C) Neither party shifts the financial burden of the agreement to the extent that increased payments are claimed from a Federal health care program.

(D) The agreement between the eligible managed care organization and first tier contractor covering the items or services that are covered by the agreement between the parties does not involve:

(1) A Federally qualified health center receiving supplemental payments;

(2) A HMO or CMP with a cost-based contract under section 1876 of the Act; or

(3) A Federally qualified HMO, unless the items or services are covered by a risk based contract under sections 1854 or 1876 of the Act.

(2) For purposes of this paragraph, the following terms are defined as follows:

(i) *Downstream contractor* means an individual or entity that has a subcontract directly or indirectly with a first tier contractor for the provision or arrangement of items or services that are covered by an agreement between an eligible managed care organization and the first tier contractor.

(ii) *Eligible managed care organization*[587] means -

(A) A HMO or CMP with a risk or cost based contract in accordance with section 1876 of the Act;

(B) Any Medicare Part C health plan that receives a capitated payment from Medicare and which must have its total Medicare beneficiary cost sharing approved by CMS under section 1854 of the Act;

(C) Medicaid managed care organizations as defined in section 1903(m)(1)(A) that provide or arrange for items or services for Medicaid enrollees under a contract in accordance with section 1903(m) of the Act (except for fee-for-service plans or medical savings accounts);

(D) Any other health plans that provide or arrange for items and services for Medicaid enrollees in accordance with a risk-based contract with a State agency subject to the upper payment limits in § 447.361 of this title or an equivalent payment cap approved by the Secretary;

(E) Programs For All Inclusive Care For The Elderly (PACE) under sections 1894 and 1934 of the Act, except for for-profit demonstrations under sections 4801(h) and 4802(h) of Pub. L. 105-33; or

(F) A Federally qualified HMO.

---

587. The eligible managed care organizations in paragraphs (u)(2)(ii)(A)-(F) of this section are only eligible with respect to items or services covered by the contracts specified in those paragraphs.

(iii) *First tier contractor* means an individual or entity that has a contract directly with an eligible managed care organization to provide or arrange for items or services.

(iv) *Items and services* means health care items, devices, supplies or services or those services reasonably related to the provision of health care items, devices, supplies or services including, but not limited to, non-emergency transportation, patient education, attendant services, social services (e.g., case management), utilization review and quality assurance. Marketing and other pre-enrollment activities are not "items or services" for purposes of this section.

In 1999, OIG published an interim final rule establishing the above-quoted safe harbor, which corresponds to one of two statutory safe harbors relating to managed care arrangements found in 42 U.S.C. § 1320a-7b(b)(3)(F).[588] The first of these safe harbors, set forth in § 1001.952(t), "protects various financial arrangements between managed care entities that receive a fixed or capitated amount from the Federal health care programs and individuals and entities with whom the managed care entity contracts for the provision of health care items or services."[589] The OIG commented that both safe harbors were designed to "protect remuneration between parties where the remuneration is a price reduction for the provision of health care items or services" and that the safe harbors do not protect "[o]ther remuneration, such as profit distributions from investment interests in an entity with a risk sharing arrangement."[590] The OIG further clarified that any arrangement that protects remuneration that is covered by the safe harbors, and also remuneration that is not covered, would still receive protection for the former type of remuneration, and that "an arrangement that potentially falls within more than one safe harbor need only meet the requirements of one safe harbor."[591] The OIG also made a point of stating that the safe harbors "do not apply to other laws, such as State licensure laws, antitrust laws or other Federal and State health care fraud laws."[592]

For purposes of the safe harbor, an "eligible organization" includes federally qualified HMOs and competitive medical plans "that have entered into

588. Interim Final Rule: Federal Health Care Program, Fraud and Abuse, Statutory Exception to the Anti-Kickback Statute for Shared Risk Arrangements (64 Fed. Reg. 63504, Nov. 19, 1999).

589. *Id.* at 63505.

590. *Id.* at 63506.

591. *Id.*

592. *Id.*

either risk or cost-based managed care contracts" with the CMS since the OIG recognized that eligible organizations with risk-based contracts "presented little or no risk of overutilization or increased costs to the Federal Health care programs, given applicable payment arrangements and regulatory oversight."[593] The OIG noted that "[w]hen plans are paid a capitated amount for all of the services they provide regardless of the dates, frequency or type of services, there is no incentive to overutilize" and that "even if overutilization occurs, the Federal health care programs are not at risk for these increased costs."[594] The safe harbor "extends protection from the anti-kickback statute beyond the managed care arrangements" specifically protected under the statutory exception by including "other programs where the Federal health care programs pay on a capitated or fixed aggregate basis, such as certain Medicare Part C plans."[595] The safe harbor also extends protection downstream to "subcontracts with other providers and entities to provide items and services in accordance with a protected managed care arrangement" and "regardless of the payment methodology" underlying the subcontracting arrangement, provided that the "aggregate financial exposure [to the Federal health care program] is fixed in accordance with its contract with the managed care organization."[596]

The safe harbor, however, also contains certain limitations. The protections for subcontractors "is limited to risk-based managed care plans that do not claim any payment from a Federal health care program" other than the capitated amount set forth in the agreement between MCO and the federal program.[597] Protections are not afforded to subcontractor arrangements that are "cost-based or where the prime contract is protected solely because the contracting entity is a Federally-qualified HMO" because in the former situation, reimbursement is "based on costs," and in the latter situation reimbursement is made "on a fee-for-service basis," both of which involve scenarios in which "reimbursement will increase with utilization, thus providing the same incentive to overutilize as any fee-for-service payment methodology."[598] Additionally, the safe harbor "only applies to remuneration for health care items and services and those items or services reasonably related to the

593. *Id.*
594. *Id.*
595. *Id.* at 63507.
596. *Id.*
597. *Id.*
598. *Id.*

provision" of such services and "does not cover marketing services or any services provided prior to a beneficiary's enrollment in a health plan."[599] Furthermore, "there is no protection if the financial arrangements under the managed care agreement are implicitly or explicitly part of a broader agreement to steer fee-for-service Federal health care program business to the entity giving the discount to induce the referral of managed care business."[600] The concern underlying these comments involves "swapping," whereby in "managed care arrangements low capitation rates could be traded for access to additional fee-for-service lines of business."[601] The OIG expressed concern for arrangements in which "discounts are in exchange for access to fee-for-service lines of business, where there is an incentive to overutilize services provided to Federal health care program beneficiaries."

2.20. Price Reductions Offered by Contractors with Substantial Financial Risk to Managed Care Organizations

The safe harbor for price reductions offered by contractors with substantial financial risk to managed care organizations is codified in statute and regulation. The AKS, at 42 U.S.C. § 1320a-7b(b)(3)(F), states that the AKS will not apply to "any remuneration between an organization and an individual or entity providing items or services, or a combination thereof, pursuant to a written agreement between the organization and the individual or entity . . . if the written agreement, through a risk-sharing arrangement, places the individual or entity at substantial financial risk for the cost or utilization of the items or services, or a combination thereof, which the individual or entity is obligated to provide." Consistent with this statutory protection, 42 C.F.R. § 1001.952(u) provides as follows:

(u) *Price reductions offered by contractors with substantial financial risk to managed care organizations.*

  (1) As used in section 1128(B) of the Act, "remuneration" does not include any payment between:

    (i) A qualified managed care plan and a first tier contractor for providing or arranging for items or services, where the following five standards are met -

599. *Id.* This limitation also applies to § 1001.952(u).
600. *Id.*
601. *Id.*

(A) The agreement between the qualified managed care plan and first tier contractor must:
   (1) Be in writing and signed by the parties;
   (2) Specify the items and services covered by the agreement;
   (3) Be for a period of a least one year;
   (4) Require participation in a quality assurance program that promotes the coordination of care, protects against underutilization and specifies patient goals, including measurable outcomes where appropriate; and
   (5) Specify a methodology for determining payment that is commercially reasonable and consistent with fair market value established in an arms-length transaction and includes the intervals at which payments will be made and the formula for calculating incentives and penalties, if any.

(B) If a first tier contractor has an investment interest in a qualified managed care plan, the investment interest must meet the criteria of paragraph (a)(1) of this section.

(C) The first tier contractor must have substantial financial risk for the cost or utilization of services it is obligated to provide through one of the following four payment methodologies:
   (1) A periodic fixed payment per patient that does not take into account the dates services are provided, the frequency of services, or the extent or kind of services provided;
   (2) Percentage of premium;
   (3) Inpatient Federal health care program diagnosis-related groups (DRGs) (other than those for psychiatric services);
   (4) Bonus and withhold arrangements, provided -
      (i) The target payment for first tier contractors that are individuals or non-institutional providers is at least 20 percent greater than the minimum payment, and for first tier

contractors that are institutional providers, i.e., hospitals and nursing homes, is at least 10 percent greater than the minimum payment;

(ii) The amount at risk, *i.e.,* the bonus or withhold, is earned by a first tier contractor in direct proportion to the ratio of the contractor's actual utilization to its target utilization;

(iii) In calculating the percentage in accordance with paragraph (u)(1)(i)(C)(*4*)(*i*) of this section, both the target payment amount and the minimum payment amount include any performance bonus, e.g., payments for timely submission of paperwork, continuing medical education, meeting attendance, etc., at a level achieved by 75 percent of the first tier contractors who are eligible for such payments;

(iv) Payment amounts, including any bonus or withhold amounts, are reasonable given the historical utilization patterns and costs for the same or comparable populations in similar managed care arrangements; and

(v) Alternatively, for a first tier contractor that is a physician, the qualified managed care plan has placed the physician at risk for referral services in an amount that exceeds the substantial financial risk threshold set forth in 42 CFR 417.479(f) and the arrangement is in compliance with the stop-loss and beneficiary survey requirements of 42 CFR 417.479(g).

(D) Payments for items and services reimbursable by Federal health care program must comply with the following two standards -

(1) The qualified managed care plan (or in the case of a self-funded employer plan that contracts with a qualified managed care plan to provide administrative services, the self-funded employer plan) must submit the claims directly to the Federal health care program, in accordance with a valid reassignment agreement, for items or services reimbursed by the Federal health care program. (Notwithstanding the foregoing, inpatient hospital services, other than psychiatric services, will be deemed to comply if the hospital is reimbursed by a Federal health care program under a DRG methodology.)

(2) Payments to first tier contractors and any downstream contractors for providing or arranging for items or services reimbursed by a Federal health care program must be identical to payment arrangements to or between such parties for the same items or services provided to other beneficiaries with similar health status, provided that such payments may be adjusted where the adjustments are related to utilization patterns or costs of providing items or services to the relevant population.

(E) In establishing the terms of an arrangement -

(1) Neither party gives or receives remuneration in return for or to induce the provision or acceptance of business (other than business covered by the arrangement) for which payment may be made in whole or in part by a Federal health care program on a fee-for-service or cost basis; and

(2) Neither party to the arrangement shifts the financial burden of such arrangement to the extent that increased payments are claimed from a Federal health care program.

(ii) A first tier contractor and a downstream contractor, or between downstream contractors, to provide or arrange for items or services, as long as the following three standards are met -

(**A**) Both parties are being paid for the provision or arrangement of items or services in accordance with one of the payment methodologies set out in paragraph (u)(1)(i)(C) of this section;

(**B**) Payment arrangements for items and services reimbursable by a Federal health care program comply with paragraph (u)(1)(i)(D) of this section; and

(**C**) In establishing the terms of an arrangement -

(**1**) Neither party gives or receives remuneration in return for or to induce the provision or acceptance of business (other than business covered by the arrangement) for which payment may be made in whole or in part by a Federal health care program on a fee-for-service or cost basis; and

(**2**) Neither party to the arrangement shifts the financial burden of the arrangement to the extent that increased payments are claimed from a Federal health care program.

(2) For purposes of this paragraph, the following terms are defined as follows:

(i) *Downstream contractor* means an individual or entity that has a subcontract directly or indirectly with a first tier contractor for the provision or arrangement of items or services that are covered by an agreement between a qualified managed care plan and the first tier contractor.

(ii) *First tier contractor* means an individual or entity that has a contract directly with a qualified managed care plan to provide or arrange for items or services.

(iii) *Is obligated to provide* for a contractor refers to items or services:

(**A**) Provided directly by an individual or entity and its employees;

(**B**) For which an individual or entity is financially responsible, but which are provided by downstream contractors;

(**C**) For which an individual or entity makes referrals or arrangements; or

(**D**) For which an individual or entity receives financial incentives based on its own, its provider group's, or its qualified managed care plan's performance (or combination thereof).

(**iv**) *Items and services* means health care items, devices, supplies or services or those services reasonably related to the provision of health care items, devices, supplies or services including, but not limited to, non-emergency transportation, patient education, attendant services, social services (e.g., case management), utilization review and quality assurance. Marketing or other pre-enrollment activities are not "items or services" for purposes of this definition in this paragraph.

(**v**) *Minimum payment* is the guaranteed amount that a provider is entitled to receive under an agreement with a first tier or downstream contractor or a qualified managed care plan.

(**vi**) *Qualified managed care plan* means a health plan as defined in paragraph (l)(2) of this section that:

(**A**) Provides a comprehensive range of health services;

(**B**) Provides or arranges for -

(**1**) Reasonable utilization goals to avoid inappropriate utilization;

(**2**) An operational utilization review program;

(**3**) A quality assurance program that promotes the coordination of care, protects against underutilization, and specifies patient goals, including measurable outcomes where appropriate;

(**4**) Grievance and hearing procedures;

(**5**) Protection of enrollees from incurring financial liability other than copayments and deductibles; and

(**6**) Treatment for Federal health care program beneficiaries that is not different than treatment for other enrollees because of their status as Federal health care program beneficiaries; and

(**C**) Covers a beneficiary population of which either -

(1) No more than 10 percent are Medicare beneficiaries, not including persons for whom a Federal health care program is the secondary payer; or

(2) No more than 50 percent are Medicare beneficiaries (not including persons for whom a Federal health care program is the secondary payer), provided that payment of premiums is on a periodic basis that does not take into account the dates services are rendered, the frequency of services, or the extent or kind of services rendered, and provided further that such periodic payments for the non-Federal health care program beneficiaries do not take into account the number of Federal health care program fee-for-service beneficiaries covered by the agreement or the amount of services generated by such beneficiaries.

(vii) *Target payment* means the fair market value payment established through arms length negotiations that will be earned by an individual or entity that:

(A) Is dependent on the individual or entity's meeting a utilization target or range of utilization targets that are set consistent with historical utilization rates for the same or comparable populations in similar managed care arrangements, whether based on its own, its provider group's or the qualified managed care plan's utilization (or a combination thereof); and

(B) Does not include any bonus or fees that the individual or entity may earn from exceeding the utilization target.

In 1999, the OIG published an interim final rule establishing the above-quoted safe harbor, which corresponds to one of two statutory safe harbors relating to managed care arrangements found in 42 U.S.C. § 1320a-7b(b)(3)(F).[602] The second of these safe harbors, set forth in § 1001.952(u), "protects contractual relationships between managed care entities and their

602. Interim Final Rule: Federal Health Care Program, Fraud and Abuse, Statutory Exception to the Anti-Kickback Statute for (64 Fed. Reg. 63504, Nov. 19, 1999).

contractors and subcontractors where the contractors and subcontractors are at *substantial financial risk* for the cost or utilization of items or services they provide or order for Federal health care program beneficiaries."[603] The OIG recognized that "there are few existing managed care arrangements that would qualify under [this safe harbor] that are not otherwise covered by the safe harbor in [§ 1001.952(t)]" because most such arrangements "do *not* place their contractors and subcontractors at substantial financial risk for the cost or utilization of items or services to Federal health care program beneficiaries" and usually such contractors and subcontractors "are reimbursed directly by the Federal payor on a fee-for-service basis."[604]

Notwithstanding this fact, the OIG decided to adopt this safe harbor in order to protect "a category of arrangements that *could* qualify for protection."[605] The OIG commented that both safe harbors were designed to "protect remuneration between parties where the remuneration is a price reduction for the provision of health care items or services" and that the safe harbors do not protect "[o]ther remuneration, such as profit distributions from investment interests in an entity with a risk sharing arrangement."[606] The OIG further clarified that any arrangement that protects remuneration that is covered by the safe harbors, and also remuneration that is not covered, would still receive protection for the former type of remuneration, and that "an arrangement that potentially falls within more than one safe harbor need only meet the requirements of one safe harbor."[607] The OIG also made a point of stating that the safe harbors "do not apply to other laws, such as State licensure laws, antitrust laws or other Federal and State health care fraud laws."[608]

2.21. Ambulance Replenishing

The safe harbor for ambulance replenishment services, codified at 42 C.F.R. § 1001.952(v), states:

> (v) Ambulance replenishing
>
> > (1) As used in section 1128B of the Act, "remuneration" does not include any gift or transfer of drugs or medical supplies

603. *Id.* at 63505.
604. *Id.* at 63505-06.
605. *Id.*
606. *Id.* at 63506.
607. *Id.*
608. *Id.*

(including linens) by a hospital or other receiving facility to an ambulance provider for the purpose of replenishing comparable drugs or medical supplies (including linens) used by the ambulance provider (or a first responder) in connection with the transport of a patient by ambulance to the hospital or other receiving facility if all of the standards in paragraph (v)(2) of this section are satisfied and all of the applicable standards in either paragraph (v)(3)(i), (v)(3)(ii) or (v)(3)(iii) of this section are satisfied. However, to qualify under paragraph (v), the ambulance that is replenished must be used to provide emergency ambulance services an average of three times per week, as measured over a reasonable period of time. Drugs and medical supplies (including linens) initially used by a first responder and replenished at the scene of the illness or injury by the ambulance provider that transports the patient to the hospital or other receiving facility will be deemed to have been used by the ambulance provider.

(2) To qualify under paragraph (v) of this section, the ambulance replenishing arrangement must satisfy all of the following four conditions -

(i) (A) Under no circumstances may the ambulance provider (or first responder) and the receiving facility both bill for the same replenished drug or supply. Replenished drugs or supplies may only be billed (including claiming bad debt) to a Federal health care program by either the ambulance provider (or first responder) or the receiving facility.

(B) All billing or claims submission by the receiving facility, ambulance provider or first responder for replenished drugs and medical supplies used in connection with the transport of a Federal health care program beneficiary must comply with all applicable Federal health care program payment and coverage rules and regulations.

(C) Compliance with paragraph (v)(2)(i)(B) of this section will be determined separately for the receiving facility and the ambulance provider (and first responder, if any), so long as the receiving facility, ambulance provider (or first responder) refrains from doing anything that would impede the other party or parties from meeting their obligations under paragraph (v)(2)(i)(B).

(ii) (A) The receiving facility or ambulance provider, or both, must

(1) Maintain records of the replenished drugs and medical supplies and the patient transport to which the replenished drugs and medical supplies related;

(2) Provide a copy of such records to the other party within a reasonable time (unless the other party is separately maintaining records of the replenished drugs and medical supplies); and

(3) Make those records available to the Secretary promptly upon request.

(B) A pre-hospital care report (including, but not limited to, a trip sheet, patient care report or patient encounter report) prepared by the ambulance provider and filed with the receiving facility will meet the requirements of paragraph (v)(2)(ii)(A) of this section, provided that it documents the specific type and amount of medical supplies and drugs used on the patient and subsequently replenished.

(C) For purposes of paragraph (v)(2)(ii) of this section, documentation may be maintained and, if required, filed with the other party in hard copy or electronically. If a replenishing arrangement includes linens, documentation need not be maintained for their exchange. If documentation is not maintained for the exchange of linens, the receiving facility will be presumed to have provided an exchange of comparable clean linens for soiled linens for each ambulance transport of a patient to the receiving facility. Records required under paragraph (v)(2)(ii)(A) of this section must be maintained for 5 years.

(iii) The replenishing arrangement must not take into account the volume or value of any referrals or business otherwise generated between the parties for which payment may be made in whole or in part under any Federal health care program (other than the referral of the particular patient to whom the replenished drugs and medical supplies were furnished).

(**iv**) The receiving facility and the ambulance provider otherwise comply with all Federal, State, and local laws regulating ambulance services, including, but not limited to, emergency services, and the provision of drugs and medical supplies, including, but not limited to, laws relating to the handling of controlled substances.

(**3**) To qualify under paragraph (v) of this section, the arrangement must satisfy all of the standards in one of the following three categories:

(**i**) General replenishing

(**A**) The receiving facility must replenish medical supplies or drugs on an equal basis for all ambulance providers that bring patients to the receiving facility in any one of the categories described in paragraph (v)(3)(i)(A)(1), (2), or (3) of this section. A receiving facility may offer replenishing to one or more of the categories and may offer different replenishing arrangements to different categories, so long as the replenishing is conducted uniformly within each category. For example, a receiving facility may offer to replenish a broader array of drugs or supplies for ambulance providers that do no not charge for their services than for ambulance providers that charge for their services. Within each category, the receiving facility may limit its replenishing arrangements to the replenishing of emergency ambulance transports only. A receiving facility may offer replenishing to one or more of the categories -

(**1**) All ambulance providers that do not bill any patient or insurer (including Federal health care programs) for ambulance services, regardless of the payor or the patient's ability to pay (i.e., ambulance providers, such as volunteer companies, that provide ambulance services without charge to any person or entity);

(2) All not-for-profit and State or local government ambulance service providers (including, but not limited to, municipal and volunteer ambulance services providers); or

(3) All ambulance service providers.

(B) (1) The replenishing arrangement must be conducted in an open and public manner. A replenishing arrangement will be considered to be conducted in an open and public manner if one of the following two conditions are satisfied:

(i) A written disclosure of the replenishing program is posted conspicuously in the receiving facility's emergency room or other location where the ambulance providers deliver patients and copies are made available upon request to ambulance providers, Government representatives, and members of the public (subject to reasonable photocopying charges). The written disclosure can take any reasonable form and should include the category of ambulance service providers that qualifies for replenishment; the drugs or medical supplies included in the replenishment program; and the procedures for documenting the replenishment. A sample disclosure form is included in appendix A to subpart C of this part for illustrative purposes only. No written contracts between the parties are required for purposes of paragraph (v)(3)(i)(B)(1)(i) of this section; or

(ii) The replenishment arrangement operates in accordance with a plan or protocol of general application promulgated by an Emergency Medical Services (EMS) Council or comparable entity, agency or organization,

provided a copy of the plan or protocol is available upon request to ambulance providers, Government representatives and members of the public (subject to reasonable photocopying charges). While parties are encouraged to participate in collaborative, comprehensive, community-wide EMS systems to improve the delivery of EMS in their local communities, nothing in this paragraph shall be construed as requiring the involvement of such organizations or the development or implementation of ambulance replenishment plans or protocols by such organizations.

(2) Nothing in this paragraph (v)(3)(i) shall be construed as requiring disclosure of confidential proprietary or financial information related to the replenishing arrangement (including, but not limited to, information about cost, pricing or the volume of replenished drugs or supplies) to ambulance providers or members of the general public.

(ii) Fair market value replenishing

(A) Except as otherwise provided in paragraph (v)(3)(ii)(B) of this section, the ambulance provider must pay the receiving facility fair market value, based on an arms-length transaction, for replenished medical supplies; and

(B) If payment is not made at the same time as the replenishing of the medical supplies, the receiving facility and the ambulance provider must make commercially reasonable payment arrangements in advance.

(iii) Government mandated replenishing. The replenishing arrangement is undertaken in accordance with a State or local statute, ordinance, regulation or binding protocol that requires hospitals or receiving facilities in the area subject to such requirement to replenish ambulances that deliver patients to the hospital with drugs or medical supplies (including linens) that are used during the transport of that patient.

(4) For purposes of paragraph (v) of this section -

(i) A receiving facility is a hospital or other facility that provides emergency medical services.

(ii) An ambulance provider is a provider or supplier of ambulance transport services that provides emergency ambulance services. The term does not include a provider of ambulance transport services that provides only non-emergency transport services.

(iii) A first responder includes, but is not limited to, a fire department, paramedic service or search and rescue squad that responds to an emergency call (through 9-1-1 or other emergency access number) and treats the patient, but does not transport the patient to the hospital or other receiving facility.

(iv) An emergency ambulance service is a transport by ambulance initiated as a result of a call through 9-1-1 or other emergency access number or a call from another acute care facility unable to provide the higher level care required by the patient and available at the receiving facility.

(v) Medical supplies includes linens, unless otherwise provided.

The safe harbor provision for Ambulance Replenishing was enacted in 2001. Ambulance restocking deals before the passage of this safe harbor were often deemed to violate the AKS by giving a material benefit to those that bring in patients to hospitals. HHS noted that there was a potential for abuse with these arrangements, even though the vast majority of ambulance restocking arrangements are believed to be lawful under the AKS.[609] HHS acknowledged the need for this safe harbor in the final version by saying, "We fully recognize the importance of ambulances being restocked and ready for emergency use at all times. Properly structured restocking arrangements contribute to this laudable goal without significant risk of fraud or

609. Final Rule: OIG Ambulance Replenishing Safe Harbor Under the Anti-Kickback Statute, 66 Fed. Reg. 233, 62979, 62980 (Dec. 4, 2001).

abuse."[610] The intention of this safe harbor was to provide protection for the "vast majority of ambulance restocking arrangements" and subsequently enhance the ability of EMS to benefit the entire community.[611] The safe harbor covers drugs, supplies, and linens used for the care of patients either on the scene or in transit in an ambulance. The final rule was written as an expansion of the scope of the safe harbor, with less ambiguity, and granted more autonomy for those who enter a replenishing agreement.[612]

The federal government's first public mention of ambulance replenishing arrangements was in a 1997 advisory opinion that indicated that a certain ambulatory restocking arrangement would be in violation of the AKS.[613] This led to fear among the medical community that ambulance replenishment would not be a protected agreement.[614] However, following this negative document, the OIG offered several positive advisory opinions on the matter. A proposal for an ambulance replenishing safe harbor was offered in a 2000 advisory opinion, before the final rule was enacted.[615]

The final rule outlines regulations for three categories of replenishing arrangements: (1) general restocking, (2) fair market value restocking, and (3) government-mandated restocking. "Parties need only satisfy the conditions applicable to any one of these categories."[616] All three categories are first governed by certain overarching regulations, codified at § 1001.952(v)(2), and then by the arrangement-specific regulations, codified at § 1001.952(v)(3).[617]

There are four conditions that apply to all replenishing arrangements:

1. Appropriate billing of federal health care programs. The ambulance provider and the hospital are not allowed to both bill for the same restocked drugs or supplies. However, improper billing by one party does not necessitate improper billing by the other party. "For example, if a hospital improperly bills for restocked supplies, the ambulance provider who received the supplies may still be protected, so long as the

610. *Id.*

611. Proposed Rule: OIG Ambulance Replenishing Safe Harbor Under the Anti-Kickback Statute, 65 Fed. Reg. 99, 32060, 32061 (May 22, 2000).

612. Final Rule: OIG Ambulance Replenishing Safe Harbor Under the Anti-Kickback Statute, 66 Fed. Reg. 233, 62979,62980 (Dec. 4, 2001).

613. OIG Advisory Opinion No. 97-6 (Oct. 8, 1997).

614. Final Rule: OIG Ambulance Replenishing Safe Harbor Under the Anti-Kickback Statute, 66 Fed. Reg. 233, 62979,62982 (Dec. 4, 2001).

615. OIG Advisory Opinion No. 00-9 (Dec. 8, 2000).

616. Final Rule: OIG Ambulance Replenishing Safe Harbor Under the Anti-Kickback Statute, 66 Fed. Reg. 233, 62979,62981 (Dec. 4, 2001).

617. 42 C.F.R. § 1001.952.

provider has not done anything to impede the hospital's compliance with the billing rules."[618]

2. Documentation requirements. "Under the final rule, either the hospital or the ambulance provider may generate the necessary documentation, so long as the other party receives and maintains a copy of it for 5 years."[619]
3. No ties or referrals. This condition is a safeguard that prohibits any restocking arrangement from being predicated on, or taking into account, the volume or value of referrals or other business between the parties.
4. Compliance with all other laws. Both the receiving facility and ambulance provider must comply with all other federal and state laws.[620]

For general restocking, an agreement in which a provider pays either nothing or some discounted amount for restocked drugs and supplies, the agreement must adhere to two conditions. First, the receiving party must restock supplies and drugs on an equal basis for ambulance providers in one or more of the following three categories: "(i) All ambulance providers; (ii) all non-profit and governmental providers; or (iii) all non-charging providers (typically volunteers and municipal providers)."[621] A receiving facility can offer restocking to any number of the three categories and may offer different programs to the different categories. However, within each category, the program must be the same for any provider.

Second, all restocking agreements must be made public. An agreement will be considered public if, "(i) The arrangement is memorialized in a conspicuously posted writing that outlines the terms of the restocking program and copies are available publicly (a sample disclosure form is included in the regulations); or (ii) The restocking program operates in accordance with a plan or protocol of general application promulgated by an EMS council or comparable organization."[622] Confidential or proprietary information does not need to be disclosed in these writings.[623]

618. Final Rule: OIG Ambulance Replenishing Safe Harbor Under the Anti-Kickback Statute, 66 Fed. Reg. 233, 62979, 62981 (Dec. 4, 2001).

619. *Id.*

620. *Id.*

621. *Id.*

622. *Id.*

623. *Id.*

Fair market value restocking, agreements that have ambulance providers paying fair market value for restocked medical supplies (though the resale of drugs is not included, as that is covered by the Prescription Drug Marketing Act), must satisfy two conditions: "(i) The restocking must be at fair market value, and (ii) payment arrangements must be commercially reasonable and made in advance."[624]

Government-mandated restocking, agreements that are ordered by local statutes, has no additional conditions to be met other than adherence to the regulation.[625]

As with all safe harbors, failure to meet the terms of the ambulance replenishment safe harbor does not necessarily mean an arrangement would be in violation of the AKS. Instead, such arrangements must be evaluated on a case-by-case basis.[626] Further, HHS clarified that participation in restocking agreements by either party is not required. "All ambulance providers in a service area are not required to participate in order for an arrangement to fit in the safe harbor. Under the proposed rule, we did not intend to require all ambulance providers and receiving facilities in a service area actually to participate in a restocking arrangement in order for the arrangement to qualify for safe harbor protection."[627]

Two Advisory Opinions have been issued regarding this safe harbor since its enactment. The first, Advisory Opinion No. 02-2, addressed concerns about free replenishing for emergency ambulances from a receiving facility. The arrangement was deemed acceptable because of the general replenishment subsection, which allows for free or discounted rates of restocking, provided that the offer is made to all ambulance providers.[628] This opinion further solidifies the comprehensive and clear language of the statute at § 1001.952(v)(3)(i).[629] The second, Advisory Opinion No. 02-3, further clarifies the general replenishment category of arrangements. A formal region-wide policy of ambulance replenishment was implemented that satisfied the criteria of the safe harbor. All of the ambulances of the same category were offered the same arrangement, and the definition of emergency transports met the standards of the safe harbor.[630]

624. *Id.* at 62981-82.
625. *Id.* at 62982.
626. *Id.*
627. *Id.* at 62984.
628. OIG Advisory Opinion No. 02-2 (Apr. 11, 2002).
629. 42 C.F.R. § 1001.952(v)(3)(i).
630. OIG Advisory Opinion No. 02-3 (Apr. 11, 2002).

2.22. Health Centers

The safe harbor for health centers is codified at 42 C.F.R. § 1001.952(w):

(w) *Health centers.* As used in [the AKS], "remuneration" does not include the transfer of any goods, items, services, donations or loans (whether the donation or loan is in cash or in-kind), or combination thereof from an individual or entity to a health center (as defined in this paragraph), as long as the following nine standards are met -

(1)

(i) The transfer is made pursuant to a contract, lease, grant, loan, or other agreement that -

(A) Is set out in writing;

(B) Is signed by the parties; and

(C) Covers, and specifies the amount of, all goods, items, services, donations, or loans to be provided by the individual or entity to the health center.

(ii) The amount of goods, items, services, donations, or loans specified in the agreement in accordance with paragraph (w)(1)(i)(C) of this section may be a fixed sum, fixed percentage, or set forth by a fixed methodology. The amount may not be conditioned on the volume or value of Federal health care program business generated between the parties. The written agreement will be deemed to cover all goods, items, services, donations, or loans provided by the individual or entity to the health center as required by paragraph (w)(1)(i)(C) of this section if all separate agreements between the individual or entity and the health center incorporate each other by reference or if they cross-reference a master list of agreements that is maintained centrally, is kept up to date, and is available for review by the Secretary upon request. The master list should be maintained in a manner that preserves the historical record of arrangements.

(2) The goods, items, services, donations, or loans are medical or clinical in nature or relate directly to services provided by the health center as part of the scope of the health center's section 330 grant (including, by way of example, billing

services, administrative support services, technology support, and enabling services, such as case management, transportation, and translation services, that are within the scope of the grant).

(3) The health center reasonably expects the arrangement to contribute meaningfully to the health center's ability to maintain or increase the availability, or enhance the quality, of services provided to a medically underserved population served by the health center, and the health center documents the basis for the reasonable expectation prior to entering the arrangement. The documentation must be made available to the Secretary upon request.

(4) At reasonable intervals, but at least annually, the health center must re-evaluate the arrangement to ensure that the arrangement is expected to continue to satisfy the standard set forth in paragraph (w)(3) of this section, and must document the re-evaluation contemporaneously. The documentation must be made available to the Secretary upon request. Arrangements must not be renewed or renegotiated unless the health center reasonably expects the standard set forth in paragraph (w)(3) of this section to be satisfied in the next agreement term. Renewed or renegotiated agreements must comply with the requirements of paragraph (w)(3) of this section.

(5) The individual or entity does not
   (i) Require the health center (or its affiliated health care professionals) to refer patients to a particular individual or entity, or
   (ii) restrict the health center (or its affiliated health care professionals) from referring patients to any individual or entity.

(6) Individuals and entities that offer to furnish goods, items, or services without charge or at a reduced charge to the health center must furnish such goods, items, or services to all patients from the health center who clinically qualify for the goods, items, or services, regardless of the patient's payor status or ability to pay. The individual or entity may impose reasonable

limits on the aggregate volume or value of the goods, items, or services furnished under the arrangement with the health center, provided such limits do not take into account a patient's payor status or ability to pay.

(7) The agreement must not restrict the health center's ability, if it chooses, to enter into agreements with other providers or suppliers of comparable goods, items, or services, or with other lenders or donors. Where a health center has multiple individuals or entities willing to offer comparable remuneration, the health center must employ a reasonable methodology to determine which individuals or entities to select and must document its determination. In making these determinations, health centers should look to the procurement standards for beneficiaries of Federal grants set forth in 45 CFR 75.326 through 75.340.

(8) The health center must provide effective notification to patients of their freedom to choose any willing provider or supplier. In addition, the health center must disclose the existence and nature of an agreement under paragraph (w)(1) of this section to any patient who inquires. The health center must provide such notification or disclosure in a timely fashion and in a manner reasonably calculated to be effective and understood by the patient.

(9) The health center may, at its option, elect to require that an individual or entity charge a referred health center patient the same rate it charges other similarly situated patients not referred by the health center or that the individual or entity charge a referred health center patient a reduced rate (where the discount applies to the total charge and not just to the cost-sharing portion owed by an insured patient).

Note to paragraph (w):

For purposes of this paragraph, the term "health center" means a Federally Qualified Health Center under section 1905(l)(2)(B)(i) or 1905(l)(2)(B)(ii) of the Act, and "medically underserved population" means a medically underserved population as defined in regulations at 42 CFR 51c.102(e).

The OIG proposed this safe harbor in 2005[631] in compliance with section 431 of the Medicare Prescription Drug, Improvement, and Modernization Act of 2003 (MMA). As explained by the OIG in the Final Rule:

> Section 431 of MMA amended the anti-kickback statute to create a new safe harbor for certain agreements involving health centers. Specifically, section 431(a) of MMA excludes from the reach of the anti-kickback statute any remuneration between: (i) A health center described under section 1905(l)(2)(B)(i) or 1905(l)(2)(B)(ii) of the Act; and (ii) an individual or entity providing goods, items, services, donations, loans, or a combination of these to the health center pursuant to a contract, lease, grant, loan, or other agreement, provided that such agreement contributes to the health center's ability to maintain or increase the availability, or enhance the quality, of services provided to a medically underserved population served by the health center.
>
> In other words, Congress intended to permit health centers to accept certain remuneration that would otherwise implicate the anti-kickback statute when the remuneration furthers a core purpose of the Federal health centers program: ensuring the availability and quality of safety net health care services to otherwise underserved populations.[632]

The OIG further explained the history of the federal health center initiative:

> Beginning in the 1960s, Congress enacted various health center programs to assist the large number of individuals living in medically underserved areas, as well as the growing number of special populations with limited access to preventive and primary health care services. . . .
>
> . . .
>
> Health centers receiving section 330 grant funding must provide, either directly or through contracts or cooperative arrangements, a broad range of required primary health care services, including clinical services by physicians, and, where appropriate, physician assistants, nurse practitioners, and nurse midwives; diagnostic laboratory and radiological services; preventive health services; emergency medical

631. Proposed Rule: Safe Harbor for Federally Qualified Health Centers Under the Anti-Kickback Statute (70 Fed. Reg. 38081; July 1, 2005).

632. Final Rule: Safe Harbor for Federally Qualified Health Centers Arrangements Under the Anti-Kickback Statute (72 Fed. Reg. 56632, 56634; Oct. 4, 2007).

> services; certain pharmaceutical services; referrals to other providers (including substance abuse and mental health services); patient case management; services that enable individuals to use the services of the health center (*e.g.*, outreach, transportation, and translation services); and patient and community education services. 42 U.S.C. 254b(b)(1). They may also provide certain additional health services that are appropriate to serve the health needs of the population served by the health center. 42 U.S.C. 254b(b)(2). These additional health services may include mental health and substance abuse services; recuperative care services; environmental health services; special occupation-related health services for migratory and seasonal agricultural workers; programs to control infectious disease; and injury prevention programs.
>
> Consistent with their mission and the terms of their PHS grants, section 330 grant recipients serve predominantly low-income individuals, including some beneficiaries of the Medicare and Medicaid programs. . . .
>
> . . .
>
> Frequently, health centers are provided with, or seek out, opportunities to enter into arrangements with hospitals or other providers or suppliers to further the health centers' patient care mission. For example, providers or suppliers may agree to provide health centers with capital development grants, low cost (or no cost) loans, reduced price services, or in-kind donations of supplies, equipment, or space.
>
> Some providers and suppliers expressed concern that remuneration offered to health centers might be viewed as suspect under the anti-kickback statute, because the health centers are frequently in a position to refer Federal health care program beneficiaries to the provider or supplier. Accordingly, Congress enacted section 431 of MMA to enable some health centers to conserve section 330 and other monies by accepting needed goods, items, services, donations, or loans for free or at reduced rates from willing providers and suppliers.[633]

As adopted, the safe harbor regulation "protects remuneration in the form of goods, items, services, donations or loans (whether the donation or loan is in cash or in-kind), or a combination thereof provided by a Donor to a qualifying health center."[634] The remuneration "must be medical or clinical in nature or relate directly to services provided by the health center as

633. *Id.* at 56633-34.
634. *Id.* at 56635.

part of the scope of the health center's section 330 grant," and a "protected arrangement must contribute to the ability of the health center to maintain or increase the availability of, or enhance the quality of, services provided to a medically underserved population."[635] The OIG further explains:

> Protected arrangements must be pursuant to a contract, lease, grant, loan, or other agreement that is written, signed by the parties, and covers all of the remuneration to be provided. The amount of the remuneration must be specified and not be conditioned on the volume or value of Federal health care program business generated between the parties.
>
> Health centers must reasonably expect before entering into an agreement that the arrangement is likely to contribute to the health center's ability to maintain or increase the availability, or enhance the quality, of services provided to a medically underserved population as defined at 42 U.S.C. 254b(b)(3). Health centers must document the basis for their determination that the arrangement will yield such a benefit. Health centers must periodically reevaluate agreements to ensure ongoing compliance with the benefit standard. These determinations must be contemporaneously documented.
>
> Health centers must not be required to refer patients to a particular provider or supplier under the arrangement, and must be free to refer patients to any provider or supplier. In addition, Donors that offer to furnish goods, items, or services for health center patients must furnish those goods, items, or services to all health center patients who clinically qualify for them, regardless of payor status or ability to pay.
>
> Health centers are required to provide effective notification to patients of their freedom to choose any willing provider or supplier and to disclose to patients, upon request, the existence and nature of the arrangement with the Donor.
>
> The safe harbor makes clear that a health center may, at its option, require a Donor that enters into a protected arrangement to charge a referred health center patient the same rate it charges other similarly situated persons not referred by the health center or furnish items or services to health center patients at a reduced rate (where the discount applies to the total charge and not just the cost-sharing portion owed by an insured patient).[636]

---

635. *Id.*
636. *Id.*

The OIG clarified that protected remuneration under the safe harbor "would generally extend to community benefit grants or similar payments, even where such grants or payments are subject to a reconciliation provision . . . [if] the reconciliation methodology is fixed in advance and does not hinge on the volume or value of referrals from the health center to the Donor."[637] Further, "[d]onations and loans need not be limited to in-kind goods or services, and indeed may be in monetary form."[638] Donations, however, must be for the purpose of benefiting the health center to receive protection. According to the OIG, "Congress did not intend the safe harbor to protect arrangements where the donation primarily creates a benefit to the Donor instead of to the health center."[639] Likewise, the OIG stated that the safe harbor "would not protect an arrangement where a Donor used the health center as a conduit to transfer remuneration to a particular recruited physician; to transfer remuneration specifically for the purpose of recruiting a physician to join the Donor's medical staff, or to practice in the Donor's service area; or to transfer remuneration to existing group practices."[640] Nor does the safe harbor "protect remuneration transferred to an individual affiliated with a health center" or "remuneration transferred from a health center to an individual or entity."[641]

The OIG also set forth guidelines for health centers to follow when evaluating arrangements with potential donors for funds to support physician recruitment, commenting that "health centers should consider whether the remuneration would be used for expenses commonly or typically borne by the health center, such that the arrangement results in measurable savings that will benefit a medically underserved population, or would be used to recruit a health care professional needed by the health center to serve a medically underserved population, or would be used to recruit a health care professional needed by the health center to serve a medically underserved population."[642] The OIG noted that if a recruited physician joined a health center's staff, that "would be some evidence that the benefit primarily runs to medically underserved populations served by the health center as opposed to the Donor."[643]

637. *Id.* at 56637.
638. *Id.*
639. *Id.*
640. *Id.*
641. *Id.*
642. *Id.*
643. *Id.*

Regarding the transfer of goods, items, services, donations, or loans that are "medical or clinical in nature," the OIG explained that this category

> broadly covers all medical or clinical services (*e.g.*, physician services, nurse practitioner and physician assistant services, diagnostic services, therapeutic services, etc.); medical or clinical goods and items (*e.g.*, pharmaceuticals, knee braces, stethoscopes, x-ray machines, etc.); donations of money or other forms of remuneration that the health center can use to furnish medical or clinical services or to acquire goods, items, or services that are medical or clinical in nature; and loans of money or other forms of remuneration that the health center can use to furnish medical or clinical services or to acquire goods, items, or services that are medical or clinical in nature.[644]

Commenting on the safe harbor's writing requirement, the OIG clarified that the safe harbor "requires the documentation of all arrangements for the transfer of goods, items, services, donations, or loans from a Donor to a health center."[645]

As to the requirement in subparagraph (3) that the center "reasonably expects the arrangement to contribute meaningfully to the health center's ability to maintain or increase the availability, or enhance the quality, of services provided to a medically underserved population served by the health center," the OIG confirmed that the rule "does not require a financial gain to the health center and does not require direct savings of [health center] funding."[646] Satisfying this requirement will depend on the "specific facts and circumstances," but the OIG believes that "health centers are well-situated in the first instance to make a reasonable determination whether an arrangement contributes meaningfully to the health center's ability to maintain or increase the availability, or enhance the quality of, services provided to a medically underserved population," and that they "should have flexibility in making these determinations."[647] The OIG listed several "exemplar" considerations that could factor into this determination, although it made clear that it is not necessary to satisfy each one:

- Does the arrangement directly benefit a medically underserved population?
- Does the arrangement involve goods, items, or services of a type that are commonly or typically purchased by the health center, such that the

644. *Id.* at 56638.
645. *Id.*
646. *Id.* at 56639.
647. *Id.*

arrangement results in measurable savings that will benefit a medically underserved population?

- If the arrangement involves a donation to the health center, would the donation result in the increased availability of an item, good, device, service, technology, or treatment needed by a medically underserved population but not previously available in sufficient quantities due to financial limitations?
- Does the health center need the donated items, goods, or services, or the loaned funds to satisfy the scope of its section 330 grant?[648]

Regarding the requirement in (w)(3) that the health center document the basis for its reasonable expectation of benefits to a medically underserved population, the OIG indicated that it "may, as a matter of prudent business practice, develop standards that are reasonable, uniform, and consistently applied as part of the methodology [it uses] in assessing the expected benefit to a medically underserved population."[649] In this regard, the OIG noted that a "health center can document its determination of a meaningful benefit to a medically underserved population . . . by maintaining written or electronic records of the data and methodology used to assess the expected maintenance of, increase in, or enhanced quality of services to a medically underserved population and the outcome of such assessment."[650] Further, if the arrangement falls out of compliance with this requirement, "the continuation of such an arrangement would fall outside of the safe harbor and its legality under the anti-kickback statute would be determined on a case-by-case basis, based on all the facts and circumstances, including intent of the parties."[651]

The OIG clarified that nothing in the safe harbor "limits a health center's ability to contract with one supplier consistent with the procurement rules."[652] Nor does the safe harbor "prohibit the health center from entering into an exclusive arrangement with a provider or supplier when the health center so chooses, and when it can do so in compliance with relevant procurement rules."[653] As an example, the OIG stated that a health center could enter into an exclusive contract with one laboratory supplier to the

648. *Id.* at 56639.
649. *Id.*
650. *Id.*
651. *Id.* at 56640.
652. *Id.*
653. *Id.*

exclusion of other suppliers in order to accept an offer of free laboratory services for uninsured patients, "provided all other safe harbor conditions are met."[654] The OIG stressed, however, that the safe harbor was "unique to Federally Qualified Health Centers" and that "[i]n general, arrangements where a provider or supplier offers free or discounted items or services to a potential referral source that would otherwise incur out-of-pocket costs for such items or services pose a substantial risk of fraud under the anti-kickback statute."[655]

Regarding the requirement in (w)(6) that donors that are offering free or reduced charge goods or services furnish them to all patients of the health center who clinically qualify without regard for payer status or ability to pay, the OIG commented that the safe harbor "does not protect arrangements through which Donors limit their financial risk by cherry picking which health center patients will receive their goods or services based on the patient's insurance status."[656] The OIG further clarified that this requirement applies only to goods, items, or services furnished by donors, and not donations or loans.[657]

Regarding the patient notification requirement in (w)(8), the OIG clarified that "health centers can satisfy the notification requirement through broad disclosures" such as "directing patients to a written disclosure notice posted in a conspicuous place in the health center . . . provided that the written notice is reasonably calculated to provide effective notice and to be understood by the parties."[658] Broad disclosures, however, "are not required."[659]

The provision set forth in (w)(9), which affords health centers the option of requiring that donors charge a referred health center patient either a reduced rate or the same rate charged other similarly situated patients, was intended to "allow health centers to protect their patients from price gouging" by "being charged prices higher than they would be charged in the absence of the health center's participation in the safe harbored arrangement."[660] The OIG indicated its concern that, without such an option, donors "might otherwise seek to recoup part of the cost of remuneration offered to a health center by charging health center patients inflated

654. *Id.*
655. *Id.* at 56640-41.
656. *Id.* at 56641.
657. *Id.*
658. *Id.* at 56642.
659. *Id.*
660. *Id.*

rates."[661] The OIG further confirmed that the safe harbor would not keep health centers "from offering health center patients waivers or reductions of cost sharing obligations, as permitted in the safe harbor for waiver of beneficiary coinsurance and deductible amounts [1001.952(k)]" or reducing patient cost sharing amounts "based on individualized good faith assessments of financial need."[662]

This safe harbor was the subject of Advisory Opinion No. 08-01.[663] That opinion addressed the program of a nonprofit corporation that arranged for pharmaceutical manufacturer patient assistance programs (PAPs) to provide donated drugs to free clinics and FQHCs for use by needy patients without outpatient prescription drug coverage. The program was not open to Medicare or Medicaid patients; therefore, donated pharmaceuticals could not be dispensed to such patients. The OIG analyzed the arrangement under § 1001.952(w), concluding that the safe harbor was "potentially applicable" to the portion of the arrangement involving FQHCs. The OIG concluded, however, that the arrangement, while sharing "many features of the safe harbor," did not "fit squarely for several reasons," including that the arrangement does not require the FQHC "to make the requisite determinations regarding benefit to underserved populations" and "the free drugs offered by [donors] are not offered to all FQHC patients regardless of payer status."[664]

Notwithstanding these failings, however, the OIG elected not to impose sanctions. Although the OIG recognized that the arrangement could be a vehicle through which a pharmaceutical donor offers or pays remuneration to "induce FQHCs to purchase or order" donor products reimbursable by a federal health care program or to "influence the prescribing patterns of the FQHC physicians with respect to" such products, the OIG concluded that certain other characteristics of the arrangement mitigated this risk. Specifically, the OIG first noted that "the FQHCs receive no compensation from any [donor] for dispensing or administrative services under the Arrangement, and the FQHCs are not permitted to bill any insurer or patient for the [donor] drugs," making any remuneration to the FQHC indirect, such as

661. *Id.*

662. *Id.*

663. Advisory Opinion No. 08-01 (Issued Feb. 1, 2008). The safe harbor also was referenced in United States v. IASIS Healthcare LLC, 2016 WL 6610675 at *7 (D. Ariz. Nov. 9, 2016) (under safe harbor, "FQHCs may receive payments pursuant to written contracts designated for administrative and case management services").

664. *Id.* at p. 4.

"through the offsetting of drug costs otherwise borne by the FQHC."[665] The OIG further commented that the arrangement did not warrant the imposition of sanctions for the following additional reasons:

- The structure of the arrangement mitigated the risk that the FQHCs "might obtain excess stocks of drugs" by limiting drug supplies to the provision of outpatient prescription drugs that are shipped monthly "based on amounts dispensed to eligible patients during the previous month or based on projected usage (with subsequent reconciliation)."[666]
- The arrangement was transparent and documented in a signed agreement covering all the free drugs to be provided, the drugs were shipped to each FQHC "pursuant to a fixed methodology that is unrelated to the volume or value of referrals of Federal business generated by the FQHC for the [donor]," and the FQHCs were required to segregate inventory and maintain detailed records that create an audit trail for the distribution of PAP drugs to eligible patients.[667]
- The donors do not control the selection of FQHCs which participate in the arrangement, and pharmaceutical donors that participate in the arrangement must provide drugs "uniformly to all participating affiliated FQHCs." As a result, the arrangement "prevents [donors] from cherry-picking certain FQHCs to receive donated drugs." The nonprofit certified that "the availability of drugs . . . is not conditioned on the volume or value of Federal health care program business generated by an FQHC or on the inclusion of other non-[patient assistance program] products of the [donors] on the FQHC's formulary."[668]
- The physicians prescribing drugs for FQHC patients "do not receive any compensation that takes into account in any manner the physicians' prescribing patterns for [donor] products and the FQHCs do not track any physician's prescribing patterns." Physicians are encouraged to choose PAP drugs for eligible patients to minimize financial hardship, but only when the drug would be clinically appropriate. The nonprofit certified that the affiliated FQHCs would adopt a policy ensuring that physicians "are made aware of these protections by written

665. *Id.* at p. 6.
666. *Id.*
667. *Id.*
668. *Id.*

notice provided annually" in order to protect physician independent professional judgment.[669]

- The nonprofit insulates the FQHCs from the donors by not permitting "any of its staff or the staff of any participating [donors] to be involved in the formulary decision-making process of any affiliated FQHC," the participating FQHCs adopted conflict of interest policies "[prohibiting] employees involved in the formulary decision-making process from accepting employment with, or remuneration from, any participating [donor]," and the nonprofit "does not permit sales or marketing representatives of any participating [donor] to communicate with affiliated FQHCs, or their physicians, with respect to the Arrangement."[670]
- The ultimate recipients of the drugs are limited to "financially-needy patients who lack outpatient prescription drug coverage," "the PAP drugs are targeted at precisely the type of vulnerable, financially-needy patients the FQHCs are commissioned to serve," and so the arrangement did "not involve the kind of cherry-picking of patients on the basis of payer status or ability to pay that raises concerns in other contexts."[671]
- The nonprofit certified that there were no other undeclared arrangements or understandings among the parties that might result in FQHC physicians prescribing donor products to insured patients or FQHCs agreeing to place donor products on their formularies.[672]
- The arrangement related "directly to the core clinical services provided by the FQHCs and helps ensure the availability of safety net health services for otherwise underserved populations."[673]

2.23. Electronic Prescribing Items and Services

The safe harbor provision for electronic prescribing items and services is codified at 42 C.F.R. § 1001.952(x), including a supplemental definition paragraph:

> (x) *Electronic prescribing items and services.* As used in section 1128B of the Act, "remuneration" does not include nonmonetary remuneration (consisting of items and services in the form of hardware, software, or information technology and training services)

669. *Id.* at p. 7.
670. *Id.*
671. *Id.*
672. *Id.*
673. *Id.*

necessary and used solely to receive and transmit electronic prescription information, if all of the following conditions are met:

(1) The items and services are provided by a -
   (i) Hospital to a physician who is a member of its medical staff;
   (ii) Group practice to a prescribing health care professional who is a member of the group practice; and
   (iii) A PDP sponsor or MA organization to pharmacists and pharmacies participating in the network of such sponsor or organization and to prescribing health care professionals.
(2) The items and services are provided as part of, or are used to access, an electronic prescription drug program that meets the applicable standards under Medicare Part D at the time the items and services are provided.
(3) The donor (or any person on the donor's behalf) does not take any action to limit or restrict the use or compatibility of the items or services with other electronic prescribing or electronic health records systems.
(4) For items or services that are of the type that can be used for any patient without regard to payor status, the donor does not restrict, or take any action to limit, the recipient's right or ability to use the items or services for any patient.
(5) Neither the beneficiary nor the recipient's practice (or any affiliated individual or entity) makes the receipt of items or services, or the amount or nature of the items or services, a condition of doing business with the donor.
(6) Neither the eligibility of a beneficiary for the items or services, nor the amount or nature of the items or services, is determined in a manner that takes into account the volume or value of referrals or other business generated between the parties.
(7) The arrangement is set forth in a written agreement that -
   (i) Is signed by the parties;
   (ii) Specifies the items and services being provided and the donor's cost of the items and services; and
   (iii) Covers all of the electronic prescribing items and services to be provided by the donor (or affiliated parties). This requirement will be met if all separate agreements

between the donor (and affiliated parties) and the beneficiary incorporate each other by reference or if they cross-reference a master list of agreements that is maintained and updated centrally and is available for review by the Secretary upon request. The master list should be maintained in a manner that preserves the historical record of agreements.

(8) The donor does not have actual knowledge of, and does not act in reckless disregard or deliberate ignorance of, the fact that the beneficiary possesses or has obtained items or services equivalent to those provided by the donor.

Note to paragraph (x):
For purposes of paragraph (x) of this section, *group practice* shall have the meaning set forth at 42 CFR 411.352; *member of the group practice* shall mean all persons covered by the definition of "member of the group or member of a group practice" at 42 CFR 411.351, as well as other prescribing health care professionals who are owners or employees of the group practice; *prescribing health care professional* shall mean a physician or other health care professional licensed to prescribe drugs in the State in which the drugs are dispensed; *PDP sponsor or MA organization* shall have the meanings set forth at 42 CFR 423.4 and 422.2, respectively; *prescription information* shall mean information about prescriptions for drugs or for any other item or service normally accomplished through a written prescription; and *electronic health record* shall mean a repository of consumer health status information in computer processable form used for clinical diagnosis and treatment for a broad array of clinical conditions.

This safe harbor was finalized simultaneously with the Electronic Health Records safe harbor, 42 C.F.R. § 1001.952(y), with the intention of expanding the use and modernization of technology in the health care field. These safe harbors were passed following the adoption of the MMA of 2003. Following this new drug benefit, Congress required that HHS establish standards for electronic prescriptions in an effort to improve the efficiency and effectiveness of patient care. This direction came with the assumption of donations of electronic prescription-capable technology to hospitals and other health care groups, which would create the potential for AKS violations. Therefore, a safe harbor was added to protect the growth of technology in the medical field that had to be in compliance with the new law.[674]

The rule that was initially proposed in 2005 was significantly more restrictive than the final rule. The scope of the safe harbor and the latitude afforded to the donor and donee were expanded with the passage of the final rule in 2006.[675] The limit on the value of donated goods was removed along with the required written statement ensuring that donated technology was not equivalent to technology already possessed by the recipient, or was instead a significant upgrade over said possessed technology.[676]

The proposed written certification was originally included to make the donation process as transparent as possible, in an effort to reduce the potential for abuse. However, this was omitted from the final rule because it was "unnecessarily burdensome" for the recipient.[677] It is difficult to distinguish between "significant" improvements as opposed to other beneficial improvements, and the difficult distinction made the certification overly complex.[678] The potential abuse of this system is severely mitigated by the burden shifting to the donor not to "have actual knowledge of, and . . . [not to] act in reckless disregard or deliberate ignorance of, the fact that the beneficiary possesses or has obtained items or services equivalent to those provided by the donor."[679] It is further mitigated by the use of the term "necessary," further defined later in this section.[680]

The OIG expressed concern over the lack of a hard limit for value of donated goods, stating, "in our experience, the risk of fraud and abuse generally (although not always) increases with the value of the remuneration

674. Final Rule: Medicare and State Health Care Programs: Fraud and Abuse; Safe Harbors for Certain Electronic Prescribing and Electronic Health Records Arrangements Under the Anti-Kickback Statute, 71 Fed. Reg. 45110, 45110 (Aug. 8, 2006).

675. Proposed Rule: Medicare and State Health Care Programs: Fraud and Abuse; Safe Harbor for Certain Electronic Prescribing Arrangements Under the Anti-Kickback Statute, 70 Fed. Reg. 59015, 59015 (Oct. 11, 2005).

676. Final Rule: Medicare and State Health Care Programs: Fraud and Abuse; Safe Harbors for Certain Electronic Prescribing and Electronic Health Records Arrangements Under the Anti-Kickback Statute, 71 Fed. Reg. 45110, 45115 (Aug. 8, 2006).

677. *Id.* at 45123.

678. *Id.* at 45116.

679. 42 C.F.R.§ 1001.952(x)(8).

680. Final Rule: Medicare and State Health Care Programs: Fraud and Abuse; Safe Harbors for Certain Electronic Prescribing and Electronic Health Records Arrangements Under the Anti-Kickback Statute, 71 Fed. Reg. 45110, 45123 (Aug. 8, 2006).

offered."[681] Despite this, the OIG agreed that the fair market value of certain goods would be difficult to ascertain, particularly in the rapidly developing field of technology. In an effort to stay within the spirit of the law and to not stunt the growth of technology in the health care field, the limit was removed, with the provision that "necessary and used solely" should be sufficient to prevent abuse. "Under the final safe harbor, any upgrade that is necessary and used solely to transmit and receive electronic prescribing information will be protected."[682]

The final rule allows for the donation of electronic prescribing technology including, but not limited to, hardware, software, and information technology and/or training services that are necessary and solely used for receiving and sending electronic prescription information.[683] The OIG declined to be more specific in its terminology for this rule. "While a specific list would provide a 'bright line' rule, in this case it would also impede the ability of the safe harbor to accommodate novel or rapidly evolving technologies in the marketplace. For these reasons, we are not promulgating a specific list of protected items and services."[684] The terms "necessary" and "used solely" were more narrowly defined by the OIG. "We believe . . . that Congress intended for all donated technology to be necessary for the receipt and transmission of electronic prescription information and to be used solely for that purpose."[685] This definition removes devices that can be used for prescription purposes but also serve other uses from the acceptable list of donations. The OIG stated that this was done intentionally so as to reduce the risk of abuse by donors. Further, the electronic prescription technology must meet the applicable standards under Medicare Part D.[686]

This safe harbor covers four donor-recipient relationships: "hospital to its medical staff; . . . medical group practice to its members; . . . a [prescription drug plan] sponsor or [Medicare Advantage] organization to prescribing health care professionals, as well as to pharmacies and pharmacists in

681. *Id.* at 45118.

682. *Id.* at 45116.

683. 42 C.F.R.§ 1001.952(x).

684. Final Rule: Medicare and State Health Care Programs: Fraud and Abuse; Safe Harbors for Certain Electronic Prescribing and Electronic Health Records Arrangements Under the Anti-Kickback Statute, 71 Fed. Reg. 45110, 45116 (Aug. 8, 2006).

685. *Id.* at 45115.

686. 42 C.F.R. § 1001.952(x)(2).

the plan's network."[687] Having this relationship does not necessarily confer safe harbor protection unless all of the remaining requirements are satisfied. The goal of this safe harbor was to promote technological use and development in health care, which led to the broad scope of protected donors. The intention was to "protect any donor that is an individual or entity that provides patients with health care items or services covered by a Federal health care program and submits claims or requests for payment for those items or services (directly or pursuant to reassignment) to Medicare, Medicaid, or other Federal health care programs."[688] The OIG still held reservations about the potential for abuse, particularly with respect to "laboratories, durable medical equipment suppliers, and others."[689] It was clarified that these protected donors will be under particular scrutiny for abuse, and the OIG may revisit the issue should the need arise, though no revisions have been made since the safe harbor's enactment.[690] This is a "bright-line" rule, intended to directly clarify who the protected donors are, while simultaneously achieving the goal of the safe harbor.

The donor is not allowed to attach restrictions to the donation it provides. The donor may not donate in a manner that takes into account the volume or value of referrals generated between the two parties, nor can the donor take action to limit the use of the electronic prescribing technology. Likewise, the recipient is not allowed to condition doing business with the donor based on the receipt of electronic prescribing technology.[691] These restrictions are made clear by the OIG:

> The safe harbor would not protect arrangements that seek to induce a recipient to change loyalties from other providers or plans to the donor (e.g., a hospital using an electronic prescribing technology arrangement to induce a physician who is on the medical staff of another hospital to join the donor hospital's medical staff), because such arrangements take into account business generated for the donor.[692]

---

687. Final Rule: Medicare and State Health Care Programs: Fraud and Abuse; Safe Harbors for Certain Electronic Prescribing and Electronic Health Records Arrangements Under the Anti-Kickback Statute, 71 Fed. Reg. 45110, 45114 (Aug. 8, 2003).

688. *Id.* at 45127.

689. *Id.* at 45128.

690. *Id.*

691. 42 C.F.R. §§ 1001.952(x)(4), (5), (6).

692. Final Rule: Medicare and State Health Care Programs: Fraud and Abuse; Safe Harbors for Certain Electronic Prescribing and Electronic Health Records Arrangements Under the Anti-Kickback Statute, 71 Fed. Reg. 45110, 45118 (Aug. 8, 2003).

2.24. Electronic Health Records

The safe harbor for electronic health records (EHR), modified by 85 FR 77684, is codified at 42 C.F.R. § 1001.952(y):

(y) *Electronic health records items and services.* As used in section 1128B of the Act, "remuneration" does not include nonmonetary remuneration (consisting of items and services in the form of software or information technology and training services, including cybersecurity software and services) necessary and used predominantly to create, maintain, transmit, receive, or protect electronic health records, if all of the conditions in paragraphs (y)(1) through (13) of this section are met:

(1) The items and services are provided to an individual or entity engaged in the delivery of health care by:

(i) An individual or entity, other than a laboratory company, that:

(A) Provides services covered by a Federal health care program and submits claims or requests for payment, either directly or through reassignment, to the Federal health care program; or

(B) Is comprised of the types of individuals or entities in paragraph (y)(1)(i)(A) of this section; or

(ii) A health plan.

(2) The software is interoperable at the time it is provided to the recipient. For purposes of this paragraph (y)(2) of this section, software is deemed to be interoperable if, on the date it is provided to the recipient, it is certified by a certifying body authorized by the National Coordinator for Health Information Technology to certification criteria identified in the then-applicable version of 45 CFR part 170.

(3) [Reserved by 85 FR 77887]

(4) Neither the recipient nor the recipient's practice (or any affiliated individual or entity) makes the receipt of items or services, or the amount or nature of the items or services, a condition of doing business with the donor.

(5) Neither the eligibility of a recipient for the items or services, nor the amount or nature of the items or services, is determined in a manner that directly takes into account

the volume or value of referrals or other business generated between the parties. For the purposes of this paragraph (y)(5), the determination is deemed not to directly take into account the volume or value of referrals or other business generated between the parties if any one of the following conditions is met:

(i) The determination is based on the total number of prescriptions written by the beneficiary (but not the volume or value of prescriptions dispensed or paid by the donor or billed to a Federal health care program);

(ii) The determination is based on the size of the recipient's medical practice (for example, total patients, total patient encounters, or total relative value units);

(iii) The determination is based on the total number of hours that the recipient practices medicine;

(iv) The determination is based on the recipient's overall use of automated technology in his or her medical practice (without specific reference to the use of technology in connection with referrals made to the donor);

(v) The determination is based on whether the recipient is a member of the donor's medical staff, if the donor has a formal medical staff;

(vi) The determination is based on the level of uncompensated care provided by the recipient; or

(vii) The determination is made in any reasonable and verifiable manner that does not directly take into account the volume or value of referrals or other business generated between the parties.

(6) The arrangement is set forth in a written agreement that

(i) Is signed by the parties;

(ii) Specifies the items and services being provided, the donor's cost of those items and services, and the amount of the recipient's contribution; and

(iii) Covers all of the electronic health records items and services to be provided by the donor (or any affiliate). This requirement will be met if all separate agreements between the donor (and affiliated parties) and the beneficiary incorporate each other by reference or if they cross-reference a master list of agreements that is maintained and updated centrally and is available for review by the Secretary upon request. The master list should be maintained in a manner that preserves the historical record of agreements.

(7) [Reserved by 85 FR 77887]

(8) For items or services that are of the type that can be used for any patient without regard to payor status, the donor does not restrict, or take any action to limit, the recipient's right or ability to use the items or services for any patient.

(9) The items and services do not include staffing of the recipient's office and are not used primarily to conduct personal business or business unrelated to the recipient's clinical practice or clinical operations.

(10) [Reserved by 78 FR 79219]

(11) The recipient pays 15 percent of the donor's cost for the items and services. The following conditions apply to such contribution:

(i) If the donation is the initial donation of EHR items and services, or the replacement of part or all of an existing system of EHR items and services, the recipient must pay 15 percent of the donor's cost before receiving the items and services. The contribution for updates to previously donated EHR items and services need not be paid in advance of receiving the update; and

(ii) The donor (or any affiliated individual or entity) does not finance the recipient's payment or loan funds to be used by the recipient to pay for the items and services.

(12) The donor does not shift the costs of the items or services to any Federal health care program.

(13) [Reserved by 85 FR 77887]

(14) For purposes of this paragraph (y), the following definitions apply:

(i) Cybersecurity means the process of protecting information by preventing, detecting, and responding to cyberattacks.

(ii) Health plan shall have the meaning set forth at § 1001.952(l)(2).

(iii) Interoperable shall mean able to:
  (A) Securely exchange data with and use data from other health information technology; and
  (B) Allow for complete access, exchange, and use of all electronically accessible health information for authorized use under applicable state or federal law.
(iv) Electronic health record shall mean a repository of consumer health status information in computer processable form used for clinical diagnosis and treatment for a broad array of clinical conditions.

The EHR safe harbor modifications, effective January 19, 2021, removed the prior sunset provision, updated and removed certain interoperability requirements, removed the prohibition on donation of equivalent technology, and clarified that certain cybersecurity technology and services are protected under the EHR safe harbor.[693]

The prior version of the EHR safe harbor contained a sunset provision that limited the applicability of the safe harbor to only the transfer of items and services and satisfaction of all conditions of the EHR safe harbor on or before December 31, 2021. In response to the nearly universal support to remove the sunset provision, OIG eliminated such provision, rather than extending it, so that donors and recipients may have certainty regarding the ongoing protection of donations of EHR items and services.[694]

In its recent final rule, OIG made numerous modifications and additions to incorporate protections addressing cybersecurity. In addition to the inclusion of a new cybersecurity safe harbor codified at 1001.952(jj), OIG has added an explicit reference to cybersecurity software and services in the EHR safe harbor and clarifies that cybersecurity software and services were always covered under the EHR safe harbor, so long as the donation met all applicable conditions. In addition to the newly included reference to cybersecurity software and services, OIG has explicitly added safe harbor protection for those software or information technology and training services used predominantly to "protect" EHRs. OIG has noted the overlap between the EHR safe harbor modifications and the new cybersecurity safe harbor

693. Final Rule: Medicare and State Health Care Programs: Fraud and Abuse; Revisions to Safe Harbors Under the Anti-Kickback Statute, and Civil Monetary Penalty Rules Regarding Beneficiary Inducements 85 Fed. Reg. 77684, 77686 (Dec. 2, 2020).

694. *Id.* at 77832.

codified at 1001.952(jj),[695] stating that "[r]egardless of this acknowledged overlap, it is useful to clarify in the EHR safe harbor that cybersecurity software and services with the predominant purpose of protecting electronic health records can be protected under the EHR safe harbor provided the donation satisfies all other safe harbor conditions."[696] In the EHR safe harbor, OIG has included the definition of "cybersecurity," which mirrors the definition found in the cybersecurity safe harbor.

OIG revised the EHR safe harbor to provide one clear example of acceptable interoperable software. Software is "deemed to be interoperable if, on the date it is provided to the recipient, it is certified by a certifying body authorized by the National Coordinator for Health Information Technology to certification criteria identified in the then-applicable version of 45 CFR part 170."[697] The reference to certification by an applicable certifying body is only one way in which donors and recipients can ensure the technologies are "interoperable" as contemplated under the EHR safe harbor. OIG asserts that the interoperability requirement can be satisfied by technologies not certified by an authorized certifying body, so long as the technologies meet the definition of interoperability at the time it is provided to the recipient.[698] The definition of "interoperable" was also updated to more closely align with the definition contained in the 21st Century Cures Act (Cures Act), but OIG purposefully chose to not directly incorporate reference to the definition of "interoperable" in the Cures Act so as to not inadvertently include a condition that prohibits a donor from restricting the use, compatibility, or interoperability of the EHR items and services with other electronic prescribing or EHR systems.[699]

OIG has deleted paragraph 1001.952(y)(3), which prohibited the donor or any person on the donor's behalf from taking any action to limit or restrict the use, compatibility, or interoperability of the donated EHR items or services. OIG notes that "there are now other enforcement authorities designed to address information blocking."[700] For example, the Cures Act provides

695. *See* discussion *supra* 2.33 Cybersecurity.

696. Final Rule: Medicare and State Health Care Programs: Fraud and Abuse; Revisions to Safe Harbors Under the Anti-Kickback Statute, and Civil Monetary Penalty Rules Regarding Beneficiary Inducements 85 Fed. Reg. 77684, 77830 (Dec. 2, 2020).

697. 42 CFR § 1001.952(y)(2).

698. Final Rule: Medicare and State Health Care Programs: Fraud and Abuse; Revisions to Safe Harbors Under the Anti-Kickback Statute, and Civil Monetary Penalty Rules Regarding Beneficiary Inducements 85 Fed. Reg. 77684, 77831 (Dec. 2, 2020).

699. *Id.* at 77838.

700. *Id.* at 77832.

the Office of the National Coordinator for Health Information Technology (ONC) and OIG with direct authority to investigate and address claims of information blocking.[701]

OIG also added new paragraphs at §1001.952(y)(11)(i) and (ii). OIG has clarified that the recipient of EHR items and services must pay 15 percent of the donor's costs prior to receiving an initial donation and prior to replacement of part or all of an existing system of EHR items and services, yet advance payment of the recipient's contribution is *not required* to receive updates to previously donated EHR items and services.[702] OIG acknowledged that "updates may need to take place quickly to remedy security or other problems in an EHR system" and they "believe it is reasonable and does not create additional risk to bill a recipient for its contribution after providing the update."[703] Recipient contribution is required but it need not delay updates to previously donated EHR items and services.

The EHR safe harbor no longer includes a provision that requires that the donor not have actual knowledge of, and not act in reckless disregard or deliberate ignorance of, the fact that a recipient already possessed or had obtained items or services equivalent to those provided by the donor. OIG recognized that "there may be valid business or clinical reasons for a recipient to replace an entire system rather than update existing technology. Under this safe harbor, it should be noted that replacement technology is treated the same as a new donation and would need to meet all conditions of the safe harbor to receive protection."[704]

OIG has expanded the types of donors that can take advantage of the EHR safe harbor so that not only those individuals that provide federal health care program covered services, submit claims to, or request payment from (either directly or through reassignment) a federal health care program benefit from the safe harbor. With the recent changes, an individual or entity (other than a laboratory company) that is comprised of the types of individuals or entities that provide services covered by, submit claims to, or request payment from a federal health care program can seek protection under the EHR safe harbor so long as they meet the other applicable conditions. This expansion allows entities such as health systems, accountable care organizations (ACOs), and clinically integrated entities to make use of

701. *Id.*
702. *Id.* at 77834.
703. *Id.*
704. *Id.* at 77835.

the EHR safe harbor.[705] OIG continues to raise fraud and abuse concerns regarding EHR donations made by laboratories and manufacturers or suppliers of items, and as such, these donations are not protected under the EHR safe harbor.[706]

2.25. Federally Qualified Health Centers and Medicare Advantage Organizations

The regulatory safe harbor for FQHCs and Medicare Advantage Organizations is codified at 42 C.F.R. § 1001.952(z), which states:

> (z) *Federally Qualified Health Centers and Medicare Advantage Organizations*. As used in [the AKS], "remuneration" does not include any remuneration between a federally qualified health center (or an entity controlled by such a health center) and a Medicare Advantage organization pursuant to a written agreement described in section 1853(a)(4) of [the Social Security Act].

Section 1853(a)(4) of the Social Security Act[707] states that when a patient is enrolled in a Medicare Advantage plan and receives services from an FQHC that has a written agreement in place with the Medicare Advantage Organization, HHS will pay the amounts owed for such services directly to the FQHC on at least a quarterly basis.

This is a relatively new safe harbor that was enacted in December 2016 and became effective in January 2017. When enacting the safe harbor, HHS explained that the level and amount of payment made to the FQHC for patient services must be "not less than the level and amount of payment that the [Medicare Advantage Organization] would make for such services if the services had been furnished by an entity other than an FQHC."[708] HHS further clarified that this requirement sets a minimum, but not a maximum, with respect to the payments received by an FQHC.[709] Medicare Advantage Organizations and FQHCs can sign agreements that specify various payment levels and amounts, so long as they meet this minimum threshold. HHS also noted that this safe harbor

705. *Id.* at 77836.

706. *Id.*

707. Codified at 42 U.S.C. § 1395w-23(a)(4).

708. Final Rule: Revisions to the Safe Harbors Under the Anti-Kickback Statute and Civil Monetary Penalty Rules, 81 Fed. Reg. 88368, 88377 (Dec. 7, 2016).

709. *Id.*

does not include a fair market value requirement, unlike many other safe harbors under the AKS.[710]

Moreover, this safe harbor applies only to payments received by an FQHC for services rendered to patients enrolled in a Medicare Advantage plan. Other types of arrangements between an FQHC and a Medicare Advantage Organization, such as leasing of office space or provision of administrative services, would have to be analyzed independently and may need to rely on other safe harbors for protection under the AKS.[711]

2.26. Medicare Coverage Gap Discount Program

The safe harbor for Medicare coverage gap discount program is codified at 42 C.F.R. § 1001.952(aa):

> (aa) *Medicare Coverage Gap Discount Program.* As used in [the AKS], "remuneration" does not include a discount in the price of a drug when the discount is furnished to a beneficiary under the Medicare Coverage Gap Discount Program established in section 1860D-14A of the Act, as long as all the following requirements are met:
> (1) The discounted drug meets the definition of "applicable drug" set forth in section 1860D-14A(g) of the Act;
> (2) The beneficiary receiving the discount meets the definition of "applicable beneficiary" set forth in section 1860D-14A(g) of the Act; and
> (3) The manufacturer of the drug participates in, and is in compliance with the requirements of, the Medicare Coverage Gap Discount Program.

Under the Medicare Coverage Gap Discount Program (MCGDP), "prescription drug manufacturers enter into an agreement with the Secretary to provide certain beneficiaries access to discounts on drugs at the point of sale."[712] The Patient Protection and Affordable Care Act (PPACA) amended the AKS by adding a provision "to protect the discounts provided for under the [MCGDP]" and this safe harbor was proposed to "codify this

---

710. *Id.*

711. *Id.* For example, if an FQHC leased office space from the Medicare Advantage Organization, such an arrangement would fall under the space rental safe harbor.

712. Proposed Rule: Medicare and State Health Care Programs: Fraud and Abuse; Revisions to Safe Harbors Under the Anti-Kickback Statute, and Civil Monetary Penalty Rules Regarding Beneficiary Inducements and Gainsharing (79 Fed. Reg. 59717, 59721; Oct. 3, 2014).

self-implementing exception" in the law.[713] The safe harbor is designed "to protect a discount in the price of an 'applicable drug' of a manufacturer that is furnished to an 'applicable beneficiary' under the [MCGDP]."[714] The safe harbor incorporates by reference the definitions of "applicable beneficiary" and "applicable drug" MCGDP statute.[715]

In adopting the final rule, the OIG clarified that "minor administrative or technical non-compliance [with the requirements of the MCGDP] should not preclude safe harbor protection."[716] However, the OIG also stated that "[w]hile we do not contemplate that missing a payment deadline by one day would subject a manufacturer to sanctions under the anti-kickback statute, the safe harbor only protects discounts offered in connection with this program" and that "[a] manufacturer that knowingly and willfully provided discounts without complying with the requirements of the [MCGDP] could be subject to sanctions, unless such discounts are protected by another safe harbor."[717]

---

713. *Id.*

714. Final Rule: Medicare and State Health Care Programs: Fraud and Abuse; Revisions to the Safe Harbors Under the Anti-Kickback Statute and Civil Monetary Penalty Rules Regarding Beneficiary Inducements (81 Fed. Reg. 88368, 88378; Dec. 7, 2016).

715. (1) Applicable beneficiary.—The term "applicable beneficiary" means an individual who, on the date of dispensing an applicable druga covered part D drug—

(A) is enrolled in a prescription drug plan or an MA–PD plan;

(B) is not enrolled in a qualified retiree prescription drug plan;

(C) is not entitled to an income-related subsidy under section 1860D–14(a);

(D) who—

(i) has reached or exceeded the initial coverage limit under section 1860D–2(b) (3) during the year; and

(ii) has not incurred costs for covered part D drugs in the year equal to the annual out-of-pocket threshold specified in section 1860D–2(b)(4)(B).

(2) Applicable drug.—The term "applicable drug" means, with respect to an applicable beneficiary, a covered part D drug—

(A) approved under a new drug application under section 505(b) of the Federal Food, Drug, and Cosmetic Act or, in the case of a biologic product, licensed under section 351 of the Public Health Service Act (other than a product licensed under subsection (k) of such section 351); and

(B) (i) if the PDP sponsor of the prescription drug plan or the MA organization offering the MA–PD plan uses a formulary, which is on the formulary of the prescription drug plan or MA–PD plan that the applicable beneficiary is enrolled in;

(ii) if the PDP sponsor of the prescription drug plan or the MA organization offering the MA–PD plan does not use a formulary, for which benefits are available under the prescription drug plan or MA–PD plan that the applicable beneficiary is enrolled in; or

(iii) is provided through an exception or appeal.

716. *Id.*

717. *Id.*

2.27. Local Transportation

The safe harbor for local transportation, modified by 85 FR 77684, is codified at 42 C.F.R. § 1001.952(bb):

(bb) *Local Transportation.* As used in section 1128B of the Act, "remuneration" does not include free or discounted local transportation made available by an eligible entity (as defined in this paragraph (bb)):

(1) To Federal health care program beneficiaries if all the following conditions are met:

(i) The availability of the free or discounted local transportation services

(A) Is set forth in a policy, which the eligible entity applies uniformly and consistently; and

(B) Is not determined in a manner related to the past or anticipated volume or value of Federal health care program business;

(ii) The free or discounted local transportation services are not air, luxury, or ambulance-level transportation;

(iii) The eligible entity does not publicly market or advertise the free or discounted local transportation services, no marketing of health care items and services occurs during the course of the transportation or at any time by drivers who provide the transportation, and drivers or others arranging for the transportation are not paid on a per-beneficiary-transported basis;

(iv) The eligible entity makes the free or discounted transportation available only:

(A) To an individual who is:

(1) An established patient (as defined in this paragraph (bb)) of the eligible entity that is providing the free or discounted transportation, if the eligible entity is a provider or supplier of health care services; and

(2) An established patient of the provider or supplier to or from which the individual is being transported;

(B) Within 25 miles of the health care provider or supplier to or from which the patient would be transported, or within 75 miles if the patient resides in a rural area, as defined in this paragraph (bb) except that, if the patient is discharged from an inpatient facility following inpatient admission or released from a hospital after being placed in observation status for at least 24 hours and transported to the patient's residence, or another residence of the patient's choice, the mileage limits in this paragraph (bb)(1)(iv)(B) shall not apply; and

(C) For the purpose of obtaining medically necessary items and services.

(v) The eligible entity that makes the transportation available bears the costs of the free or discounted local transportation services and does not shift the burden of these costs onto any Federal health care program, other payers, or individuals; and

(2) In the form of a "shuttle service" (as defined in this paragraph (bb)) if all of the following conditions are met:

(i) The shuttle service is not air, luxury, or ambulance-level transportation;

(ii) The shuttle service is not marketed or advertised (other than posting necessary route and schedule details), no marketing of health care items and services occurs during the course of the transportation or at any time by drivers who provide the transportation, and drivers or others arranging for the transportation are not paid on a per-beneficiary-transported basis;

(iii) The eligible entity makes the shuttle service available only within the eligible entity's local area, meaning there are no more than 25 miles from any stop on the route to any stop at a location where health care items or services are provided, except that if a stop on the route is in a rural area, the distance may be up to 75 miles between that stop and any providers or suppliers on the route;

(iv) The eligible entity that makes the shuttle service available bears the costs of the free or discounted shuttle services and does not shift the burden of these costs onto any Federal health care program, other payers, or individuals.

(3) For purposes of this paragraph (bb), the following definitions apply:
   (i) An eligible entity is any individual or entity, except for individuals or entities (or family members or others acting on their behalf) that primarily supply health care items.
   (ii) An established patient is a person who has selected and initiated contact to schedule an appointment with a provider or supplier, or who previously has attended an appointment with the provider or supplier.
   (iii) A shuttle service is a vehicle that runs on a set route, on a set schedule.
   (iv) A rural area is an area that is not an urban area, as defined in paragraph (bb)(3)(v) of this section.
   (v) An urban area is:
      (A) A metropolitan statistical area (MSA) or New England County Metropolitan Area (NECMA), as defined by the Executive Office of Management and Budget; or
      (B) The following New England counties, which are deemed to be parts of urban areas under section 601(g) of the Social Security Amendments of 1983 (Pub. L. 98–21, 42 U.S.C. 1395ww (note)): Litchfield County, Connecticut; York County, Maine; Sagadahoc County, Maine; Merrimack County, New Hampshire; and Newport County, Rhode Island.

Modifications to the local transportation safe harbor went into effect January 19, 2021.

The new rule expanded rural area mileage limits eligible for safe harbor protection and removed mileage limits for transportation of patients to their residence after an inpatient stay. OIG clarified that the safe harbor is available for transportation provided through rideshare arrangements. The modified transportation safe harbor still does not extend protection to transportation for nonmedical purposes. Below is a further discussion on the various components of the modified local transportation safe harbor.

A. *Expansion of Mileage Limit*

The modified rule expanded the mileage limits for local transportation to patients residing in rural areas—now covering transportation up to 75 miles. The 25-mile limit for nonrural areas remains the same.

The aim of the modification is to "balance the needs of rural patients to have access to quality health care" with potential concerns that "patients could be transported for unnecessary care or be swayed to use a more distant provider even when they may prefer to receive items or services from a local provider."[718] OIG reiterated that the current safe harbor design of a single, uniform mileage limit for rural areas offers bright-line guidance and reduces administrative burden, including the administrative burden associated with the need to obtain certifications or other evidence of need determinations or both.[719]

A bright-line rule does not mean that programs offering transportation for rural area patients at greater distances are unlawful. To the contrary, OIG noted that such programs may be lawful depending on their facts and circumstances and would need to be evaluated on a case-by-case basis under the statute, including with respect to the intent of the parties.[720] Lack of access to care in a particular geographic area could be a relevant factor in determining on a case-by-case basis whether a particular local transportation arrangement involves an improper inducement to a beneficiary under the federal anti-kickback statute or Beneficiary Inducements Civil Monetary Penalty (CMP). Depending on the specific facts and circumstances of the arrangement, arrangements could comply with the statutes even if they do not fit in the safe harbor.

B. *Elimination of Distance Limitations on Transportation of Discharged Patients to Their Residence*

The modified local transportation safe harbor eliminates mileage limits for transportation to patients discharged from a hospital to the patient's residence or another residence of the patient's choice.[721] As discussed below, this also applies when a patient is placed in observation status for at least 24 hours. This flexibility applies to patients in rural and nonrural areas.[722] As noted by OIG, a residence of the patient's choice can include the residence of a friend or relative who is caring for the patient post-discharge.[723] The term "residence" as used in the safe harbor includes custodial care facilities, provided that the patient established the custodial care facility as a residence before receiving treatment at the facility from which the patient

718. *Id.* at 77859.
719. *Id.* at 77858.
720. *Id.* at 77860.
721. *Id.* at 77861.
722. *Id.* at 77861.
723. *Id.* at 77861.

is being transported.[724] In addition, OIG intended the term "residence" to include a homeless shelter when "a patient is homeless or established the homeless shelter as a residence prior to hospital admission."[725] The post-discharge analysis is not dependent on whether the patient resides in a rural or urban setting.[726]

C. *Transportation to Locations Other Than a Patient's Residence or a Residence of the Patient's Choice*

The modifications do not protect transportation of patients to any location, such as, for example, another provider or facility. OIG stated that "we believe that protecting transportation between health care providers in a position to refer to each other is not sufficiently low risk to warrant safe harbor protection because of the risk that such transportation arrangements could be used to steer patients to health care facilities that may not be in the patients' best interests."[727]

It should be noted that OIG did finalize a new safe harbor paragraph, 1001.952(hh),[728] which, according to OIG "may protect certain patient engagement tools and supports including transportation when the offeror of the transportation is a value based enterprise (VBE) participant."[729]

D. *Elimination of Distance Limitations for Patients Other Than Those Discharged After an Inpatient Admission*

The mileage limitation of the modified transportation safe harbor does not apply in two circumstances: when a patient is discharged after being admitted as an inpatient; and when a patient is released after spending 24 hours in observation status.[730] OIG stated that it believes that transportation home after an extended stay in observation status at a hospital is sufficiently similar to transportation home after an inpatient discharge and to prevent any safe harbor compliance challenges resulting from a patient's status as an inpatient or outpatient in the hospital.[731]

---

724. *Id.* at 77861.
725. *Id.* at 77861.
726. *Id.* at 77861.
727. *Id.* at 77861.
728. *See* discussion *supra* 2.31 Patient Engagement and Support.
729. Final Rule: Medicare and State Health Care Programs: Fraud and Abuse; Revisions to Safe Harbors Under the Anti-Kickback Statute, and Civil Monetary Penalty Rules Regarding Beneficiary Inducements 85 FED. REG. 77684, 77861 (Dec. 2, 2020).
730. *Id.* at 77862.
731. *Id.* at 77862.

OIG made clear that the rule maintains the mileage limitation "for other patients categorized as outpatients, including patients who are seen in the emergency room but not under observation for at least 24 hours, or patients discharged from an ambulatory surgical center."[732]

E. *Local Transportation for Health-Related, Nonmedical Purpose*

The modified rule does not expand the local transportation safe harbor to protect patient transportation for nonmedical purposes. As noted in the main volume, OIG reiterated that in the case of beneficiaries being improperly induced to obtain items or services when the transportation is for nonmedical purposes, the risk is too high for safe harbor protection.[733] Although a transportation program offered by a provider or supplier inherently poses a risk of inducing patients to get items or services that they might otherwise not have obtained and to get services from that provider or supplier, such risk is acceptable.

OIG did finalize a new safe harbor at paragraph 1001.952(hh)[734] that protects nonmedical transportation offered by VBE participants if such transportation has a direct connection to the coordination and management of care of the target patient population and meets the other conditions of the safe harbor.

F. *Use of Ride-Sharing Services*

OIG noted that, despite requests from commenters to do so, the regulatory text need not be amended to protect ride-sharing arrangements under the safe harbor. Although the regulatory text does not explicitly refer to ride-sharing services, OIG sees "no meaningful differences between these services and taxis, or other similar technology that serve as a taxi service should they become available in the future."[735] A taxi company, ride-sharing service, or other provider of transportation may advertise that it provides transportation to medical appointments and suggest to patients that they contact their medical providers to determine whether free or discounted transportation is available, but such providers of transportation cannot advertise that they provide free or discounted transportation to a particular health care provider or group of providers.[736]

---

732. *Id.* at 77862.
733. *Id.* at 77863.
734. *See* discussion *supra* 2.31 Patient Engagement and Support.
735. *Id.* at 77863.
736. *Id.*

Background for Value-Based Safe Harbor Revisions

In a final rule that became effective on January 19, 2021, the OIG, Department of Health and Human Services (HHS), as part of an HHS initiative branded "Regulatory Sprint to Coordinated Care," added seven new safe harbors and modified four existing ones focusing on care coordination and value-based care. The purpose of the changes was to further the goal of transforming the health care system from one "which rewards providers for the volume of care delivered" to "a value-driven health care system . . . that pays for health and outcomes."[737] According to OIG, the changes were designed "to encourage and improve patients' experience of care, providers' coordination of care, and information sharing to facilitate efficient care and preserve and protect patients' access to data."[738] Additionally, "the new and modified safe harbors were designed to further the goals of access, quality, patient choice, appropriate utilization, and competition, while protecting against increased costs, inappropriate steering of patients, and harms associated with inappropriate incentives tied to referrals."[739]

Three of the new safe harbors aim to protect value-based arrangements that enhance patient care and deliver value. These safe harbors were designed to "offer flexibility for innovation and customization of value-based arrangements to the size, resources, needs, and goals of the parties to them" and also "allow for emerging arrangements that reflect up-to-date understandings in medicine, science, and technology."[740] Although all three value-based safe harbors offer protection for in-kind remuneration, such as technology or services, OIG noted that "only the safe harbors for value-based arrangements with substantial assumption of risk (paragraphs 1001.952(ff) and (gg)) protect monetary remuneration. The care coordination arrangements safe harbor at paragraph 1001.952(ee), which requires little or no assumption of risk, does not."[741] Specific requirements for each of the three value-based safe harbors will

---

737. Final Rule: Medicare and State Health Care Programs: Fraud and Abuse; Revisions to Safe Harbors Under the Anti-Kickback Statute, and Civil Monetary Penalty Rules Regarding Beneficiary Inducements 85 Fed. Reg. 77684 (Dec. 2, 2020).

738. *Id.*

739. *Id.* at 77688.

740. *Id.* at 77685.

741. *Id.*

be addressed in turn, along a summary of insight provided by OIG in response to comments on the proposed rule implementing the value-based safe harbors.

OIG noted that several safe harbors, including the value-based arrangements safe harbors, "intersect with the physician self-referral law exceptions that CMS is finalizing as part of the Regulatory Sprint," and that it has "sought to align value-based terminology and safe harbor conditions with those being adopted by CMS in its physician self-referral regulations" wherever possible.[742] However, OIG also recognized that due to important differences in the laws, "complete alignment is not feasible."[743] Specifically, the physician self-referral law (Stark Law) is a more narrowly focused strict liability law that includes exceptions designed to "define the full universe of acceptable arrangements that implicate" the law, whereas the AKS is an intent-based law pursuant to which compliance with a safe harbor is voluntary and not evidence of an AKS violation.[744] Accordingly, OIG noted that the value-based safe harbors "need not capture the full universe of value-based arrangements" and that "rather than mirror CMS's exceptions, [OIG] included safe harbor conditions designed to ensure that protected arrangements are not disguised kickback schemes."[745] Where arrangements implicate the AKS and the Stark Law, "the value-based safe harbors may therefore protect a narrower universe of such arrangements than CMS's exceptions," and an arrangement may comply with the Stark Law and still violate the AKS.[746] However, OIG expressed the view that both laws "create pathways" for parties to value-based arrangements to avoid liability, and that "the same value-based enterprise or value-based arrangement can seek protection under both regulatory schemes, provided the relevant conditions of a safe harbor and an exception are satisfied."[747]

The three new value-based safe harbors exist in a tiered structure to support the transformation of industry payment systems "and in recognition that arrangements involving higher levels of downside financial

742. *Id.* at 77689.
743. *Id.*
744. *Id.*
745. *Id.*
746. *Id.*
747. *Id.* at 77689, 77690.

risk for those in a position to make referrals or order products or services could curb, at least to some degree, fee-for-service (FFS) incentives to order medically unnecessary or overly costly items and services."[748] The tiers offer varied flexibilities to parties based on the party's capability to take on certain degrees of risk in a value-based arrangement.[749] In this regard, OIG commented that those who are unable to assume risk or are not willing to assume substantial or full downside risk "may look to the care coordination arrangements safe harbor, which does not require the assumption of risk, structure arrangements to fit in another safe harbor that might apply, or enter into arrangements that are not protected by a safe harbor."[750]

It is important to note that there are certain entities deemed ineligible for value-based safe harbor protection. Those ineligible entities are pharmaceutical companies, PBMs, laboratory companies, compounding pharmacies, manufacturers of devices or medical supplies, durable medical equipment, prosthetics, orthotics, and supplies (DMEPOS) companies, and medical device distributors and wholesaler. However, there is an exception, in the case of device and DME companies, for care coordination arrangements involving in-kind remuneration consisting of digital health technology.[751]

The value-based safe harbors are prospective only; no retroactive protection is available.[752] As noted by OIG, "it is neither feasible nor desirable to confer safe harbor protection retrospectively under a criminal statute."[753]

Although OIG recognized that the value-based safe harbors, as finalized, do not include the traditional fraud and abuse safeguards of fair market value or a broad prohibition on taking into account the volume or value of any referrals, it noted that certain safeguards have been included that are discussed in the upcoming chapters. OIG further commented that "the risk sharing required by the substantial downside financial risk and full financial risk safe harbors reduces some

748. *Id.* at 77690.
749. *Id.*
750. *Id.* at 77691.
751. *Id.* at 77685–86, 77708.
752. *Id.* at 77693–94.
753. *Id.*

fraud and abuse concerns associated with a traditional fee-for-service payment system" and that the "care coordination arrangements safe harbor does not protect monetary payments, including payments for services such as radiology or imaging."[754] OIG also noted that "nothing in the risk-based safe harbors prevents parties from negotiating fair market value arrangements for services or from using the personal services and management contracts and outcomes-based payments safe harbor at paragraph 1001.952(d), which includes fair market value requirements."[755]

Responding to concerns that the care coordination focus of the value-based safe harbors could drive further industry consolidation, OIG replied that "it is not the intent of this final rule to foster industry consolidation," that value-based arrangements "can be among many participants or as few as two" and that "[t]he safe harbors are available to large and small systems and to rural and urban providers."[756]

In response to comments urging OIG to extend the value-based safe harbors to participants in arrangements involving only commercial payer patients and to clarify that the AKS is not implicated by such arrangements, OIG made clear that while the AKS ordinarily does not apply to arrangements involving patients who are not federal health care program beneficiaries, "to the extent the offer of remuneration pursuant to an arrangement involving only non-Federal health care program beneficiaries is intended to pull through referrals of Federal health care program beneficiaries or business, the Federal anti-kickback statute would be implicated and potentially violated."[757] According to OIG, such a "pull-through arrangement" would not meet the requirements in the value-based safe harbors "that the offeror of remuneration does not take into account the volume or value of, or condition the remuneration of referrals of, patients who are not part of the target patient population, or business not covered under the value-based arrangement."[758]

754. *Id.* at 77691.
755. *Id.*
756. *Id.* at 77692.
757. *Id.* at 77693.
758. *Id.*

Value-Based Terminology

The final rule defines certain terms within the care coordination safe harbor found at paragraph 1001.952(ee) that are cross-referenced in the other value-based safe harbors found at (d)(2), (ff), (gg), and (hh). These terms include "value-based enterprise" (VBE), "value-based arrangement," "target patient population," "value-based activity," "VBE participant," "value-based purpose," "coordination and management of patient care," "limited technology participant," "digital health technology," and "manufacturer of a device or medical supply."

Value-Based Enterprise

Value-based enterprise or *VBE* means two or more VBE participants:

(A) Collaborating to achieve at least one value-based purpose;

(B) Each of which is a party to a value-based arrangement with the other or at least one other VBE participant in the value-based enterprise;

(C) That have an accountable body or person responsible for financial and operational oversight of the value-based enterprise; and

(D) That have a governing document that describes the value-based enterprise and how the VBE participants intend to achieve its value-based purpose(s).

OIG commented that the VBE definition "is intended to be broad and flexible to encompass a wide range of VBEs, from smaller VBEs comprised of only two or three parties to large VBEs, such as entities that function similar to ACOs [accountable care organizations]."[759] OIG declined to expand the definition to include VBE affiliates that are not otherwise VBE participants so as to "ensure the remuneration that the safe harbors protect is exchanged pursuant to a value-based arrangement where all parties are striving to achieve value-based purposes."[760] Regarding how VBE participants can prove that they are collaborating to achieve a value-based purpose, OIG commented that "time spent

759. *Id.* at 77695.
760. *Id.*

on value-based activities, records of collaboration between parties, and participation in applicable meetings, could all be relevant factors, depending on the unique nature and circumstance of the VBE and the arrangements among the VBE participants."[761] OIG further confirmed that a VBE could have as few as two participants, and that "VBE participants may join and leave a VBE throughout the existence of the VBE."[762]

Responding to a comment inquiring how the VBE definition applies to already existing integrated delivery systems, OIG noted that "an existing integrated delivery system, ACO, or comparable entity could potentially qualify as a 'value-based enterprise' and meet all of the requirements of the definition to use the value-based safe harbors" and that "[a]rrangements for shared savings or losses and certain bundled payments could be protected under the substantial downside and full financial risk safe harbors, which protect in-kind and monetary remuneration exchanged between a VBE and a VBE participant."[763] As an example, OIG stated that "a hospital that is a VBE participant could enter into a value-based arrangement with a VBE, pursuant to which the VBE shares savings or losses with the hospital VBE participant."[764] OIG further explained that while the care coordination safe harbor found at (ee) could not apply since it does not protect the exchange of monetary remuneration, "[m]onetary remuneration, including payments linked to outcomes, could qualify for protection under the safe harbor for personal services and management contracts and outcomes-based payments at paragraph 1001.952(d)(2)." OIG cautioned, however, that "[n]either the substantial downside financial risk safe harbor nor the full financial risk safe harbor protects the exchange of remuneration between entities downstream of the VBE (i.e., between VBE participants, a VBE participant and a downstream contractor, or downstream contractors)."[765]

Regarding the requirement for an "accountable body," OIG acknowledged that it did "not expect that small VBEs would have the same resources as larger VBEs for this function or would structure the

761. *Id.*
762. *Id.*
763. *Id.* at 77696.
764. *Id.*
765. *Id.*

function in the same way."[766] Rather, a VBE "should have an accountable body or responsible person that is appropriate for its size and resource and is capable of carrying out the associated responsibilities."[767] OIG further noted that "[w]here parties already have a governing body that constitutes an accountable body or responsible person, such parties are not required to form a new accountable body or designate a responsible person for purposes of creating a VBE."[768] Responding to an inquiry concerning whether VBE participants would be expected to conduct oversight in addition to that of the accountable body, OIG explained that "where a VBE participant or VBE has done everything that it reasonably could to comply with the safe harbor requirements applicable to that party but the remuneration exchanged loses safe harbor protection as a result of another party's noncompliance, the compliant party's efforts to take all reasonable steps would be relevant in a determination of whether such party had the requisite intent to violate the Federal anti-kickback statute."[769] OIG also commented that while it was not requiring a duty of loyalty to the VBE, it did believe that the accountable body or responsible person "necessarily must act in furtherance of the VBE's value-based purpose(s) to fulfill its oversight responsibilities" and that "[p]arties are free to include this duty in their contractual arrangements."[770] Also, while not imposing the administrative burden of adopting a process through which patients could express concerns or ensure that informed consent is obtained for each patient treated within a VBE, OIG noted that "[s]uch requirements may be useful processes for VBEs to consider in ensuring safe harbor compliance."[771]

OIG also provided comments on the "governing document" requirement, explaining its purpose is to "[provide] transparency regarding the structure of the VBE, the VBE's value-based purpose(s), and the VBE participants' roadmap for achieving the purpose(s)."[772] OIG stated that "[a] single document could constitute both the VBE's governing

766. *Id.* at 77697.
767. *Id.*
768. *Id.* at 77698.
769. *Id.*
770. *Id.* at 77699.
771. *Id.*
772. *Id.* at 77700.

document and the writing required for a value-based arrangement so long as it includes all of the requisite requirements for each writing."[773] OIG further confirmed that "an existing payor contract could qualify as a governing document so long as it describes the value-based enterprise and how the VBE participants intend to achieve the VBE's value-based purpose(s)," but OIG declined to permit the governing documents to be comprised of multiple writings, concluding that the "[c]reation of one governing document, that may be amended over time as the value-based activities, VBE participants, or other features of the VBE evolve, will help ensure that there is a clearly identifiable governance structure for the VBE."[774] No matter the format, OIG stressed that the "core requirement" for the governing document is a description of the value-based enterprise and how the VBE participants intend to achieve the VBE's value-based purpose. According to OIG, "[t]his definition offers parties significant flexibility to craft a value-based enterprise and a governing document commensurate with the scope and sophistication of the VBE."[775]

Value-Based Arrangement

Value-based arrangement means an arrangement for the provision of at least one value-based activity for a target patient population to which the only parties are:

(**A**) The value-based enterprise and one or more of its VBE participants; or

(**B**) VBE participants in the same value-based enterprise.

Value-based arrangements are arrangements between VBEs and one or more of the enterprise's participants. These safe harbors are designed to protect certain remuneration exchanged between or among eligible participants in a value-based arrangement that fosters better coordinated and managed patient care.[776]

OIG expressed its view that "the definition of 'value-based arrangement' is broad enough to capture commercial and private insurer

773. *Id.* at 77699.
774. *Id.*
775. *Id.* at 77700.
776. *Id.* at 77881.

arrangements" and is "intended to afford parties significant flexibility."[777] Replying to a commenter's concern that parties to value-based arrangements not be precluded from using nondisclosure agreements to prevent one party from using information gleaned from the arrangement against another party, OIG confirmed that such nondisclosure agreements are permitted.[778]

OIG further stressed that "qualification as a value-based arrangement is necessary, but not sufficient, to protect remuneration exchanged pursuant to that arrangement."[779] OIG explained further that "value-based arrangements are not *de facto* safe harbor protected" but rather an arrangement that meets the definition of that term "is eligible to seek protection in a value-based safe harbor" and must then satisfy all elements.[780] OIG also offered a reminder that not every provider furnishing value-based care needs the protection of a safe harbor, and that "the value-based arrangements in which it participates might not need safe harbor protection if they do not implicate the [anti-kickback] statute."[781]

Target Patient Population

Target patient population means an identified patient population selected by the VBE or its VBE participants using legitimate and verifiable criteria that:

(A) Are set out in writing in advance of the commencement of the value-based arrangement; and

(B) Further the value-based enterprise's value-based purpose(s).

OIG explained that the definition of target patient population requires the use of "legitimate" criteria "to ensure the target patient population selection process is based upon bona fide criteria that further a value-based arrangement's value-based purpose(s)" and that "legitimate criteria could be based on social determinants of health, such as safe housing or transportation needs."[782] OIG further observed that

777. *Id.* at 77700.
778. *Id.* at 77701.
779. *Id.* at 77700.
780. *Id.* at 77701.
781. *Id.*
782. *Id.* at 77702.

requiring "legitimate and verifiable" criteria "will afford parties comparatively greater flexibility in determining the target patient population and aligns with CMS's definition of the same term."[783] OIG explained that the patient population must be identified "in advance of the commencement of the value-based arrangement" and that the "selection criteria – not the individual patients – must be identified in advance."[784] Although modifications to selection criteria may only be done "prospectively (and upon amending [the] existing value-based arrangement), no amendment would be required to attribute patients retroactively to the target patient population," provided they meet selection criteria established prior to the start of the value-based arrangement.[785]

Responding to a concern that VBE participants not be permitted to manipulate the target patient population based on inappropriate criteria, OIG confirmed that if participants "establish criteria to target particularly lucrative patients ('cherry-picking') or avoid high-cost or unprofitable patients ('lemon-dropping'), such criteria would not be legitimate for purposes of the target patient population definition."[786] OIG further explained that "if VBE participants selectively include patients in a target patient population for purposes inconsistent with the objectives of a properly structured value-based arrangement, we would not consider such a selection process to be based on a legitimate and verifiable criteria that further the VBE's value-based purposes, as required by the definition."[787]

OIG also clarified that nothing in the definition precludes "identifying the target patient population as the entire patient population that a VBE participant serves," but OIG cautioned that "depending on the value-based arrangement, selecting a target patient population by selecting the parties' entire patient population would need to be closely scrutinized for compliance with the definition to ensure that such broad selection criteria is 'legitimate' and necessary to achieve the arrangement's value-based purpose."[788] OIG confirmed that certain categories

783. *Id.*
784. *Id.* at 77702, 77703.
785. *Id.*
786. *Id.* at 77702.
787. *Id.*
788. *Id.* at 77703.

of patients could form a target patient population as, for example, "patients who have been diagnosed with a particular disease."[789] Concerning the possibility of identifying all patients of a particular payer as the target patient population, OIG commented that while that may be appropriate in some circumstances (such as arrangement involving the assumption of full financial risk), "relying on this criterion, without sufficient justification for such a broad approach, could raise questions regarding whether it is legitimate or, instead, is a way to capture referrals of, for example, Medicare business."[790]

Value-Based Activity

Value-based activity:

(A) Means any of the following activities, provided that the activity is reasonably designed to achieve at least one value-based purpose of the value-based enterprise:

(1) Provision of an item or service;

(2) Taking action; or

(3) Refraining from taking an action; and

(B) Does not include the making of a referral.

OIG explained that the definition of value-based activity "is intended to be broad and to include the actions parties take or refrain from taking pursuant to a value-based arrangement and in furtherance of a value-based purpose."[791] As an example, the offering of health care technology to track patient data to improve patient care could be a value-based activity, as could the use of the technology to track patient data.[792] Further, "[a]n inaction that constitutes a value-based activity might be refraining from ordering certain items or services in accordance with a medically appropriate care protocol that reduces the number of required steps in a given procedure."[793] OIG further noted that "giving something of value to patients, such as a fitness tracker, also may constitute a value-based activity if doing so is reasonably designed

789. *Id.*
790. *Id.*
791. *Id.* at 77704.
792. *Id.*
793. *Id.*

to achieve a value-based purpose."[794] However, if remuneration is exchanged between VBE participants and one of the VBE participants then transfers the remuneration to a patient, "the care coordination arrangements safe harbor [is] available only to protect the remuneration exchanged between the VBE participants," and one must look to the patient engagement and support safe harbor to protect the remuneration given to the patient.[795]

OIG cautioned that, while the definition of value-based activity is intended to afford significant flexibility, "it is not intended to facilitate parties' attempts to mask fraudulent referral schemes presented under the guise of value-based activity."[796] In this regard, OIG stressed that the "definition provides that merely making a referral, without more, is not a value-based activity for purposes of this rule."[797] Although "[m]aking referrals, or documenting reasons for referrals, would not constitute value-based activities," it is also true that "[p]arties to a value-based arrangement may make referrals and document the reasons for the referrals as part of a value-based arrangement without losing safe harbor protection under an applicable safe harbor," provided the parties are performing one or more value-based activities.[798] This exclusion of referrals from the definition of value-based activity is intended "to require parties to engage in activities other than making referrals . . . to be eligible for safe harbor protection."[799]

VBE Participant

> ***Value-based enterprise participant*** or VBE participant means an individual or entity that engages in at least one value-based activity as part of a value-based enterprise, other than a patient acting in their capacity as a patient.

OIG explained that its approach to this definition "effectively divides the universe of VBE participants into three categories: (i) VBE participants that are eligible to rely on the value-based safe harbors for all

794. *Id.*
795. *Id.*
796. *Id.* at 77705.
797. *Id.*
798. *Id.*
799. *Id.*

types of arrangements that meet safe harbor conditions; (ii) limited technology participants that are only eligible to rely on the care coordination arrangements safe harbor for arrangements involving digital health technology; and (iii) VBE participants that are ineligible to rely on any of the value-based safe harbors for any types of arrangements."[800] By design, OIG excluded patients (as well as patient family members and others acting on behalf of patients) from the scope of the definition, with OIG commenting that "[e]ntities seeking safe harbor protection for remuneration provided to patients should look to the patient engagement and support safe harbor for protection, not to the value-based safe harbors."[801] By way of explanation, OIG noted that "[t]he role of VBE participants in health care business activities of VBEs is not a role assumed by patients and families, who play a critical role in patient care in other ways."[802]

Although all entities other than patients are eligible to be VBE participants, "each value-based safe harbor and the patient engagement and support safe harbor incorporates a list of entities that are ineligible for safe harbor protection."[803] Determination of which entities would be ineligible was "based on multiple factors, including the extent to which the entities are involved in front line care coordination and program integrity concerns."[804] OIG explained that the VBE participant will not stop meeting the definition merely because it "merges with or acquires a different type of entity or develops a new business line" or because "it acquires an entity that is not eligible," but if a VBE participant itself became an ineligible entity as a result of a transaction, "the safe harbor would no longer be available to protect any remuneration exchanged by that entity under a value-based arrangement."[805] OIG further clarified that the value-based safe harbors "do not prohibit the VBE from entering into contractual arrangements with any type of entity, including an entity that is not a VBE participant," but that "[r]emuneration exchanged by certain types of entities, including non-VBE participants,

800. *Id.* at 77706.
801. *Id.* at 77705–06.
802. *Id.* at 77707.
803. *Id.*
804. *Id.*
805. *Id.*

and VBE participants on the carve-out list, will not be protected by a value-based safe harbor, and parties would need to look to other safe harbors to the extent they want to protect it."[806]

Value-Based Purpose

Value-based purpose means:

(A) Coordinating and managing the care of a target patient population;

(B) Improving the quality of care for a target patient population;

(C) Appropriately reducing the costs to or growth in expenditures of payors without reducing the quality of care for a target patient population; or

(D) Transitioning from health care delivery and payment mechanisms based on the volume of items and services provided to mechanisms based on the quality of care and control of costs of care for a target patient population.

OIG explained that the definition "was crafted to provide parties with flexibility to develop innovative care arrangements and strategies specific to the needs of their target patient populations."[807] OIG further noted, however, that "compliance with the value-based purpose definition does not necessarily qualify parties or arrangements for safe harbor protection."[808]

Replying to comments, OIG declined to clarify how "quality" should be defined or measured, or to opine on whether certain measures would be seen as reducing quality, explaining that "[w]hether certain measures reduce quality is a fact-specific inquiry."[809] OIG did clarify that "neither the definition of 'value-based purpose' nor the value-based safe harbors requires parties to achieve the VBE's value-based purpose(s); rather, the definition of 'value-based purpose' should be read in conjunction with the definition of 'value-based activity,' which requires value-based activities to be reasonably designed to achieve the VBE's value-based purpose(s)."[810]

806. *Id.* at 77708.
807. *Id.* at 77720.
808. *Id.* at 77721.
809. *Id.* at 77720.
810. *Id.*

Replying to a request for more guidance on the fourth listed value-based purpose, OIG explained that it was based on a "recognition that parties transitioning to value-based care may need to provide infrastructure and perform other activities necessary to transition to the assumption of downside financial risk."[811]

Coordination and Management of Care

> ***Coordination and management of care (or coordinating and managing care)*** means the deliberate organization of patient care activities and sharing of information between two or more VBE participants, one or more VBE participants and the VBE, or one or more VBE participants and patients, that is designed to achieve safer, more effective, or more efficient care to improve the health outcomes of the target patient population.

OIG commented that the definition "helps ensure that protected arrangements serve patients and the goals of coordinated care" and also "provides a standard against which safe harbor compliance can be measured."[812] OIG further commented that "actual achievement of safer, more effective, or more efficient care that improves health outcomes is not required," but "the parties must ensure that their efforts" are designed to achieve such goals.[813] Replying to a commenter's inquiry regarding whether patient monitoring, diagnostic activities, treatment, and related communications and predictive analytics would qualify under the definition, OIG explained that each such activity could qualify depending on the facts and circumstances:

> We intend for the coordination and management of care to require beneficial activities beyond the mere referral of a patient or ordering of an item or service. Coordination and management of care requires some additional, deliberate effort and sharing of information, across two or more parties, that is designed to augment care delivery to achieve safer, more effective, or more efficient care to improve health outcomes.[814]

---

811. *Id.*
812. *Id.* at 77721.
813. *Id.* at 77722.
814. *Id.*

Although the mere ordering of an imaging study and reporting results back to the ordering provider would not qualify under the definition, if such an activity were "part of a more deliberate, organized effort between or among parties to achieve safer and more effective care and improve health outcomes," such as by actions intended to reduce redundant testing or ensuring the sharing of tests results with patients and caregivers to inform medical decision-making, "then the arrangement may constitute coordination and management of care."[815] OIG stressed that "the definition requires not only the deliberate organization of patient care activities, but also the sharing of information between (or among) the parties who are coordinating and managing care" and such information sharing "must be part of a design to achieve safer, more effective, or more efficient care to improve the health outcomes of the target population."[816] OIG pointed to a "clear distinction between coordinating and managing patient care transitions for the purpose of improving the quality of care or improving efficiencies, which would fit in the definition, and churning patients through care settings to capitalize on a reimbursement scheme or otherwise generate revenue, which would not fit in the definition."[817]

OIG also noted, in response to a comment about cybersecurity, that "[a]s a general matter, the use or sharing of cybersecurity items and services alone would not meet the definition" because it viewed "the use or sharing of such items and services to be focused on ensuring the security of patient care items and related information exchange, rather than the deliberate organization of patient care activities and sharing of information. . . ."[818] However, OIG did allow for the possibility that such items and services could be incorporated into an arrangement involving the exchange of health information technology to facilitate the coordination and management of care.[819] Even so, OIG pointed out that meeting the definition does not automatically afford safe harbor protection.[820]

815. *Id.*
816. *Id.*
817. *Id.*
818. *Id.*
819. *Id.* at 77695.
820. *Id.* at 77722.

OIG also emphasized that "any billing or financial management services arrangement that is characterized as facilitating the coordination and management of patient care [is] outside the scope of this definition." Financial management services such as "bookkeeping operations, contract management, revenue cycle management, or other similar activities," while they might complement the organization of patient care activities, "are not the type of care coordination activities" covered by the definition.[821] OIG pointed out that arrangements focused on billing and financial management services could be structured to take advantage of a different safe harbor, such as the one for personal services and management contracts, but that the value-based safe harbors were "not intended to protect billing and financial management services arrangements . . . that are not fair market value under the guise of a value-based arrangement."[822] Moreover, any benefit that the remuneration exchanged by the parties has on administrative activities of the recipient should be "incidental, at most" so that any "value-based arrangements eligible for safe harbor protection focus on the delivery of care to patients."[823]

821. *Id.* at 77723.
822. *Id.*
823. *Id.*

2.28. Point-of-Sale Reductions in Price for Prescription Pharmaceutical Products

On November 30, 2020, OIG published a final rule for point-of-sale reductions in price offered by manufacturers on prescription pharmaceutical products payable under Medicare Part D or Medicaid managed care organizations meeting certain criteria.[824] The safe harbor states:

(cc) *Point-of-sale reductions in price for prescription pharmaceutical products.*

(1) As used in section 1128B of the Act, "remuneration" does not include a reduction in price from a manufacturer to a plan sponsor under Medicare Part D or a Medicaid Managed Care Organization for a prescription pharmaceutical product that is payable, in whole or in part, by a plan sponsor under Medicare Part D or a Medicaid Managed Care Organization, provided the following conditions are met with regard to that reduction in price:

(i) The manufacturer and the plan sponsor under Medicare Part D, a Medicaid MCO, or the PBM acting under contract with either, set the reduction in price in advance, in writing, by the time of the first purchase of the product at that reduced price by the plan sponsor or Medicaid MCO on behalf of an enrollee;

(ii) The reduction in price does not involve a rebate unless the full value of the reduction in price is provided to the dispensing pharmacy by the manufacturer, directly or indirectly, through a point-of-sale chargeback or series of point-of-sale chargebacks, or is required by law; and

(iii) The reduction in price must be completely reflected in the price of the prescription pharmaceutical product at the time the pharmacy dispenses it to the beneficiary.

(2)

(i) For purposes of this paragraph (cc), the terms manufacturer, pharmacy benefit manager or PBM, prescription

824. The original effective date of this safe harbor was January 1, 2022. However, as a result of a lawsuit challenging the final rule that was filed in the U.S. District Court for the District of Columbia, the effective date of the safe harbor was delayed by court order to January 1, 2023. Congress then extended that date in a series of legislative enactments ending with the Inflation Reduction Act of 2022, which, on August 16, 2022, extended the moratorium on implementation, administration, or enforcement of the final rule until January 1, 2032.

pharmaceutical product, and rebate have the meanings ascribed to them in paragraph (h) of this section.

(ii) For purposes of this paragraph (cc), a point-of-sale chargeback is a payment by a manufacturer made directly or indirectly (through a PBM or other entity) to a dispensing pharmacy equal to the reduction in price agreed upon in writing between the Plan Sponsor under Part D, the Medicaid MCO, or a PBM acting under contract with either, and the manufacturer of the prescription pharmaceutical product.

(iii) For purposes of this paragraph (cc), the term Medicaid Managed Care Organization or Medicaid MCO carries the meaning ascribed to it in section 1903(m) of the Social Security Act.

As proposed, this safe harbor was intended "to protect reductions in price on prescription pharmaceutical products offered to plan sponsors under Medicare Part D, Medicaid MCOs, or through a PBM acting under contract with either" if:

(**1**) The reduction in price is set in advance;

(**2**) The reduction in price does not involve a rebate, unless the full value of the price reduction is accomplished through chargebacks or is a rebate required by law; and

(**3**) The reduction in price is completely reflected in the price the pharmacy charges to the beneficiary at the point of sale.[825]

Accordingly, under the safe harbor, "Medicaid MCOs seeking safe harbor protection for discounts have the option to use either the discount safe harbor or the new safe harbor for point-of-sale reductions in price at § 1001.952(cc)."[826] However, "neither the discount safe harbor nor the new safe harbor protects rebates or other reductions in price from a manufacturer that are retained by a PBM, even if that PBM is operating on behalf

825. Final Rule: Removal of Safe Harbor Protection for Rebates Involving Prescription Pharmaceuticals and Creation of New Safe Harbor Protection for Certain Point-of-Sale Reductions in Price on Prescription Pharmaceuticals and Certain Pharmacy Benefit Manager Service Fees, 85 FED. REG. 76666, 76668 (Nov. 30, 2020).

826. *Id* at 76675.

of a Medicaid MCO."[827] Further, nothing in the final rule "alter(s) obligations under statutory provisions for Medicaid prescription drug rebates . . . including without limitation the provisions related to best price, the additional rebate amounts required for certain drugs based on the rate of increase in AMP [average manufacturer price] and the increase in the consumer price index for all urban consumers . . . or provisions regarding supplemental rebates negotiated between states and manufacturers."[828]

OIG further noted that reductions in price that are given to Part D plan sponsors or Medicaid MCOs that are conditioned on formulary placement of a particular drug "can qualify for protection under the new safe harbor for point-of-sale reductions in price" and that "reductions in price contingent on formulary placement can foster competition among manufacturers to the ultimate benefit of beneficiaries and Federal health care programs, provided that safety and efficacy considerations are not disregarded."[829] OIG therefore confirmed that "point-of-sale reductions in price can be conditioned on formulary placement and nonetheless qualify for protection under the new safe harbor at § 1001.952(cc), provided that there are no required services (e.g., marketing or switching), and all conditions of the safe harbor are met."[830] OIG, however, reiterated that "any type of 'fee' (which would include any payment retained by a PBM) is not a discount or other reduction in price and therefore will not meet the discount safe harbor at § 1001.952(h) or the new safe harbor for point-of-sale reductions at § 1001.952(cc) if it is tied to formulary placement."[831] Also, because development of a formulary is a service that a PBM provides to a plan, and not a service provided to manufacturers, such fees tied to formulary placement are not protected by the safe harbor.[832]

Responding to a commenter's concern that the safe harbor's protection of point-of-sale reductions might lead beneficiaries to use more expensive brand drugs instead of generics, which may have adverse consequences by increasing program costs, decreasing use of generics, and limiting the choice of brand drugs, OIG commented that the safe harbor "provides a pathway to protect certain types of price reductions, but it does not require price

827. *Id.*
828. *Id* at 76676.
829. *Id* at 76683.
830. *Id.*
831. *Id.*
832. *Id.*

reductions."[833] Furthermore, the safe harbor "does not affect other drug utilization tools that plans have at their disposal, such as moving generics to a lower tier or moving brands to higher tiers."[834] OIG also noted that plan sponsors have an incentive to promote lower cost drugs, "regardless of whether the drug is a generic or brand" and the safe harbor "will remove an incentive for plan sponsors to game rebates in their bidding, as well as create an incentive for plans to include more generic drugs of equal safety and efficacy on their formularies."[835]

Addressing a comment questioning whether the new safe harbor would encourage increased use of coinsurance in Part D drug plans rather than copayments, OIG pointed out that the safe harbor does not compel plans "to discontinue their use of copayments, which many consumers prefer," and that "upfront discounts on drug subject to copayments can comply with the final point-of-sale safe harbor, so long as the discounts are reflected in the point-of-sale price the beneficiary is paying and accounted for when setting the copayment amount at the time of bidding."[836] OIG further expressed the view that "enhanced transparency of premiums and out-of-pocket costs that the safe harbor encourages will support beneficiaries in making more actuarially sound decisions" and that even if the safe harbor has "a differing impact on certain patient groups," OIG believes "many patients will experience benefits."[837]

Replying to a commenter's concern that a PBM might require that the fees associated with a third-party performing point-of-sale chargeback administration be paid by a pharmaceutical manufacturer as a condition of formulary placement or position, OIG agreed that "only the party performing the point-of-sale chargeback administration should be paid for that service," that such fees are not covered under the safe harbor "regardless of whether such fees are fair market value," and that "[payments] for formulary placement, or any kind of payment for a service, are not covered" by this safe harbor or the discount safe harbor.[838]

OIG agreed with commenters' observations that removing rebates and moving to upfront discounts "should promote a more transparent

833. *Id* at 76684.
834. *Id.*
835. *Id.*
836. *Id.*
837. *Id.*
838. *Id* at 76685.

and rational pharmaceutical market that may reduce drug prices through competition."[839] OIG further noted that "[r]ebate arrangements in the prescription drug supply chain have been cited as a barrier to lowering drug costs," and that it views rebates as "an important driver of increased list prices," with "[r]ebates and price protection payments increas[ing] when list prices increase."[840] OIG believes that the safe harbor "will result in lower list prices and lower out-of-pocket costs for patients through point-of-sale reductions in price."[841]

2.29. PBM Service Fees

On November 30, 2020, OIG published a final rule for fixed fees that manufacturers pay to PBMs for services rendered to the manufacturers that meet specified criteria.[842] The safe harbor states:

> (dd) *PBM service fees.*
>
> (1) As used in section 1128B of the Act, "remuneration" does not include any payment by a pharmaceutical manufacturer to a pharmacy benefit manager (PBM) for services the PBM provides to the pharmaceutical manufacturer related to the pharmacy benefit management services that the PBM furnishes to one or more health plans as long as the following conditions are met:
>
> (i) The PBM has a written agreement with the pharmaceutical manufacturer, signed by the parties, that covers all of the services the PBM provides to the manufacturer in connection with the PBM's arrangements with health plans for the term of the agreement and specifies each of the services to be provided by the PBM and the compensation associated with such services.
>
> (ii) The services performed under the agreement do not involve the counseling or promotion of a business

839. *Id* at 76686.

840. *Id.*

841. *Id* at 76687.

842. The original effective date of this safe harbor was January 1, 2022. However, as a result of a lawsuit challenging the final rule that was filed in the U.S. District Court for the District of Columbia, the effective date of the safe harbor was delayed by court order to January 1, 2023. Congress then extended that date in a series of legislative enactments ending with the Inflation Reduction Act of 2022, which, on August 16, 2022, extended the moratorium on implementation, administration, or enforcement of the final rule until January 1, 2032.

arrangement or other activity that violates any state or federal law.

(iii) The compensation paid to the PBM is:

(A) Consistent with fair market value in an arm's-length transaction;

(B) A fixed payment, not based on a percentage of sales; and

(C) Not determined in a manner that takes into account the volume or value of any referrals or business otherwise generated between the parties, or between the manufacturer and the PBM's health plans, for which payment may be made in whole or in part under Medicare, Medicaid, or other Federal health care programs.

(iv) The PBM discloses in writing to each health plan with which it contracts at least annually the services rendered to each pharmaceutical manufacturer related to the PBM's arrangements to furnish pharmacy benefit management services to the health plan, and to the Secretary upon request, the services rendered to each pharmaceutical manufacturer related to the PBM's arrangements to furnish pharmacy benefit management services to the health plan and the fees paid for such services.

(2) For purposes of safe harbor in this paragraph (dd), the terms manufacturer, pharmacy benefit manager or PBM, and prescription pharmaceutical product have the meanings ascribed to them in paragraph (h) of this section, and health plan has the meaning ascribed to it in paragraph (l) of this section.

The impetus for the safe harbor was to "protect certain PBM service fees that were flat service fees manufacturers make to PBMs for services the PBMs provide to the pharmaceutical manufacturers, for the manufacturers' benefit, when those services relate in some way to the PBMs' arrangements to provide pharmacy benefit management services to health plans."[843]

---

843. Final Rule: Removal of Safe Harbor Protection for Rebates Involving Prescription Pharmaceuticals and Creation of New Safe Harbor Protection for Certain Point-of-Sale Reductions in Price on Prescription Pharmaceuticals and Certain Pharmacy Benefit Manager Service Fees, 85 FED. REG. 76666, 76710 (Nov. 30, 2020).

OIG expressed the view that the safe harbor would "reduce the risks associated with remuneration that may be tied to referrals" since fees must be consistent with fair market value and not determined in a manner that takes into account referrals or other business generated between the parties or between the manufacturer and the PBM's health plans that is reimbursable by a federal health care program.[844] OIG also noted that "protected fees would be only for services that the PBM provides to the manufacturer, not for services provided to health plans," with the latter potentially eligible for protection under the personal services and management contracts safe harbor.[845]

OIG commented that the requirement that the PBM service fees "relate to" pharmacy benefit management services furnished to health plans "fosters transparency for health plans" which is important because "PBMs are agents of the health plans with which they contract" and it is "important to ensure that a PBM's arrangements with pharmaceutical manufacturers are not in tension with the services it provides to the health plans for which it is acting as an agent."[846] OIG further noted that "[d]isclosures of specific services will allow a plan to see what services a PBM is contracting with a manufacturer that relate to the health plan."[847] For that reason, OIG proposed only to protect "fixed fee arrangements between manufacturers and PBMs where plans could have visibility into the arrangements."[848] The final rule "clarifies that the fees for which safe harbor protection is available are fees for services provided for the benefit of the manufacturer who is paying for them."[849] Only "legitimate services" are protected and that safe harbor does not protect arrangements for services "that are not necessary, are worthless, or are duplicative."[850] OIG also noted that since PBMs are required to disclose the services and related fees to HHS "upon request," it would be a "best practice" for them to "maintain documentation that could demonstrate how each element of the safe harbor (e.g., fair market value, fixed fees) is met."[851]

Responding to a comment on the validity of per unit fees that fluctuate based on volume or value of the services being furnished, OIG acknowledged that "compensation for services may be determined on a per-unit

844. *Id.*
845. *Id.*
846. *Id* at 76711.
847. *Id.*
848. *Id.*
849. *Id.*
850. *Id* at 76713.
851. *Id* at 76711.

of work basis and thus vary with the volume of work performed."[852] OIG further observed that "if a per-unit-of-work fee is fixed in advance at fair market value for services actually provided to the manufacturer and is not based on volume or value of federal health care business, then that arrangement could be protected, so long as the unit-based compensation does not vary during the course of the compensation arrangement in any manner that takes into account referrals or other Federal business generated."[853] However, the safe harbor "would not protect per unit compensation that varies with either increases or decreases in volume (e.g., X amount per unit for the first 1,000 units, X+1 per unit for additional units)" as, according to OIG, such an arrangement "is not low risk."[854] OIG also stressed that the safe harbor "would not protect any per-unit-of-work fee that is based on or otherwise connected with drug prices."[855]

Although OIG did not include a specific condition requiring that the aggregate services contracted for be reasonably necessary to accomplish the commercially reasonable business purpose of the services, OIG acknowledged that consideration of that fact "would likely be useful in meeting the condition that payments protected by the safe harbor be 'for services the PBM provides to the pharmaceutical manufacturer related to the pharmacy benefit management services that the PBM furnishes to . . . health plans,' and not for favorable treatment of the manufacturers' products."[856] OIG further confirmed that "provided that all other requirements of the safe harbor are met, and provided that the manufacturer party to an agreement with a PBM has taken no steps to discourage or impede the PBM from meeting the disclosure requirements, the PBM's failure to meet the disclosure requirement will not, by itself, cause the manufacturer to lose the protection of the safe harbor."[857] However, OIG noted that "if the manufacturer were aware of a failure to disclose and took no steps to remedy it, liability might attach to the manufacturer through various legal theories, depending on all the facts of the arrangement and the conduct of the parties."

852. *Id* at 76712.
853. *Id.*
854. *Id.*
855. *Id.*
856. *Id* at 76716.
857. *Id.*

2.30. Care Coordination Arrangements to Improve Quality, Health Outcomes, and Efficiency

The regulatory safe harbor for care coordination arrangements to improve quality, health outcomes, and efficiency, codified at 42 C.F.R. § 1001.952(ee), states:

(ee) *Care coordination arrangements to improve quality, health outcomes, and efficiency.* As used in section 1128B of the Act, "remuneration" does not include the exchange of anything of value between a VBE and VBE participant or between VBE participants pursuant to a value-based arrangement if all of the standards in paragraphs (ee)(1) through (13) of this section are met:

(**1**) The remuneration exchanged:

(*i*) Is in-kind;

(*ii*) Is used predominantly to engage in value-based activities that are directly connected to the coordination and management of care for the target patient population and does not result in more than incidental benefits to persons outside of the target patient population; and

(*iii*) Is not exchanged or used:

(**A**) More than incidentally for the recipient's billing or financial management services; or

(**B**) For the purpose of marketing items or services furnished by the VBE or a VBE participant to patients or for patient recruitment activities.

(**2**) The value-based arrangement is commercially reasonable, considering both the arrangement itself and all value-based arrangements within the VBE.

(**3**) The terms of the value-based arrangement are set forth in writing and signed by the parties in advance of, or contemporaneous with, the commencement of the value-based arrangement and any material change to the value-based arrangement. The writing states at a minimum:

(*i*) The value-based purpose(s) of the value-based activities provided for in the value-based arrangement;

(*ii*) The value-based activities to be undertaken by the parties to the value-based arrangement;

(*iii*) The term of the value-based arrangement;

(iv) The target patient population;
(v) A description of the remuneration;
(vi) Either the offeror's cost for the remuneration and the reasonable accounting methodology used by the offeror to determine its cost, or the fair market value of the remuneration;
(vii) The percentage and amount contributed by the recipient;
(viii) If applicable, the frequency of the recipient's contribution payments for ongoing costs; and
(ix) The outcome or process measure(s) against which the recipient will be measured.

(4) The parties to the value-based arrangement establish one or more legitimate outcome or process measures that:
(i) The parties reasonably anticipate will advance the coordination and management of care for the target patient population based on clinical evidence or credible medical or health sciences support;
(ii) Include one or more benchmarks that are related to improving or maintaining improvements in the coordination and management of care for the target patient population;
(iii) Are monitored, periodically assessed, and prospectively revised as necessary to ensure that the measure and its benchmark continue to advance the coordination and management of care of the target patient population;
(iv) Relate to the remuneration exchanged under the value-based arrangement; and
(v) Are not based solely on patient satisfaction or patient convenience.

(5) The offeror of the remuneration does not take into account the volume or value of, or condition the remuneration on:
(i) Referrals of patients who are not part of the target patient population; or
(ii) Business not covered under the value-based arrangement.

(6) The recipient pays at least 15 percent of the offeror's cost for the remuneration, using any reasonable accounting methodology, or the fair market value of the in-kind remuneration.

If it is a one-time cost, the recipient makes such contribution in advance of receiving the in-kind remuneration. If it is an ongoing cost, the recipient makes such contribution at reasonable, regular intervals.

(7) The value-based arrangement does not:
 (i) Limit the VBE participant's ability to make decisions in the best interests of its patients;
 (ii) Direct or restrict referrals to a particular provider, practitioner, or supplier if:
  (A) A patient expresses a preference for a different practitioner, provider, or supplier;
  (B) The patient's payor determines the provider, practitioner, or supplier; or
  (C) Such direction or restriction is contrary to applicable law under titles XVIII and XIX of the Act; or
 (iii) Induce parties to furnish medically unnecessary items or services, or reduce or limit medically necessary items or services furnished to any patient.

(8) The exchange of remuneration by a limited technology participant and another VBE participant or the VBE must not be conditioned on any recipient's exclusive use or minimum purchase of any item or service manufactured, distributed, or sold by the limited technology participant.

(9) The VBE, a VBE participant in the value-based arrangement acting on the VBE's behalf, or the VBE's accountable body or responsible person reasonably monitors and assesses the following and reports the monitoring and assessment of the following to the VBE's accountable body or responsible person, as applicable, no less frequently than annually or at least once during the term of the value-based arrangement for arrangements with terms of less than 1 year:
 (i) The coordination and management of care for the target patient population in the value-based arrangement;
 (ii) Any deficiencies in the delivery of quality care under the value-based arrangement; and
 (iii) Progress toward achieving the legitimate outcome or process measure(s) in the value-based arrangement.

(10) If the VBE's accountable body or responsible person determines, based on the monitoring and assessment conducted pursuant to paragraph (ee)(9) of this section, that the value-based arrangement has resulted in material deficiencies in quality of care or is unlikely to further the coordination and management of care for the target patient population, the parties must within 60 days either:
  (i) Terminate the arrangement; or
  (ii) Develop and implement a corrective action plan designed to remedy the deficiencies within 120 days, and if the corrective action plan fails to remedy the deficiencies within 120 days, terminate the value-based arrangement.

(11) The offeror does not and should not know that the remuneration is likely to be diverted, resold, or used by the recipient for an unlawful purpose.

(12) For a period of at least 6 years, the VBE or VBE participant makes available to the Secretary, upon request, all materials and records sufficient to establish compliance with the conditions of this paragraph (ee).

(13) The remuneration is not exchanged by:
  (i) A pharmaceutical manufacturer, distributor, or wholesaler;
  (ii) A pharmacy benefit manager;
  (iii) A laboratory company;
  (iv) A pharmacy that primarily compounds drugs or primarily dispenses compounded drugs;
  (v) Except to the extent the entity is a limited technology participant, a manufacturer of a device or medical supply;
  (vi) Except to the extent the entity or individual is a limited technology participant, an entity or individual that sells or rents durable medical equipment, prosthetics, orthotics, or supplies covered by a Federal health care program (other than a pharmacy or a physician, provider, or other entity that primarily furnishes services); or
  (vii) A medical device distributor or wholesaler that is not otherwise a manufacturer of a device or medical supplies.

(14) For purposes of this paragraph (ee), the following definitions apply:

(i) Coordination and management of care (or coordinating and managing care) means the deliberate organization of patient care activities and sharing of information between two or more VBE participants, one or more VBE participants and the VBE, or one or more VBE participants and patients, that is designed to achieve safer, more effective, or more efficient care to improve the health outcomes of the target patient population.

(ii) Digital health technology means hardware, software, or services that electronically capture, transmit, aggregate, or analyze data and that are used for the purpose of coordinating and managing care; such term includes any internet or other connectivity service that is necessary and used to enable the operation of the item or service for that purpose.

(iii) Limited technology participant means a VBE participant that exchanges digital health technology with another VBE participant or a VBE and that is:

(A) A manufacturer of a device or medical supply, but not including a manufacturer of a device or medical supply that was obligated under 42 CFR 403.906 to report one or more ownership or investment interests held by a physician or an immediate family member during the preceding calendar year, or that reasonably anticipates that it will be obligated to report one or more ownership or investment interests held by a physician or an immediate family member during the present calendar year (for purposes of this paragraph, the terms "ownership or investment interest," "physician," and "immediate family member" have the same meaning as set forth in 42 CFR 403.902); or

(B) An entity or individual that sells or rents durable medical equipment, prosthetics, orthotics, or supplies covered by a Federal health care program (other than a pharmacy or a physician, provider, or other entity that primarily furnishes services).

(iv) Manufacturer of a device or medical supply means an entity that meets the definition of applicable manufacturer in 42 CFR 403.902 because it is engaged in the production, preparation, propagation, compounding, or conversion of a device or medical supply that meets the definition of covered drug, device, biological, or medical supply in 42 CFR 403.902, but not including entities under common ownership with such entity.

(v) Target patient population means an identified patient population selected by the VBE or its VBE participants using legitimate and verifiable criteria that:

(A) Are set out in writing in advance of the commencement of the value-based arrangement; and

(B) Further the value-based enterprise's value-based purpose(s).

(vi) Value-based activity.

(A) Means any of the following activities, provided that the activity is reasonably designed to achieve at least one value-based purpose of the value-based enterprise:

(1) The provision of an item or service;

(2) The taking of an action; or

(3) The refraining from taking an action; and

(B) Does not include the making of a referral.

(vii) Value-based arrangement means an arrangement for the provision of at least one value-based activity for a target patient population to which the only parties are:

(A) The value-based enterprise and one or more of its VBE participants; or

(B) VBE participants in the same value-based enterprise.

(viii) Value-based enterprise or VBE means two or more VBE participants:

(A) Collaborating to achieve at least one value-based purpose;

(B) Each of which is a party to a value-based arrangement with the other or at least one other VBE participant in the value-based enterprise;

(C) That have an accountable body or person responsible for financial and operational oversight of the value-based enterprise; and

(D) That have a governing document that describes the value-based enterprise and how the VBE participants intend to achieve its value-based purpose(s).

(ix) Value-based enterprise participant or VBE participant means an individual or entity that engages in at least one value-based activity as part of a value-based enterprise, other than a patient acting in their capacity as a patient.

(x) Value-based purpose means:

(A) Coordinating and managing the care of a target patient population;

(B) Improving the quality of care for a target patient population;

(C) Appropriately reducing the costs to or growth in expenditures of payors without reducing the quality of care for a target patient population; or

(D) Transitioning from health care delivery and payment mechanisms based on the volume of items and services provided to mechanisms based on the quality of care and control of costs of care for a target patient population.

The new safe harbor is codified at 42 C.F.R. 1001.952(ee), effective January 19, 2021, to protect in-kind remuneration exchanged between a VBE and VBE participant or between VBE participants pursuant to a value-based arrangement.[858] For remuneration to be protected, it must be used to engage in value-based activities directly connected to the coordination and management of care for the target patient population.[859] Arrangements may not induce VBE participants to furnish unnecessary care, nor reduce or limit necessary care; limit medical decision-making or patient freedom of choice; or take into account the volume or value of business outside the value-based arrangement.[860] This safe harbor is only designed to protect in-kind remuneration.

858. *Id.* at 77723.
859. *Id.* at 77724.
860. *Id.*

A. General Comments

This new safe harbor is intended to protect arrangements by parties who are transitioning to higher levels of risk or who are engaging in care coordination that improves quality and efficiency, without assuming risk.[861] To mitigate the risk of fraud, there are requirements to ensure that arrangements protected by the safe harbor do not result in the traditional FFS fraud and abuse risks. Cost-sharing waivers furnished to patients would not qualify for protection under this safe harbor because such waivers "are not in-kind remuneration" and the safe harbor is "limited to exchanges of in-kind remuneration" and, moreover, OIG "did not intend patients to be VBE participants who could engage in value-based arrangements under the value-based safe harbors."[862]

Compliance with this safe harbor is dependent upon a fact-specific assessment.[863] This applies even in situations where there are multiple streams of remuneration flowing under a single value-based arrangement, in which case "the parties would need to evaluate each such stream separately to assess compliance with the safe harbor. . . ."[864] The same process would be followed by the government in the context of an enforcement action, with the government analyzing each stream separately and considering "the totality of the arrangement, to assess potential liability under the Federal anti-kickback statute."[865] OIG provided a nonexhaustive list of high-level examples to illustrate arrangements that could meet the requirements of the care coordination arrangements safe harbor:

1. A specialty physician practice that provides data analytics to a primary care practice with which it has a close working relationship and from which it receives referrals for federally reimbursable items and services, if the data analytics is used to identify nonevidence-based practice patterns or confirm whether recommended care is being sought or furnished;
2. Hospitals and physician working together in new ways to coordinate and manage care for discharged patients, including the hospital providing a physician group with care managers to ensure appropriate

861. *Id.*
862. *Id.* at 77725.
863. *Id.*
864. *Id.* at 77726.
865. *Id.*

post-discharge follow-up care, data analytics systems to help ensure better health outcomes, and remote monitoring technology to alert the physicians when a patient needs a health intervention to mitigate ER visits and hospital readmissions; and

3. A medical technology company partnering with physicians to better coordinate and manage patient care for those discharged from a hospital by providing digitally equipped devices that collect and transmit data to monitor patient recovery and issue an alert when intervention is needed.

B. Outcome Measures

Parties to a value-based arrangement are required to establish one or more legitimate outcome or process measures that the parties reasonably anticipate will advance the coordination and management of care for the target patient population based on clinical evidence or credible medical or health science support.[866] This provision is designed to increase flexibility in arrangements, while protecting against fraud and abuse. OIG clarified that the parties do not need to successfully achieve the outcome or process measure they select to qualify for safe harbor protection.[867] Notably, the exception requires a periodic assessment and, as necessary based on such assessment, a revision of the outcome or process measures and benchmarks. This is implemented because different measures should be assessed on different timelines.[868]

OIG commented that, unlike the personal services and management contracts safe harbor for outcomes-based payments, in establishing outcome or process measures, "parties may rely on credible health science as well as credible medical support, reflecting that this safe harbor covers a wider variety of care coordination arrangements (including remuneration in the form of health technology) and protects only in-kind remuneration, rather than monetary payments, presenting relatively lower overall risk."[869] The requirements encompasses "both clinical and non-clinical measures, and internal or externally generated measures, and will allow participants to select up-to-date outcome or process measures over time."[870] OIG noted that

866. *Id.* at 77727.
867. *Id.* at 77729.
868. *Id.* at 77731.
869. *Id.* at 77728.
870. *Id.*

the "specific addition of health science as a basis for selection reflects our intent, among other things, to allow remuneration in the form of information technology under the care coordination safe harbor."[871]

The outcome or process measures selected "do not need to be independently validated by a medical or other journal or another third-party source," although OIG noted that "[w]here available, use of measures validated by a credible third party would be a prudent practice."[872] OIG also confirmed that "parties can select a measure applicable to the entire target patient population" or select different outcome or process measures applicable to different segments of the population.[873] In the event, the parties must reasonably anticipate that all measures will collectively advance coordination and management of care for the entire population.[874]

Noting its concern with measures reflecting only the status quo without driving meaningful change in patient care, OIG commented that "measures must relate to the remuneration exchanged under the value-based arrangement so that there is a close nexus" between the value-based activities and what is being measured.[875] OIG stressed that measures "cannot be based solely on patient satisfaction or patient convenience, both of which can be subjective, uninformative with respect to quality or efficiency of care, and gamed with relative ease, including through use of rewards or incentives to patients."[876] OIG nonetheless acknowledged that tools to measure patient satisfaction or patient convenience can provide valuable information to government programs and "can be tied to other legitimate measures or can exist alongside such other measures."[877] OIG further clarified that parties "need not successfully achieve the outcome or process measure they select to qualify for safe harbor protection (and if they select more than one, they need not meet any of the them)," recognizing that despite best efforts, "parties to a value-based arrangement may not always achieve their selected measures due to a variety of factors."[878] In this respect, OIG noted a "key distinction" between this safe harbor and the "outcomes-based payments under the personal services and management contracts safe harbor," noting that

871. *Id.* at 77731.
872. *Id.* at 77728.
873. *Id.*
874. *Id.* at 77729
875. *Id.*
876. *Id.*
877. *Id.* at 77730.
878. *Id.* at 77729.

the latter "requires that agents achieve the outcome measure established for their payments in order to receive those payments."[879] In response to one comment concerning the adoption of payor-identified outcome measures, OIG clarified that parties may, but are not required to, use "payor-driven or developed outcome measures" and that they "are free to use [such measures] if they find them useful or if doing so is required by a payor."[880]

C. *Commercial Reasonableness*

The value-based arrangement in which the remuneration is exchanged must be commercially reasonable, considering the arrangement itself, as well as all value-based arrangements within the VBE.[881] The commercial reasonableness requirement helps ensure that the value-based arrangement serve legitimate objectives; mandates that parties structure the terms of their value-based arrangement in a manner calibrated to achieve the parties' legitimate business purposes; and reduces the likelihood that the arrangement might be a payment-for-referral scheme.[882] OIG noted its concern that, without the commercial reasonableness requirement, "the other conditions in this safe harbor will not sufficiently mitigate the risk of one party offering more remuneration than is necessary . . . to reward the other party for referrals of target patient population patients."[883] OIG further explained that this requirement "is the only safeguard in the care coordination arrangements safe harbor that directly addresses the risk that parties might use a series of value-based arrangements to effectuate a payment-for-referral scheme."[884] OIG also explained that by requiring that the value-based arrangement be "calibrated to achieve the parties' legitimate business purposes," the commercial reasonableness requirement safeguards against the risk that the remuneration furnished will lead to "overutilization, corruption of practitioners' medical judgment, inappropriate patient steering, or unfair competition."[885] By way of example, OIG explained that a value-based arrangement, which provides remuneration "in excess of what is reasonably necessary to coordinate and manage the care of the target patient population, as contemplated by the terms of that arrangement, would not

879. *Id.*
880. *Id.* at 77731–32.
881. *Id.*
882. *Id.*
883. *Id.* at 77732.
884. *Id.*
885. *Id.*

be commercially reasonable."[886] Furthermore, "terms that are calibrated to secure referrals, rather than to achieve the value-based purposes of the value-based arrangement, would result in an arrangement that is not commercially reasonable."[887]

D. *Writing*

The writing requirement for this safe harbor requires the terms of the value-based arrangement must be established in advance of, or contemporaneous with, the commencement of the value-based arrangement and any material change to the value-based arrangement. This requirement is intended to promote transparency, "both at its commencement and when there is a material change."[888] OIG further clarified that to promote transparency and accountability, "each value-based arrangement must be set forth in writing and signed by all parties to the value-based arrangement."[889] The writing need not be a single document, however, as "the parties can sign separate documents."[890] OIG further commented that the requirement that the parties document the value-based purposes of the value-based activities provided for in the value-based arrangement "effectuates [OIG's] intent" and that OIG view "the documentation of the value-based purpose(s) – and specifically, documentation of the care coordination and management of care purpose – to be an important component of a writing designed to ensure transparency and accountability."[891]

E. *Limitations on Remuneration*

Protected remuneration must be in-kind, as providing safe harbor protection to monetary remuneration exchanged under arrangements where the parties are not required to assume financial risk, and the protected remuneration is not required to be fair market value and may take into account the volume or value of referrals for the target patient population, presents fraud and abuse risks outweighing the potential benefits to federal health care programs and patients.[892] OIG commented that "longstanding guidance makes clear that remuneration in the form of cash and cash equivalents

886. *Id.* at 77733.
887. *Id.*
888. *Id.* at 77734.
889. *Id.*
890. *Id.*
891. *Id.* at 77735.
892. *Id.*

pose a higher risk of interfering with clinical decision-making, incentivizing overutilization or inappropriate utilization, and increasing costs to Federal health care programs."[893] The policy underlying this limitation to in-kind remuneration further addresses the "heightened risk that fungible monetary remuneration could be misused to make intentional kickback payments and would be more difficult to track."[894]

Regarding the requirements that the remuneration exchanged be used predominantly to engage in value-based activities that are directly connected to the coordination and management of care for the target patient population, and that such remuneration result in no more than incidental benefits to persons outside that population, OIG acknowledged that "in-kind remuneration exchanged for value-based activities may indirectly benefit patients out of the scope of the associated value-based arrangement and that parties may find it difficult to anticipate or project the extent of such 'spillover' benefits."[895] The language of the safe harbor reflects OIG's intent "to permit safe harbor protection for care coordination arrangements that predominantly benefit the target patient population."[896]

OIG further commented that the condition requiring that the remuneration exchange not induce the furnishing of medically unnecessary care or reduce or limit medically necessary items or services reflects its intent not to protect such arrangements, but that this requirement "is not intended to interfere with medical decision-making" but only "to support decision-making in the best interests of patients without inappropriate financial influence."[897] The requirement, according to OIG, is "a hallmark safeguard against fraudulent and abusive practices that could lead to inappropriate utilization, inappropriate steering of patients, or stinting on care."[898]

F. *Taking into Account the Volume or Value of, or Conditioning Remuneration on, Business or Patients Not Covered Under the Value-Based Arrangement*

Value-based care, including coordinated care, may take into account the volume of patients in the target patient population or value of referrals or

893. *Id.*
894. *Id.* at 77736.
895. *Id.*
896. *Id.*
897. *Id.* at 77738.
898. *Id.*

other business generated between the parties resulting from referrals of the target patient population. OIG stated that a complete prohibition on this could operate as an actual or perceived barrier to safe harbor protection for the kinds of innovative care coordination arrangements that are the goal of this rulemaking.[899]

However, the safe harbor prohibits the offeror of the remuneration from taking into account the volume or value of, or conditioning an offer of remuneration on, patient referrals that are ***not*** part of the value-based arrangement's target patient population or on business not covered by such an arrangement. OIG characterized this as "an important safeguard to protect against remuneration offered under the guise of a value-based arrangement that is intended to induce the recipient's referrals of patients or business not covered" by the value-based arrangement.[900]

G. Contribution Requirement

There is a minimum contribution requirement of 15 percent of the offeror's cost of the remuneration or fair market value of the remuneration for purposes of the care coordination arrangements safe harbor. This requirement is designed to increase the likelihood a recipient uses the care coordination items and services, to ensure the remuneration be well tailored to the recipient, and to promote the recipient's vested interest in achieving the intended purpose of the value-based arrangement.[901] OIG commented that "the contribution requirement serves as an important guardrail to prevent fraud and abuse under the guise of a value-based arrangement and an incentive for parties to develop arrangements that are both effective in coordinating and managing care and economically prudent."[902]

OIG further noted that where, in a care coordination arrangement, nonmonetary contributions flow from the offeror to the recipient and from the recipient to the offeror, the parties "would need to assess any potential Federal anti-kickback statute implications for both streams of contributions" and would have to "satisfy the contribution requirement for each stream of remuneration."[903] Additionally, "[t]here may be circumstances under which the parties could appropriately offset payments made to satisfy the

---

899. *Id.* at 77739.
900. *Id.*
901. *Id.*
902. *Id.* at 77740.
903. *Id.* at 77741.

contribution requirement for each stream, but any such assessment would be fact specific."[904]

OIG also clarified that if the participants in a value-based arrangement are sharing in-kind remuneration provided by VBE or another VBE participant, "it would be reasonable—under both methodologies that parties can use to determine the contribution requirement—to reasonably and in good faith allocate the 'offeror's cost for the in-kind remuneration' or the 'fair market value' of the shared resources between the various VBE participants sharing in the resources."[905] In that regard, OIG stated its expectation that parties seeking the safe harbor's protection "would use reasonable accounting methodologies and generally accepted valuation methodologies and principles in determining any appropriate allocation of the shared resources for the purposes of determining the 'offeror's cost for the in-kind remuneration' or the 'fair market value' in relation to the contribution requirement."[906] OIG acknowledged that "reasonable accounting methodologies and commonly accepted valuation principles would allow for consideration of the shared nature of the in-kind remuneration."[907]

H. Preserving Clinical Decision-Making

The rule prohibits any limitation of VBE participants' ability to make decisions in the best interests of their patients and limits the circumstances in which parties to a value-based arrangement may direct or restrict referrals.[908] These are implemented to support patient choice, as well as independent professional judgment. It is OIG's intention that a patient can express a preference for a different practitioner, provider, or supplier without the value-based arrangement restricting or limiting that choice.[909] Protection does not extend to an arrangement where the value-based arrangement directs or restricts referrals to a particular provider "if the patient's payor determines the provider, practitioner, or supplier or the direction or restriction is contrary to applicable law. . . ."[910]

Abusive, pay-for-referral arrangements, such as an arrangement where an individual or entity is required to offer remuneration to a provider to receive

904. *Id.*
905. *Id.*
906. *Id.*
907. *Id.*
908. *Id.* at 77743.
909. *Id.* at 77744.
910. *Id.*

that provider's referrals or an arrangement that encourages providers to steer patients in ways that are not in the patients' best interests, will not be able to meet the requirements of the safe harbor.[911] Further, "[f]acts and circumstances demonstrating that the value-based arrangement has limited a VBE participant's ability to make decisions in the best interest of its patients would disqualify the remuneration exchanged pursuant to the value-based arrangement from protection under this safe harbor."[912]

I. Marketing of Items or Services or Patient Recruitment Activities

This rule prohibits the use of remuneration for the purpose of marketing items or services provided by the VBE or VBE participants or for patient recruitment activities. OIG did not define these terms, choosing to promote flexibility and favor the commonly understood definitions.[913] OIG commented that it did "not consider remuneration exchanged between parties to a value-based arrangement to (i) provide objective patient educational materials or (ii) engage in objective patient informational activities to constitute marketing or patient recruitment activities for purposes of this safe harbor condition."[914] Further, "[a] determination regarding whether remuneration is being exchanged or used for the purposes of marketing items or services or patient recruitment activities or for an educational activity requires a fact-specific analysis."[915] For example, "[r]emuneration exchanged between parties to a value-based arrangement may be used to inform patients in the target patient population that the VBE participant participates in the value-based arrangement without such information being considered a marketing or recruitment activity."[916] Likewise, OIG "would not consider the publication of quality and cost data to constitute marketing or patient recruitment activity."

OIG further noted that arrangements do not necessarily need to have safe harbor protection to be lawful and that "many legitimate health care entities lawfully market services without benefit of a safe harbor."[917] In relation to

911. *Id.*
912. *Id.*
913. *Id.* at 77745.
914. *Id.*
915. *Id.*
916. *Id.* at 77746.
917. *Id.*

this safe harbor, however, remuneration that is exchanged "for the purpose of marketing or patient recruitment would not be eligible for protection."[918]

J. Monitoring and Assessment

The VBE or the VBE's accountable body must reasonably monitor and assess, no less than annually, the coordination and management of care for the target patient population in the value-based arrangement; any deficiencies in the delivery of care under the arrangement; and progress toward achieving the legitimate outcome in the arrangement.[919] The rule as implemented does not require the establishment of specific protocols, nor does it prescribe how VBEs must receive and address any patient concerns, although OIG noted that it would be a good compliance practice "to establish a mechanism through which patients and others could submit reports related to, for example, deficiencies in the delivery of quality care under the value-based arrangement."[920] OIG described this requirement as "a critical safeguard to ensure oversight of the value-based arrangement."[921] OIG further commented that "monitoring and assessment should be reasonable in relation to the complexity and sophistication of the VBE participants, the VBE, and the value-based arrangement and available resources."[922]

K. Termination of the Arrangement

Regarding the requirement that a value-based arrangement be terminated within 60 days, or that a corrective action plan be developed to correct deficiencies within 120 days, if the value-based arrangement has resulted in material deficiencies in quality of care or is unlikely to further the coordination and management of care of the target patient population, OIG stated that its goal is "a reasonable but also prompt termination of arrangements that are no longer serving the goals for which safe harbor protection is offered."[923] OIG stressed that the safe harbor "does not require the recipient to achieve an outcome or process measure" or require termination if it is determined that an outcome or process measure is unlikely to be achieved.[924] If a corrective action plan is developed and identified deficiencies are not

918. *Id.*
919. *Id.* at 77748.
920. *Id.* at 77749.
921. *Id.* at 77748.
922. *Id.*
923. *Id.* at 77750.
924. *Id.*

remedied, the arrangement would need to be terminated and, at that point, "safe harbor protection for remuneration exchanged pursuant to the value-based arrangement would no longer be available."[925] OIG further clarified that "at a minimum, the party or parties responsible for monitoring and assessment must monitor the matters listed in the regulation . . . and report the results so that the accountable body or person can make a determination as to whether any of the events that trigger the termination or corrective action provision have occurred."[926]

2.31. Value-Based Arrangements with Substantial Downside Financial Risk

A new safe harbor for value-based arrangements with substantial downside financial risk, added by 85 FR 77684, is codified at 42 C.F.R. § 1001.952 (ff):

> **(ff)** *Value-based arrangements with substantial downside financial risk.* As used in section 1128B of the Act, "remuneration" does not include the exchange of payments or anything of value between a VBE and a VBE participant pursuant to a value-based arrangement if all of the following standards in paragraphs (ff)(1) through (8) of this section are met:
>
> **(1)** The remuneration is not exchanged by:
>
> **(i)** A pharmaceutical manufacturer, distributor, or wholesaler;
>
> **(ii)** A pharmacy benefit manager;
>
> **(iii)** A laboratory company;
>
> **(iv)** A pharmacy that primarily compounds drugs or primarily dispenses compounded drugs;
>
> **(v)** A manufacturer of a device or medical supply;
>
> **(vi)** An entity or individual that sells or rents durable medical equipment, prosthetics, orthotics, or supplies covered by a Federal health care program (other than a pharmacy or a physician, provider, or other entity that primarily furnishes services); or
>
> **(vii)** A medical device distributor or wholesaler that is not otherwise a manufacturer of a device or medical supplies.

925. *Id.*
926. *Id.*

(2) The VBE (directly or through a VBE participant, other than a payor, acting on the VBE's behalf) has assumed through a written contract or a value-based arrangement (or has entered into a written contract or a value-based arrangement to assume in the next 6 months) substantial downside financial risk from a payor for a period of at least 1 year.

(3) The VBE participant (unless the VBE participant is the payor from which the VBE is assuming risk) is at risk for a meaningful share of the VBE's substantial downside financial risk for providing or arranging for the provision of items and services for the target patient population.

(4) The remuneration provided by, or shared among, the VBE and VBE participant:

(i) Is directly connected to one or more of the VBE's value-based purposes, at least one of which must be a value-based purpose defined in § 1001.952(ee)(14)(x)(A), (B), or (C);

(ii) Unless exchanged pursuant to risk methodologies defined in paragraph (ff)(9)(i) or (ii) of this section, is used predominantly to engage in value-based activities that are directly connected to the items and services for which the VBE has assumed (or has entered into a written contract or value-based arrangement to assume in the next 6 months) substantial downside financial risk;

(iii) Does not include the offer or receipt of an ownership or investment interest in an entity or any distributions related to such ownership or investment interest; and

(iv) Is not exchanged or used for the purpose of marketing items or services furnished by the VBE or a VBE participant to patients or for patient recruitment activities.

(5) The value-based arrangement is set forth in writing, is signed by the parties in advance of, or contemporaneous with, the commencement of the value-based arrangement and any material change to the value-based arrangement, and specifies all material terms including:

(i) Terms evidencing that the VBE is at substantial downside financial risk or will assume such risk in the next 6 months for the target patient population;

(ii) A description of the manner in which the VBE participant (unless the VBE participant is the payor from which the VBE is assuming risk) has a meaningful share of the VBE's substantial downside financial risk; and

(iii) The value-based activities, the target patient population, and the type of remuneration exchanged.

(6) The VBE or VBE participant offering the remuneration does not take into account the volume or value of, or condition the remuneration on:

(i) Referrals of patients who are not part of the target patient population; or

(ii) Business not covered under the value-based arrangement.

(7) The value-based arrangement does not:

(i) Limit the VBE participant's ability to make decisions in the best interests of its patients;

(ii) Direct or restrict referrals to a particular provider, practitioner, or supplier if:

(A) A patient expresses a preference for a different practitioner, provider, or supplier;

(B) The patient's payor determines the provider, practitioner, or supplier; or

(C) Such direction or restriction is contrary to applicable law under titles XVIII and XIX of the Act; or

(iii) Induce parties to reduce or limit medically necessary items or services furnished to any patient.

(8) For a period of at least 6 years, the VBE or VBE participant makes available to the Secretary, upon request, all materials and records sufficient to establish compliance with the conditions of this paragraph (ff).

(9) For purposes of this paragraph (ff), the following definitions apply:

(i) Substantial downside financial risk means:

(A) Financial risk equal to at least 30 percent of any loss, where losses and savings are calculated by comparing current expenditures for all items and services that are covered by the applicable payor and furnished to the target patient population to a bona fide benchmark designed to approximate the expected total cost of such care;

(B) Financial risk equal to at least 20 percent of any loss, where:

(1) Losses and savings are calculated by comparing current expenditures for all items and services furnished to the target patient population pursuant to a defined clinical episode of care that are covered by the applicable payor to a bona fide benchmark designed to approximate the expected total cost of such care for the defined clinical episode of care; and

(2) The parties design the clinical episode of care to cover items and services collectively furnished in more than one care setting; or

(C) The VBE receives from the payor a prospective, per-patient payment that is:

(1) Designed to produce material savings; and

(2) Paid on a monthly, quarterly, or annual basis for a predefined set of items and services furnished to the target patient population, designed to approximate the expected total cost of expenditures for the predefined set of items and services.

(ii) Meaningful share means the VBE participant:

(A) Assumes two-sided risk for at least 5 percent of the losses and savings, as applicable, realized by the VBE pursuant to its assumption of substantial downside financial risk; or

(B) Receives from the VBE a prospective, per-patient payment on a monthly, quarterly, or annual basis for a predefined set of items and services furnished to the target patient population, designed to approximate the expected total cost of expenditures for the predefined set of items and services, and does not claim payment in any form from the payor for the predefined items and services.

(iii) Manufacturer of a device or medical supply, target patient population, value-based activity, value-based arrangement, value-based enterprise, value-based purpose, and VBE participant shall have the meaning set forth in paragraph (ee) of this section.

OIG established a new safe harbor codified at 42 CFR 1001.952(ff), effective January 19, 2021, to protect remuneration exchanged between a VBE and a VBE participant pursuant to a value-based arrangement where the VBE participant is obligated to assume substantial downside risk. For a value-based arrangement to be protected under this safe harbor, a VBE must assume substantial downside financial risk from a payor under one of the three methodologies at 42 C.F.R. 1001.952(ff)(9)(i). Although there is a separate safe harbor now finalized at 42 CFR 1001.952(ii) for CMS-sponsored models, the final safe harbor at paragraph 1001.952(ff) may be used by participants in CMS-sponsored models as well, if safe harbor conditions are met. OIG noted however, that the paragraph at 1001.952(ff) is primarily for other kinds of value-based arrangements, including arrangements in the commercial market.[927]

A. *General Comments*

This safe harbor has been simplified and clarified to address concerns of overcomplication. OIG, in making this safe harbor unique from CMS's methodology, noted that CMS's methodology focuses on physician risk arrangements and remuneration rather than risk assumed at the VBE level, and is therefore not appropriate.

B. *Substantial Downside Risk*

Substantial downside risk for purposes of this safe harbor is defined by one of three methodologies at 42 C.F.R. 1001.952(ff)(9)(i). The first payment methodology is the "Shared Savings and Losses Methodology," the second is the "Episodic Payment Methodology," and the third is the "VBE Partial Capitation Methodology." The definition of "substantial downside financial risk" requires, among other criteria, that the VBE assume the potential for realizing losses.[928] The risk thresholds in the final rule are intended to reflect substantial downside financial risk under the three methodologies. The risk thresholds are required to mitigate traditional fraud and abuse risks associated with payments systems that incorporate fee-for-service reimbursement methodologies. OIG stated that despite opposition from commenters who suggested the risk thresholds were unduly burdensome on smaller providers,

927. Final Rule: Medicare and State Health Care Programs: Fraud and Abuse; Revisions to Safe Harbors Under the Anti-Kickback Statute, and Civil Monetary Penalty Rules Regarding Beneficiary Inducements 85 Fed. Reg. 77684, 77754 (Dec. 2, 2020).

928. 85 Fed. Reg. 77684, 77760.

the risk levels set in this value-based safe harbor are necessary and will "be substantial enough to reduce any traditional volume-driven incentives to overutilize or increase program costs by ordering and referring providers and to increase incentives to promote efficient delivery of health care."[929] The safe harbor does not prevent the VBE from assuming other types of risk from the payor such as investment risk, contractual risk, and clinical risk related to treating complex patients, as long as the VBE also assumes substantial downside risk from a payor.[930] However, risk methodologies that only include upside risk are not sufficient. There is no limit on the number of providers that can participate in the VBE and work together to assume substantial downside financial risk.

The Shared Savings and Losses Methodology requires any losses and savings calculations take into account all items and services that are covered by the payor and furnished to the target population, not simply those items and services furnished by specified VBE participants.[931] This methodology permits the assumption of risk prospectively or retrospectively. 1001.952(ff)(9)(i)(B)(2) requires the parties to design the clinical episode of care to cover items and services collectively furnished in more than one care setting. The VBE and the payor can meet this requirement as long as they design the clinical episode of care to cover a collection of items and services that they anticipate will be provided in more than one care setting even if a particular patient in the target patient population undergoing a clinical episode of care ultimately does not receive items and services in more than one care setting. We believe this requirement is consistent with episodic or bundled payment methodologies that involve services delivered by more than one provider and promotes collaboration across providers and suppliers that may otherwise operate independently and deliver care in silos.

C. *Meaningful Risk Sharing*

A VBE participant must be at risk for a meaningful share of the VBE's substantial downside financial risk.[932] The requirement to assume a meaningful share of the VBE's risk is foundational to the structure of the safe harbor, and any risk assumed by a VBE participant pursuant to this methodology must be two-sided risk. This is because this safe harbor does not

929. *Id.* at 77756.
930. *Id.*
931. *Id.* at 77757.
932. 42 C.F.R. 1001.952(ff)(3).

include certain established safeguards, such as a fair market value requirement, or a bar on monetary compensation or a contribution requirement.[933]

The Meaningful Share Partial Capitation Methodology requires a VBE participant to: (i) receive from the VBE a prospective, per-patient payment on a monthly, quarterly, or annual basis for a predefined set of items and services furnished to the target patient population by the VBE participant designed to approximate the expected total cost of those expenditures for the predefined items or services; and (ii) not separately claim payment from the payor for the predefined set of items and services covered by the partial capitated payment. OIG stated this methodology ensures that VBE participants assuming a meaningful share of the VBE's risk do so in a manner that is aligned with the payor's cost-reduction goals.[934] This methodology would not include fee-for-service payments under the Medicare inpatient prospective payment system or other fee-for-service payments under Medicare Parts A or B. Further, payments must be made on a monthly, quarterly, or annual basis.[935] A VBE participant may be at risk through this methodology where the VBE is at substantial downside financial risk through the VBE Partial Capitation Methodology or through any other substantial downside financial risk methodology.[936]

Regarding the reasoning for differing standards for the assumption of downside risk ("substantial downside financial risk" and "meaningfully sharing in the VBE's substantial downside financial risk"), OIG stated that the VBE is contracting into a value-based arrangement with a payor to assume substantial downside financial risk, most likely for items and services provided across care settings and by multiple VBE participants. Conversely, the VBE participant contracting with the VBE is one step removed from the payor contract, but its performance of value-based activities is likely to have a narrower focus. Therefore, a lower risk assumption threshold is appropriate for the VBE participant.[937]

A party may join an existing value-based arrangement as a VBE participant provided all safe harbor requirements are met, including amending the signed writing to include a description of the manner in which the new VBE participant will have a meaningful share of the VBE's substantial downside financial risk. OIG noted specifically that, other than the 6-month phase-in

933. 85 Fed. Reg. 77684, 77761.
934. *Id.*
935. *Id.*
936. *Id.*
937. 85 Fed. Reg. 77684, 77762.

period, the VBE participant must be at risk for a meaningful share of the VBE's risk throughout its participation in the value-based arrangement. This requirement does not apply if the participant is the payor from which the VBE is assuming risk.[938]

D. VBE's Assumption of Risk from a Payor

The requirement at paragraph 1001.952(ff)(2) gives two options to VBEs assuming substantial downside risk from a payor. First, a VBE can assume risk from the payor through an arrangement that meets the definition of "value-based arrangement." Alternatively, a VBE can assume risk from a payor through a contract that places the VBE at substantial downside financial risk. OIG noted that "under the second option, if a payor does not wish to be part of the VBE, the VBE can assume substantial downside financial risk from the payor through a written contract."[939]

The requirement that the VBE assume substantial downside financial risk from a payor is a safeguard against fraud and abuse. Payors are responsible for the cost of the items and services furnished, which is why they must be party to the risk arrangement that serves as the foundation for this safe harbor. The payor has a holistic view of, and a financial interest in reducing, total expenditures for the target patient population, which mitigates the overuse risks of fee-for-service systems.[940]

OIG emphasized that parties assuming substantial downside financial risk have more flexibility, and because of that, the safe harbor provides that payors and VBEs have two options for entering into the risk arrangement described above—entering into either a value-based arrangement or a written contract for the VBE to assume risk from the payor.[941]

Under the first option for risk arrangements, payors must be a VBE participant. The payor and the VBE can enter into a value-based arrangement for the VBE to assume substantial downside financial risk. Remuneration exchanged pursuant to a payor's and a VBE's value-based arrangement could be protected by this safe harbor, including remuneration exchanged to implement a substantial downside financial risk methodology (e.g., shared savings and losses).[942] This is not unduly burdensome because a value-based

938. *Id.*
939. 85 Fed. Reg. 77684, 77763.
940. *Id.*
941. *Id.*
942. *Id.* at 77764.

arrangement requires only the provision of at least one value-based activity for a target patient population, and the payor and VBE already must enter into an agreement to effectuate the VBE's assumption of risk for the target patient population.[943]

The second option allows payors that do not wish to be part of the VBE to choose to enter a written contract for purposes of the VBE assuming substantial downside financial risk. The written contract between the payor and the VBE would not be a value-based arrangement, and the payor would not be subject to the other conditions of the safe harbor. These contracts must only meet the condition at paragraph 1001.952(ff)(2): they must evidence the VBE's assumption of substantial downside financial risk from the payor. Remuneration exchanged pursuant to a risk assumption contract that is not a value-based arrangement is *not* protected by this safe harbor, and the parties must assess any potential remuneration exchanged with the federal anti-kickback statute.[944]

This safe harbor is only available for contracts or value-based arrangements where the target patient population is comprised of patients insured by a payor with which a VBE can enter into a risk arrangement. It is possible that Indian health care providers to Indian Health Service (IHS) beneficiaries might not be risk-bearing entities for purposes of this safe harbor because Indian health care is compensated through IHS appropriations and the Medicare, Medicaid, and CHIP programs. However, Indian health care providers may receive protection under other safe harbors.[945]

OIG clarified that a VBE may assume risk from the payor directly or through a single VBE participant acting on its behalf because not all VBEs may be a separate legal entity.[946]

Patients in the target patient population may select providers and suppliers inside and outside the VBE, but OIG believes that the VBE and its VBE participants can coordinate and manage the care of these patients and should be required to assume risk for these patients to benefit from this safe harbor. Further, allowing providers to remove patients from the calculation of downside risk could lead to manipulation of the target patient population in ways that could compromise the quality of patient care.[947]

943. *Id.*
944. *Id.*
945. 85 Fed. Reg. 77684, 77764.
946. *Id.*
947. *Id.*

E. Phase-In Period

To address start-up arrangements for parties preparing to take on risk, the safe harbor protects remuneration exchanged between the VBE and a VBE participant during the 6 months prior to the date by which the VBE must assume substantial downside financial risk.[948] This benchmark was implemented to alleviate concerns from newly formed or smaller entities about time needed to establish baselines against which to measure losses or savings. To illustrate the phase-in period, OIG noted that, "if a VBE enters into a contract with a payor on January 1, the VBE must assume substantial downside financial risk no later than July 1. The phase-in period runs from January 1 to July 1 (or an earlier date if the VBE assumes risk sooner)."[949]

Parties may not use the 6-month phase-in period to protect remuneration exchanged to set up a VBE because the VBE must already be in existence. In addition, there must be a value-based arrangement between the VBE and VBE participant that includes an exchange of something for which safe harbor protection is sought. The remuneration under this value-based arrangement could include efforts to set up the infrastructure to assume risk for the target patient population.[950]

Income guarantee payments do not satisfy any of the risk-based methodologies set forth in the definitions of "substantial downside financial risk" or "meaningful share." However, OIG did note that "[w]hether income guarantee payments to physicians could otherwise be protected by this safe harbor would depend on whether such remuneration satisfies all requirements of the safe harbor." They further noted this was an unlikely scenario because, while income guarantees could result in ancillary benefits to patients or contribute to appropriate cost reductions, they are unlikely to be directly connected to improvements in the quality of care or appropriate reductions in costs.[951]

F. Remuneration for Value-Based Activities

This safe harbor also requires that certain remuneration be used predominantly to engage in value-based activities that are directly connected to the items and services for which the VBE is at substantial downside financial

948. 42 CFR 1001.952(ff)(2); 85 Fed. Reg. 77684, 77765.
949. 85 Fed. Reg. 77684, 77765.
950. *Id.*
951. *Id.*

risk.[952] If the remuneration meets the definition of "substantial downside financial risk" or "meaningful share" (defined in paragraph 1001.952(ff)(9)(i) and (ii)), then the remuneration does not need to be used predominantly to engage in value-based activities. However, all other remuneration must meet the connectedness requirement of 42 C.F.R. 1001.952(ff)(4)(ii), which requires that the value-based activities are directly connected to the items and services for which the VBE is at substantial downside financial risk.[953] The safe harbor does not require the offeror to track the recipient's use to determine whether it is consistent with the safe harbor requirement to predominantly use remuneration to engage in value-based activities for the target patient population. Although OIG noted that all parties to the value-based arrangement would lose safe harbor protection if the recipient failed to satisfy the predominant use requirement, there are ways for an offeror to protect itself against this risk, such as "including terms in the signed writing requiring the recipient to use funds in a particular manner."[954]

G. Direct Connection to Value-Based Purposes

The safe harbor requires that remuneration be directly connected to at least one of the three value-based purposes defined in paragraph 1001.952(ee)(13)(x)(A)-(C).[955] Parties may elect to meet more than one of these purposes to satisfy this condition.

H. Reductions in Medically Necessary Items or Services

The value-based arrangement itself may not induce the VBE or VBE participants to reduce or limit medically necessary items or services furnished to any patient. Due to the nature of a value-based arrangement, incentives for stinting or cherry-picking may occur. To protect against this, the prohibition applies to not only the remuneration exchanged between the parties but also to all terms and conditions of a value-based arrangement.[956]

---

952. *Id.*

953. 85 FED. REG. 77684, 77766.

954. *Id.*

955. Remuneration must be directly connected to one or more of the following value-based purposes:

> The coordination and management of care for the target patient population; improving the quality of care for the target patient population; and appropriately reducing the costs to, or growth in expenditures of, payors without reducing the quality of care for the target patient population.

42 C.F.R 1001.952(ee)(14)(x)(A)-(C).

956. 85 FED. REG. 77684, 77767.

I. *Ownership or Investment Interests*

This safe harbor does not protect an ownership or investment interest in the VBE or any distributions related to an ownership or investment interest, but parties seeking to protect a particular ownership or investment interest may look to other safe harbors.[957]

J. *Remuneration from Individuals or Entities Outside the Applicable VBE*

OIG specified that the exchange of remuneration between parties other than the VBE and a VBE participant would not be protected by any value-based safe harbor. Contributions or funding from an affiliate of a VBE to that VBE is not viewed as qualifying for protection under this or any value-based safe harbor. However, the mere fact that an affiliate exchanges remuneration with the VBE would not preclude safe harbor protection for value-based arrangements between that VBE and its VBE participants.[958]

K. *Writing*

Notably, the terms of the value-based arrangement must be set forth in a signed writing containing a description of the nature and extent of the VBE's substantial downside financial risk for the target patient population and a description of the manner in which the recipient meaningfully shares in the VBE's substantial downside financial risk.[959] Because contracts between a payor and a VBE in circumstances where the payor is not a VBE participant do not constitute value-based arrangements, this writing requirement does not apply.[960] The writing requirement can be satisfied by a collection of documents, and there is no requirement of documentation of the offeror's costs. In addition, the writing must be established in advance of, or contemporaneous with, the commencement of the value-based arrangement.[961]

L. *Preserving Clinical Decision-Making*

The value-based arrangement must not limit the VBE participant's ability to make decisions in the best interests of its patients.[962]

---

957. *Id.* at 77768.
958. *Id.*
959. *Id.*
960. 85 Fed. Reg. 77684, 77768.
961. 85 Fed. Reg. 77684, 77769.
962. 42 C.F.R. 1001.952(ff)(7); 85 Fed. Reg. 77684, 77769.

M. *Materials and Records*

OIG highlighted the fact that the VBE or its VBE participants must maintain, for a period of at least six years, records and materials sufficient to establish compliance with the conditions of the safe harbor.[963] The purpose of this six-year requirement is to "transparency and facilitate alignment with CMS's parallel value-based exception."[964]

N. *Downstream Arrangements*

This safe harbor has a requirement that the exchange of remuneration be between the VBE and a VBE participant. This is because OIG did not propose to protect arrangements where remuneration is passed from one VBE participant to another VBE participant or from a VBE participant to a downstream contractor. OIG sought to limit protection under this safe harbor because this provides greater regulatory flexibility than the care coordination arrangements safe harbor, and as a result, declined to extend safe harbor protection to downstream financial arrangements to which the VBE is not a party and that may not include all of the safeguards required by this safe harbor.[965] OIG acknowledged that different VBE participants may act on behalf of the VBE at different times during the term of the value-based arrangement, but that only remuneration between a VBE participant acting on behalf of the VBE and another VBE participant may be protected.[966]

2.32. Value-Based Arrangements with Full Downside Financial Risk

The regulatory safe harbor for value-based arrangements with full financial risk is added by 85 FR 77684, and is codified at 42 C.F.R. § 1001.952(gg), which states:

> **(gg)** *Value-based arrangements with full financial risk.* As used in section 1128B of the Act, "remuneration" does not include the exchange of payments or anything of value between the VBE and a VBE participant pursuant to a value-based arrangement if all

---

963. *Id.*
964. *Id.* at 77769.
965. 85 Fed. Reg. 77684, 77770.
966. *Id.*

of the standards in paragraphs (gg)(1) through (9) of this section are met:

(1) The remuneration is not exchanged by:
  (i) A pharmaceutical manufacturer, distributor, or wholesaler;
  (ii) A pharmacy benefit manager;
  (iii) A laboratory company;
  (iv) A pharmacy that primarily compounds drugs or primarily dispenses compounded drugs;
  (v) A manufacturer of a device or medical supply;
  (vi) An entity or individual that sells or rents durable medical equipment, prosthetics, orthotics, or supplies covered by a Federal health care program (other than a pharmacy or a physician, provider, or other entity that primarily furnishes services); or
  (vii) A medical device distributor or wholesaler that is not otherwise a manufacturer of a device or medical supplies.

(2) The VBE (directly or through a VBE participant, other than a payor, acting on behalf of the VBE) has assumed through a written contract or a value-based arrangement (or has entered into a written contract or a value-based arrangement to assume in the next 1 year) full financial risk from a payor.

(3) The value-based arrangement is set forth in writing, is signed by the parties, and specifies all material terms, including the value-based activities and the term.

(4) The VBE participant (unless the VBE participant is a payor) does not claim payment in any form from the payor for items or services covered under the contract or value-based arrangement between the VBE and the payor described in paragraph (2).

(5) The remuneration provided by, or shared among, the VBE and VBE participant:
  (i) Is directly connected to one or more of the VBE's value-based purposes;
  (ii) Does not include the offer or receipt of an ownership or investment interest in an entity or any distributions related to such ownership or investment interest; and
  (iii) Is not exchanged or used for the purpose of marketing items or services furnished by the VBE or a VBE participant to patients or for patient recruitment activities.

(6) The value-based arrangement does not induce parties to reduce or limit medically necessary items or services furnished to any patient.

(7) The VBE or VBE participant offering the remuneration does not take into account the volume or value of, or condition the remuneration on:

(i) Referrals of patients who are not part of the target patient population; or

(ii) Business not covered under the value-based arrangement.

(8) The VBE provides or arranges for a quality assurance program for services furnished to the target patient population that:

(i) Protects against underutilization; and

(ii) Assesses the quality of care furnished to the target patient population.

(9) For a period of at least 6 years, the VBE or VBE participant makes available to the Secretary, upon request, all materials and records sufficient to establish compliance with the conditions of this paragraph (gg).

(10) For purposes of this paragraph (gg), the following definitions apply:

(i) Full financial risk means the VBE is financially responsible on a prospective basis for the cost of all items and services covered by the applicable payor for each patient in the target patient population for a term of at least 1 year.

(ii) Prospective basis means that the VBE has assumed financial responsibility for the cost of all items and services covered by the applicable payor prior to the provision of items and services to patients in the target patient population.

(iii) Items and services means health care items, devices, supplies, and services.

(iv) Manufacturer of a device or medical supply, target patient population, value-based activity, value-based arrangement, value-based enterprise, value-based purpose, and VBE participant shall have the meaning set forth in paragraph (ee) of this section.

OIG established a new safe harbor codified at 42 CFR 1001.952(gg), effective January 19, 2021, to protect remuneration exchanged between a VBE and a VBE participant pursuant to a value-based arrangement where the VBE is obligated to assume full financial risk. "Full financial risk" requires the VBE be at risk for the cost of all items and services covered by the payor for each patient in the target patient population for at least one year.[967] This safe harbor is designed to encourage more providers to take on full financial risk agreements.

A. *General Comments*

This safe harbor exists due to the limited number of providers assuming full financial risk. This safe harbor is intended to remove a potential barrier to providers taking on more risk and having additional financial incentives to coordinate care, and to provide flexibility in the level of financial risk assumed by the parties. The "full financial risk" definition, as well as the conditions of this safe harbor, are designed to balance the additional flexibilities with appropriate safeguards against risks associated with fee-for-service payment systems, and risks present in risk-based arrangements. We believe that the definition of "full financial risk," combined with the conditions of this safe harbor, appropriately balance the flexibilities afforded by this safe harbor with any identified program integrity risks.[968]

B. *Full Financial Risk*

Full financial risk requires the VBE to be at risk on a prospective basis for the cost of *all* items and services covered by the applicable payor for each patient in the target patient population for at least one year. "Prospective basis" means the VBE has assumed financial responsibility for the cost of all items and services covered by the applicable payor prior to the provision of items and services to patients in the target patient population. Safe harbor protection is not extended where a VBE assumed risk for only a subset of items and services, for all items and services except certain high-cost or specialty items and services, or for only the items and services to which the

967. Final Rule: Medicare and State Health Care Programs: Fraud and Abuse; Revisions to Safe Harbors Under the Anti-Kickback Statute, and Civil Monetary Penalty Rules Regarding Beneficiary Inducements 85 FED. REG. 77684, 77770 (Dec. 2, 2020).

968. 85 FED. REG. 77684, 77771.

remuneration relates; however, the substantial downside of financial risk safe harbor may be available for such arrangements.[969]

A VBE can assume full financial risk for patients with a particular condition by selecting a target patient population only with said condition; however, the VBE must cover all items and services for those patients.[970] As such, the VBE can limit the number of patients it assumes full financial risk for through its selection of the target patient population, but it must be at risk for all items and services furnished to the target patient population.[971] For parties seeking protection for remuneration exchanged pursuant to risk arrangements with a lower level of risk, the substantial downside financial risk safe harbor or the care coordination arrangements safe harbor may be available.[972]

A VBE is a collection of two or more VBE participants. Some or all of the VBE participants that comprise the VBE can combine their respective risk to satisfy the definition of full financial risk.[973]

OIG clarified that global budget or capitation payment methodologies would satisfy the definition of "full financial risk" if the global budget or capitation payments covered the cost of all items and services covered by the applicable payor for the target patient population for a term of at least one year.[974]

The requirement for the assumption of risk being on a prospective basis is in recognition of the flexibilities offered by this safe harbor because risk assumption can serve to limit the potential harms that may result from financial incentives inherent to fee-for-service payments systems.[975]

A payor can pay the VBE at any point in the coverage period and engage in retrospective reconciliations, providing that the VBE has assumed full financial risk for a term of at least one year prior to the provision of items and services to patients in the target patient population.[976] This safe harbor does not protect payments from a payor to a VBE participant that is a physician practice to offset losses the practice incurred.[977]

969. *Id.* at 77772.
970. *Id.*
971. *Id.*
972. 85 Fed. Reg. 77684, 77773.
973. *Id.*
974. *Id.*
975. *Id.*
976. *Id.*
977. 85 Fed. Reg. 77684, 77774.

The safe harbor seeks to increase options to create a range of arrangements eligible for safe harbor protection. All parties providing items and services to the target patient population are not required to be VBE participants and the rule does not require the VBE to enter into value-based arrangements with all such parties.[978] Accordingly, individuals and entities are not required to meet the definition of VBE, or to be a VBE participant, to rely on this safe harbor. Offering the VBE as an option is designed to increase flexibility.[979]

C. *Items and Services*

Items and services are defined only as health care items, devices, supplies, and services. A VBE may assume risk for items and services reasonably related to the provision of health care items, devices, supplies, or services such as nonemergency transportation, patient education, and social services, but doing so is not a safe harbor requirement.[980] The scope of items and services for which a VBE must be at risk depends on the items and services covered by the payor.[981] This provision does not change the scope of items and services a payor must cover to meet the definition of full financial risk. That is to say, this safe harbor does not protect partial capitated arrangements that require the VBE to assume risk for only a limited set of items and services. This includes, to the extent the payor with which the VBE contracts covers prescription drugs, the VBE's risk must encompass prescription drugs.[982]

D. *VBE's Assumption of Risk from a Payor*

A VBE can assume risk from the payor through a value-based arrangement, or through a contract that places the VBE at full financial risk. The first option requires the payor to be a VBE participant before the two may enter a value-based arrangement for the VBE to assume full financial risk that can be protected under this safe harbor.[983] Under the second option, payors would not be VBE participants, and the payor would not be subject to the other conditions of the safe harbor. These contracts must show

978. *Id.*
979. *Id.*
980. 85 Fed. Reg. 77684, 77774.
981. 85 Fed. Reg. 77684, 77775.
982. *Id.*
983. *Id.*

the VBE's assumption of full financial risk from the payor.[984] Remuneration exchanged pursuant to a risk assumption contract that is not a value-based arrangement is not protected by this safe harbor and needs to be assessed separately in accordance with the federal anti-kickback statute.[985]

Under the terms of this safe harbor, a payor and VBE may utilize this safe harbor to protect remuneration exchanged pursuant to their value-based arrangement, though the payor is a VBE participant. The safe harbor provides that the payor is exempt from the prohibition against a VBE participant claiming payment in any form from the payor for items or services covered under the value-based arrangement.[986] However, OIG stated that the payor cannot act on behalf of the VBE, and the VBE must be a distinct legal entity or represented by a separate, nonpayor, VBE participant.[987]

A VBE can assume full financial risk for all items and services provided to *all* of a VBE participant's patients if the VBE and VBE participant have defined the target patient population to include all of the VBE participant's patients. Further, if the VBE participant's patients are insured by multiple payors, the VBE has assumed full financial risk from each payor. The risk that a VBE assumes may not be limited to the items and services covered by the applicable payor that a VBE participant provides but must instead encompass all items and services covered by the applicable payor, regardless of whether they or another provider provide such items and services.[988]

E. Phase-In Period

The protected phase-in period for parties that have entered into a contract or a value-based arrangement to assume full financial risk is one year, in contrast to the substantial downside financial risk safe harbor, which offers a six-month phase-in period. OIG believes that a one-year phase-in period is warranted where a VBE is preparing to assume full financial risk for the total cost of items and services covered by the applicable payor for the target patient population.[989]

---

984. *Id.*
985. *Id.*
986. 85 Fed. Reg. 77684, 77776.
987. *Id.*
988. *Id.*
989. *Id.*

F. *Writing*

The value-based arrangement must be set forth in writing, signed by the parties, and specify all material terms, including the value-based activities and the term of the arrangement.[990] As with the substantial downside financial risk safe harbor, OIG does not specify how parties must document their value-based arrangements.[991]

G. *Direct Connection to Value-Based Purposes*

All remuneration exchanged between the VBE and a VBE participant under this safe harbor must be connected to one or more value-based purposes.[992] This requirement does allow for arrangements for bonus payments based on quality outcomes or shared savings and losses arrangements, among other arrangements, even if the other safe harbor requirements are satisfied. This requirement does not state the manner of payment between the VBE and the VBE participant. For example, the VBE could pay the VBE participant on a fee-for-service basis.[993]

It is a fact-specific determination whether a VBE could give remuneration to an owner of the VBE, where the owner is a VBE participant. The terms do not preclude remuneration exchanged between a VBE and an owner of the VBE where the owner is a VBE participant, but OIG noted that this safe harbor does not protect an ownership or investment interest in the VBE or any distributions related to an ownership or investment interest.[994]

Notably, this safe harbor has no requirement for a direct connection to any specific value-based purpose. OIG made this safe harbor with the purpose of protecting the broadest scope of remuneration. A VBE assuming full financial risk is given greater flexibility to determine the value-based purpose to which the exchange of remuneration is directly connected.[995]

H. *No Reduction in Medically Necessary Items or Services*

The value-based arrangement itself may not induce the VBE or VBE participants to reduce or limit medically necessary items or services furnished to any patient. Due to the nature of a value-based arrangement, incentives for

990. 85 Fed. Reg. 77684, 77777.
991. *Id.*
992. 1001.952(gg)(5)(i).
993. 85 Fed. Reg. 77684, 77778.
994. *Id.*
995. *Id.*

stinting or cherry-picking may occur. To protect against this, the prohibition applies to not only the remuneration exchanged between the parties but also all terms and conditions of a value-based arrangement.[996]

I. Offer or Receipt of Ownership or Investment Interests

As mentioned above, protection for ownership or investment interests in a VBE are not protected under this safe harbor. Protecting such remuneration streams serves only to align financial interests of the parties without benefiting the payor or target patient population. This further presents a risk of offers of investment interests or returns on investment being intended to induce referrals, without attendant care coordination, quality, or cost-reduction benefits related to the target patient population or the payor.[997]

J. Utilization Review and Quality Insurance Programs

A VBE must provide for a program to protect against underutilization and specify patient goals.[998] Such program must do the following: "(i) [p]rotects against underutilization of items and services furnished to the target patient population; and (ii) assesses the quality of care furnished to the target patient population."[999] Parties may determine how to best assess the quality and appropriateness of care furnished to the target patient population, a condition OIG allowed for because VBEs may be subject to varying requirements related to quality assurance programs based on state law or the terms of its value-based arrangement with the payor.[1000] The VBE need not establish such a program itself, but may arrange for such programs.[1001]

K. No Marketing of Items or Services or Patient Recruitment Activities

OIG crafted the marketing requirement to preclude protection for remuneration exchanged or used for the purpose of marketing items or services furnished by the VBE or a VBE participant to patients or patient recruitment activities.[1002] Although the VBE's assumption of full financial risk generally warrants greater flexibility in this safe harbor, the prohibition on certain marketing and patient recruitment practices is an important fraud and

996. 85 Fed. Reg. 77684, 77778.
997. *Id.*
998. 1001.952(gg)(6).
999. 85 Fed. Reg. 77684, 77779.
1000. *Id.*
1001. *Id.*
1002. 85 Fed. Reg. 77684, 77780.

abuse safeguard across all three value-based safe harbors.[1003] In particular, OIG was concerned that remuneration under the value-based arrangement may be exchanged or used to engage in inappropriate patient recruitment activities to incentivize, for example, beneficiary enrollment in, or alignment to, a particular health plan.[1004]

L. Materials and Records

Consistent with the other value-based safe harbors, OIG requires the VBE or its VBE participants to maintain, for a period of at least six years, records and materials sufficient to establish compliance with the conditions of the safe harbor.[1005]

M. Downstream Arrangements

This safe harbor does not protect remuneration that passes from one VBE participant to another VBE participant or a downstream contractor.[1006] OIG stated the importance of providing the protection and regulatory flexibility of the risk-based safe harbors *only* where the VBE is a party to the value-based arrangement. Without the VBE as a party, where neither party has assumed full financial risk and may continue to bill the applicable payor on a fee-for-service-basis, OIG stated they believe there is concern about traditional FFS fraud and abuse risks.[1007]

N. Potential Additional Safeguards

There is no requirement that value-based arrangements include outcome measures because OIG believes the conditions of this safe harbor offer sufficient protection.[1008]

2.33. Patient Engagement and Support

The regulatory safe harbor for patient engagement and support is added by 85 FR 77684 and is codified at 42 C.F.R. § 1001.952(hh) which states:

> **(hh)** *Arrangements for patient engagement and support to improve quality, health outcomes, and efficiency.* As used in section 1128B

1003. *Id.*
1004. *Id.*
1005. *Id.*
1006. 85 Fed. Reg. 77684, 77780.
1007. *Id.*
1008. 85 Fed. Reg. 77684, 77781.

of the Act, "remuneration" does not include a patient engagement tool or support furnished by a VBE participant to a patient in the target patient population of a value-based arrangement to which the VBE participant is a party if all of the conditions in paragraphs (hh)(1) through (9) of this section are met:

(1) The VBE participant is not:

- **(i)** A pharmaceutical manufacturer, distributor, or wholesaler;
- **(ii)** A pharmacy benefit manager;
- **(iii)** A laboratory company;
- **(iv)** A pharmacy that primarily compounds drugs or primarily dispenses compounded drugs;
- **(v)** A manufacturer of a device or medical supply, unless the patient engagement tool or support is digital health technology;
- **(vi)** An entity or individual that sells or rents durable medical equipment, prosthetics, orthotics, or supplies covered by a Federal health care program (other than a pharmacy, a manufacturer of a device or medical supply, or a physician, provider, or other entity that primarily furnishes services);
- **(vii)** A medical device distributor or wholesaler that is not otherwise a manufacturer of a device or medical supply; or
- **(viii)** A manufacturer of a device or medical supply that was obligated under 42 CFR 403.906 to report one or more ownership or investment interests held by a physician or an immediate family member during the preceding calendar year, or that reasonably anticipates that it will be obligated to report one or more ownership or investment interests held by a physician or an immediate family member during the present calendar year, even if the patient engagement tool or support is digital health technology (for purposes of this paragraph, the terms "ownership or investment interest," "physician," and "immediate family member" have the same meaning as set forth in 42 CFR 403.902).

(2) The patient engagement tool or support is furnished directly to the patient (or the patient's caregiver, family member, or other individual acting on the patient's behalf) by a VBE participant that is a party to the value-based arrangement or its eligible agent.

(3) The patient engagement tool or support:
  (i) Is an in-kind item, good, or service;
  (ii) That has a direct connection to the coordination and management of care of the target patient population;
  (iii) Does not include any cash or cash equivalent;
  (iv) Does not result in medically unnecessary or inappropriate items or services reimbursed in whole or in part by a Federal health care program;
  (v) Is recommended by the patient's licensed health care professional; and
  (vi) Advances one or more of the following goals:
    (A) Adherence to a treatment regimen determined by the patient's licensed health care professional.
    (B) Adherence to a drug regimen determined by the patient's licensed health care professional.
    (C) Adherence to a follow-up care plan established by the patient's licensed health care professional.
    (D) Prevention or management of a disease or condition as directed by the patient's licensed health care professional.
    (E) Ensure patient safety.

(4) The patient engagement tool or support is not funded or contributed by:
  (i) A VBE participant that is not a party to the applicable value-based arrangement; or
  (ii) An entity listed in paragraph (hh)(1) of this section.

(5) The aggregate retail value of patient engagement tools and supports furnished to a patient by a VBE participant on an annual basis does not exceed $500. The monetary cap set forth in this paragraph (hh)(5) is adjusted each calendar year to the nearest whole dollar by the increase in the Consumer Price Index - Urban All Items (CPI-U) for the 12-month period ending the preceding September 30. OIG will publish guidance after September 30 of each year reflecting the increase in the CPI-U for the 12-month period ending September 30 and the new monetary cap applicable for the following calendar year.

(6) The VBE participant or any eligible agent does not exchange or use the patient engagement tools or supports to market other reimbursable items or services or for patient recruitment purposes.

(7) For a period of at least 6 years, the VBE participant makes available to the Secretary, upon request, all materials and records sufficient to establish that the patient engagement tool or support was distributed in a manner that meets the conditions of this paragraph (hh).

(8) The availability of a tool or support is not determined in a manner that takes into account the type of insurance coverage of the patient.

(9) For purposes of this paragraph (hh), the following definitions apply:

   (i) Eligible agent means any person or entity that is not identified in paragraphs (hh)(1)(i) through (viii) of this section as ineligible to furnish protected tools and supports under this paragraph.

   (ii) Coordination and management of care, target patient population, value-based arrangement, VBE, VBE participant, manufacturer of a device or medical supply, and digital health technology shall have the meaning set forth in paragraph (ee) of this section.

OIG established a new safe harbor codified at 1001.952(hh), effective January 19, 2021, to protect remuneration in the form of patient engagement tools and supports furnished directly by VBE participants in a target patient population. The safe harbor is designed to protect only in-kind preventive items, goods, or services, or in-kind items, goods, or services.[1009]

A. *Entities Ineligible for Protection*

OIG determined the following entities as ineligible to use the safe harbor to furnish protected remuneration to patients: (i) pharmaceutical manufacturers, wholesalers, and distributors; (ii) PBMs; (iii) laboratory companies;

1009. Final Rule: Medicare and State Health Care Programs: Fraud and Abuse; Revisions to Safe Harbors Under the Anti-Kickback Statute, and Civil Monetary Penalty Rules Regarding Beneficiary Inducements 85 Fed. Reg. 77684, 77781 (Dec. 2, 2020).

(iv) pharmacies that primarily compound drugs or primarily dispense compounded drugs; (v) manufacturers of devices or medical supplies (except with respect to digital health technology, as described below); (vi) entities or individuals that sell or rent DMEPOS (other than a pharmacy, a medical device or supply manufacturer that also sells or rents DMEPOS, or a physician, provider, or other entity that primarily furnishes services, all of whom remain eligible); (vii) medical device distributors or wholesalers that are not otherwise manufacturers of devices or medical supplies; and (viii) medical device manufacturers, distributors, or wholesalers with ownership or investment interests held by physicians.[1010]

OIG does, however, permit manufacturers to furnish patient engagement tools or supports that constitute digital health technology.[1011] This expanded list was made to address the concerns that certain entities present a higher risk of misusing this safe harbor to offer remuneration to beneficiaries as a means to market products and services rather than to improve the coordination and management of patient care.[1012] However, this safe harbor does not encompass a financial risk requirement in an effort to promote flexibility and innovation related to patient engagement and support.

B. Limitations on Recipients

Safe harbor protection is limited to tools and supports provided to patients in a target patient population.[1013] The intent is to clarify that, to qualify for safe harbor protection, a tool or support must be furnished by a VBE participant to a patient in the target patient population of a value-based arrangement to which the VBE participant is a party. OIG declines to protect remuneration furnished to patients outside a specified target patient population in an effort to ensure that the tools and supports have a nexus to the VBE's underlying value-based purpose.[1014] If parties wish to modify their target patient population selection criteria, they may amend their existing value-based arrangement.[1015]

1010. *Id.* at 77782.
1011. *Id.*
1012. *Id.*
1013. *Id.* at 77785.
1014. *Id.* at 77786.
1015. *Id.*

C. *Furnished Directly to the Patient*

The tool or support must be furnished directly to the patient by a VBE participant, or a third party that qualifies as an "eligible agent" of the VBE participant.[1016] This requirement was included to help patients understand who is furnishing the tool or support and why. The eligible agent must be an individual or entity that could furnish protected tools and supports under this safe harbor, though the eligible agent does not itself need to become a VBE participant.[1017] Further, OIG believes that a tool or support should be eligible for safe harbor protection if it is furnished to a caregiver or family member of a patient in the target population if it satisfies all the conditions of the safe harbor.[1018] OIG declined to impose a notification requirement, finding that VBE participants are incentivized to clearly communicate about the tools and supports that they provide.[1019]

D. *Funding Limitations*

The patient engagement tool or support must not be funded or contributed by an ineligible entity or by a VBE participant that is not a party to the value-based arrangement.[1020] The patient receiving the tool or support must be a member of the target patient population of a VBE to which the VBE participant is a party.[1021] The purpose of this regulation is to ensure that the remuneration has a direct connection to the coordination and management of care of the target patient population. OIG believes that limiting the types of entities that can fund protected tools and supports serves as a safeguard against circumvention schemes such as arrangements involving foundations or charities.[1022] Nothing in this condition shall prevent a charity or foundation from providing tools and supports directly to patients, so long as the arrangement complies with the federal anti-kickback statute and Beneficiary Inducements CMP, if either statute is implicated.[1023] However, free services that are offered through a third-party that provide federally reimbursable

1016. *Id.*
1017. *Id.*
1018. *Id.* at 77787.
1019. *Id.*
1020. 85 FED. REG. 77787.
1021. *Id.*
1022. *Id.*
1023. *Id.* at 77788.

items and services, such as a hospital, shall be analyzed on a case-by-case basis under the statute.[1024]

E. Nature of the Remuneration/In-Kind Remuneration

This safe harbor protects patient engagement tools and supports that are in-kind items, goods, and services.[1025] This is designed to protect a broad range of tools and supports, including, but not limited to, health-related technology, patient health-related monitoring tools and services, and supports and services designed to identify and address a patient's social determinants of health. OIG confirmed that preventive items, goods, or services can be protected under this safe harbor by including the phrase "prevention or management of a disease or condition" into the text.[1026] OIG declined to list specific examples of tools and supports eligible under the safe harbor, instead listing goals for the tools and supports to work toward, to promote flexibility for VBE participants.[1027]

a. Cash, Cash Equivalents, and Gift Cards

Given that this safe harbor is limited to in-kind remuneration, cash and cash equivalents, including most gift cards, are excluded in the final rule.[1028] This safe harbor is restricted to in-kind remuneration due to OIG's "long standing concern" about the potential for fraud and abuse that is inherent to providing cash, cash equivalents, or gift cards to beneficiaries.[1029] Although OIG would consider a voucher for a particular tool or support to be protected potentially,[1030] it does consider debit cards, rebate checks, and most gift cards to be cash equivalents and, thus, not a protected form of in-kind remuneration.[1031]

The only instance in which gift cards would meet the in-kind requirement is if their potential use is limited to certain categories of items or services that meet the conditions of the safe harbor.[1032] Additionally, discount cards and coupons may qualify as protected in-kind remuneration

1024. *Id.*
1025. *Id.*
1026. *Id.*
1027. *Id.*
1028. *Id.* at 77789.
1029. *Id.*
1030. For example, a meal voucher or a voucher for a taxi.
1031. *Id.* at 77789–90.
1032. *Id.* at 77790.

if the other conditions of this safe harbor are satisfied.[1033] However, this safe harbor is not intended to protect waivers or reductions in patient cost-sharing obligations, and will not be expanded to include "cash and cash-equivalent payments offered as part of contingency management interventions or other programs to motivate beneficial behavioral changes."[1034] Although this does not mean that all cash or cash-equivalent payments are necessarily unlawful, they would be subject to a case-by-case review under the federal anti-kickback statute and Beneficiary Inducements CMP.

There is a common misunderstanding of OIG's guidance that cash and cash-equivalent incentive payments up to $75 are permitted; however, this is not the case.[1035] Congress expressed an intent in the conference committee report accompanying the enactment of the Beneficiary Inducements CMP that inexpensive gifts of nominal value be permitted.[1036] OIG believes inexpensive gifts of nominal value are "in-kind items and services with a retail value of no more than $15 per item or $75 in the aggregate per beneficiary on an annual basis."[1037] Although gifts that exceed these dollar limits and implicate the Beneficiary Inducements CMP are not necessarily prohibited, they instead are analyzed on a case-by-case basis for compliance under the statute."[1038] Further, there is not a $75 limitation on contingency management program incentives imposed by OIG.[1039]

b. *Waiver or Reduction of Cost-Sharing Obligations*

This safe harbor will not protect cost-sharing waivers or other tools and supports designed to effectuate a waiver of beneficiary cost-sharing.[1040] OIG does not believe that this safe harbor would be a proper mechanism to protect a waiver or reduction of a programmatic requirement, nor that it would be appropriate to protect cost-sharing waivers, which could preclude a programmatic requirement created by statute.[1041]

1033. *Id.*
1034. *Id.*
1035. *Id.*
1036. *Id.* at 77791.
1037. *Id.*
1038. *Id.*
1039. *Id.*
1040. *Id.* at 77793.
1041. *Id.*

c. Social Determinants of Health

OIG did not list specific examples of health-monitoring tools that identify and address social determinants of health, finding that an explicit list is not necessary and could potentially limit innovation related to such tools, or constrain entities from offering the most beneficial types of tools and supports.[1042] Thus, OIG did not implement a rigid definition of social detriments of health.[1043] OIG does offer a nonexhaustive list designed to serve as an example of tools that could be structured to fit in the safe harbor.[1044]

d. Health-Related Technology and Patient Monitoring

Protected remuneration may encompass health-related technology and patient health-related monitoring tools and supports, so long as all safe harbor conditions are met.[1045] Although the safe harbor does not specifically reference health-related monitoring tools, and instead requires that tools or supports are in the form of an in-kind item, good, or service that meets the other requirements of the safe harbor, OIG does not intend "to limit the scope of remuneration protected by the safe harbor to exclude or otherwise limit health-related technology."[1046]

The intention behind this broadened language in the safe harbor is to provide greater opportunities for innovation and patient support, including remote patient monitoring.[1047] For example, tools that may be protected if all other conditions of the safe harbor are satisfied include "scales or blood pressure monitors that track and transmit data to a patient's licensed health

1042. *Id.* at 77794.

1043. *Id.*

1044. *Id.* (OIG's nonexhaustive list of tools that may fit in the safe harbor include: (i) provision of in-kind transportation, such as transit vouchers or rideshares organized by the VBE participant; (ii) home modifications such as grab bars, air filters or purifiers, and other physical or structural modifications that allow patients to live safely at home; (iii) temporary housing for an individual experiencing homelessness or living far from a hospital after a surgical discharge; (iv) providing broadband access to a patient to enable remote patient monitoring or virtual care; grocery or meal delivery services, nutrition supplements, and nutrition education; (v) exercise or fitness programs or equipment; (vi) vehicle modifications; incentives as part of addiction recovery programs, including peer-to-peer programs and contingency management programs; (vii) incentives as part of mental health programs; and (viii) supports related to interpersonal violence. For the preceding examples to fit in the safe harbor, all safe harbor conditions must be met, including that the tool or support must advance a goal enumerated in paragraph 1001.952(hh)(3)(vi)).

1045. *Id.* at 77796.

1046. *Id.*

1047. *Id.*

care professional, or applications that allow a patient's mobile devices to monitor activity or other health data."[1048] Another example of a support that may be protected is in-kind telehealth, such as "a smartphone that facilitates telehealth services with a patient's licensed health care professional, or a platform or software that facilitates telehealth services," so long as all of the safe harbor's conditions are satisfied.[1049]

e. Not Duplicative

OIG will not require that the VBE participant confirm that the tool or support is not "duplicative or, or substantially the same as, tools and services the patient already has," as it would be challenging for a participant to make this determination.[1050] However, a tool or support that is duplicative of one that a patient already owns may not be eligible for safe harbor protection, as it may not advance one of the goals listed at 1001.952(hh)(3)(vi).[1051] Protection under this safe harbor is not conditioned on achieving one of these goals, but "a tool or support would not be eligible for safe harbor protection without a reasonable basis that it would advance at least one of the enumerated goals."[1052]

For example, a VBE participant providing a patient with a new smartphone, when the patient already has a sufficiently functional smartphone, would not necessarily advance any of the enumerated goals.[1053] This would be the case if, for instance, a licensed health care professional recommended a smartphone to transmit medication adherence reminders, yet this is already achievable with the patient's existing cell phone, as this would not advance the patient's adherence to a drug regimen.[1054] However, if a new smartphone added functionality needed for remote monitoring that was not available on the patient's existing phone, and thus promoted adherence to a treatment regimen determined by the patient's licensed health care professional, this may advance the goal listed at paragraph 1001.952(hh)(3)(vi)(A).[1055]

1048. *Id.*
1049. *Id.*
1050. *Id.* at 77796–97.
1051. *Id.* at 77797.
1052. *Id.*
1053. *Id.*
1054. *Id.*
1055. *Id.*

F. Marketing and Patient Recruitment

Under this safe harbor, the VBE participant may not market other reimbursable items or services using the patient engagement tools or supports, nor use such tools or supports for patient recruitment purposes.[1056] OIG does not intend to protect tools or supports that solely serve as patient recruitment incentives.[1057] However, this is only applicable to the marketing of items and services that may be reimbursed by federal health care programs, otherwise such marketing would not implicate the anti-kickback statute, and thus, not require safe harbor protection.[1058] Further, this condition would not prevent VBE participants from educating patients and providing information regarding tools and supports to established patients, or "engaging in objective patient informational activities with respect to patients in the target population."[1059]

As an example, OIG states that a physician VBE participant would not violate this condition if they informed their patient with asthma that "clean air in the home is important for keeping asthma symptoms under control."[1060] The physician may explain that air conditioning and purifying mechanisms are vital for keeping air in the home clean, and that the VBE has a program that provides such filters, and the patient may be eligible to receive free filters provided by the physician.[1061]

The intention behind this condition is to prevent abusive marketing schemes that may wrongly induce patients to choose providers or use items or services because they are given free or low-cost tools and supports.[1062] Although this condition protects tools and supports to patients, it is not intended to protect any marketing, advertising, or patient recruitment arrangements.[1063]

OIG offers examples of actions that would be protected under this safe harbor, such as the operation of a nonbillable diabetes remote monitoring program by a VBE participant to help coordinate the care of a patient with diabetes in which the participant offers patients a free tablet to facilitate

---

1056. *Id.*
1057. *Id.*
1058. *Id.*
1059. *Id.*
1060. *Id.* at 77798.
1061. *Id.*
1062. *Id.*
1063. *Id.*

the remote monitoring program.[1064] This could be protected under this safe harbor if the VBE participant satisfied the marketing and patient recruitment condition at paragraph 1001.952(hh)(6).[1065] However, if the participant advertised the free tablet, this would qualify as use of the tool to recruit patients and would not be protected under this safe harbor.[1066]

The notification of the availability of tools and support to an entire target patient population may satisfy the requirements under this condition, though it would be subject to a highly fact-specific assessment.[1067] As an example, OIG suggests that if a physician advertised free air conditioning filters for patients that come for an office visit, this would constitute prohibited marketing and patient recruitment.[1068] However, if the announcement from the physician included information about "the need for asthma patients to ensure the air in the home is clean and to contact the physician for further information," this type of notification would not violate this condition.[1069]

Ultimately, this provision is geared toward preventing VBE participants from influencing patients "regarding billable health care items and services based on the offer of free tools and supports."[1070] OIG is concerned that patients may face coercion into making decisions that are not in their best medical interest, and finds that "a prohibition on marketing and patient recruitment serves as an important protection against inappropriate patient steering and overutilization of federally reimbursable items and services."[1071]

G. Direct Connection

Any tool or support that is protected under this safe harbor must have a "'direct connection' to the coordination and management of care of the

---

1064. *Id.*

1065. *Id.* (An example of an educational activity that would comply with this condition includes a VBE participant counseling a patient with diabetes about benefits of the nonbillable remote monitoring program, including a free tablet to facilitate the program. The participant could explain that the tablet may be used to communicate information such as "nutritional information, recipes, wellness tips, and appointment reminders." Note that, in this example, the participant is not using the tablet to market other reimbursable items or services.)

1066. *Id.*

1067. *Id.*

1068. *Id.*

1069. *Id.* (A hospital that posts general information, such as the hours of operation of its food pantry for patient knowledge and access is another example of an action that would not run afoul of this condition.)

1070. *Id.*

1071. *Id.* at 77799.

target patient population," and OIG does not believe that it will be challenging for a VBE participant to find a nexus between the tool or support and the coordination and management of care.[1072] OIG maintains that there must be a "direct" connection, as opposed to a "reasonable" connection, in an effort to ensure that VBE participants carefully evaluate for this connection, and "ensure that the remuneration is closely linked to the goals of the Regulatory Sprint, including promoting care coordination and value-based care."[1073]

However, to avoid unneeded clerical burdens, and because it relies on the other safeguards, OIG will not require that VBE participants make a bona fide determination of such "direct connection," and that the VBE and VBE participants may establish this connection through other means.[1074]

The protection of this safe harbor is limited to tools and supports that are directly connected to the coordination and management of care. The other three purposes enumerated, (i) improving the quality of care; (ii) appropriately reducing the costs to, or growth in expenditures of, payors without reducing the quality of care; and (iii) transitioning the health care delivery and payment systems to value-based care, are not as closely in line with the patient engagement goals of this safe harbor.[1075]

OIG does not provide a specific list of examples in which tools and supports would qualify as having a direct connection to the coordination and management of a patient's care. In doing so, OIG hopes to "foster innovation and allow VBEs and VBE participants flexibility in appropriately identifying the nexus between the tool or support and the coordination and management of care."[1076] However, OIG does provide an example, stating that a grab-bar for a patient recovering from knee surgery is a tool that has a direct connection to the coordination and management of care, as it is designed to prevent falls and consequently provides safer and more effective care for knee surgery patients.[1077]

H. Medical Necessity

The tool or support may not cause medically inappropriate or unnecessary items or services to be reimbursed by a federal health care program.[1078]

1072. *Id.* at 77780.
1073. *Id.*
1074. *Id.*
1075. *Id.* at 77781.
1076. *Id.*
1077. *Id.*
1078. *Id.*

An incentive to participate in a community-based service would also need to meet all other safe harbor conditions to be eligible for protection under this safe harbor, including the restriction of inappropriate reimbursement.[1079] These community-based services must be recommended by the licensed health care professional of the patient and have a direct connection to the coordination and management of care of the target population.[1080]

I. Licensed Health Care Professional Recommendation

This safe harbor will only provide protection for tools or supports recommended by the patient's licensed health care professional.[1081] OIG clarified that the recommendation must come from the patient's "professional" rather than "provider," as the term provider is commonly used in reference to "a hospital or other entity that furnishes institutional health care services."[1082] Because this requirement places high importance on the medical judgment of a health care professional, OIG believes that "professional" is a clearer description of this intent.[1083] Further, a tool or support recommended by a licensed provider would not necessitate protection because it would be supplied by the provider as a covered service.[1084]

The intent of this condition is to emphasize the importance of quality of care, and confirm that the remuneration is specifically focused on patient care, the health care provider's medical judgment, and the patient's relationship with their provider in creating plans for treatment and care.[1085] Further, this condition ensures that the professional recommending the tool or support is subject to some level of oversight by a licensing body and has undergone a degree of review.[1086] It is the belief of OIG that a patient's licensed health care professional is in the best position to determine whether the tool or support is directly connected to the coordination and management of the patient's care and, thus, will not result in medically unnecessary or inappropriate reimbursable items and services.[1087]

1079. *Id.*
1080. *Id.*
1081. *Id.* at 77801.
1082. *Id.*
1083. *Id.*
1084. *Id.* at 77802.
1085. *Id.*
1086. *Id.*
1087. *Id.*

OIG further clarified that, for the purposes of this safe harbor, it requires a recommendation by a licensed health care professional, not "social workers, case workers, and others who may not be licensed clinicians."[1088] OIG also provided examples of health care professionals, so long as they are properly licensed by the appropriate state licensing body.[1089] The licensed health care professional would not be required to certify that the tool or support is recommended solely to treat a documented chronic condition.[1090]

J. Advances Specified Goals

The final rule was revised from stating that the goal was "management of a disease or condition" to "prevention or management of a disease or condition," as OIG strove to incorporate the element of prevention.[1091] Further, OIG replaced references to "licensed health care providers" with "licensed health care professionals."[1092] OIG also amended the goal at paragraph 1001.952(hh)(3)(vi)(D) to read "the prevention or management of a disease or condition" so the safe harbor may "protect preventive items, goods, or services that meet the other safe harbor conditions."[1093]

OIG does not provide an exhaustive list of tools and supports to provide flexibility and the opportunity to innovate, as well as to avoid unintentionally constraining which tools and supports advance specified goals.[1094] Further, OIG emphasizes that just one tool may satisfy more than one of the enumerated goals, for example, "a device or program that reminds a patient to take a medication or attend a scheduled office visit might advance the goals related to adherence to a treatment regimen, drug regimen, or follow-up care plan, or advance goals related to prevention or management of a disease or ensuring patient safety."[1095]

1088. *Id.*

1089. The list of potential health care professionals includes: (i) physicians (including doctors of medicine, osteopathy, dental surgery, dental medicine, podiatric medicine, and optometry); (ii) osteopathic practitioners; (iii) chiropractors; (iv) physician assistants; (v) nurse practitioners; (vi) clinical nurse specialists; (vii) certified registered nurse anesthetists; (viii) physical therapists; (ix) occupational therapists; (x) clinical psychologists; (xi) qualified speech-language pathologists; (xii) qualified audiologists; and (xiii) registered dietitians or nutrition professionals.

1090. *Id.*

1091. *Id.* at 77803.

1092. *Id.*

1093. *Id.*

1094. *Id.*

1095. *Id.*

K. Prohibition on Cost-Shifting

OIG did not finalize a proposed condition that would "prohibit VBE participants that furnish patient engagement tools and supports from: (i) billing Federal health care programs, other payors, or individuals for those tools or supports; (ii) claiming the value of a tool or support as a bad debt for payment purposes under a Federal health care program; or (iii) otherwise shifting the burden of the value of a tool or support on a Federal health care program, other payors, or individuals."[1096]

OIG believed that the addition of a cost-shifting prohibition would not add "appreciable additional protection for programs or patients," and did not seek to exclude safe harbor protection for VBE participants who have a variation of arrangements with payors, "including reimbursement terms that permit certain costs to be passed on to third-party payors."[1097]

There may be a circumstance in which a VBE participant gives a federal health care program beneficiary something of value while furnishing a covered item or service, therefore implicating the anti-kickback statute.[1098] For example, if a provider waived a required cost-sharing obligation for a covered item incurred by a federal health care program beneficiary, this would implicate the anti-kickback statute.[1099] Further, this safe harbor will not exempt parties from responsibility for compliance with all applicable coverage and billing rules, nor will it transform an otherwise nonbillable item or prohibited service into a billable or allowable item or service.[1100]

L. No Selection Based on Payor

This safe harbor includes a condition that VBE participants may not take insurance coverage into account when making a determination about the availability of patient engagement tools and supports.[1101] However, this safe harbor shall not compel VBE participants to offer tools or supports where they cannot be used or accepted, nor shall it compel a patient to accept an unwanted tool or support. OIG's intention behind this condition is to prevent the discriminatory provision of tools and supports based on a patient's payor type and to ensure that a potential donor uses true needs

---

1096. *Id.*
1097. *Id.*
1098. *Id.* at 77803–04.
1099. *Id.* at 77804.
1100. *Id.*
1101. *Id.*

and characteristics separate from payor status to determine an appropriate target patient population, instead of simply valuing future federally reimbursable items and services provided to such population.[1102]

This condition would not necessarily preclude the furnishing of tools and supports by a VBE participant to patients based on clinical attributes, such as a certain chronic condition, or geographical factors, regardless of whether the patient population disproportionally has the same insurance.[1103] Nor would OIG view the furnishing of tools and supports to a population "disproportionately comprised of Medicare beneficiaries to run afoul of this condition."[1104] Further, this condition will not preclude a VBE participant from offering protected tools and supports only to uninsured individuals, as OIG will not consider this a determination based on insurance coverage.[1105] VBE participants also are not required to establish different target patient populations solely to ensure the consistent provision of tools and supports across an entire patient population.[1106]

OIG believes that VBE participants are in the best position to determine whether to offer and provide a tool or support to a patient, as this decision sits squarely within the discretion of a VBE participant, in conjunction with the VBE in which the VBE participant participates.[1107] Although VBE participants are able to "evaluate the costs and savings associated with the provision of patient engagement tools and supports, and to structure such arrangements in economically viable ways," they may not directly take a patient's payor status into account.[1108] OIG designed this condition to address cherry-picking and lemon-dropping concerns related to payor type and lack of insurance.[1109]

M. Monitoring Effectiveness

OIG did not finalize a condition that would require "offerors to use reasonable efforts to monitor the effectiveness of the tool or support in achieving the intended coordination and management of care for the patient," nor did it add a safeguard to require monitoring "to ensure that the tool or

1102. *Id.* at 77804–05.
1103. *Id.* at 77804.
1104. *Id.*
1105. *Id.* at 77805.
1106. *Id.*
1107. *Id.*
1108. *Id.*
1109. *Id.*

support does not result in diminished quality of care or patient harm."[1110] Although the final safe harbor does not include a prospective monitoring requirement, at a minimum, a VBE participant must reasonably expect the tool or support to effectively advance a goal.[1111]

N. *Retrieval of Items and Goods*

OIG did not finalize a condition that would require an offeror to make a "reasonable effort to retrieve the tool or support in certain circumstances, such as when the patient is no longer in the target patient population or the offeror is no longer a VBE participant," nor will the condition require a "minimum value [to] trigger any retrieval requirement and other issues related to the practicality of retrieval."[1112] However, an offeror may make an effort to retrieve or require the return of tools and supports where it would not be harmful to the patient, and where the decision to retrieve is consistent and not commenced in a way that takes into account the volume or value of referrals of federal health care program business.[1113] Although the final safe harbor does not include a retrieval requirement, the stipulated requirement to "advance one or more of the listed goals" means that VBA participants should not advance tools or supports if found to be ineffective.[1114]

O. *Monetary Cap*

The final rule includes an annual $500 monetary cap at paragraph 1001.952(hh)(5), as well as an inflation adjuster, but does not include an exception to this requirement that would allow exceeding the monetary cap for patients with demonstrated financial need.[1115] OIG's intention behind this rule is to provide bright-line guidance to VBE participants regarding the value of acceptable tools and supports, while keeping in mind that "different patients may have different needs," and thus, this rule does not mean it is necessarily unlawful, in individual instances, "for a provider or other party to furnish for free or below fair market value tools and supports that exceed $500 per year."[1116] However, this rule does not make remuneration below $500 "automatically immune from sanctions under the Federal

1110. *Id.*
1111. *Id.*
1112. *Id.* at 77806.
1113. *Id.*
1114. *Id.*
1115. *Id.*
1116. *Id.* at 77806–07.

anti-kickback statute and Beneficiary Inducements CMP unless it meets all safe harbor conditions."[1117]

Cases in which a patient requires tools and supports that exceed an aggregate of $500 annually may be evaluated on a case-by-case basis, and there may be lawful avenues for providers to offer such tools and supports, in particular to those experiencing financial need.[1118] In the past, OIG has issued favorable advisory opinions to those seeking to furnish free or low-cost tools and supports to patients when such tools and supports do not directly satisfy the safe harbor, an exception to the Beneficiary Inducements CMP, or both.[1119]

As the value of patient engagement tools and supports furnished by a VBE participant to a patient may not exceed $500 annually, this value shall be measured at the time such tools and supports are furnished to the patient, as though the patient had acquired the tool or support on the open market on their own.[1120] This monetary cap shall apply per VBE participant and per patient, and a patient may collect a number of tools and supports from a number of VBE participants (in one or more VBE) over the course of a year; however, no single VBE participant individually may provide more than $500 in aggregate value to the patient per year.[1121] The burden on VBE participants of tracking the value of tools may be alleviated by the fact that VBE participants are not required to monitor the value of tools and supports provided by other parties.[1122]

OIG will finalize an "annual adjustment to the monetary cap to account for inflation," which shall adjust the monetary cap for "inflation to the nearest whole dollar effective January 1 of each calendar year using the CPI-U for the 12-month period ending the preceding September 30."[1123] After September 30 of each year, OIG will post an announcement on its website to reflect "the increase in the CPI-U for the 12-month period, and the new monetary cap applicable for the following calendar year."[1124]

1117. *Id.* at 77807.

1118. *Id.* (For example, the local transportation safe harbor at paragraph 1001.952(bb) is obtainable to protect certain local transportation furnished to patients, so long as such local transportation satisfies the requirements of the safe harbor.)

1119. *Id.*

1120. *Id.*

1121. *Id.*

1122. *Id.*

1123. *Id.*

1124. *Id.*

It is the belief of OIG that this safe harbor condition reaches the proper balance between the flexibility of VBE participants to provide beneficial tools and supports to patients and the protection of programs and patients from the inappropriate influence of remuneration.[1125] OIG further believes that exceptions to the $500 cap would add complexity and raise compliance challenges and thus is not finalizing exceptions to this condition.[1126] Tools and supports with greater value have the potential to improperly influence patients to select treatments or providers not in their best interests, which may in turn lead to the very harms that the federal anti-kickback statute is designed to protect.[1127]

P. Diversion or Resale

OIG did not finalize a condition that would have excluded tools or supports from safe harbor protection if the offeror knew or should have known that the tool or support was "likely to be diverted, sold, or utilized by the patient other than for the express purpose for which the tool or support was provided."[1128] OIG reasons that this condition should not be finalized because there are other safeguards within the safe harbor to effectively address the issue of whether a recipient of a tool is receiving it for appropriate purposes.[1129] For example, a requirement that a licensed health care professional recommend the tool or support and that it be directly connected to the coordination and management of care should diminish the risk that such tool or support will likely be diverted or resold.[1130] Other provisions limit the risk or diversion or resale even further, such as the monetary cap, the requirement that a tool or support advance an enumerated goal, and the restriction on marketing and patient recruitment."[1131]

Q. Materials and Records

This safe harbor requires that the materials and records that establish compliance with the safe harbor must be made available to the secretary, and such records must be kept for at least six years.[1132] OIG does not believe

1125. *Id.* at 77807–08.
1126. *Id.* at 77808.
1127. *Id.*
1128. *Id.*
1129. *Id.*
1130. *Id.*
1131. *Id.*
1132. *Id.*

that this requirement is too rigorous, as it does not require signed writing before supplying the tools and supports to a patient and does not propose any specific parameters on the type or form of documentation.[1133] Instead, this provision simply requires that documentation be made available upon request, and must show that tools or supports were provided in accordance with the safe harbor's conditions.[1134] OIG emphasizes that any party relying on a safe harbor to protect certain arrangements should document compliance with that safe harbor.[1135]

R. Notice to Patients

OIG declines to require that "the VBE provide a patient receiving a tool or support with written notice identifying the VBE participant and describing the nature and purpose of the tool or support."[1136] The reason behind this decision is the belief of OIG that a licensed health care professional recommending a tool or support is the proper time for the patient to understand the purpose of such tool or support.[1137] Despite the fact that formal notice to the patient is not required under this rule, OIG expects that, at the time it is recommended, providers will communicate the purpose of the tool or support "in furtherance of the coordination and management of care."[1138]

2.34. CMS-Sponsored Model Arrangements and CMS-Sponsored Model Patient Incentives

The safe harbor for CMS-sponsored model arrangements and CMS-sponsored model patient incentives, added by 85 FR 77684, is codified at 42 C.F.R. § 1001.952(ii):

> (ii) *CMS–sponsored model arrangements and CMS–sponsored model patient incentives.*
>
> (1) As used in section 1128B of the Act, "remuneration" does not include an exchange of anything of value between or among CMS-sponsored model parties under a CMS-sponsored model

1133. *Id.*
1134. *Id.*
1135. *Id.*
1136. *Id.*
1137. *Id.*
1138. *Id.*

arrangement for which CMS has determined that this safe harbor is available if all of the following conditions are met:

(i) The CMS-sponsored model parties reasonably determine that the CMS-sponsored model arrangement will advance one or more goals of the CMS-sponsored model;

(ii) The exchange of value does not induce CMS-sponsored model parties or other providers or suppliers to furnish medically unnecessary items or services, or reduce or limit medically necessary items or services furnished to any patient;

(iii) The CMS-sponsored model parties do not offer, pay, solicit, or receive remuneration in return for, or to induce or reward, any Federal health care program referrals or other Federal health care program business generated outside of the CMS-sponsored model;

(iv) The CMS-sponsored model parties in advance of or contemporaneous with the commencement of the CMS-sponsored model arrangement set forth the terms of the CMS-sponsored model arrangement in a signed writing. The writing must specify at a minimum the activities to be undertaken by the CMS-sponsored model parties and the nature of the remuneration to be exchanged under the CMS-sponsored model arrangement;

(v) The parties to the CMS-sponsored model arrangement make available to the Secretary, upon request, all materials and records sufficient to establish whether the remuneration was exchanged in a manner that meets the conditions of this safe harbor; and

(vi) The CMS-sponsored model parties satisfy such programmatic requirements as may be imposed by CMS in connection with the use of this safe harbor.

(2) As used in section 1128B of the Act, "remuneration" does not include a CMS–sponsored model patient incentive for which CMS has determined that this safe harbor is available if all of the following conditions are met:

(i) The CMS-sponsored model participant reasonably determines that the CMS-sponsored model patient incentive will advance one or more goals of the CMS-sponsored model;

(ii) The CMS-sponsored model patient incentive has a direct connection to the patient's health care unless the participation documentation expressly specifies a different standard;

(iii) The CMS-sponsored model patient incentive is furnished by a CMS-sponsored model participant (or by an agent of the CMS-sponsored model participant under the CMS-sponsored model participant's direction and control), unless otherwise specified by the participation documentation;

(iv) The CMS-sponsored model participant makes available to the Secretary, upon request, all materials and records sufficient to establish whether the CMS-sponsored model patient incentive was distributed in a manner that meets the conditions of this safe harbor; and

(v) The CMS-sponsored model patient incentive is furnished consistent with the CMS-sponsored model and satisfies such programmatic requirements as may be imposed by CMS in connection with the use of this safe harbor.

(3) For purposes of this paragraph (ii), the following definitions apply:

(i) CMS-sponsored model means:

(A) A model being tested under section 1115A(b) of the Act or a model expanded under section 1115A(c) of the Act; or

(B) The Medicare shared savings program under section 1899 of the Act.

(ii) CMS-sponsored model arrangement means a financial arrangement between or among CMS-sponsored model parties to engage in activities under the CMS-sponsored model that is consistent with, and is not a type of arrangement prohibited by, the participation documentation.

(iii) CMS-sponsored model participant means an individual or entity that is subject to and is operating under participation documentation with CMS to participate in a CMS-sponsored model.

(iv) CMS-sponsored model party means:
(A) A CMS-sponsored model participant; or
(B) Another individual or entity whom the participation documentation specifies may enter into a CMS-sponsored model arrangement.
(v) CMS-sponsored model patient incentive means remuneration not of a type prohibited by the participation documentation that is furnished to a patient under the terms of a CMS-sponsored model.
(vi) Participation documentation means the participation agreement, legal instrument setting forth the terms and conditions of a grant or cooperative agreement, regulations, or model-specific addendum to an existing contract with CMS that specifies the terms of a CMS-sponsored model.

(4) For purposes of remuneration that satisfies this paragraph (ii), the safe harbor protects:
(i) For a CMS-sponsored model governed by participation documentation other than the legal instrument setting forth the terms and conditions of a grant or a cooperative agreement, the exchange of remuneration between CMS-sponsored model parties that occurs on or after the first day on which services under the CMS-sponsored model begin and no later than 6 months after the final payment determination made by CMS under the model;
(ii) For a CMS-sponsored model governed by the legal instrument setting forth the terms and conditions of a grant or cooperative agreement, the exchange of remuneration between CMS-sponsored model parties that occurs on or after the first day of the period of performance (as defined at 45 C.F.R. 75.2) or such other date specified in the participation documentation and no later than 6 months after closeout occurs pursuant to 45 C.F.R. 75.381; and
(iii) For a CMS-sponsored model patient incentive, an incentive given on or after the first day on which patient care services may be furnished under the CMS-sponsored model as specified by CMS in the participation

> documentation and no later than the last day on which patient care services may be furnished under the CMS-sponsored model, unless a different timeframe is established in the participation documentation. A patient may retain any incentives furnished in compliance with paragraph (ii)(2) of this section.

This safe harbor protects remuneration provided in connection with certain CMS-sponsored models (i.e., Medicare Shared Savings Program or other models being tested by CMS under 42 U.S.C. 1315a(b)). The CMS-sponsored model safe harbor is intended to provide greater predictability to model participants and uniformity across models. OIG received several comments noting that the safe harbor will encourage greater voluntary participation in new CMS-sponsored models.[1139] The safe harbor will reduce the need for separate OIG fraud and abuse waivers for new CMS-sponsored models, though the safe harbor does not preclude OIG from issuing such waivers in the future, nor does the safe harbor supersede OIG's existing fraud and abuse waivers.[1140]

A. *Scope of the Safe Harbor*

OIG rejected the recommendation of some commenters to expand the safe harbor beyond "CMS-sponsored models." Some examples not covered under this safe harbor include: (i) arrangements under State Innovation Waivers granted pursuant to section 1332 of the Affordable Care Act; (ii) arrangements involving commercially insured patients that operate "alongside" an arrangement related to the CMS-sponsored model if the commercial arrangement is identical in all respects to the CMS-sponsored model arrangement; (iii) arrangements needed to support CMS-approved Medicaid Alternative Payment Models and delivery system initiatives; (iv) arrangements established in the Medicare Physician Fee Schedule and Merit-based

---

1139. Final Rule: Medicare and State Health Care Programs: Fraud and Abuse; Revisions to Safe Harbors Under the Anti-Kickback Statute, and Civil Monetary Penalty Rules Regarding Beneficiary Inducements 85 Fed. Reg. 77684, 77781 (Dec. 2, 2020).

1140. *Id.* at 77810. OIG noted that for "any existing model that has a fraud and abuse waiver issued by OIG, CMS may determine that this safe harbor is available for specific CMS-sponsored model arrangements and CMS-sponsored model patient incentives that began prior to issuance of this final rule." *Id.* at 77813. If the CMS-sponsored model has an OIG waiver, the waiver can be relied on, or if CMS in their discretion issues a notice stating that such CMS model participants can seek safe harbor protection, the participants can rely on the notice, provided all of the safe harbor conditions are met. *Id.*

Incentive Payment System (MIPS); and (v) arrangements between organizations participating in any CMS-led or CMS-supported demonstration authorized by statute. OIG noted that many of the programs cited by commenters do not have the requisite CMS oversight and involvement.[1141] Therefore, the proposed rule was finalized and tailored to include those CMS-sponsored models being tested under the Innovation Center's models from section 1115A(b) of the Act (42 U.S.C. 1315A), or a model expanded under section 1115A(c) of the act; or those from the Medicare shared savings program under section 1899 of the act (42 U.S.C. 1395jjj).[1142]

OIG also received comments regarding the scope of the safe harbor as it pertains to tools and supports furnished to patients who are: (i) approved by CMS through a Medicaid section 1115 waiver; (ii) approved by CMS as a State Plan Amendment; or (iii) allowed through Supplemental Benefit for Chronically Ill Enrollees in the Medicare Advantage program.[1143] Conversely, some commenters supported limiting the scope of the safe harbor. For instance, one commenter suggested that such broadening was inappropriate and that the federal anti-kickback statute serve as the backstop.[1144]

In response, OIG pronounced that it is continuing to finalize the scope of the safe harbor, but commented that the safe harbor is designed to work collaboratively with the Innovation Center's models under section 1115A of the act and the Medicare Shared Savings Program under section 1899 of the act.[1145] Accordingly, OIG articulated that the safe harbor permits some flexibility that is low risk in that CMS also includes integrity safeguards in the Medicare Shared Savings Program and the Innovation Center models. OIG concluded that it is continuing to tailor the scope of the safe harbor.[1146]

OIG also responded to a comment as to whether the safe harbor protects incentives such as transportation, nutrition support, home monitoring technology, and gift cards. In response, OIG made it clear that CMS determines the specific types of financial arrangements and incentives to which safe harbor protection applies.[1147] This means that depending on the particular CMS-sponsored model's parameters, the safe harbor could protect a broad range of incentives, including transportation, nutrition support, home monitoring

1141. *Id.* at 77810.
1142. *Id.* 77810; 42 C.F.R. §1001.952(ii)(3).
1143. *Id.*
1144. *Id.*
1145. *Id.*
1146. *Id.*
1147. 85 FR 77684 at 77811.

technology, and gift cards.[1148] If the CMS-sponsored model prohibits a particular type of incentive, then it would not be protected by this safe harbor. In addition, OIG noted that CMS defines which entities may provide an incentive. For example, OIG noted that "if the CMS-sponsored model is a State-based model where the State or State Medicaid agency implements the model through care-delivery partners in a State, the Innovation Center may expressly specify that such State partners may provide CMS-sponsored model patient incentives under the model on behalf of the State."[1149]

OIG also noted that it is currently modifying the definition of "CMS-sponsored model patient incentive" at 1001.952(ii)(3)(v) for simplicity and to consolidate safe harbor language contained at 1001.952(ii)(2). Specifically, OIG proposed to define the phrase to mean "remuneration not of a type prohibited by the participation documentation and is furnished consistent with the CMS-sponsored model by a CMS-sponsored model participant . . . directly to a patient under the CMS-sponsored model."[1150] OIG also mentioned that they do not intend this redefinition and language manipulation to be a substantive change.[1151]

One commenter recommended expanding the safe harbor to include incentives to patients who the CMS-sponsored model participant has a good-faith belief will be covered by a CMS-sponsored model. The commenter offered the example that the Comprehensive ESRD Care Model has shown that 120 or more days may pass between the time a Medicare beneficiary begins dialysis treatment and the time by which the ESRD Seamless Care Organization receives confirmation of the beneficiary's alignment.[1152]

OIG responded by clarifying that the Innovation Center defines the scope of patients who are eligible to receive incentives, and OIG agreed that "depending on how the Innovation Center has designed the model, a CMS-sponsored model participant may not know exactly which beneficiaries are in the model or aligned to the model participant at the time the beneficiary could benefit from a patient incentive."[1153] However, as noted by OIG, a "CMS-sponsored model patient incentive" is remuneration that is not prohibited by the relevant participation documents, and an "incentive given

1148. *Id.*
1149. *Id.*
1150. *Id.*
1151. *Id.*
1152. 85 FR 77684 at 77811.
1153. *Id.*

before final alignment could still meet the condition set forth in paragraph 1001.952(ii)(2)(v) and qualify for safe harbor protection of all other terms of the safe harbor are met."[1154]

In response to a comment inquiring about whether the safe harbor would apply to "Phase II" testing of an Innovation Center model, OIG noted that the safe harbor protects CMS-sponsored models regardless of the model's phase of testing.[1155]

OIG notes that the term "participation documentation" is defined as "legal instrument setting forth the terms and conditions of a grant or cooperative agreement" instead of simply "cooperative agreements." This was done to accommodate future CMS-sponsored models that may be implemented by a type of grant that is not a cooperative agreement and to accurately characterize the relevant documentation for such forms of federal funding.[1156]

B. *Conditions for Safe Harbor Protection*

A commenter suggested that safe harbor protection should apply so long as the remuneration at issue meets all programmatic requirements and the terms of the model participation agreements or other participation documentation. Specifically, the commenter articulated a concern that incorporating additional requirements in the safe harbor of which are beyond the model's contractual and programmatic requirements could limit the ability to tailor program integrity requirements and potentially lead to conflicting formulations between the safe harbor and the internal requirements.[1157] Another commenter agreed, but expressed that such specific requirements are redundant because they are already included within most Innovation Center model participation requirements.[1158] Another commenter took concern with the additional requirements, and cautioned OIG to modify the safe harbor conditions insofar they were unclear or imposed an undue burden.[1159]

In response, OIG expressed that it appreciated the desire of the commenters to streamline the safe harbor conditions as much as possible. Yet,

1154. *Id.*
1155. *Id.*
1156. *Id.* at 77812.
1157. *Id.*
1158. *Id.*
1159. *Id.*

OIG noted that the suggested requirement of permitting the safe harbor to apply if all programmatic and contractual conditions were met may inadvertently leave some incentives unprotected because there may be potential inadvertent failures to satisfy the model requirements, which does not bear on the particular financial arrangement or patient incentive.[1160] OIG also agreed that there may be some redundancy in the safe harbor requirements, but that such redundancy far outweighed the potential for issues regarding clarity and consistency.[1161]

Safe harbor protection will not necessarily apply to every possible financial arrangement or incentive that CMS-sponsored model parties may wish to implement; rather, CMS must affirmatively state that the safe harbor would be available for specific CMS-sponsored model arrangements and CMS-sponsored model patient incentives within a particular model or initiative.[1162] As opposed to providing that the safe harbor covers all CMS-sponsored model covered, absent a specific exclusion, this approach allows the CMS Innovation Center to evaluate each model and determine whether safe harbor protection is necessary.[1163]

OIG highlighted the following safeguards in the safe harbor, which help to ensure the safe harbor operates as intended by CMS. First, the remuneration must not induce the furnishing of medically unnecessary services or reduce or limit medically necessary care or induce referrals of patients outside the CMS-sponsored model unless such outside referrals are specified by the participation documentation.[1164] Second, the parties must make materials and records available to the secretary upon request, and the parties satisfy programmatic requirements imposed by CMS.[1165] In addition, OIG stressed that under the new safe harbor, the CMS-sponsored model patient incentive must have a direct connection to the patient's health care, unless the participation documentation specifies a different standard. An example when the participation documentation may specify a different patient incentive standard is as follows: a CMS-sponsored model permitted incentives related to social determinants might not "directly" relate to a patient's health, yet the participation documentation may specify that the

1160. *Id.*
1161. *Id.*
1162. *Id* at 77813.
1163. *Id.*
1164. 85 FR 77684 at 77812; 42 U.S.C. § 1001.952(ii)(1)(ii)-(iii).
1165. 42 U.S.C. § 1001.952(ii)(1)(v)-(vi) and 1001.952(ii)(2)(iii).

incentive bear a "reasonable" connection to the patient's health, in which case compliance with the "reasonable connection" standard would satisfy the safe harbor condition.[1166]

Another commenter expressed that the safe harbor condition requiring an arrangement to satisfy "other programmatic requirements" would leave the protection for such arrangements significantly uncertain. OIG replied that such "other programmatic requirements" would be further clarified in relevant participation documentation or would otherwise become publicly available.[1167]

Another commented that OIG should specify that the safe harbor is automatically applicable to CMS-sponsored models absent any affirmative exclusion, rather than requiring the Innovation Center to specify that the safe harbor applies to a particular model. OIG expressly rejected that recommendation because safe harbor protection may not be necessary to test all models or for every possible arrangement. Therefore, this permits the Innovation Center to evaluate each model on a case-by-case basis and make a specific determination regarding the appropriateness of waivers.[1168]

C. Duration

The safe harbor specifies time frames for when protection begins and ends.[1169] In general, the first day on which services begin is often the first day of the first performance period of a model, which may be referred to in the participation documentation as the start date.[1170] OIG notes that "there are circumstances where it may be appropriate to continue protection for patient incentives given after the date on which the model concludes."[1171] However, if a model ends, or a CMS-sponsored model participation documentation terminates, "the safe harbor would not protect patient incentives indefinitely, even if the incentive benefits or improves outcomes for a particular patient."[1172] In other words, the duration of safe harbor

---

1166. 42 U.S.C. § 1001.952(ii)(2)(ii); 85 FR 77684 at 77812.

1167. *Id.*

1168. *Id* at 77813.

1169. 42 U.S.C. § 1001.952(ii)(4)(i)-(iii).

1170. 85 FR 77684 at 77813. A caveat to the start date is that "[i]f a CMS-sponsored model has an 'implementation period' included in the participation documentation, the first day on which 'services under the CMS-sponsored model begin' would be the first day of the implementation period, unless otherwise specified by CMS in the participation documentation.").

1171. *Id.* at 77813.

1172. *Id.* at 77813.

protection, including potential protection for a clinical episode that extends beyond a final performance period, is determined by the CMS participation documents.[1173]

One commenter recommended that the safe harbor protect the last payment or exchange of value made or received following the final performance period, even if the model has otherwise terminated. In response, OIG agreed, stating that it was OIG's intent that the safe harbor protect remuneration exchanged pursuant to CMS-sponsored model arrangements for a limited period of time after the CMS-sponsored model expires or is terminated to permit necessary reconciliation.[1174]

2.35. Cybersecurity

The regulatory safe harbor for cybersecurity is added by 85 FR 77684, codified at 42 C.F.R. § 1001.952(jj). The safe harbor protects arrangements that are intended to address the growing threat of cyberattacks impacting the health care ecosystem. It states:

> (jj) *Cybersecurity technology and related services.* As used in section 1128B of the Act, "remuneration" does not include nonmonetary remuneration (consisting of cybersecurity technology and services) that is necessary and used predominantly to implement, maintain, or reestablish effective cybersecurity if all of the conditions in paragraphs (jj)(1) through (4) of this section are met.
>
> (1) The donor does not:
>
> (i) Directly take into account the volume or value of referrals or other business generated between the parties when determining the eligibility of a potential recipient for the technology or services, or the amount or nature of the technology or services to be donated; or
>
> (ii) Condition the donation of technology or services, or the amount or nature of the technology or services to be donated, on future referrals.
>
> (2) Neither the recipient nor the recipient's practice (or any affiliated individual or entity) makes the receipt of technology or services, or the amount or nature of the technology or services, a condition of doing business with the donor.

1173. *Id.* at 77814.
1174. *Id.* at 77813.

(3) A general description of the technology and services being provided and the amount of the recipient's contribution, if any, are set forth in writing and signed by the parties.
(4) The donor does not shift the costs of the technology or services to any Federal health care program.
(5) For purposes of this paragraph (jj), the following definitions apply:
 (i) Cybersecurity means the process of protecting information by preventing, detecting, and responding to cyberattacks.
 (ii) Technology means any software or other types of information technology.

OIG established a new safe harbor codified at 1001.952(jj), effective January 19, 2021, to protect arrangements intended to address the growing threat of cyberattacks. The safe harbor protects nonmonetary donations of certain cybersecurity technology and related services.[1175]

A. *Purpose of Donation*

The cybersecurity technology and services safe harbor provides an opportunity for stakeholders to establish a cybersecurity network, regardless of ability to independently invest in the necessary technology. The safe harbor is limited to technology and services that are necessary and used predominantly to implement, maintain, or reestablish cybersecurity. Importantly, OIG recognized that software can have multiple functions, but, if the software has multiple functions, cybersecurity must be the predominant function for the software to be eligible for protection under the safe harbor. Notably, the safe harbor in many ways mirrors that of the EHR safe harbor set forth at 42 C.F.R. §§ 1001.952(y), which provides that donated items or services must be necessary and used predominantly to create, maintain, transmit, receive, or protect EHRs. Consistency in this regard is important because certain cybersecurity software may be donated under both safe harbors.[1176]

1175. Final Rule: Medicare and State Health Care Programs: Fraud and Abuse; Revisions to Safe Harbors Under the Anti-Kickback Statute, and Civil Monetary Penalty Rules Regarding Beneficiary Inducements 85 FED. REG. 77684, 77815 (Dec. 2, 2020).

1176. *Id.*at 77815–16.

B. Protected Donors

The safe harbor protects all donors. Provided that the conditions of the safe harbor are met, all donors, without any limitations on the type of individual or entity donating cybersecurity technology and services, are available for protection.[1177] OIG noted that the need to improve cybersecurity in the health care industry is "paramount to restrictions on donors traditionally found in other safe harbors."[1178]

C. Permitted Recipients

Donations of cybersecurity technology and related services to any individual or entity without limitation, including when the recipient is a patient, are protected by the safe harbor.[1179] The requirement that all donations be "necessary" mitigates concern over who is permitted to receive said donations.[1180] Thus, a recipient can be any individual or entity, without limitation and without any additional or different safeguards for any recipient. Importantly, while OIG did not require that the parties conduct a risk assessment prior to making the donation, OIG stated that the parties remain free and are encouraged as a general matter to obtain a risk assessment to evaluate their cybersecurity needs.[1181]

D. No Contributions from Recipients Required

Unlike the EHR safe harbor,[1182] the new safe harbor does not require that donors of cybersecurity technology and services collect a monetary contribution from recipients. OIG stated that this "frees up recipients to invest resources in other technology not protected by the safe harbor, such as updating legacy multifunctional hardware that may pose a cybersecurity risk or simply investing in their own computers."[1183] Further, OIG stated that the exception includes other conditions that prevent abuse or potential anti-competitive behavior.[1184] Donors, however, are still free to require recipients to contribute to the cost of the technology or services provided.[1185]

1177. *Id.* at 77817.
1178. *Id.*
1179. 85 Fed. Reg. 77817.
1180. *Id.* at 77818.
1181. *Id.*
1182. 42 C.F.R. §§ 1001.952(y).
1183. 85 Fed. Reg. 77826.
1184. *Id.* at 77827.
1185. *Id.*

E. Nature of the Remuneration/In-Kind Remuneration

The safe harbor protects patient engagement tools and supports that are in-kind items, goods, and services, provided they meet all applicable safe harbor conditions.[1186] The rule specifies that protection is offered only for in-kind items, goods, or services, without specifying categories of items, goods, or services. Provided that all safe harbor requirements are satisfied, the final rule protects a broad range of tools and supports that may include health-related technology, patient health-related monitoring tools and services, and supports and services designed to identify and address a patient's social determinants of health. OIG confirmed that preventive items, goods, or services can be protected under this safe harbor by including the phrase "prevention or management of a disease or condition."[1187] Notably, OIG declined to protect monetary remuneration or reimbursement for cybersecurity technology and services. OIG viewed cash and cash-equivalent remuneration to potential referral sources as inherently higher risk under the federal anti-kickback statute and the Beneficiary Inducements CMP.[1188]

F. Other Safe Harbors May Apply

The donation of cybersecurity software and services may also be covered under the EHR safe harbor.[1189] The EHR safe harbor is more limiting regarding eligible donors and recipients, scope of software and services that can be donated, the requirement of a recipient contribution, and exclusion of hardware. Accordingly, any entity donating cybersecurity technology and services needs to consider each of the potentially applicable safe harbors.

G. Written Documentation Required

The safe harbor requires written documentation memorializing the arrangement. However, OIG has stressed flexibility regarding how the documentation requirement can be met. The writing does not have to be set forth in a single document.[1190]

1186. *Id.* at 77788.
1187. 42 C.F.R. § 1001.952(hh)(3)(vi).
1188. 85 Fed. Reg. at 77816.
1189. 42 C.F.R. § 1001.952(y).
1190. 85 Fed. Reg. 77827.

2.36. ACO Beneficiary Incentive Program

A new safe harbor for ACOs operating a beneficiary incentive program, added by 85 FR 77684, is codified at 42 C.F.R. § 1001.952(kk), which states:

> (kk) *ACO Beneficiary Incentive Program.* As used in section 1128B of the Act, "remuneration" does not include an incentive payment made by an ACO to an assigned beneficiary under a beneficiary incentive program established under section 1899(m) of the Act, as amended by Congress from time to time, if the incentive payment is made in accordance with the requirements found in such subsection.[1191]

This safe harbor applies to ACOs that operate a beneficiary incentive program that is approved by the CMS under the Medicare Shared Savings Program, which was established under Section 1899(m) of the Social Security Act and codified at 42 U.S.C. § 1395jjj(m). The safe harbor protects any incentive payments made by the ACO to its beneficiaries, provided that such incentive payments are made in accordance with the requirements of the Medicare Shared Savings Program.[1192]

The safe harbor only requires the incentive payments to satisfy the statutory requirements of the Medicare Shared Savings Program under Section 1899(m) of the Social Security Act, as codified at 42 U.S.C. § 1395jjj(m), and not necessarily additional regulatory requirements of the Medicare Shared Savings Program that have been established by CMS. Nonetheless, OIG noted: "[w]hile compliance with these regulations is not a condition of satisfying the safe harbor, it would be prudent for ACOs to review these regulations to ensure that their ACO Beneficiary Incentive Programs meet

---

1191. Final Rule: Medicare and State Health Care Programs: Fraud and Abuse; Revisions to Safe Harbors Under the Anti-Kickback Statute, and Civil Monetary Penalty Rules Regarding Beneficiary Inducements 85 Fed. Reg. 77684, 77864 (Dec. 2, 2020).

1192. The Medicare Shared Savings Program only applies to incentives paid by an ACO to beneficiaries with respect to certain "qualifying primary care services" provided to the beneficiary. 42 U.S.C. § 1395jjj(m). The incentive payments must satisfy several requirements, including that they must be: (i) in an amount up to $20, with such maximum amount updated annually by the percentage increase in the consumer price index for all urban consumers; (ii) in the same amount for each beneficiary eligible for the payment; (iii) paid for each qualifying service provided to the beneficiary; and (iv) paid no later than 30 days after the qualifying service was provided to the beneficiary. 42 U.S.C. § 1395jjj(m)(2)(D). The ACO must also abide by several reporting obligations to CMS. 42 U.S.C. § 1395jjj(m).

all applicable programmatic requirements."[1193] Further, OIG clarified that the safe harbor does not waive any of the requirements set forth under any applicable CMS regulations and guidelines.[1194]

It is also worth noting that this safe harbor only applies to ACO beneficiary programs that have been approved under the existing Medicare Shared Savings Program, but OIG also finalized a new safe harbor for CMS-sponsored model arrangements and patient incentives, codified at 42 C.F.R. § 1001.952(ii), that would have broader applicability to future CMS-sponsored incentive programs and payment models.[1195]

Several commenters expressed support for this new safe harbor, indicating that it can help improve quality of overall care. For example, the safe harbor allows ACOs to incentivize patients to not skip primary care visits, which can have a significant impact on improving patient outcomes and reducing downstream costs of care.[1196]

1193. 85 Fed. Reg. 77684, 77864-65 (Dec. 2, 2020).
1194. *Id.*
1195. *Id.*
1196. *Id.*

3
Interplay Between the Anti-Kickback Statute and Other Laws

3.1. The False Claims Act

The False Claims Act (FCA) (31 U.S.C. §§ 3729 *et seq.*), known as the "Lincoln Law," was passed during the Civil War in response to profiteering by companies that sold worthless supplies to the Union Army like guns that did not shoot, ammunition filled with sawdust, and uniforms that disintegrated in the rain. President Lincoln advocated passage of the law, which contained "*qui tam*" provisions that allowed private citizens to sue on the government's behalf. "*Qui tam*" is short for a Latin phrase meaning "he who brings an action for the king as well as for himself." The FCA is the federal government's primary enforcement tool to recover monies lost to health care fraud and other government fraud. In 2017, the federal government recovered more than $3.7 billion in judgments and settlements under the FCA.[1197] Of that amount, $2.4 billion came from the health care industry.[1198] Between 2009 and 2017, the federal government recovered about $22.1 billion in fraudulent health care claims under the FCA.[1199]

1197. Press Release, Department of Justice, Justice Department Recovers Over $3.7 Billion from False Claims Act Cases in Fiscal Year 2017 (Dec. 21, 2017).

1198. *Id.*

1199. *Id.*

The FCA creates civil liability for knowingly submitting, *or* causing others to submit, *or* agreeing with others to submit, false claims seeking reimbursement from the government.[1200] "Claim" is defined extremely broadly to include any request for money or property that is presented to the government or made to a contractor or grantee if the money or property is being spent on the government's behalf or to advance a governmental interest, and the government either funds or reimburses the contractor or grantee for any portion of the money or property being requested.[1201] Failing to return overpayments received from the government can also be a false claim; this is called a "reverse false claim."[1202] Proving an intent to defraud is not required, provided that the action was undertaken knowingly, which means acting with actual knowledge or in deliberate ignorance or reckless disregard of the truth.[1203]

The FCA authorizes recovery of three times the amount of the damages actually sustained by the government.[1204] The FCA also imposes a mandatory civil penalty of not less than $5,500 (or $11,181 for claims submitted after November 2, 2015) or more than $11,000 (or $22,363 for claims submitted after November 2, 2015) for each false claim submitted.[1205] Violators are also subject to possible exclusion from participating in federal health care programs.[1206] If a violator promptly self-discloses its misconduct to government, and cooperates in the investigation prior to any criminal prosecution, civil action, or administrative action being commenced, and if that person had no knowledge of an investigation at the time such information was provided, damages may be reduced to twice the amount of loss.[1207]

Pursuant to the statute's *qui tam* provisions, a person with knowledge of government fraud may bring an action on behalf of the government.[1208] That person, referred to as a "relator," will collect a portion of the government's recovery if the action results in a settlement or verdict. The complaint is filed under seal, and a copy of the complaint and a disclosure statement of all material information possessed by the relator is served on

1200. 31 U.S.C. § 3729(a).
1201. 31 U.S.C. § 3729(b)(2).
1202. 31 U.S.C. § 3729(b)(3).
1203. 31 U.S.C. § 3729(b)(1).
1204. 31 U.S.C. § 3729(a).
1205. 15 C.F.R. § 6.3(a)(3).
1206. 42 U.S.C. § 1320a-7(a)(7).
1207. 31 U.S.C. § 3729(a)(2).
1208. 31 U.S.C. § 3730(b).

the government.[1209] The initial seal is for 60 days while the government considers whether to intervene in the action. Extensions of the initial seal are routinely requested and granted while the government investigates.

The government may choose to intervene in the action and assume control over the litigation, or it may choose to decline intervention. When the government declines intervention, the relator may proceed with the action independently, although the government continues to monitor the case as it proceeds and retains ultimate control over the government's claim, including the power to approve or reject any settlement reached between the parties. Even if the government declines intervention, it may reenter the case at a later date for good cause.[1210] If the FCA action is successful (whether by settlement or judgment), the relator's share of the recovery is between 15 and 25 percent if the government intervenes and between 25 and 30 percent if the government declines intervention.[1211] If the relator planned and initiated the activity underlying the violation, the court may reduce the relator's share of the recovery. If the relator is convicted of an offense arising from an FCA violation, the relator receives nothing under the FCA.[1212]

The AKS can form the basis of an FCA claim and is frequently cited as the legal predicate for FCA lawsuits and settlements. All claims for services submitted to Medicare or Medicaid include express certifications that such claims comply with the AKS, rendering such claims false when they instead arose as a result of kickbacks paid to induce patient referrals. Furthermore, the AKS includes a provision that states that "a claim that includes items or services resulting from a violation of [the AKS] constitutes a false or fraudulent claim for purposes of [the FCA]."[1213]

3.2. The Civil Monetary Penalties Law

The Civil Monetary Penalties Law (CMPL) was enacted in 1981 to provide the US Department of Health and Human Services (HHS) with an administrative remedy corresponding to the FCA to combat Medicare and Medicaid fraud.[1214] The Health Insurance Portability and Accountability Act of 1996 (HIPAA) made the CMPL applicable to virtually all federal health

1209. *Id.*
1210. 31 U.S.C. § 3730(c).
1211. 31 U.S.C. § 3730(d).
1212. *Id.*
1213. 42 U.S.C. § 1320a-7b(g).
1214. Omnibus Budget Reconciliation Act of 1981, Pub. L. No. 97-35, §2105(a). *See* S. Rep. No. 97-139, 97th Cong., 1st Sess. 461-2 (1981), reprinted in 1981 U.S.C.C.A.N. 727-28.

care programs.[1215] The CMPL covers a broad range of misconduct, including violations of the AKS.[1216] Each such AKS violation, under the CMPL, carries a penalty of $50,000, plus damages of not more than three times the total amount of remuneration offered, paid, solicited, or received without regard to whether such act was done for a lawful purpose.[1217]

In addition, HHS may exclude the violator from participating in federal health care programs and direct the relevant state agency to do the same for state programs.[1218]

3.3. Administrative Exclusions

Another administrative remedy available to combat Medicare and Medicaid fraud is the exclusion authority granted HHS in 42 U.S.C. § 1320a-7. There are both mandatory and permissive exclusions for misconduct enumerated in the statute.[1219] In the case of mandatory exclusions, the period of exclusion must be for at least five years but will be for at least ten years if the individual was previously convicted of a mandatory exclusion offense and will be permanent if the individual had two or more such prior convictions.[1220] In many ways, the exclusion authority is the most powerful weapon available to the government because the ability to seek reimbursement from federal health care programs is frequently essential in order for a health care provider to maintain a viable business operation. Exclusion thus can effectively end a corporate provider's business and an individual provider's career. A conviction under the AKS would require mandatory exclusion under 42 U.S.C. § 1320a-7(a)(1) or (3).

3.4. Physician Self-Referral Law ("Stark Law")

The Stark Law is a civil statute that, together with its accompanying regulations, generally prohibits physicians[1221] from making referrals for certain

1215. The only exception is the Federal Employees Health Benefits Program (FEHBP). The CMPL incorporates the definition of federal health care program contained in 42 U.S.C. § 1320a-7b(f), which excludes the FEHBP.

1216. 42 U.S.C. § 1320a-7a(a)(7) (CMPL covers conduct "described in paragraph (1) or (2) of section 1320a-7b(b)").

1217. 42 U.S.C. § 1320a-7a(a).

1218. *Id.*

1219. 42 U.S.C. § 1320a-7(a) and (b).

1220. 42 U.S.C. § 1320a-7(c)(3)(B) and (G).

1221. Physician is defined as "a doctor of medicine or osteopathy, a doctor of dental surgery or dental medicine, a doctor of podiatric medicine, a doctor of optometry, or a chiropractor." 42 C.F.R. § 411.351.

designated health services (DHSs) payable by Medicare or Medicaid[1222] to an entity with which he or she has a financial relationship, unless an exception to the law applies.[1223] The Stark Law prohibits entities from presenting a claim to Medicare or Medicaid for those referred services.[1224] A "financial relationship" of a physician includes (1) an ownership or investment interest in the entity or (2) a compensation arrangement between the physician and the entity.[1225]

DHS includes the following services: (i) clinical laboratory services; (ii) physical therapy, occupational therapy, and outpatient speech-language pathology services; (iii) radiology and certain other imaging services; (iv) radiation therapy services and supplies; (v) durable medical equipment and supplies; (vi) parenteral and enteral nutrients, equipment, and supplies; (vii) prosthetics, orthotics, and prosthetic devices and supplies; (viii) home health services; (ix) outpatient prescription drugs; and (x) inpatient and outpatient hospital services.

The Stark Law is a strict liability statute, meaning that liability does not depend on the knowledge or intent of the individual violating the law. No payment may be made for any DHS billed in violation of the Stark Law, and any person who collects amounts billed in violation of the Stark Law is liable for and must refund such amounts. Moreover, anyone knowingly presenting a claim in violation of the Stark Law is subject to a civil monetary penalty of up to $15,000 for each service unlawfully billed. The Stark Law provides more severe penalties for engaging in a "circumvention scheme," described as "an arrangement or scheme (such as a cross-referral arrangement) which the physician or entity knows or should know has a principal purpose of assuring referral by the physician to a particular entity which, if the physician directly made referrals to such entity, would" violate the law. A physician or entity engaging in a circumvention scheme is subject to a civil monetary penalty of up to $100,000 for each such scheme.

The Stark Law and the AKS are frequently implicated in the same fact patterns, as both laws regulate financial relationships with patient referral sources. Like the AKS, the Stark Law may support liability under the FCA,

---

1222. The Stark Law is extended to Medicaid claims through 42 U.S.C. § 1396b(s), which denies federal funding for claims submitted to state Medicaid programs in violation of the Stark Law.

1223. 42 USC § 1395nn.

1224. *Id.*

1225. *Id.*

and *qui tam* cases brought against health care providers frequently include allegations under both statutes. The Stark Law, however, is considerably narrower in scope than the AKS, as it only applies to referrals made by physicians (whereas the AKS applies to anyone), and the Stark Law covers only DHS, and not all items and services reimbursable by a federal health care program as with the AKS.

3.5. State Analogs

Many jurisdictions have adopted state-law versions of the AKS, which focus on the payment of kickbacks in Medicaid and/or commercial payer cases.[1226] Additionally, similar prohibitions are frequently incorporated into professional misconduct rules barring licensed professionals from paying, offering, soliciting, or receiving payment for referrals.

1226. See e.g.,

AK ST § 09.58.010

CA GOVERNMENT CODE SECTIONS 12650-12656

CO Added by Laws 2010, Ch. 296, § 14, eff. May 26, 2010. Amended by Laws 2017, Ch. 175, § 3, eff. Aug. 9, 2017CO C. R. S. A. § 25.5-4-310, CO ST § 25.5-4-310. CT ST Title 4, CHAPTER 55e

DE ST tit. 6, subtit. II, ch. 12. D.C. Law 19-317, 60 DCR 2064. FL False Claims Act tit. 6, § 68.081-68.092. GA Taxpayer Protection False Claims Act, codified at 23-3-120 to 23-3-127 (as amended Ga. L. 2014, p. 866, SB 340). GA State False Medicaid Claims Act, codified at 49-4-168 TO 49-4-168.6 (as amended Ga. L. 2014, p. 77, HB 973). HI False Claims to the State (**661-21** *et seq.*) (as amended by Laws 2012 ch. 294.). HI False Claims to the Counties (46-171 *et seq.*) (as amended by Laws 2012 ch. 294.). IL False Claims Act 740 ILCS 175/1 from ch. 127, ¶ 4101.

IL 740 ILCS 175/2 from Ch. 127, ¶ 4102. IN False Claims and Whistleblower Protection Act, codified at 5-11-5.5 *et seq.* (as amended through P.L. 109-2014); and IN Medicaid False Claims and Whistleblower Protection Act, codified at 5-11-5.7 *et seq.* (as amended through P.L. 109-2014). IA False Claims Act Title XV, Subtitle 5, ch. 685. LA ST Title 46, Part VI-A, Subpart A, § 437.1 and 437.2. MD False Health Claims Act, Health, tit. 2, subtit. 6, § 2-601– 2-611. MA False Claims Act, Part 1, tit. II, ch. 12, § 5-50. MI the Medicaid False Claim Act, 400.601, § 1-15. MN False Claims Act § 15C.01–15C.145. MT False Claims Act ch. 388, L.2013. 17-8-401. NV False Claims Act ch. 357. NH False Claims Act § 167. NJ False Claims Act § 1-15, 17-18, 2A:32C-1 Short title. NM Medicaid False Claims Act §§ 27-14-1 to 27-14-15, as enacted by Laws 2004, ch. 49. NM Fraud Against Taxpayers Act §§ 44-9-1 to 44-9-14, as amended by Laws 2015, ch. 128. NY False Claims Act, NYS Finance Law, Chapter 56, Article XIII, § 187-194. NC False Claims Act § 1-605–1-618. OK 63 Okl. St. Ann. § 5053.1. RI False Claims Act ch. 1.1, § 9-1.1-1 through 9-1.1-9. TN False Claims Act 4-18-101 *et seq.* (through Acts 2012, ch. 1061). TN Medicaid False Claims Act 71-5-181 *et seq.* (through Acts 2013, ch. 99). TN False Claims Act as amended by Acts 2012, ch. 1061. TX Human Resources Code ch. 36, subch. A, § 36.0001. VT False Claims Act (H.120) Sec. 1. 32 V.S.A. ch. 7, subch. 8

VA Fraud Against Taxpayers Act § 8.01-216.1-18. WA Medicaid Fraud False Claims Act RCW 74.66.0005 [2012 c 241 § 214.].

Index

Note: Page numbers followed by "*f*" indicate figures.

D

E

G

H

N

O

P

S

V